PRICE
THEORY
AND ITS USES

PRICE
THEORY

AND ITS USES
FOURTH EDITION

DONALD S. WATSON
The George Washington University

MARY A. HOLMAN
The George Washington University

HOUGHTON MIFFLIN COMPANY *BOSTON*

Atlanta   Dallas   Geneva, Illinois   Hopewell, New Jersey   Palo Alto   London

BY DONALD S. WATSON

Price Theory in Action

Printed in the U.S.A.

Library of Congress Catalog Card Number: 76-14003

ISBN: 0-395-24422-6

CONTENTS

PART 2   THE THEORY OF THE FIRM   139

PART 4   MONOPOLY PRICING   283

PART 5   PRICING IN IMPERFECT COMPETITION   327

PART 6   PRICES OF FACTORS   377

PREFACE

The Fourth Edition of this text on intermediate price theory retains the features of the Third Edition. To strengthen the clarity we have made many small changes by rewriting several passages, altering slightly the book's organization, and introducing some new material.

One of the organizational changes is a regrouping of some of the materials on demand. Chapter 3 now contains price elasticity of demand and Chapter 4 contains the other major elasticity concepts. The more advanced welfare analysis has been moved from the old Chapter 14 to the new Chapter 23. In this edition Chapter 15 now contains illustrations and applications of competitive equilibrium, some of which are new material. A minor rearrangement shifted the indifference curves for income and leisure to the chapter on wages. The Fourth Edition also has new and revised diagrams, updated references, numerous small additions, and more than twice as many exercises and problems.

The highest level reached by most of the students who take the course on intermediate price, or microeconomic, theory is the intermediate level. To meet these students' needs and to stimulate their interests, it is important to show the relevance and uses of price theory. Thus this edition continues to have many illustrations and applications. In addition, much of the theory that is useful in practical problems of government and business belongs on the intermediate level rather than the advanced level. And, by keeping the applications and uses of the theory short, we hold them subordinate to the exposition of the theory.

In preparing the Fourth Edition we received much good advice. The many useful suggestions and comments from reviewers and users of earlier editions continues to influence the overall direction of the book. Thorough criticism of the previous edition, together with constructive counsel on improvement, was furnished by Mary L. Eysenbach of the University of Utah and David N. Hyman of

North Carolina State University at Raleigh. Penetrating reviews of the manuscript of the Fourth Edition came from Donald P. Cole of Drew University, C. A. Knox Lovell of the University of North Carolina, and David L. Shapiro of the Hoover Institution. Several constructive suggestions were offered by Kanji Haitani of State University College, Fredonia, New York. At The George Washington University, help came to us from C. Edward Galbreath; from Richard H. Sines, who showed us how to overhaul the mathematical notes; from S. Scott Sutton; and from Theodore Suranyi-Unger. Because we did not follow all of the advice, the remaining faults are ours.

Donald Stevenson Watson

Mary A. Holman

The George Washington University

1
Introduction

The flood of material things enjoyed by Americans does not make them contented. The desire for more, and still more, runs always ahead of the rising level of living. How to get more and how to make the best use of what is available is *the* economic problem, the everlasting problem of every family, every business firm, and every unit of government.

The economic problem is the subject of price theory. In a free economy, prices are the instruments that allocate resources—material things and human services—among the ends that they can serve. Prices determine what goods and services are produced, how they are produced, and who gets them.

SCARCITY AND CHOICE

If we look at what people actually want, instead of passing judgment on what they ought to want, it is clear that there is no affluence, no abundance, no plenty, no embarrassment of riches. The test is simple. Imagine that every person in the United States was told that he could have everything he wants, and in any quantity. Imagine that every business executive, every farmer, every self-employed person was also told that he could have all the new equipment and all the personal services he wants, free, and in any quantity. Imagine that the heads of the armed services, of all the colleges and school systems, of the health services, police forces, and of the other multifarious public bodies and activities were told that they too could have all the materials, equipment, and people they would ask for. Then think of the sum total of the three lists—what consumers, producers, and governmental bodies would want. Who can doubt that the total would exceed, by many times, the amounts of material and human resources that are available?

Because they fall short of wants, resources are said to be *scarce*. The usual everyday meaning of scarcity is "physical nonavailability"; in a serious drought, water might not be available in customary

1

quantities in some communities. But in economic literature, scarcity means "availability in amounts less than sufficient to satisfy all wants or desires." The test of scarcity is price. Only goods that are not scarce, such as air, do not command a price. Resources have alternative uses. A consumer's resources are money and time. Both can be put to many uses, some more urgent than others. The consumer's economic choices allocate his limited amounts of money and time among his competing ends, or purposes. A business firm's resources are labor, materials, and equipment, which also have many uses of varying importance. The business firm's resources must also be allocated. Units of government use their budgets as the formal procedures for allocating their scarce resources among alternative ends.

PRICE THEORY AND INCOME THEORY

The two main branches of modern economic theory are *price theory* and *income theory*. Another name for price theory is *microeconomics*—the theory of the small, of the behavior of consumers, producers, and markets. The corresponding name for income theory is *macroeconomics*—the theory of the large, of the behavior of hundreds of billions of dollars of consumer expenditures, business investments, and government purchases. Microeconomics, then, is the analysis of individual behavior, whereas macroeconomics is the analysis of mass, or aggregate, behavior.

Price theory explains the composition, or allocation, of total production—why more of some things are produced than of others. Income theory explains the level of total production and why the level rises and falls.

For two centuries, price theory has been the center of attention of economists. In the eighteenth and nineteenth centuries, it was known as the *theory of value*. The theory of value played a leading role as one of the intellectual foundations of the new freedoms that came after 1776. The theory of value was also at the heart of the old controversies over capitalism and socialism. The price theory presented in this book is the standard, established body of theory. Some parts are old, others are new. Many minds have tried and tested the logic of the theory. On nearly all of it, economists substantially agree. Such disagreement as exists is on points of emphasis.

THEORY AND REALITY

Why bother with theory, why not go to the real world itself and study it? Why not get the facts?

There are two troubles with facts. It is not always easy to say just what a fact is. Anyone who has been in a laboratory or in a court of law can testify to that. The other trouble with the facts of economic life is that there are too many of them, too many hundreds of millions of them. Tens of millions of families in the United States consume goods and services every day. In some way, each family differs from the others. Goods and services are provided by millions of producers; these too are all different from one another. Goods and services are exchanged for money in tens of thousands of markets. Obviously, it is quite impossible to get "all of the" facts of economic life.

Theory is the systematic description of reality. Theory selects the essential features and shows the connections among them. Theory consists of generalizations and of causal relationships.

Models   Economic theory consists of the building and using of economic *models*, which are sets of interconnected economic relationships. Suppose that severe freezing weather damages most of the citrus crop. Everyone would then agree that the price of citrus fruits will go up. Here is an example of a model and its use. The model consists of what people think are the relations among *demand*, *supply*, and *price*. The bad weather affects supply. The model predicts the rise in price. This kind of economic model, which exists in just about everyone's mind, is not necessarily identical with the corresponding model of formal price theory. The models of theory are clear and exact. Their foundations are carefully specified, as are the relations among the variables. As simplifications of reality, models have their limitations which theory recognizes.

A model airplane lacks many of the features of a real airplane, but the model exhibits the essentials of what an airplane is and what it does. So too, economic models are stripped down to the essentials. A model of the pricing of beef does not include tens of thousands of the facts that have to do with beef. The demand-price relationship in the model does not have to mention whether more people prefer their steaks rare than well done. Nor does the supply-price relationship in the model have to mention whether ranch hands prefer jeeps to horses. A model contains only the essential and the relevant relationships that can explain an aspect of how prices function in a private enterprise economy.

Just because things are left out of them, there must be caution in using models. In a particular application, one of the omitted things might turn out to be crucially important. A model in which business executives always act so as to maximize their profits has to be modified when it is applied in circumstances where they don't.

Alert readers will be able to think of exceptions to many of the statements made in this book. But the exceptions will turn out to be complications or refinements of simple statements, rather than contradictions. More complicated models are needed to handle the exceptions. A feather blowing along in the breeze does not really contradict the law of gravity. An explanation of the movements of the feather has to be furnished by a model much more intricate than the standard and simple one for falling bodies.

The proper contrast, accordingly, is not between theory and the facts of real life. To select facts, to align them, to give them meaning is to theorize. The proper contrast is between good theory and bad theory, between useful theory and irrelevant theory.

More and more, economists are building models that can be tested by statistical analyses of factual data, which now can be executed quickly, thanks to the computer. A model or a theory cannot be confirmed by an appeal to fact; but it can be refuted. If the refutation is conclusive, then the model should be thrown away and a new and better one devised.

THE USES OF PRICE THEORY

The uses of price theory are many. Of these the greatest is the understanding of the operation of the economy. The United States is usually said to have a mixed economy, a mixture of public and private enterprise. But the private enterprise sector is still about three times as large as the public sector. Knowledge of price theory is indispensable to anyone who wants depth of understanding of how the private enterprise sector of the economy functions. Such understanding is important as a foundation for an intelligent position on the ideological and political conflicts in the world in the present age.

When it confines itself to statements about causes and their effects and to statements of functional relations, theory is said to be *positive*. When, in contrast, it embraces norms or standards, mixing them with cause-effect analyses, theory is said to be *normative*. Positive economic theory consists of propositions of this type: If *A*, then *B*. Normative economic theory seeks rules for improving the working of the economy. The distinction is akin to that between pure science and applied science.

In fact, however, the distinction between positive and normative economic theory is never drawn as a clear line. In part this is due to language itself. To say, for example, that "the function of prices is . . ." is to confer some approval, however mild, on the work that prices do. Nor can the word *monopoly* be mentioned without some overtones of evil. The same thing is true in macroeconomics, where no matter how technical the analysis, it is always plain that full employment and stable growth are good, whereas unemployment, depression, and inflation are bad.

Welfare Economics

Normative price theory is more commonly known as welfare economics. The subject of welfare economics is the economic well-being of persons as consumers and as producers, and the possible ways of improving that well-being, or welfare. Welfare economics proper has only a remote connection with "the welfare state," that vast complex of social service activities of modern governments in providing for the aged, the blind, the disabled, the unemployed, and others who cannot care for themselves. The social service activities embrace selected groups of the population, whose unique common characteristic is their low incomes.

In contrast, the theory of welfare economics examines the conditions of the economic welfare of all persons, considered as individuals. Economic welfare consists of the subjective satisfactions that individuals get from consuming goods and services, and from enjoying leisure. The force of the word *economic* is that economic welfare is confined to those subjective satisfactions that, in fact or in principle, can be put under the measuring rod of money. More economic welfare, or a higher level of economic welfare, means more satisfaction, or a higher level of satisfaction.

Here is an illustration of what welfare economics does. Consider the price that a profit-hungry monopolist charges. Everyone would probably agree that the monopoly price is high and that the consumers who pay the price are injured. But the monopoly price is higher than what? And just how great is the injury to the consumers? Of what does it consist? Can it be measured? Is the injury to the consumers greater or less than the benefit the monopolist enjoys? The theory of welfare economics tries to answer these questions. It also goes on to make proposals for dealing with monopoly.

One of the main tasks of modern welfare economics is to define and analyze the rules of *economic efficiency*. For present purposes it suffices to say that an economy is efficient if goods and services are produced in such amounts as to yield a maximum of satisfaction to consumers; any other than the efficient amounts would reduce the satisfactions of some persons. The American economy falls short of the ideal optimum efficiency in many ways, though by no means hopelessly so. Thus a companion task of welfare economics is to point to methods of bringing the actual closer to the ideal. Furthermore, the rules of economic efficiency apply to any kind of economy—capitalist or socialist or anything else. The people managing the economy of the Soviet Union have been delegating more and more decisions to prices and profits, i.e., to the decisions of consumers and plant managers. This trend is not really a move "toward capitalism." Rather it is the belated recognition of the usefulness of (western) price theory and its principles of economic efficiency.

Much of welfare economics is highly abstract, as a discussion of the ideal must be. And welfare economics operates with an idealistic conception of government as an all-seeing Olympian intelligence. By doing so, welfare economics furnishes standards. Yet the economic controls actually exercised by government fall short of ideal standards in many ways. Forming no consistent pattern, the controls are a mixture of the wise and the foolish. Let them now be classified under the heading of economic policy. Another use of price theory is as a foundation of logical analysis for economic policy.

Economic Policy

As we just said, economic policy means all of the actions of government—federal, state, and local—that are intended to influence the economy. The multitudes of economic controls that now exist have a wide range of objectives. One group of controls is aimed at stabilizing the economy. These controls rest on and can be evaluated by macroeconomic theory. Other controls directly and indirectly cause changes in the allocation of resources. Government fixes some prices, and tries to influence others. Taxes, tariffs, loans, and subsidies all have various effects on prices and production.

Price theory furnishes the analytical tools for economic policies affecting prices and production. These tools are not always used by policy makers in government; and when they are, they are often not used wisely. Price theory then becomes an apparatus of criticism, its standards of criticism being drawn from its view of the ideal economy.

Microeconomic Problems of the 1970s

Every decade has its economic problems and its succession of major economic crises. Some of the economic crises of the 1970s had far-reaching effects on the demands, supplies, and prices of a number of important commodities, such as crude oil from the Arab countries, gasoline, natural gas, coal, wheat, and beef. These microeconomic problems were compounded because they became tangled with the macroeconomic problem of inflation. And when the federal government tried to stop inflation with price controls, it found itself grappling with another set of microeconomic problems—limiting the sizes of price increases of individual products and the sizes of wage increases awarded by individual employers.

The tools of price theory are available for use in tackling such other contemporary microeconomic problems as the issues facing consumers, the employment contracts of athletes in professional sports, and the efforts to cut down the amount of government regulation of transportation. Resale price maintenance—"fair trade" pricing—was hobbled in 1975, but other problems of retailing continue. The control of pollution has impacts on prices, costs, and employment. Higher minimum wage rates and programs to alleviate poverty influence the sizes of incomes and the demand for and the supply of labor.

Managerial Economics

Still another use of price theory is the application of its methods of analysis to certain of the problems continually faced by business enterprises. Since the end of World War II, the business community has been drawing upon the organized knowledge and the analytical techniques of the social sciences to an extent far greater than ever before. Price theory in the service of business executives is known as managerial economics. Its main contributions to improved decision making in business are in demand analysis, cost analysis, and in methods of calculating prices. Even though it might be supposed that business people always know what their profits are, events have shown that the consulting economist can often give useful advice to business executives on how they should think about their profits and how these profits should be measured.

The postwar period has also seen the emergence of a powerful new analytical tool in price theory. This tool is linear programming, which is described in Chapter 12. Linear programming is a mathematical method that has already proved itself as a major innovation in theory and in the practical application of theory to business problems. The contribution of linear programming is that of finding actual numerical solutions to problems calling for optimum choices when the problems have to be solved within definite bounds.

Operations research, also known as operations analysis, has many affinities with managerial economics, and indeed overlaps it. Operations research was born during World War II, when physicists, mathematicians, and other specialists solved such problems as how best to lay mines to destroy enemy ships. Since the end of the war, operations research has grown much. Government and industry continue to use operations research for new and difficult problems. The special feature of operations research is its use of mathematical tools in tackling practical problems. Usually, also, operations research is conducted by teams of technicians with varied specializations—engineering, mathematics, statistics, psychology, economics. When it tackles economic problems, operations research draws upon the methods of price theory.

Economy and Efficiency

What once was often said to be a weakness of price theory has turned out to be perhaps its greatest strength. The supposed weakness is the reliance on the notion that business executives and consumers behave rationally—that they survey possible courses of action, measure the expected benefits and costs of each course of action, and then choose those promising the greatest surpluses of benefits over costs.

Even if it were true that many persons do not always behave rationally in making decisions about material things, it would still be important to know what rational behavior is, because rational behavior is the kind that results in the best uses of scarce resources. The best uses are what price theory demonstrates. They are the meaning of welfare economics, of managerial economics, and of linear programming. Another way to express the same thought is to say that price theory deals with decisions and their consequences on economy and efficiency. Economy, or economizing, means to achieve a given objective with the fewest resources—at the least costs. (Economizing does not mean doing things the cheap way. The least cost of a given objective might be very expensive—in the everyday sense.) Efficiency means to achieve the maximum possible benefits from given resources. Economy and efficiency are therefore mirrors of each other.

For many years after the end of World War II, the greatest single concentration of applied economic knowledge was to the problems of the national defense. Clearly, the size of the gross national product is important to the national defense, and so is the stable growth of the gross national product. But the special contributions of economists in the many research organizations working directly and indirectly with the armed services were to demonstrate how to attain economy and efficiency in the allocation of resources among defense programs and weapons systems.

Economic knowledge is being applied of course to a wide range of domestic problems. Economists in government, in the universities, and in private research organizations are making benefit-cost analyses that will help make better decisions in programs for the development of natural resources, for outdoor recreation, for health care, for urban renewal, for improved transportation (especially in the cities), for training and education, and above all, for improvements in the quality of the physical environment. Economists do not pretend to have superior wisdom on all these matters. But they do have tested methods of analyzing benefits and costs and of showing decision makers how to achieve the best uses of scarce resources.

Price theory does not of course yield immediate solutions to real problems. Solutions require the hard work of gathering and interpreting facts and the still harder work of making estimates for an uncertain future. The essential role of theory is to tell what facts to look for and what to do with them once they have been found. Facts do not speak for themselves; they convey meaning only when they are selected, arranged, and interpreted by systematic thought.

SUMMARY

Price theory investigates *the* economic problem: how prices function so as to allocate scarce resources among competing, or alternative, purposes. Price theory, or microeconomics, is one of the two main branches of modern economic theory, the other being income theory, or macroeconomics. Price theory has many uses. The greatest of these is depth in understanding of how a free private enterprise economy operates. When it is adapted to the task of stating the norms and standards of an ideal economy, price theory is called welfare economics, because an ideal economy provides the maximum of economic welfare—subjective satisfaction—obtainable from the economy's resources. Price theory also offers the analytical tools for evaluating and criticizing the everyday economic controls of government over prices and production. Price theory in the service of business is known as managerial economics. Because it is a tested way of thinking about economy and efficiency, price theory has wide uses in decision making in the employment of resources in government programs.

SELECTED REFERENCES

On scope and method: Lionel Robbins, *An Essay on the Nature and Significance of Economic Science,* 2d ed. (Macmillan, London, 1935); Oskar Morgenstern, "Thirteen Critical Points in Contemporary Economic Theory: An Interpretation," *Journal of Economic Literature*, 10 (December 1972), 1163-1189.

On integration of modern theory with its origins: William Fellner, *Emergence and Content of Modern Economic Analysis* (McGraw-Hill, New York, 1960).

On the uses of microeconomic theory: Charles J. Hitch, "The Uses of Economics," in *Research for Public Policy,* Brookings Dedication Lectures (Brookings Institution, Washington, D.C., 1961); Mary A. Holman, *The Political Economy of the Space Program* (Pacific Books, Palo Alto, Calif., 1974).

On the nature of economic theory: William S. Vickrey, *Microstatics* (Harcourt, New York, 1964), chap. 1; Kenneth E. Boulding, *Economics as a Science* (McGraw-Hill, New York, 1970).

1
THE THEORY OF
DEMAND

2
Demand,
SUPPLY, AND MARKET PRICE

People have been talking about demand and supply for centuries. They still do, in everyday conversation as well as in such places as the financial pages and the editorial columns of newspapers. It was long ago remarked, however, that if the ups and downs of prices can be explained simply by uttering the two words *demand* and *supply*, economics could be taught to parrots.

This chapter and the next four cover the theory of demand. This chapter also contains some materials on supply and market price, mainly to help put demand into clearer perspective. More extended analysis of supply comes in later chapters. The modern theory of market demand rests on the structure built by Alfred Marshall (1842–1924). He taught at Cambridge University and through his *Principles of Economics*[1] molded the thinking of his and the following generations of British and American economists.

The demand for a commodity is the total of the demands of the individual buyers in a market. The voice of logic would say that the theory of the behavior of the individual consumer ought to come first. Because the theory of market demand is simple, however, there are advantages in introducing the techniques of theoretical analysis with the simpler relations and problems.

THE DEMAND FUNCTION

Theory deals with concepts and functions. A function states the relationship between two or more variables, such as prices and physical quantities. If two variables are related in such a way that for each value of one of the variables (the independent variable) there corresponds only one value of the other variable (the dependent variable), then the second variable is said to be a function of the first one. Important in price theory are demand functions, cost functions, production functions, and supply functions. The word *function* is

[1] Macmillan, London; 1st ed. 1890; 8th ed. 1920.

just a shorthand way of referring to the things that determine demand, cost, production, and supply.

In a given market in a given period of time, the demand function for a commodity is the relation between the various amounts of the commodity that might be bought and the determinants of those amounts. The determinants are: (1) the possible prices of the commodity, (2) the incomes of the buyers, (3) their tastes, and (4) the prices of closely related commodities. (Note 1 in the Appendix to Part 1 gives some examples of mathematical demand functions.)

The role of price will be taken up shortly. At this point, a few preliminary remarks will be made about the other determinants. Clearly, the incomes of buyers influence their purchases of a commodity. Though suitable enough for consumers making purchases at retail, the word *tastes* is hardly right for the state of mind of the purchasing agent of a business corporation. Presumably, the agent buys commodities on the basis of their specifications and of their estimated productivities for the company. The business demand for commodities is however immediately or ultimately dependent on consumer demand. Accordingly, a general analysis need not keep a high wall between consumer demand and business demand.

The commodities closely related to any one commodity are its substitutes and complements. The substitutes for any one commodity are the other commodities that can take its place, i.e., its alternatives. One brand of beer is a substitute for another. Complements are commodities that go together; for example, shoelaces and shoes, gasoline and lubricating oil, olives and martinis. In practical problems, the closely related commodities are nearly always easy to identify. Purchases of a commodity can be highly sensitive to changes in the prices of its substitutes and complements.[2] But the substitutes of a commodity have *their* substitutes, which in turn have *their* substitutes, etc. Much depends on how a commodity is defined.

Commodities, Markets, and Time

The word *commodity* can mean a broad or narrow class of objects, as well as some one unique object. The meaning of the word is nearly always plain from its context. Whether the meaning is broad or narrow depends on the problem at hand. Thus, the demand for meat can be a subject of investigation; so can the demand for beef, and the demand for sirloin steaks. Tobacco, automobiles, and housing are other examples of broad classes of commodities that can be subdivided into narrower classes. When commodities are successively subdivided into narrower classes, their demands undergo

---

[2] This point is elaborated in Chapter 4 under the heading of cross elasticity of demand.

changes, mainly because their substitutes take different forms. If the commodity is tobacco, it has no close substitutes. If the commodity is cigarettes, the substitutes are cigars and pipe tobacco. But if the commodity happens to be a brand of filter-tip cigarettes, then it has several even closer substitutes—the other brands.

How to define a commodity is by no means a problem thought up by academic hairsplitters. The problem comes up constantly in the enforcement of the antitrust laws. Millions of dollars can ride on the final decisions of the federal courts on how particular commodities should be defined. For example, suppose the commodity is baseballs. Should "the" commodity include *all* baseballs, those meeting major league specifications as well as the cheap rubber-covered baseballs bought for children? Or should baseballs be divided into three or four groups, each one a separate commodity? Remember that a children's ball is not a substitute for a major league ball, although a major league ball is an enthusiastically accepted substitute for a children's ball. The importance of the legal definition can be illustrated in this hypothetical example: Suppose 50 companies make baseballs of all kinds and that 2 of them merge. A merger may be unlawful if it substantially lessens competition. If there are now 49 companies instead of 50, competition is not reduced much. But if the 2 companies that merge turn out to be the only ones making major league baseballs, competition is not just substantially lessened; it is eliminated. If the courts decide that major league balls, not baseballs generally, are a distinct commodity, they will prohibit such a merger, thus denying to the companies the possible monopoly profits from merging.

The word commodity need not mean only physical objects, or classes of them. Services, such as entertainment and medical care, can also be included as commodities. After all, what people want from physical objects are the services they render. This is obviously true of durable goods, which provide services to their owners over periods of time. But it is also true of nondurable goods; food is there to be eaten, clothes are there to be worn, and so on.

A note on terminology: Economic literature does not distinguish, unvaryingly, between *commodities* and *products*. In some contexts the two words are interchangeable, but in others they convey different shades of meaning. In general, *commodity* is the broader term. Automobiles are commodities, but Chevrolets are products of General Motors Corporation. That is, the outputs of industries are commodities, whereas the outputs of individual business firms are products. In the national income and product accounts, however, all final goods and services are known as "products." The items in the gross national product are distinguished from "intermediate goods" and from "factors." Labor and capital[3] are the factors that produce a typewriter, which is a final product, if it is a personal typewriter. The steel in the typewriter is an intermediate good.

The demand for a commodity exists in a market. The word *market* also has a flexible meaning, and markets can also be subdivided. In general, a market is a set of points of contact between buyers and sellers. A market can, but need not, be a definite geographical area. The market for college professors does not exist at any one place, nor is it confined within national boundaries. Where markets are primarily geographical, they can also be local, regional, national, and international.

The demand for a commodity in a market must also be specified for a period of time. It obviously makes a difference whether demand is for a day, or a month, or a year, or longer. Because commodities, markets, and time periods can each be specified in many ways, and because the idea of demand requires all three of them, it follows that demand can take on an endless number of forms. What can be said about "the" demand for "a" commodity in "a" market in "a" period of time consists of the generalizations that apply to demand in all of the forms it can take.

Demand and Price

As a determinant of the demand for a commodity, price can have the simple meaning of money value per physical unit, e.g., 10¢ per pound. The wider meaning of price is the terms on which the commodity is available. The more expensive consumer durable goods are available on terms that include not only the quoted price, but also such matters as down payments, trade-in allowances, financing charges, and lengths of loans. Such matters do influence demand; for the sake of simplicity they will be treated here as having a cash equivalent which is part of "price."

DEMAND SCHEDULES AND DEMAND CURVES

The relation between demand and price occupies the center of the stage of price theory. Demand schedules and demand curves are the techniques for describing the demand-price relationship. The three other determinants of demand—tastes, incomes, and the prices of substitutes and complements—are held constant while attention focuses on demand and price. In other words, the willingness and the ability of buyers to buy are held constant while attention focuses on how the buyers would react to different prices.

Demand Schedules

A demand schedule, one of Alfred Marshall's many contributions to the techniques of price theory, is a list of prices and quantities. At

[3] In this book, land is not treated as a separate factor of production. The tendency in modern theory is to subsume land under capital. See the opening pages of Chapter 21.

each price, the corresponding quantity is the amount of the commodity that would be bought at that price. A simple demand schedule is shown in Table 2-1.

A demand schedule states the relation between the two variables of price and quantity. Economic theory employs many other relations between two variables; all are similar in form. The demand schedule in Table 2-1 should be read in this way: If the price were 10¢, the quantity bought would be 1,000 units; if instead the price were 9¢, the quantity bought would be 2,000 units, and so on. A demand schedule does not say what the price is. It only says what amounts would be bought at different possible prices. The lower the price, the larger is the quantity that is bought. Similarly, the higher the price, the smaller the quantity.

This inverse relationship between price and quantity is often called the *law of demand*. The law rests upon firm logic (the theory of consumer behavior presented in Chapters 5 and 6). The law also stands confirmed by many empirical investigations. For present purposes an intuitive explanation of the law of demand can suffice. At a given time in a given market, people will not buy more of a commodity unless its price becomes lower. The lower price makes it attractive for those persons who are already buying some of the commodity to buy more of it, and causes other persons to start buying some of the commodity.

Demand Curves

The price-quantity relation can be illustrated with numbers as in Table 2-1. It can also be displayed geometrically. The demand schedule is then transformed into a demand curve. The demand curve is always so called, even when it happens to be a straight line.

Figure 2-1 shows a demand curve. Price is plotted on the vertical axis and quantity on the horizontal axis.[4] The little circles in Figure 2-1 are obtained by using the numbers in Table 2-1. The circle in the upper left shows the price of 10¢ and the 1,000 units that would be bought at that price. The next one, down and to the right, shows 9¢ and 2,000 units, and so on. The heavy line is drawn from one circle to the next. This line is the demand curve.

Demand curves, supply curves, cost curves, and many others are used throughout economic theory. Once they are mastered, these visual aids become a convenient shorthand that can quickly and accurately portray the logic of economic relations. But demand curves, and the others, contain an important implicit assumption,

---

[4] Some mathematical economists reverse the axes, on the ground that quantity is the dependent variable, which belongs on the vertical axis. To put price on the vertical axis and quantity on the horizontal axis is a convention established by Alfred Marshall.

TABLE 2-1   **A DEMAND SCHEDULE**

Price	Quantity
10¢	1,000 units
9	2,000
8	3,000
7	4,000

FIGURE 2-1   **A DEMAND CURVE**

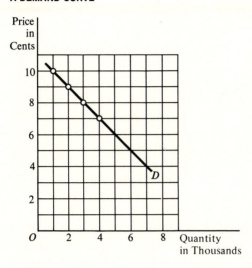

namely, that price and quantity vary continuously. This assumption is not realistic, but it has the great advantages of simplicity and of convenience.[5]

In Figure 2-2, a demand curve is constructed from bars instead of from the little circles in Figure 2-1. In Figure 2-2, the horizontal lengths of the bars represent the quantities bought at each of the prices shown. The vertical widths of the bars represent the gradations of price. The demand curve is drawn through the midpoints of the vertical widths at the right. The appearance of the bars suggests a set of steps. Imagine that the height of the steps becomes smaller and smaller—that the gradations of price become finer and finer. Ultimately, the height of the steps would become so small that the bars would become thin horizontal lines. The smooth curve would then give a perfect fit.

[5] The assumption of continuity is easily justified for demand curves that are statistically constructed from prices that are averages of discrete individual quotations.

FIGURE 2–2

ANOTHER DEMAND CURVE

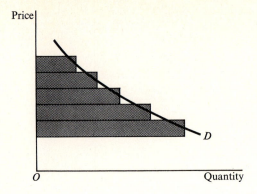

THE SLOPE OF A CURVE   With unimportant exceptions to be noted later, a demand curve always goes downward from left to right. The slope of a demand curve is negative. The notion of the *slope of a curve* is important in economic theory; there are many other kinds of curves besides demand curves. Hence a few words are in order on the meaning of the slope of a curve.

Figure 2–3 contains curves with different slopes. In this three-part figure, P and Q are price and quantity, but they could be any two other related variables. The curves *1, 2, 3,* and *4* show four of the possible relations between the two variables. Loosely speaking, the slope of a curve is its steepness. Strictly speaking, the slope of a curve has to be measured at a point on the curve. This is done by finding the slope of the tangent (i.e., the tangent line) to the curve at a point.

In Figure 2–3A, curve *1* goes downhill from left to right. So does the tangent at point A. The actual slope at point A is the line AB divided by the line BC. The lengths of the two lines are equal, so that

FIGURE 2–3   **THE SLOPES OF CURVES**

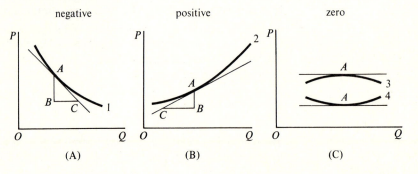

the slope at A is $1:1$, or unity. For a slope of unity, however, both axes have to have indentical unit scales. The slope of curve *1* is negative, because P decreases while Q increases.

In Figure 2-3B, curve *2* goes up and to the right. Here the slope at point A is AB divided by BC. Since AB is half as long as BC, the slope at A is $1:2$, or $\frac{1}{2}$. The slope of curve *2* is positive, because P increases as Q increases.

In Figure 2-3C, curves *3* and *4* are neither falling nor rising at their points A. Both tangents are horizontal; when they are, slopes are said to be zero.

The slope of a demand curve can vary from one point to another. But whether it is large or small, as measured by the slopes of tangents at different points, the slope of a demand curve is negative. Finally, if a demand curve is a straight line, it has the same negative slope at all points.

CHANGES
IN DEMAND

A change in demand is a change in an entire demand schedule; it is a shift in a demand curve. A change in demand comes from changes in buyers' tastes or in their incomes or in the prices of substitutes— singly or in combination. When demand increases, all of the quantities opposite each of the prices become larger. Or to say the same thing in another way: When demand increases, buyers are willing to pay a higher price than before for any given quantity.

An increase in demand should not be confused with an increase in the quantity bought because of a fall in price. Consider the hypothetical data in Table 2-2. In Schedule A, the quantity bought at the price of 9¢ is 2,000 units, and at 8¢ more is bought. But this is not an increase in demand. The demand remains the same—it is the whole schedule. But from Schedule A to Schedule B, the amount bought at 9¢ increases from 2,000 units to 3,000 units. And at each other price the amount increases. The meaning of an increase (or a decrease) in demand, then, is a change in the entire schedule.

The meaning of a change in demand is also shown in Figure 2-4. In the figure are two demand curves, D_1 and D_2. An increase in demand is a shift of the curve to the right. (That the two curves are parallel has no special meaning.) At the price OP_1, the amount

TABLE 2-2   **TWO DEMAND SCHEDULES**

| | Schedule A | | Schedule B | |
	P	Q	P	Q
	10¢	1,000 units	10¢	2,000 units
	9	2,000	9	3,000
	8	3,000	8	4,000

FIGURE 2-4

CHANGE IN DEMAND

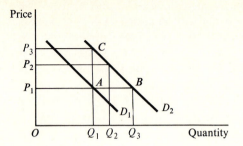

bought with D_1 is the quantity $P_1A(= OQ_1)$. When the demand increases to D_2, the quantity $P_1B(= OQ_3)$ is bought at the same price. Observe also that the quantity P_1A, equal to P_3C, is bought at the higher price OP_3, when demand is D_2. All of this, of course, applies in reverse, if demand decreases from D_2 to D_1.

A rise in price and an increase in demand often go together. In Figure 2-4, point A shows the quantity OQ_1, which is the quantity bought when demand is D_1 and price is P_1. Now look at point B: It shows the larger quantity OQ_3, which is bought at the same price P_1, after demand increases to D_2. Point C is directly above point A. The meaning of point C is that after the increase in demand, the buyers would buy the same quantity OQ_1 at the higher price P_3. The price P_2 is higher than P_1 but lower than P_3. At the price P_2 the quantity bought is OQ_2, which is a larger quantity than the quantity bought at P_1 on demand curve D_1. Thus the effect of an increase in demand can offset the effect of a rise in price. That is to say, when the price of a good or service goes up, you can expect that people will buy less. But if demand grows, it is quite possible that they will buy more, despite the higher price.

Causes of Changes in Demand

A demand curve is like a still photograph. Behind the price-quantity relation are always the tastes of the buyers, their incomes, and the prices of substitute and complementary commodities. When they change, the demand curve changes, shifting to the right or to the left. Demand curves are thus in constant motion; motion pictures would be far better than still photographs.

The causes of changes in demand will be more fully discussed in the next few chapters. At this point, a brief summary statement can be made. Table 2-3 contains it. The four causes of increases and decreases in demand can work in the same direction, or can offset one another. Each one can also have a different strength.

Exceptions to the Law of Demand

Full proof of the inverse relation between price and quantity appears in later chapters. For the time being, let it simply be assumed that the law of demand is valid.

TABLE 2-3

CAUSES OF CHANGES IN DEMAND

Increase	Decrease
Consumer desires become stronger	Consumer desires become weaker
Consumer incomes rise[a]	Consumer incomes fall[a]
Prices of substitutes rise	Prices of substitutes fall
Prices of complements fall	Prices of complements rise

[a] Exceptions to this statement are treated in Chapters 4 and 6.

Only two possible exceptions to the law of demand have been discovered, both of them quite unimportant. One is associated with the name of Thorstein Veblen (1857–1929), the sharp-tongued social critic, and his doctrine of conspicuous consumption. If consumers measure the desirability of a commodity entirely by its price, and if nothing else influences consumers, then they will buy less of the commodity at a low price, and more at a high price. Diamonds are often mentioned as an example. Here the demand curve has to be consumer demand, not the industrial demand for diamonds as cutting edges in machine tools. The other exception is associated with the name of Sir Robert Giffen (1837–1910), who is supposed to have said that a rise in the price of bread caused low-paid British wage earners, early in the nineteenth century, to buy more bread, not less. These wage earners subsisted on a diet of mainly bread. When its price rose, and when therefore they had to spend more money for a given quantity of bread, they could not afford to buy as much meat as before. To maintain their intake of food, they bought more bread at higher prices.

Other exceptions to the law of demand are apparent, not real. Remember local gasoline price wars? When motorists saw prices start to go down, they expected the prices to fall even farther. Then, if their tanks still held a few days' gasoline, people waited for the expected lower prices before buying more. Thus for a short while, buyers' *price expectations* dominated their behavior, causing their demand curves to shift to the left. The reverse is also true—higher prices with the expectation of further rises cause demand curves to shift to the right, with increases in the amounts bought. Then too, the statistical data for many commodities show large amounts bought at high prices and small amounts at low prices over the course of the business cycle. But such data do not contradict the law of demand; they mean only that the demands for many commodities increase in times of prosperity because of rising incomes, and decrease in times of depression, when incomes are falling. Still another false exception is the article sold under two brand names at the same time. Consumers often buy more of the higher-priced brand than of the low-priced, even though the articles are otherwise identical. But consumers who act in this way *think* that the two brands are different. Hence the two brands must be analyzed as if they were two different commodities.

The meaning of supply is symmetrical with the meaning of demand; thus there is no need to go into the definition of supply at length. In economics, the word *supply* always means a schedule—a schedule of possible prices and of amounts that would be sold at each price. A supply function is the relation between different quantities sold and the determinants of the quantities. In ordinary conversation, however, the word supply often signifies some single definite amount, such as the number of bushels of wheat produced last year or the number of barrels of heating oil in storage tanks last month.

Supply Schedules

Like a demand schedule, a supply schedule is a relation between prices and quantities for a given commodity, in a given market, and in a given period of time. Quantity is made to depend on price, the other variables that can affect quantity being held constant. No simple statement about the other variables can be made because the analysis of supply is much more complex than that of demand. At this point, however, some of the other variables can be mentioned. The prices of closely related commodities must be taken into account. The supply of hogs is affected by the price of corn. In general, the supply of any one product is influenced by the prices of others. The supply schedule for any one kind of labor depends on the earnings (which are also a price) this labor could obtain in another employment. In short periods of time, the supply of a commodity can be dominated by the sellers' expectations of future prices. Over longer periods of time, changes in technology cause changes in costs, which in turn influence supply. The supplies of many commodities are affected by forces such as the weather, strikes, and other temporary and ephemeral incidents and disturbances.

A hypothetical supply schedule is shown in Table 2–4. The numbers in the table can be imagined as applying to the sellers of some kind of grain in a particular market on a particular day. Notice that the higher the price, the larger the quantity. This relation generally

TABLE 2–4   A SUPPLY SCHEDULE

Price	Quantity
$2.00	40 million bushels
1.95	38
1.90	36
1.80	34

FIGURE 2-5

CHANGE IN SUPPLY

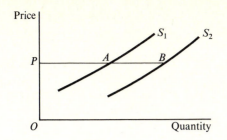

holds in supply schedules, but not always, because there can be supply schedules where larger quantities are sold at *lower* prices. More will be said on this in later chapters.

Supply Curves Like demand curves, supply curves are also drawn to present a smooth continuous relation between price and quantity. They too can be straight lines and still be called curves. Figure 2-5 shows two supply curves, S_1 and S_2. They have positive slopes; that is, they go up and to the right. Consider curve S_1 first. One price is shown in the figure, the price OP. At this price, the amount sold is PA. The quantity supplied *at* the price OP is PA. It is evident that more would be sold at a higher price and less at a lower price. The curve S_2 is there to illustrate the meaning of a change in supply. An increase in supply is a shift of the whole curve to the right—the shift from S_1 to S_2. With an increased supply, more is sold at any price— the amount PB instead of PA, at price OP. The meaning of a decrease in supply is simply the reverse. (See Note 2 in the Appendix to Part 1.)

An expression often used by economists because of its convenient brevity is "supply price." The supply price of anything is the price that will call forth a certain supply, or amount, of the commodity or service under some given circumstances. A supply price is the price corresponding to a point on a supply curve. For example, the supply price of pianists who can play cocktail music in bars is probably low, because it seems that there are always many such persons who are willing to perform for comparatively little money. On the other hand, the supply price of double the number of neurosurgeons who now specialize in one of the new exotic fields is probably very high, because additional neurosurgeons would have to be attracted away from other new, exciting, and well-paid fields of medicine.

MARKET PRICE Demand and supply can now be brought together in the determination of market price. Imagine a market such as the wheat market in

Chicago, where there are many buyers and sellers who want to buy and to sell quantities of a standardized commodity. Each person in the market acts independently. Each buys or sells such a small fraction of the quantities traded that this action has no visible effect on the market as a whole. That is what *many* means.

Here we have the simplest and most general model of the process of price determination. The main feature of the model is that stocks of the commodity are already in existence. They are not in the process of being produced—they are there, on hand, in the possession of the sellers. Therefore, market supply schedules are not influenced by costs of production. Estimates of prices and of costs made in the past—weeks ago, or months ago, or perhaps even years ago—caused the quantities to be what they are today, or this week, or this month. Meanwhile, much has happened. Past estimates are usually wrong, if only by a little; past costs may or may not be recouped in today's selling price.

The market supply schedule, then, shows the amounts the sellers would sell at different possible prices. The perishability of the commodity, its storage costs if it is storable, the price it might fetch in another market if one exists—these matters, together with the sellers' price expectations and their cash positions, determine the shapes of market supply schedules.

Market demand schedules must be defined for similarly short periods. Buyers are also influenced by their expectations of future prices. Is now the time to buy? Or should purchases be postponed because prices will probably fall in the next few weeks? The availabilities and prices of substitute commodities also influence buyers, as well as their cash positions.

The Equilibrium Price

The equilibrium price in the market period is the price that equates the quantity demanded with the quantity supplied. At this price, the buyers are willing to buy a certain amount. The sellers are willing to sell exactly the same amount. The market is cleared, there being no surplus and no shortage. Of course, some buyers and some sellers are disappointed; the equilibrium price is too high or too low for them.

Figure 2-6 shows how to visualize the determination of the equilibrium market price. In some market in some short period of time, D and S are the demand and supply curves, the graphic versions of the market demand and supply schedules just discussed. The two curves intersect at point A, which corresponds to the price OP_1 and to the quantity, bought and sold, P_1A. At price OP_1, demand and supply are equal. At a higher price such as OP_2, the quantity demanded is P_2B, whereas the quantity supplied is P_2C. The excess supply of BC forces the price down. The higher price

FIGURE 2-6

EQUILIBRIUM OF DEMAND AND SUPPLY

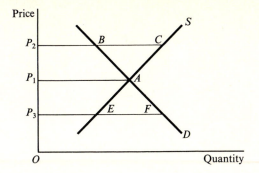

can prevail only briefly because the sellers try to sell more than the buyers want to buy at the same price. Similarly, a price lower than the equilibrium can exist only briefly because the excess demand *EF* pushes the price up. The buyers try to buy more than the sellers want to sell.

The model displayed in Figure 2-6 is simple, but being simple it is also general. As a first approximation, the model is accordingly applicable to a wide range of markets—the organized markets in which farm products are sold, the produce markets in large cities, the stock exchanges, the government-bond market, the foreign exchange markets where rates are free. The model is a generalization about these and similar markets. These markets differ among themselves in many ways; any one generalization about them omits much. Still, the model draws attention to the forces common and basic in all markets. It is best to think of the demand and supply curves as being in ceaseless motion so that, always, new equilibrium prices are coming into being. A diagram such as Figure 2-6 is like a snapshot of a scene of action.

SOME APPLICATIONS

The first and greatest use of the concept of the demand curve is in understanding part of the mechanism of a whole economy. The gross national product consists of many billion dollars' worth of many thousands of final products. What the products are and the relative amounts of each are decided in part by demand. Rattlesnake meat and beef are both foodstuffs; both are produced and sold. But much less of one is sold than of the other, the difference in demand being a good enough explanation.

Surpluses and Shortages

Surpluses and shortages of commodities appear here and there in the American economy much of the time. Until the 1970s, the word *surplus* was likely to suggest farm products such as wheat and cotton and the problems that government faced when it tried to raise

FIGURE 2-7

SURPLUSES AND SHORTAGES

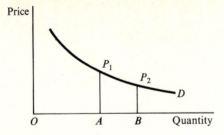

their prices. In its turn, the word *shortage* brings to mind one of the main consequences of wartime and peacetime price controls. Even when there are no government price controls, temporary surpluses and shortages arise from mistakes in pricing by business firms. These surpluses and shortages can be illustrated by a simple application of the demand curve.

Figure 2-7 can be interpreted to show the meaning of both surpluses and shortages. Suppose that the amount of a commodity offered for sale in some period of time is *OB*. Suppose too that the prevailing price is P_1A. At the price P_1A, however, the consumers will buy only the amount *OA*, for this is the information conveyed by the demand curve *D*. The amount *AB* is not sold—it is the surplus. The surplus remains on shelves or in warehouses during the time period in question. Unless the demand increases, so that at price P_1A the whole amount *OB* will be bought, the sellers of the commodity must either keep the unsold surplus or lower the price. If they had chosen the price P_2 to begin with, there would of course have been no surplus at all.

Next, let Figure 2-7 show the meaning of a shortage. Suppose the amount offered for sale is *OA*, and that the price is P_2B. Hence buyers try to buy the amount *OB*, with the result that a shortage equal to *AB* exists. When the quantity available is *OA* and when the price is P_2B, the price is "too low." Too low a price creates a shortage. Examples of shortages arising from prices that are too low are the natural gas sold in interstate commerce in the 1960s and early 1970s, camping sites in busy seasons in national parks, and retail gasoline in the first few months of 1974. Shortages can take different forms. Retailers might have the commodity in stock only part of the time. If dealers establish waiting lists, the length of the waiting period becomes another measure of the size of the shortage.

Prices are often said to perform a rationing function. A large crop sells at a low price, a small one at a high price. The idea of the demand curve shows at once why and how this is so.

Price Fixing   Federal, state, and local governments engage in many forms of price fixing. For the most part, price fixing by government is confined to monopolistic industries—transportation, electric power, natural gas, telephone service, etc. But there is also some price fixing in industries that can be analyzed with the simple model of demand and supply. Price fixing, i.e., the establishment of definite prices, must be distinguished from activities designed to raise or lower the prices determined by demand and supply in free markets. In practice, price fixing means that a government agency sets either maximum or minimum prices.

Maximum   Maximum prices are imposed either as one of many economic con-
Prices   trols in a period of national emergency or as a means of redistributing income from one group of persons to another. Wartime price controls are one prominent example; peacetime rent controls are another.

   To become a problem, a maximum price must necessarily lie *below* the equilibrium price of the commodity or service in question, that is, of course, the equilibrium price that would prevail in the absence of price control. In the past, the common method of fixing maximum prices was to declare them to be the prices actually being paid and received on a given date. To pay or receive higher prices after that date was unlawful.

   Figure 2-8 gives a simplified illustration. Initially, D_1 and S are demand and supply. Suppose that the quantities demanded and supplied are in equilibrium at A; the equilibrium price is therefore P_m. Imagine that this price is declared to be the maximum. Then imagine that demand increases to D_2, the supply curve remaining constant. The quantity supplied is still P_mA, but would-be consumption at this price is P_mB. Therefore, the unfilled demand, i.e., the shortage, is the quantity AB.

FIGURE 2–8   **EFFECT OF A MAXIMUM PRICE**

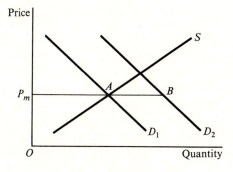

In Figure 2-8, three prices are to be distinguished: two equilibrium prices and the maximum price. The "old" equilibrium price is given by the intersection of D_1 and S. The "new" equilibrium price is determined by the intersection of D_2 and S. At the new equilibrium price, however, transactions do not take place, because government establishes the maximum price at the old equilibrium level.

The size of the shortage when the maximum price is below the new equilibrium price depends on the change in demand. If the shortage is not handled by the imposition of perfectly enforced rationing on the buyers, a black market is likely to spring into life. Black markets (or white markets, if they are sanctioned by government) are always and everywhere the result of the setting of maximum prices by governments. An analytical question is this: Is the black market price identical with the new equilibrium price? It could be if the government made little effort to enforce its maximum, if buyers and sellers alike unhesitatingly flouted the government, and if they had the same information in the black market as in the formerly free market. The black market price could, however, be below the new equilibrium price if some buyers or sellers, or both, were unwilling or afraid to trade in the black market. This can be shown by drawing black market demand and supply curves, above the maximum price, each one to the left of the ordinary curves. Their point of intersection could, though it need not, lie below the new equilibrium level.

To use the model for the rental dwelling market is, perhaps, going a little too far. Though they are far from homogeneous, dwellings can be lumped together as "housing" in a broad-brush treatment. Rent controls are also maximum prices. They too cause shortages and networks of little black markets. In some countries, rent controls have been kept in force so long that they dried up the construction of new dwellings. Typically in such countries, governments have had to undertake public housing projects of great size.

TWO MORE EXAMPLES: BUSES AND LIBRARIES   Suppose a city operates its own bus system. The passengers will of course have to pay a fare. The people who use the city's public library, however, do not have to pay any fees for the library's normal services. In other words, the residents of the city pay a price for bus service but pay zero for library service. Why does this difference exist? One kind of answer to this question could be a complex discussion of the public interest that is attached to public libraries and to municipal transportation. A simple way to answer the question, however, is to bring forward the concept of the demand curve. The demand curve for library service must touch the quantity axis at some point. This means that, at price = zero, the quantity is some definite number of, say, books borrowed per average day. This number is within the capacity of the library. In contrast, the demand curve for bus rides would, it seems certain, flatten out at low fares (say, 10¢ and 5¢), and, at price zero the quantity demanded would be huge, far in excess of the bus system. With nothing to pay, many people would want to ride a block or two. The buses would be so crowded, at least at some times of the day, that the elderly and the infirm might not be able to get on at all. Such indeed was the experience in one of the communist countries when the new rulers operated a street car system without charging fares. Chaos ensued. To eliminate it, the rulers had to reinstate fares, so as to bring the quantity demanded within the feasible limits of the system.

Like a public library, a college library charges no fees for its ordinary services. The demand for these services fluctuates; it is high before examination periods and low at the beginning of the academic year, when everyone has something else to do. The reserve book room can be a problem because of the congestion just before exams, with accompanying irritation and frustration. One way to reduce the congestion, so it has been seriously proposed, would be to charge a fee for the use of each reserve book during the periods that experience shows are congested. Figure 2-9 illustrates how this proposal would work ideally. The normal or average daily demand for reserve books is D_A. There is no fee for normal use. With the price at zero, the number of books taken out is OA. The demand in congested periods is D_B. With no fee in such periods, students would want to use OB books, which causes problems. With a fee equal to price OP in congested periods, students would take out PC books. Rather than pay the price, some students would reschedule their reading plans. Whether or not this is a good proposal is, no doubt, a debatable subject.

FIGURE 2-9   THE DEMAND FOR RESERVE BOOKS

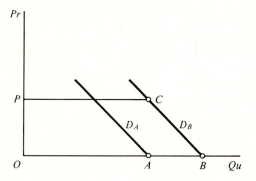

When a government agency sets a minimum price for a commodity, the result is nearly always a "surplus" of the commodity. The surplus is often called "overproduction," but this means nothing more than the excess of the quantity supplied over the quantity demanded *at* the minimum price.

When it results in a surplus, a minimum price is *above* the equilibrium of demand and supply. The size of the surplus depends on the gap between the minimum and the equilibrium prices and on the shapes of the demand and supply curves. If the minimum price is maintained at a constant figure, the size of the surplus varies from period to period as demand and supply change. In some periods, the equilibrium price may rise above the minimum so that the surplus temporarily disappears.

The disposal of a surplus is always a problem. The government agency fixing a minimum price must take some action to keep the excess supply off the market, for otherwise the minimum price cannot be made effective. One technique is for the government agency to buy and hold the surplus quantities of the commodity. Or, government can buy and destroy the surplus. Occasionally, surplus foodstuffs have been rendered physically unfit for human consumption by deliberate action. Another technique for handling the surplus resulting from a minimum price is to divert the surplus quantity to other markets. Milk is an example. In many areas of the United States, the federal government lends its auspices to the establishment of minimum prices for fluid milk. The surplus milk, whose amount has a strong seasonal fluctuation, is diverted to the markets where milk is converted into butter, cheese, ice cream, and other products.

DEMAND AND "NEED"

The demand concept is often ignored or overlooked by those who should know better, with the result that some great issues of public policy become beclouded and confused. Take the example of water. Water shortages have occurred in many communities, and from time to time, forecasts of a future water shortage for the whole nation are made. Population is growing, so are the urban communities, and so is industrial production. At present rates of consumption—per household, per ton of steel, per acre of irrigated land, etc.—the future "needs" for water will exceed the physical amounts available. Such is the common pattern of thought, which operates with the idea of the need for water as if the need were a fixed (or almost a fixed) number of gallons of water, per household, per ton of steel, etc. The common view looks to the need for water, not to the demand for it.

That there is a need for water is beyond dispute, but for how much? Does the suburbanite need enough so that the garden hose can run for a few more hours because it's too much trouble to go out and turn it off? Do the owners of an industrial plant need so much that they can always draw fresh amounts and not have to install equipment to reuse water?

Obviously, if the price of water were higher, less of it would be used in households, in industry, and in agriculture. When the price of water is adjusted so that the amount available is equal to the quantity demanded *at that price*, there can be no shortage. The future might hold the prospect of more expensive water, but proper pricing policies will prevent "shortages." This is not to say that pricing alone should be relied upon to handle the water problem of the future. Larger facilities to furnish water will be constructed; that is, there will be adjustments on the supply side, too. The flaw in looking only at "need" is that the entire burden of adjustment is placed on supply. The correct policy is to use both supply and demand.

SUMMARY

The *demand function* for a commodity is the relation between the various amounts of the commodity that might be bought and (1) the possible prices of the commodity, (2) the incomes of the buyers, (3) their tastes, and (4) the prices of closely related commodities. A *commodity* can be broadly or narrowly defined; how to do so depends on the purpose of analysis. Similarly, *markets* can be broadly or narrowly defined, and *time periods* can be long or short.

When buyers' incomes and tastes as well as the prices of closely related commodities are held constant, attention centers on the relation between demand and price. A *demand schedule* is a list of possible prices and of quantities that would be bought at each possible price in a market in a period of time. A *demand curve* portrays the quantity-price relation. The *law of demand* causes a demand curve to have a *negative slope*; exceptions are rare and unimportant. An *increase in demand* means that the entire demand curve shifts to the right; a decrease in demand is a shift to the left. Demand curves shift or change because of changes in consumer tastes, in consumer incomes, and in the prices of substitutes and complements. *Supply schedules* and *supply curves* also show relations between quantities and prices. The *equilibrium price* equates the quantity demanded with the quantity supplied.

SELECTED REFERENCES

Alfred Marshall, *Principles of Economics*, 8th ed. (Macmillan, London, 1920), III, chaps. 1, 2, 3. Demand analysis for the business firm is presented by W. Warren Haynes and William R. Henry, *Managerial Economics: Analysis and Cases,* 3d ed. (Business Publications, Dallas, 1974), chap. 3. The classic work on empirical demand study is Henry Schultz, *The Theory and Measurement of Demand* (University of Chicago Press, Chicago, 1938).

For an economic analysis of the water problem, see Donald Stevenson Watson, ed., *Price Theory in Action: A Book of Readings,* 3d ed. (Houghton Mifflin, Boston, 1973), chap. 55.

EXERCISES AND PROBLEMS

1. Practice drawing demand curves. For example, take the nationwide annual demand for new automobiles. Start a demand curve with 8 million cars at $3,500. Then, with price assumed to be the only variable affecting purchases, make guesses about other points on the demand curve. Practice reading a demand curve from both axes: How many cars would be bought at $4,800? What would the price have to be if 10 million cars are to be bought?

2. Construct a hypothetical demand curve for pay television. Suppose there are 100,000 television sets in private homes in a metropolitan area and that all of the sets are equipped to receive special programs on payment of a fee. Suppose too that pay television has been in existence long enough for its novelty to wear off. Let the "commodity" be high-quality, first-run movies, one being broadcast each week. Let the possible fees for seeing any one of these movies on pay television be 25¢, or 50¢, or 75¢, or $1.00, etc. Make up a plausible demand schedule—number of thousands of sets turned on to pay TV in an average week.

3. People need medical care. Of that, there can be no doubt. But what about demand? For simplicity and convenience, let a unit of medical care be defined as one consultation with a physician. Would people buy the same number of units of medical care at $10 each as they would at $2 each? As many at $25 each as at $10? Construct a hypothetical demand schedule for medical care in a community of 10,000 families. In your demand schedule, include a fee of $0, i.e., free medical care. Write a short statement in explanation of your hypothetical estimate.

4. Suppose that the price of a commodity declines from one month to the next and that more is bought in the second month. Draw a diagram to show that demand could have increased, or decreased, or remained the same.

5. Draw demand and supply curves that show a severe water shortage in a metropolitan area when the price of water is 50¢ per 1,000 gallons, and a surplus of water when the price is 75¢.

6. Explain why elegant restaurants usually require reservations,

whereas cafeterias and family restaurants rarely accept reservations.

7. Draw a diagram to show what would happen if the government imposed a ceiling on the retail price of gasoline. Why do some advocates of price controls also recommend rationing?

8. Although many people are not aware of it, clean water and clean air have market prices just as other goods and services do. Draw hypothetical demand curves for clean water, with various possible prices, for the following kinds of communities: (a) a community whose main source of income comes from tourism, (b) a community whose main source of income comes from finance and insurance activities, and (c) a community whose main source of income comes from steel and automobile production.

9. Draw demand and supply curves that show an equilibrium price and an equilibrium quantity. Now assume an increase in demand. What compensating change in supply would be needed to keep the same equilibrium price? What have the changes in demand and supply done to the equilibrium quantity?

3

PRICE

Elasticity

OF DEMAND

So far, demand has been described as the inverse relation between price and quantity. At lower prices, more is bought. But how much more? A great deal or just a little? Similarly, at higher prices, less is bought. Much less or only a little less? If the price of gasoline went up by 50 per cent, would people buy 50 per cent less gasoline or would they buy 5 per cent less, or what? To answer questions like these is to make use of the concept of price elasticity of demand. Broadly, demand is elastic if quantity is highly responsive to price, and inelastic if it is not.

THE MEANING OF ELASTICITY

Price elasticity of demand is one of a family of concepts of elasticity. In economics, elasticity always has the same meaning; it is the *ratio* of the *relative* change in a dependent to the *relative* change in an independent variable. In other words, elasticity is the relative change in the dependent variable divided by the relative change in the independent variable. The subject of this chapter is price elasticity of demand. The dependent variable is quantity demanded; the dependent variable is price. Other elasticity concepts to be taken up in the next chapter are income elasticity, cross elasticity, the elasticity of price expectations, and price elasticity of supply. Advanced theory makes use of still other elasticity concepts. They are all ratios of relative changes.

Alfred Marshall was the first economist to give a clear formulation of price elasticity as the ratio of a relative change in quantity to a relative change in price. Let E stand for elasticity. Then

$$E = \frac{\text{relative change in quantity}}{\text{relative change in price}}.$$

Equivalently, elasticity is the percentage change in quantity divided by the percentage change in price. If the percentages are known—they can often be estimated—then the numerical value of E can be calculated. Suppose the percentages are 2 for quantity and 1 for price, and that the price falls. Since it falls, price changes by minus 1 per cent. Then

$$E = \frac{2\%}{-1\%} = -2.$$

If, instead, price goes up, the *quantity* change is minus 2 per cent. Therefore E, the price elasticity of demand, is always negative; because it is, the minus sign can henceforth be disregarded. To do so is common practice.

Why does the definition of elasticity express the changes in quantity and price as *relative* changes? The reason is that a given absolute change can be relatively large or relatively small. Suppose a price goes up by 5¢. This is a relatively large increase for chewing gum or for a newspaper. But a 5¢ price increase is relatively small if it applies to an electric appliance or to a suit of clothes. Similarly, a change in quantity of a thousand bushels is relatively large if it applies to a rare herb and is extremely small if it applies to wheat.

The Coefficient of Elasticity

E is also called the *coefficient* of elasticity of demand. It is a pure number; that is, it stands by itself, being independent of units of measurement. When numerical estimates are possible, the coefficients of elasticity of different commodities can be directly compared. Another common way to state the coefficient of elasticity of demand is

$$E = \frac{\Delta Q}{Q} \bigg/ \frac{\Delta P}{P} = \frac{\Delta Q}{Q} \times \frac{P}{\Delta P} = \frac{P}{Q} \frac{\Delta Q}{\Delta P}.$$

Here, Q is quantity, P is price, and Δ (delta) is the symbol meaning "a change in." Thus, $\frac{\Delta Q}{Q}$ is a relative change in quantity, and $\frac{\Delta P}{P}$ is a relative change in price.

To continue with definitions: If the coefficient E is greater than 1, demand is said to be elastic. If E equals 1, demand has unit elasticity. If E is less than 1, but more than 0, demand is inelastic. If the coefficient is zero, demand is said to be perfectly inelastic. A zero coefficient means that a change in price is accompanied by no change—at all—in the quantity bought. Hence ΔQ is zero, making the whole fraction zero.

If a change in price causes an infinitely large change in quantity, then ΔQ in the fraction is infinitely large. This gives the coefficient the value of infinity. When the coefficient is infinity, demand is said to be infinitely, or perfectly, elastic. Because he sells so small a part of the total, the demand for the wheat of any *one* wheat farmer is perfectly elastic at the prevailing price. This means that the farmer

TABLE 3-1   **DEMAND SCHEDULES WITH DIFFERENT ELASTICITIES**

Elastic Demand			Unit Elastic Demand			Inelastic Demand		
P	Q	PQ	P	Q	PQ	P	Q	PQ
$10	1,000 units	$10,000	$10	1,000 units	$10,000	$10	1,000 units	$10,000
9	2,000	18,000	9	1,111	10,000	9	1,050	9,450
8	3,000	24,000	8	1,250	10,000	8	1,100	8,800

Note: *PQ* is price multiplied by quantity, and is therefore the total dollar expenditure by consumers, at each price.

can sell all he has at that price without causing the price to change. He could sell nothing at all at any higher price.

ELASTICITY AND EXPENDITURE

If demand is elastic, a given fall in price causes a relatively larger increase in the amount bought. From this it follows that a drop in price causes consumers to make a larger money expenditure on a commodity whose demand is elastic. If demand is inelastic, a fall in price causes consumers to spend less money on the commodity. And if demand has unit elasticity, a fall in price causes no change in expenditures.

These relations can be illustrated with simple hypothetical demand schedules. This is done in Table 3-1, which contains three demand schedules. Each has the same set of prices, but the quantities are different, being so chosen as to make the demand schedules elastic, unit elastic, and inelastic. Table 3-1 has one flaw, though an unavoidable one. In the unit elastic demand schedule, the relative changes in price and in quantity are close but are not exactly identical. A change in price from $10 to $9 is a drop of 10 per cent, but the corresponding increase in quantity bought is 11.1 per cent. The discrepancy results from the choice of discrete numbers—after all, 9 and 10 are far apart, farther apart than 9.9 and 10, which are farther apart than 9.99 and 10, and so on. Often popping up in arithmetical illustrations of economic relations, such discrepancies are not serious, but they cause arithmetic to be an awkward servant.

The relations between elasticity and expenditure are stated in more general form in Table 3-2.

The expenditures of consumers are of course the same amounts as the revenues of the sellers. If demand is elastic (inelastic), a lower price brings more (less) revenue to the sellers. A higher price causes revenue to be smaller (larger) if demand is elastic (inelastic).

Suppose you own a small movie theater located in a new shopping mall in an affluent suburb. With the price of admission at $3, you sell 1,200 tickets a week. But most of the time many seats in your theater are empty. You cut the price to $1 and find that you sell

TABLE 3–2   **ELASTICITY AND EXPENDITURE**

	Elastic	Unit Elastic	Inelastic	Perfectly Inelastic
Value of coefficient	$E > 1$	$E = 1$	$0 < E < 1$	$E = 0$
Effect of fall in price	$\dfrac{\Delta Q}{Q} > \dfrac{\Delta P}{P}$ larger expenditure	$\dfrac{\Delta Q}{Q} = \dfrac{\Delta P}{P}$ constant expenditure	$\dfrac{\Delta Q}{Q} < \dfrac{\Delta P}{P}$ smaller expenditure	$\Delta Q = 0$ fall in expenditure is proportional to fall in price
Effect of rise in price	$\dfrac{\Delta Q}{Q} > \dfrac{\Delta P}{P}$ smaller expenditure	$\dfrac{\Delta Q}{Q} = \dfrac{\Delta P}{P}$ constant expenditure	$\dfrac{\Delta Q}{Q} < \dfrac{\Delta P}{P}$ larger expenditure	$\Delta Q = 0$ rise in expenditure is proportional to rise in price

Note: In the first row above, under inelastic, $0 < E < 1$ means that E is less than 1 but greater than 0. The coefficient can be anywhere between but not including 1 and 0.

5,000 tickets a week. Here the demand is obviously elastic; at the lower price the customers—as a group—spend more money. And you have larger gross revenue.

Here is an actual example of an inelastic demand: In Washington, D.C., the private transit company was permitted in July 1970 to raise its bus fare from 32¢ to 40¢. In August 1970 there were 8.2 million passengers as compared with 9.3 million passengers in August 1969. Fewer riders spent more money. Another way to see that the demand here was inelastic is this: The 25 per cent fare increase caused a 12 per cent decline in the use of buses.

Another example is the rise in rates per kilowatt hour for electricity brought on by the energy crisis that began in the mid–1970s. Monthly electric bills went up substantially. Consumer protests were more than normally angry because, in the name of conservation, many households had dutifully cut back their usage of kilowatt hours. But the higher rates, or prices, more than offset the slight leftward shift of the demand curves. With demands being inelastic, the higher prices yielded more revenue to the utility companies and bigger bills to the consumers.

ELASTIC AND INELASTIC DEMAND CURVES

Elasticity and inelasticity of demand can be easily portrayed through demand curves. Figure 3–1 shows five demand curves of differing elasticities. Elastic demand is drawn as a curve that is relatively flat, whereas the curve for an inelastic demand is relatively steep. Price changes are shown in the upper part of Figure 3–1. Suppose that price falls from P_1 to P_2. Then quantity increases from Q_1 to Q_2. Total dollar expenditures of the buyers are the *rectangles*—prices multiplied by quantities. In the elastic demand, the rectangle P_2Q_2 is

FIGURE 3-1

DIFFERING ELASTICITIES OF DEMAND

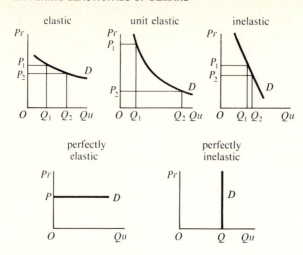

bigger than the rectangle P_1Q_1, signifying a larger total expenditure at the lower price. The opposite is true of the inelastic demand. When demand is unit elastic at all prices, the rectangles have exactly the same areas. A demand curve with unit elasticity is called a *rectangular hyperbola*. The lower part of Figure 3-1 shows a perfectly elastic demand curve which is a horizontal line, and a perfectly inelastic demand curve which is a vertical line.

Four warnings must now be uttered. The first is that to portray elastic demand as a relatively flat curve and inelastic demand as a relatively steep curve is a convention accurate enough for some purposes, but not for others. If, as is often true, it matters in an economic problem only whether demand is elastic or inelastic, a flat curve or a steep curve will do. But if a problem makes it important to take a close look at elasticity, slope turns out to be a poor or even a wrong measure.[1] After all, the slope of a demand curve is $\dfrac{\Delta P}{\Delta Q}$, whereas elasticity is $\dfrac{P\Delta Q}{Q\Delta P}$. These reminders lead to the idea of varying elasticities on the same demand curve, an idea that will be discussed shortly.

The second warning is about the scales on the axes of the diagram. If elastic demand is to be represented by a flat curve, the scales have to be in order. If the price axis has the scale 10, 9, 8, etc., and if the quantity axis has the scale 1, 2, 3, etc., for, say, each

---

[1] When a demand curve is plotted on double logarithmic paper, slope does become an exact measure of elasticity, because double log scales compare percentage changes. See Note 4 in the Appendix to Part 1.

quarter inch, then the curve is relatively flat—over that range of prices and quantities. But if the same prices are coupled with quantities of 101, 102, 103, for each quarter inch, etc., demand of course would be inelastic, though the curve would still be relatively flat.

A third warning is on the interpretation of changes in prices. Suppose that the price of a commodity rises from one month to the next and that less is bought at the higher price. From these facts alone, no certain inference about elasticity can be drawn. In Figure 3-2, the price rise is from P_1 to P_2. These two prices can be observed, along with the quantities bought at each of the prices. What demand curve or curves do the prices lie on? The two prices *could* lie on one stable demand curve, which is D_3. Or quite possibly, P_1 is a point on demand curve D_1 and P_2 is a point on curve D_2. In other words, the observed rise in price could take place along the one unchanged and inelastic demand D_3, or the rise in price could go along with an *increase* in demand from D_1 to D_2. Both of these curves happen to be relatively elastic. Which is it, then? A stable demand or an increasing demand? This is something to be estimated with the help of additional information—on buyers' incomes and tastes, and on the movements of the prices of substitutes during the month in question.

The fourth warning is about another kind of misinterpretation, namely, drawing wrong conclusions from reflection on personal experience. Suppose, for example, that the bus fare goes up 10 cents and that despite this, you keep on riding the bus just as often as before. It is wrong to leap to the conclusion that the demand for bus service is *therefore* perfectly or highly inelastic. The demand for bus service comes from thousands of people in the city. Their mass response to the change in fare is the demand behavior under examination here. One of the differences between the behavior of people en masse and as individuals is in the response to changes in price. The mass, or market, demand for a commodity can be elastic, even though the demands of some of the buyers are inelastic.

FIGURE 3-2   ELASTIC OR INELASTIC DEMAND?

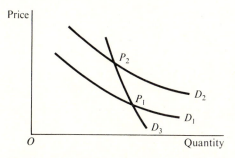

FIGURE 3-3

ELASTICITIES AND PRICE RANGES

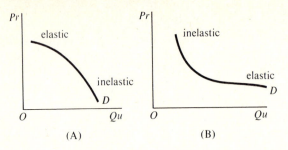

(A)   (B)

So far, the terms *elastic* and *inelastic* have been applied to the whole demand for a commodity. This is accurate enough for some purposes, but not for others, because the demand for a commodity can be elastic in one price range and inelastic in another. The degree of elasticity or of inelasticity—as indicated by the size of the coefficient—can also vary from one price range to another.

Figure 3-3 shows two demand curves. Notice that the demand curve in Figure 3-3A is elastic at high prices and inelastic at low prices. The demand curve in Figure 3-3B is just the opposite. Both kinds of demand curves are possible.

By itself, "price range" is not a precise expression. The coefficient of elasticity could vary within some given range, as well as from one price range to another. Precision requires that elasticity be measured at a *point* on a demand curve.

Figure 3-4 shows how to find the elasticity at a point on a demand curve. On the demand curve D, take any point, such as P. Draw a tangent to the demand curve at point P. Then the ratio $\dfrac{PA}{PB}$ is an exact measure of elasticity at point P.[2] In Figure 3-4A, demand at P is elastic because PA is longer than PB. It is about twice as long, so that the coefficient is about 2. In Figure 3-4B, in contrast, demand at point P is inelastic because PB is about twice as long as PA. The coefficient is therefore about 0.5.

Point elasticity is the ratio of an infinitesimally small relative change in quantity to an infinitesimally small change in price. If a price range is made as small as possible, i.e., shrunk to a point, then the relative changes must be made as small as possible—

[2]Proof: $E = \dfrac{P}{Q}\dfrac{\Delta Q}{\Delta P}$. The term $\dfrac{\Delta Q}{\Delta P}$ is the reciprocal of the slope. The slope of the line BA in Figure 3-4A is $\dfrac{PC}{CA}$. In Figure 3-4A, P is PC, Q is OC, and $\dfrac{\Delta Q}{\Delta P}$ is $\dfrac{CA}{PC}$. Therefore, $E = \dfrac{PC}{OC} \times \dfrac{CA}{PC} = \dfrac{CA}{OC}$. And since the triangles PCA and BOA are similar, $\dfrac{CA}{OC} = \dfrac{PA}{PB}$.

FIGURE 3–4   **POINT ELASTICITY OF DEMAND**

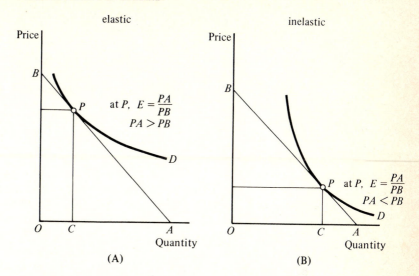

at P, $E = \dfrac{PA}{PB}$

$PA > PB$

at P, $E = \dfrac{PA}{PB}$

$PA < PB$

(A)   (B)

infinitesimally small. Though the logic of point elasticity is exact, the concept might not at first seem useful. In fact, however, it is useful and has been used many times. In the statistical measurement of demand, quantitative data are fed into mathematical formulas that often contain the point elasticity idea.[3] (See Notes 2 and 3 in the Appendix to Part 1.) If the formulas do a good job of describing the demand for a commodity, they can be used for prediction.

Arc Elasticity   The precise measure, point elasticity, is used when a demand curve is known, either by assumption or through a statistical calculation based on many observations of prices and quantities. Often, however, only scanty data are available, the data being a few price-quantity observations of purchases of a commodity. Then another measure of price elasticity comes to the fore. The measure is *arc elasticity*; an arc is a portion or a segment of a demand curve.

---

[3] Elasticity as a ratio of percentages and point elasticity are identical only for linear demand curves. In empirical work, calculated demand functions often contain a constant price elasticity assumption; that is, point elasticity is constant at all points on a curvilinear demand. To illustrate how the percentage and point methods can give different results: Let the demand function be $q = ap^{-1}$, where q is quantity, p is price, and a is a constant that locates the demand curve. The exponent, -1, is the coefficient of elasticity (see Note 3 in the Appendix to Part 1). Now let price fall by 20 per cent. The percentage formula says that quantity increases by 20 per cent. But with the demand function of this footnote, $q_2/q_1 = p_1/p_2 = 10/8 = 1.25$, which is an increase of quantity of 25 per cent. For many practical purposes, however, the difference is not particularly important. See the reference to Pigou at the end of this chapter.

The question now is the appropriate formula for arc elasticity. The percentage formula, $\dfrac{\Delta Q}{Q}\bigg/\dfrac{\Delta P}{P}$, gives different results depending on whether the price is raised or lowered. Suppose the prices are 10 and 8 and the quantities 1 and 3. A price reduction is a drop of 20 per cent, but a price rise is 25 per cent. And an increase in quantity is 200 per cent, whereas a decline in quantity is $66\frac{2}{3}$ per cent. With the formula $\dfrac{\Delta Q}{Q}\bigg/\dfrac{\Delta P}{P}$, the price reduction results in a coefficient of $\frac{2}{1}/\frac{2}{10} = 2 \times \frac{10}{2} = 10$. A price increase results in a coefficient of $\frac{2}{3}/\frac{2}{8} = \frac{2}{3} \times \frac{8}{2} = 2\frac{2}{3}$.

The way out of this difficulty is to take an average of prices and quantities, and thus to measure elasticity at the midpoint of the arc. The formula then becomes $\dfrac{\Delta Q}{\frac{1}{2}(Q_1 + Q_2)}\bigg/\dfrac{\Delta P}{\frac{1}{2}(P_1 + P_2)}$. Although the $\frac{1}{2}$ cancels out in the formula, it is put there to stress the fact that by using the *average* values of the quantities and prices, the elasticity coefficient is the same whether price goes up or goes down.[4] With the same numbers as before, the formula yields the coefficient

$$\frac{2}{\frac{1}{2}(1 + 3)}\bigg/\frac{2}{\frac{1}{2}(10 + 8)} = \frac{9}{2} = 4\frac{1}{2}.$$

Elasticity When Demand is Linear

The law of demand requires only that a demand curve slope downward to the right. When discussion is abstract, describing "the" demand for "a" commodity, it is legitimate to take the simplest form of a demand curve. This is the straight line. Demand is then said to be linear. Empirical studies have sometimes found that demands for some actual commodities are linear. Hence the assumption that demand is linear is sometimes realistic. But more important, the assumption offers the convenience of simplicity. In later chapters, the assumption of linear demand will be used frequently.

But the elasticity of linear demand is tricky at first and has to be looked into. There are two features to notice. One is that the (point) elasticity of demand on a straight line is different at every point. Elasticity at any one point is the ratio of the lower part of the straight line to the upper part. Elasticity is highest at the highest prices shown, declines as prices go down, and is lowest at the lowest prices. The other feature, which is important in some applications to be taken up in later chapters, is this: If a linear demand moves to the right, shifting parallel to itself, elasticity at any given price diminishes as demand increases.

[4] The closer the numbers, the more accurate the coefficient when calculated from this formula. It is not the only one, but the circumstances and particular facts of a practical problem help to dictate the choice of a formula for calculating arc elasticity.

FIGURE 3-5

ELASTICITY OF LINEAR DEMAND

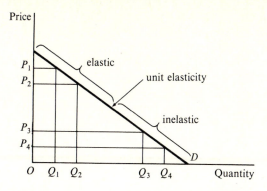

Figure 3-5 shows the differing elasticities of a linear demand curve. Elasticity is unity at the midpoint between the axes, because the two parts of the line are of course equal in length, with a ratio of unity. Above the midpoint, demand is elastic, because the lower part is longer than the upper part. Below the midpoint, demand is inelastic, the lower part being shorter than the upper. Another way to prove this, and to reinforce the notion of elasticity as a ratio of relative changes, is as follows: Take a price reduction from P_1 to P_2 and another from P_3 to P_4. The price changes are equal *absolutely* and so are the corresponding quantity changes. But they are *not* equal *relatively*. The first price change, P_1P_2, has to be measured against OP_1; the second change, P_3P_4, against OP_3. Similarly with the quantity changes: Q_1Q_2 against OQ_1, and Q_3Q_4 against OQ_3. Another glance at Figure 3-5 shows that the first price change is relatively smaller than the corresponding quantity change. Hence, demand here is elastic. The second price change, P_3P_4, is relatively larger than the corresponding change in quantity; therefore, demand is inelastic.

Figure 3-5 has four rectangles, showing consumer expenditures at each of the four prices. The second expenditure rectangle ($OP_2 \times OQ_2$) is larger than the first, but the fourth ($OP_4 \times OQ_4$) is smaller than the third. The sizes of the rectangles therefore also show the differences in elasticities.

Figure 3-6 shows a shift in a linear demand from D_1 to D_2. The two demand curves are parallel, signifying that the quantity increases at each price are equal. But at any price or range of prices, D_2 is less elastic (or more inelastic) than D_1. Here is the proof: The quantity change Q_1Q_2 is relatively larger than Q_3Q_4 although their absolute sizes are the same, because Q_1Q_2 is larger, measured against OQ_1, than Q_3Q_4 measured against OQ_3. To generalize:

FIGURE 3–6

ELASTICITY AND CHANGE IN LINEAR DEMAND

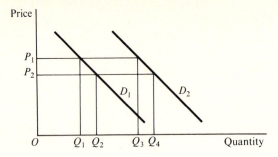

Rightward shifts in demand cause the elasticities at a price to become steadily smaller. So expressed, the generalization holds for curved as well as for straight lines.

An example of a decline in elasticity with a growth in demand is air transportation. Empirical studies showed that this demand was elastic in the period just after World War II. It was therefore to the interest of the airlines to lower their fares, so as to obtain larger revenues. Then came the enormous growth in demand in the 1950s and 1960s. By 1970 the airlines had begun to ask permission to *raise* their fares to yield more revenue. Demand had become inelastic. In the expression $\frac{P}{Q}\frac{\Delta Q}{\Delta P}$, what happened between the late 1940s and the early 1970s was such a huge increase in the size of Q that the value of E had to become less than unity.

THE DETERMINANTS OF ELASTICITY

What makes the demand for one commodity elastic and the demand for another inelastic? The determinants of the price elasticity of demand for a commodity can be put under three headings: (1) the number and closeness of its substitutes, (2) the commodity's importance in buyers' budgets, and (3) the number of its uses.

Of the three determinants, the substitutes for a commodity are the most important. If a commodity has many close substitutes, its demand is almost certain to be elastic, perhaps highly so. If price goes up, consumers buy less of the commodity and buy more of its substitutes. If its price goes down, consumers desert the substitutes and buy the commodity in (relatively) much larger quantities. So far, so good. But again, the real question is the definition of a commodity. The more narrowly and the more specifically a commodity is defined, the more close substitutes it has and the more elastic is the demand for it. The demand for a particular brand of mentholated toothpaste is more elastic than the demand for mentholated toothpaste, which is more elastic than the demand for toothpaste in general, which is more elastic than the demand for dentifrices (pastes, powders, and liquids). The pattern is similar throughout the entire range of commodities.

If a commodity is so defined that it has perfect substitutes, then its elasticity of demand is perfect, or infinite. Suppose the commodity is the wheat produced by one wheat farmer. This particular wheat does have perfect substitutes, namely, the wheat produced by other wheat farmers. If the one wheat grower tried to sell his wheat above the going price at any one time, he could sell none at all. The coefficient of elasticity of demand for *his* wheat is infinity.

The importance of a commodity in buyers' budgets also influences its elasticity. "Importance" means the fraction of total expenditures devoted to a single commodity. The demands for soap, salt, matches, ink, and for many other similar commodities are highly inelastic, because the typical household spends only a few cents a week on each of them. The percentages of family budgets devoted to such commodities are exceedingly small. Observe, however, that the demands for such commodities are inelastic, not perfectly inelastic.

The more uses a commodity can be put to, the more elastic its demand. If a commodity has only a few uses, its demand is likely to be inelastic. The various uses of any commodity can be imagined as standing in a hierarchy. If the price of a commodity is very high, consumers will put the few units they buy only to the most important use of the commodity. At successively lower prices, more of the commodity is bought, to be devoted to the less important uses. Any cookbook shows a multitude of uses for eggs, and this is a fact that tends to make the demand for them elastic.

Any judgment of the elasticity of the demand for a commodity must take all three determinants into account. They can reinforce one another, or work in opposite directions. A commodity can have several uses, but no close substitutes. Another commodity with many substitutes can have a low position in consumers' budgets.

Time and Elasticity

The demand for a commodity always exists in some period of time, which can be a day, a week, a month, a season, a year, or a period of several years. Elasticity of demand varies with the length of time periods. In general, demand is more elastic (or less inelastic) the longer the period of time. The longer the period of time, the greater is the ease of substitution for both consumers and business firms. If, for example, the price of fuel oil should rise more than the prices of other fuels, it is likely that the consumption of fuel oil in the month after the price increase would diminish very little. The demand for fuel oil in any one month, then, is probably highly inelastic. But the demand over a year is certain to be less inelastic or perhaps slightly elastic, because a year is long enough for people building new houses and renovating old houses to change their plans about the kinds of furnaces to install. Over a period of, say, five years or more, the demand for fuel oil is probably highly elastic, because such a period is long enough to permit full substitution.

Another illustration of the importance of time as an influence on elasticity comes from a statistical study of the demand for meat.[5] The study shows that the retail demand for meat is slightly inelastic in the short run. The short run here means the year-to-year demand.[6] But the long-run retail demand for meat is elastic. One of the meanings of these findings is this: Suppose something happened to cause the amount of meat produced to be curtailed and held at a lower level for several years. If the demand for meat were stable, the price would first rise and would then eventually fall, relatively less than the decline in the amount. Consumers would spend less on meat (because the demand in the long run is elastic), and therefore of course the meat industry would have smaller receipts. These matters are illustrated in Figure 3–7. The year-to-year demand is D_S and the long-run demand is D_L. Let the initial price and quantity be P_1 and OQ_1. Then the quantity falls to OQ_2, remaining there a long time. The price first rises from P_1 to P_2. But over the course of time, the demand curve swings to its long-run position, and the price falls to P_3. Something like this seems to have happened in 1973 and 1974: At first the prices of beef soared, with widespread complaints from housewives, but then prices dropped so much that many beef producers cried out for help from the government.

APPLICATIONS

Many of the applications of the concept of price elasticity of demand have to do with pricing decisions of business firms or of government

FIGURE 3–7   INFLUENCE OF TIME ON ELASTICITY

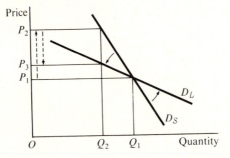

[5] Elmer J. Working, *Demand for Meat,* Institute of Meat Packing, Chicago, 1954, pp. xi, 79, 87. This study was a result of a cooperative research project of the Institute of Meat Packing, the University of Chicago, and the University of Illinois.
[6] Later chapters will give the expressions *short run* and *long run* somewhat different meanings.

agencies that directly or indirectly regulate prices. All too often decisions on prices fail to take elasticity into account, or give it insufficient attention. Changes in costs usually dominate decisions on prices; costs can be calculated, and higher costs usually seem to be a valid justification for higher prices. Even if demand and its elasticity cannot always be calculated, they should not be ignored or taken for granted.

Estimating
Elasticities

If a decision to raise or lower a price is going to be based in part on the elasticity of demand for the commodity or service, then of course the decision makers have to have some idea of the size of the coefficient. They need not think of elasticity quite in this way, but they do have to have an estimate of how a change in price affects the expenditures of the buyers. These expenditures of course are the same amounts as the total revenues of the seller (or sellers).

Quantitative estimates of coefficients of elasticity can be made if there are enough data on past prices and quantities, and if there are no obstacles to interpretation. Hundreds of such estimates have been made. Some of them are the fruits of sophisticated statistical analyses that yield precise numerical estimates of coefficients of elasticity. Others are simple direct tests to see merely if a demand is elastic or inelastic. Occasionally, experiments are possible. Bottles of ink can be sold at 15¢ retail in some cities and at 25¢ in other cities during the same period of time. The differences in sales show if the demand is elastic or inelastic in this range of prices. The main analytical task is to isolate the effects of price changes on quantities bought. These effects must be isolated from those of the other influences—changes in income, changes in the prices of related goods, and changes in taste.

Studies made for the Bell Telephone system have produced a family of coefficients of elasticity for telephone calls. The coefficients differ for local and long distance calls and by time of day. Although the elasticities for local calls are said not to be "significantly different from zero," the coefficient 0.1 is used in calculations. For Chicago-New York calls, the coefficients range from 0.23 during the day to 0.57 in the evening.[7]

Economic
Policy

The farm policies of the federal government include the objective of raising farm prices. Higher prices result in higher gross incomes for farmers because the demands for most farm products are inelastic; as is well known from empirical studies. If government keeps part of a crop off the market, the ensuing rise in gross income to the farmers

[7]S. C. Littlechild, "Peak-load Pricing of Telephone Calls," *Bell Journal of Economics and Management Science* (Autumn 1970), 201, 207.

depends on just *how* inelastic the demand that year actually is. Inelasticity of demand is also the explanation of "the paradox of plenty," namely, that a bountiful crop brings a *smaller* total revenue to its growers. Suppose for the moment that the demand for a particular farm product were elastic. To raise the gross incomes of these farmers, would the federal government try to raise the price of this product by keeping some of it off the market? No, because to do this with an elastic demand would be to lower gross incomes.

Economic policies directed to increasing exports must also take account of elasticities of demand. Suppose that a country expands the physical volume of its exports by lowering their prices, e.g., by devaluation of its currency. If the country is unlucky, the demands for its exports are inelastic. If they are inelastic, the money receipts from more physical exports become smaller, not larger.

In the middle 1930s, the Interstate Commerce Commission (ICC) ordered the railroads in the eastern part of the country to lower their passenger coach fares. The railroads resisted the order, believing that they would suffer a loss of gross revenue. But the ICC insisted, and proved to be right. In that period, the demand for coach service was indeed elastic, the coefficient being approximately 2.0. Hence the eastern railroads enjoyed a larger, not a smaller, gross revenue from the cut in fares they were at first reluctant to make. Another example from the 1930s was the dispute over the elasticity of demand for electricity in the Tennessee Valley and neighboring regions. The Tennessee Valley Authority thought that the demand was elastic and proceeded to set its prices low. The neighboring private power companies at first disagreed, but later they too found advantage in reducing their rates. True enough the demand was growing, but it was also elastic. Like anyone else, however, government agencies can make wrong estimates of elasticity. In 1960, the Commonwealth of Virginia raised the prices of alcoholic beverages sold in its stores by 10 per cent. In the first year, total revenue fell off, the demand evidently being elastic. In the next year, however, total revenue went up; the demand curve was probably shifting to the right, owing to the growth of population and income.

Business

Business executives often seem to think that demand is inelastic. Such, at least, is the impression conveyed by many public and private statements by business executives on their pricing policies. The common experience has been to see price increases followed by larger gross revenues and to see price decreases associated with smaller gross revenues. But price increases often occur when demand curves shift to the right, just as price decreases are often made when demand curves shift to the left. It was shown earlier, with the help of Figure 3–2 on page 39, that people can easily misinterpret experience, confuse shifts of demand curves with differences in position on a demand curve, and therefore fall into the belief that demand is inelastic.

A business firm producing and selling many different products usually finds marked differences in elasticities from one product to another. The products sell in different markets and face different kinds of substitutes in each. For example, take three steel products. There is no close substitute for steel rails. Hence the demand for them is highly inelastic, but it is not perfectly inelastic because a response to high prices could be to make old rails last longer. Stainless steel, on the other hand, does have close substitutes in some of its uses. Tin plate faces close competition from plastics, glass, aluminum, and other materials employed to package beer, oils, paint, and some food products.

Just as business executives sometimes err in their beliefs about elasticity, so do the critics of business. The prices and price policies of the key industries, particularly those dominated by large corporations, are under constant public scrutiny. From time to time, public criticism hits on elasticity, though of course the word *elasticity* is seldom heard. The critics urge that this or that industry or large corporation should, in its own interest, lower its prices, because to do so would much expand consumption, with consumers benefiting from lower prices and employees benefiting from higher levels of employment. In short, demand is believed to be elastic. In the late 1930s, the steel industry came under a barrage of criticism for failing to price its products so as to stabilize production and employment. But careful statistical investigations showed that the demand for "steel"—all the thousands of steel products considered as if they were one commodity—is probably fairly inelastic. In 1957, Walter Reuther of the United Automobile Workers publicly urged the automobile industry to reduce prices by $100 per car, adding that a million more cars would therefore be sold. This amounted to saying that the coefficient of the elasticity of demand for automobiles is about 4.0 ($100 was a price cut of about 4 per cent, and one million more cars was an increase in sales of about 16 per cent). Statistical studies of the demand for automobiles show, however, that elasticity varies from year to year, with the coefficient ranging from about 0.5 to about 1.5. The coefficient has been more often above 1.0 than below it.

SUMMARY

Price elasticity of demand is the ratio of a percentage change in quantity to a percentage change in price. The *coefficient of elasticity, E,* is found by dividing the percentage change in quantity by the corresponding percentage change in price. If $E > 1$, demand is *elastic*. If $E = 1$, demand has *unit elasticity*. If $E < 1$, demand is *inelastic*. If E equals infinity, demand is *perfectly elastic*. And if E equals zero, demand is *perfectly inelastic*. Elasticity is related to expenditure: If a decline in price causes an increase in expenditure, demand is elastic; if a decrease, demand is inelastic.

A demand curve can have different elasticities. *Arc elasticity* measures elasticity at the midpoint of an arc of a demand curve. *Point elasticity* is a measure at a point on a demand curve; the ratio of the lower to the upper part of a tangent to a demand curve is the elasticity at the point of tangency. A *linear demand curve* has a different elasticity at every point.

Whether the demand for a commodity is elastic or inelastic depends on the number and closeness of its *substitutes*. A commodity's *importance in consumers' budgets* and the *number of its uses* also influence its elasticity. *Time* is another determinant; the longer the period of time, the more elastic (or the less inelastic) is the demand for a commodity.

Knowledge of elasticity is important in business pricing decisions and in the execution, as well as the appraisal, of economic policies affecting prices.

SELECTED REFERENCES

Alfred Marshall, *Principles of Economics,* 8th ed. (Macmillan, London; 1920), III, chap. 4; A. C. Pigou, *Alfred Marshall and Current Thought* (Macmillan, London, 1953), part I, lecture III; W. Warren Haynes and William R. Henry, *Managerial Economics: Analysis and Cases,* 3d ed. (Business Publications, Dallas, 1974), chap. 3; Ruby Turner Norris, *The Theory of Consumer's Demand,* rev. ed. (Yale University Press, New Haven, 1952), chap. 9; Donald Stevenson Watson, ed., *Price Theory in Action: A Book of Readings,* 3d ed. (Houghton Mifflin, Boston, 1973), chaps. 1–8; Lester D. Taylor, "The Demand for Electricity: A Survey," *Bell Journal of Economics,* 6 (Spring 1975), 74–110. This article gives price and income elasticity coefficients.

EXERCISES AND PROBLEMS

1. Water is essential to life. But the demand for it at prices now prevailing is probably highly elastic. Why?
2. The demand for salt in some countries has been found to be elastic. Explain how this could be so.
3. Suppose that in year 1 the federal excise tax on cigarettes is doubled, and that in year 3 the total revenue from the cigarette tax is

twice as high as in year 1. What conclusions about the demand for cigarettes can be drawn?

4. A useful exercise: Take the demand schedule where prices are 10¢, 9¢, 8¢, etc., and quantities are 1, 2, 3, etc., units. Imagine that the price falls. Use the arc elasticity formula to work out the elasticities for each drop in price from 10¢ to 9¢, etc., all the way down to 2¢ to 1¢.

5. Consider this demand schedule:

P	Q
5.00	7.0
4.75	8.0
4.50	9.5
4.00	10.0

Imagine that this is the demand for bus transportation in an area. The prices are the average fares in cents per passenger mile; the quantities are millions of passenger miles per month. Suppose the practical problem is one of raising fares. What is the coefficient of elasticity of demand when the fare is raised from 4.00¢ to 4.50¢? From 4.50¢ to 4.75¢? (Use the arc elasticity formula.) What could cause the difference in the values of the coefficients?

6. Assume that a business firm drops its price by 10 per cent. Show the change in the total revenue of that firm if the coefficient of price elasticity of demand were 0.5, if it were 1.0, and if it were 2.0. Draw the diagrams.

7. Explain the difference, if any, between the slope of a demand curve and its elasticity.

8. Suppose a linear demand curve increases, i.e., shifts to the right. If elasticity at one price is to increase, what kind of a shift in the curve must take place?

9. Demand curves can have different elasticities at high and at low prices. Can you give examples of goods or services that are likely to have high coefficients at high prices and low coefficients at low prices? What are the probable causes at work here?

10. What changes can you foresee that will make the demand for gasoline less inelastic?

11. The demand for gasoline in the United States is probably more inelastic than it is in Western Europe. Why?

4
Other Elasticity
CONCEPTS

Four more concepts of elasticity are still to be covered. The last two chapters on demand place most of their emphasis on price. This chapter goes farther into the roles played by consumer incomes, by the prices of other commodities, and by time. This chapter also examines the concept of elasticity of supply.

Of this chapter's four concepts of elasticity, two pertain to the demand for a commodity—*income elasticity*, which is the responsiveness of quantity demanded to changes in income, and *cross elasticity*, which is the responsiveness of quantity demanded to changes in the prices of a commodity's substitutes and complements. Remember, the demand for a commodity has four determinants—consumer tastes, the commodity's own price, consumer incomes, and the prices of the commodity's substitutes and complements.

With *price elasticity*, the commodity's own price varies while tastes, incomes, and the other prices are held constant. With *income elasticity*, consumer incomes vary while tastes, the commodity's own price, and the other prices are held constant. And with *cross elasticity*, the price of a substitute or a complement varies while tastes, the commodity's own price, and consumer incomes are held constant.

INCOME ELASTICITY

Suppose your income goes up by 20 per cent. Would you buy 20 per cent more food? Hardly, but you might spend more than 20 per cent more on your favorite recreation. If you would divide the percentage increase in quantity purchased by the percentage increase in income, you would be calculating your own income elasticity of demand for the good or service in question. But how and why individual consumers' purchases change when their incomes change is part of the theory of consumer behavior. Chapter 6 deals with this subject.

For a commodity sold in a market with many buyers, income elasticity is the relative change in quantity bought divided by the corresponding relative change in the incomes of the buyers. In the expression

$$E_y = \frac{\Delta Q}{Q} \bigg/ \frac{\Delta Y}{Y} = \frac{Y}{Q} \frac{\Delta Q}{\Delta Y},$$

E_y stands for the coefficient of income elasticity and Y for income.[1]

When other determinants of the demand for a commodity are held constant while consumers' incomes vary, the relationship is sometimes called *income demand*. The idea of demand as a function of income is portrayed in Figure 4-1. Here are five income-demand curves. The curve marked *high* ($E_y > 1$) shows increases in income accompanied by relatively larger increases in amounts bought. The *unit* ($E_y = 1$) curve shows that changes in income and quantity are proportional. The curve marked *low* ($E_y < 1$) shows quantity increasing relatively less than income. The curve marked *zero* ($E_y = 0$) shows that quantity bought is constant regardless of changes in income. The curve marked *neg.*, i.e., *negative* ($E_y < 0$), says that less is bought at higher incomes and that more is bought at lower incomes. Potatoes are an example. Commodities with negative income elasticities are called *inferior goods*. Chapter 6 contains a further discussion of them.

Thus, for all except inferior goods, the sign of the coefficient of income elasticity is positive, because both income and quantity change in the same direction.

Notice the difference in terminology here. If the coefficient is greater than 1, income elasticity is "high"; if the coefficient is less than 1, income elasticity is "low." In contrast, demand is "elastic"

FIGURE 4-1   **INCOME ELASTICITIES**

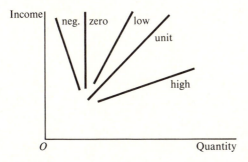

[1] In this book, the symbol E stands for price elasticity of demand. The symbols for the other elasticity concepts have subscripts, to distinguish them. Note 3 in the Appendix to Part 1 gives the simple mathematics of income elasticity of demand.

53   *Other Elasticity Concepts*

if the coefficient of *price* elasticity is greater than 1 and "inelastic" if it is less than 1.

Commodities differ widely in their income elasticities. Furs, jewelry, the better grades of steak, and automobiles are examples of commodities whose income elasticities tend to be high. In contrast, soap, salt, matches, newspapers, etc., have low income elasticities of demand. The proportion of income spent on a commodity is a major determinant of how high or how low is its income elasticity. An exception to this statement is probably housing, which takes a sizable part of anyone's income; housing seems to have a coefficient close to unity. But commodities that people regard as expensive, as luxuries, generally have high income elasticities. Indeed the simplest and best way to define luxuries is to say that they are commodities with high income elasticities of demand. Similarly, necessities can be defined as commodities with low income elasticities; cigarettes, for example. These definitions are analytical— they bypass the moral connotations that hover over the everyday ideas of luxuries and necessities.

Income Sensitivity

A rough and ready but practical companion to the concept of income elasticity is the income sensitivity of consumption expenditures. Income elasticity has to do with changes in *physical units* purchased, whereas income sensitivity deals with changes in *dollar expenditures*. The income sensitivity of a commodity in a period of time is measured by calculating the percentage change in dollar expenditures associated with a 1-per cent change in disposable income in the same period. Income sensitivity therefore also has a coefficient. In the calculations made by the United States Department of Commerce, the effects of long-term growth or decline in consumption are eliminated by statistical procedures. But the coefficients of income sensitivity are still rough and ready, because there is no way to disentangle the effects of changes in income from the effects of changes in prices and in tastes. The data on income sensitivity have some modest use in business forecasting.

The Department of Commerce has found that the following commodities and services have high income sensitivities (coefficients equal to 1.5 or more): telephone service, automobiles, air transportation, television repair, and foreign travel. These are just a few examples. Commodities and services with low income sensitivities (coefficients less than 0.5) are exemplified by shoes, clothing, local bus transportation, and dental care.

CROSS ELASTICITY

Consider some simple relations between demands and prices. Suppose the price of commodity A goes up. Hence less of A is bought.

Some of the consumers shift to a substitute, commodity B. Hence the demand for B rises, and if the price of B remains the same, more of B is bought. Next, suppose that commodity C is complementary with A. After A's price rise and the consequent decline in the purchase of A, less of C is wanted. Thus the demand for C diminishes. In general, therefore, a rise in the price of a commodity increases the demand for its substitutes and diminishes the demand for its complements.

In practical problems of demand analysis, commodities stand in more or less definite clusters of substitutes and complements. The concept of cross elasticity of demand is useful in handling inter-commodity relations. Once more, take two commodities, A and B. Let A's price go up. What is the effect on the quantity of B that is bought? The expression for cross elasticity of demand is

$$E_{BP_A} = \frac{\Delta Q_B}{Q_B} \bigg/ \frac{\Delta P_A}{P_A}.$$

The coefficient E_{BP_A} is therefore the relative (percentage) change in the quantity demanded of commodity B divided by the relative (percentage) change in the price of commodity A. The coefficient is positive if A and B are substitutes because the price change and the quantity change are in the same direction. If the price of A goes up, so does the quantity of B, and vice versa. But if A and B are complements, the coefficient is negative because changes in the price of one commodity cause opposite changes in the quantity demanded of the other.[2]

Suppose that the two commodities are margarine and butter. The cross elasticity formula shows the relative (e.g., percentage) gain in pounds of butter purchased for a rise in the price of margarine. Other things of course are held constant; they are consumer tastes for both margarine and butter, consumer incomes, and the price of butter. In some time period, the coefficient has a value, say, 0.4, which means that a 10-per cent rise in the price of margarine causes consumers to buy 4 per cent more butter. If, however, the relationship is reversed—if margarine consumption is made to depend on the price of butter—does the coefficient have the same numerical

---

[2] The statement that substitutes have positive coefficients of cross elasticity and that complements have negative coefficients is valid for commodities bought in markets, i.e., for the mass behavior of consumers. For an individual consumer, however, mathematical reasoning can demonstrate that the statement might not always be correct. Suppose a family with a low income buys much hamburger and an occasional steak. A rise in the price of hamburger makes the family so much worse off that it buys even less steak. Thus the cross elasticity coefficient here is negative, even though hamburger and steaks can be regarded as substitutes.

value? No, the coefficient is likely to be lower, say, 0.2, which would mean that a 10-per cent change in the price of butter causes a 2-per cent change in the consumption of margarine. Why the difference? Some households buy both; some buy only one. The households buying both margarine and butter probably put the two fats to different uses. Thus, substitution is a complex process; it does not work the same way in both directions. (See Note 3 in the Appendix to Part 1.)

The Relevant Market

The closer two commodities are as substitutes for each other, the greater is the size of the cross elasticity coefficient. Close substitutes have high cross elasticities of demand. Two commodities are poor substitutes for each other if the cross elasticities are low.

These ideas find important application in the enforcement of the antitrust laws. It is unlawful to monopolize, with intent to do so, the production and (interstate) sale of a commodity. But what is a commodity? Remember that a commodity can be defined broadly or narrowly, generally or specifically. So, too, in the antitrust field, the "relevant market" presents a problem of definition. Is the product of a particular business firm a monopolized product, that is, are buyers so restricted in choice that they must buy from the one business firm and have no alternatives? For *any* product, there are substitutes of one kind or another. If, however, they are poor substitutes, their cross elasticities of demand with the product are low. Here, then, is one way of defining a monopolized product. Similarly, a business firm charged with violating the laws against monopolization will try to prove that cross elasticities between its product and other similar ones are high, that therefore substitutes are close, and that buyers do indeed have effective choices.

A good illustration is given by the well-known *Cellophane* decision by the federal courts in 1953. In 1947, the Justice Department brought suit against the duPont Company for having illegally monopolized the production and sale of cellophane. The legal proceedings were long and complicated; in the end, the courts held that the government could not prove its charges. In the eyes of the law, duPont was not a monopolist in marketing cellophane. The relevant market, the courts decided, was the market for "flexible packaging materials," of which cellophane is only one, along with waxed paper, aluminum foil, pliofilm, polyethylene, and many others. In other words, the courts accepted the argument that the cross elasticities of demand between cellophane and other flexible packaging materials are high, that therefore they are all close substitutes, and that therefore duPont had no monopoly. The government argued in vain that in some of its important uses the cross elasticities of demand between cellophane and its substitutes are low, that therefore they are poor or unacceptable substitutes, and that therefore duPont really did have a monopoly.

The word *dynamics* is used here to mean simply change over time. If the demand for a commodity is a function of price, of tastes, of incomes, and of the prices of substitutes and complements, it is also a function of time. For the most part, however, price theory specifies that demand holds for some one given period of time. To do this makes it possible to draw a demand curve, whose properties and consequences can then be analyzed. So too in practical work. To lay the foundation for a business pricing decision, the analyst must expend considerable ingenuity in making an estimate of *the* demand for a product for the next six months or some such period of time.

Yet it is well to bear in mind that demand curves are much more likely to be in constant motion than to be standing still. Consumer tastes change, so do incomes, and so do the other prices. These matters have been mentioned and emphasized before. Chapter 3 stresses the influence of time upon price elasticity—the longer the time, the greater the possibilities of substitution and therefore the larger the coefficient of price elasticity.

The demand curves for many commodities steadily shift to the right over long periods of time simply because of the growth of the economy which, among other things, results in ever larger numbers of consumers. Secular gains in productivity mean that consumers have higher incomes. Some demand curves move faster to the right than others, owing to structural changes in tastes. The postwar period has seen, for example, strong increases in the demand for air transportation, automobile insurance, and electricity. The process of innovation brings wholly new products. Demands for them spring out of nowhere, expand rapidly, and sooner or later take on a more or less stable shape. Yet it is not fully accurate to say that the demands for new products come from nowhere. Once again, the meaning of commodity has to be put into play. The sudden and powerful demand for a new drug is really a part of the general demand for medical care; the new drug displaces an old one whose demand drops way off. Accordingly, though the demands for broad classes of commodities expand fairly steadily over longer periods of time, the demands for specific products can undergo strong shifts.

Price
Expectations
So far the price expectations of consumers have not been taken into account. Consumers have been described as facing given prices of the commodity in question and of its substitutes and complements. Suppose now that consumers make definite plans for their purchases

of commodities in successive periods of time stretching into the future. For the sake of simplicity, let the discussion be confined at first to one consumer. The consumer looks into the future and makes plans on how much of each commodity to buy in each period. The plans for future purchases depend on the consumer's estimates of the prices he or she expects to prevail in future periods. Let it also be assumed that the consumer's expectations are of definite prices, not probable prices or ranges of prices. She or he might expect seasonal variations in prices and accordingly will plan to buy more when prices are low and less when they are high. When this is done, the consumer is making substitutions over time. To these substitutions there are certain limits, which are set by the consumer's tastes and by the varying durabilities and storabilities of commodities.

Suppose now that the consumer believes, rightly or wrongly, that the price of some one commodity will rise steadily in the periods ahead. Acting on this belief, the consumer will buy more now, within the limits of substitution over time. Therefore, the expectation of higher prices in the future increases demand now.

Elasticity of Price Expectations

Just how much demand is affected by price expectations depends in good part upon the elasticity of price expectations. Here is another elasticity concept, devised by the English economist J. R. Hicks in 1939. People's price expectations are influenced by many things—by political news, by current and recent economic events, by the prevailing climate of opinion, and by experience with past changes in prices. Hicks's concept ties together price experience with expectations of future prices.

The elasticity of price expectations is the ratio of the relative change in expected future prices to the relative change in current prices. Suppose that a consumer or a financial manager sees that the price of a commodity has just gone up by 10 per cent. (Here, too, "relative change" can be expressed as a percentage.) If, therefore, the consumer or financial manager takes his or her original estimate of a future price of that commodity and raises the estimate by 20 per cent, then the elasticity of price expectations is 2.

Table 4–1 shows the possible ranges of elasticities of price expectations of buyers in a market.

A rise in the prices currently being paid will cause the demand curve to shift to the right, if buyers have elasticities of price expectations that are greater than unity. Demand increases because buyers want to buy more now to avoid the even higher prices they expect to prevail in the future. On the other hand, if elasticities are low or negative, a rise in price now causes demand to diminish. The demand curve shifts to the left as buyers wait for the price to come down in the future. And if elasticity is unity, a change in the prices

TABLE 4–1

ELASTICITY OF PRICE EXPECTATIONS
(ATTITUDES OF BUYERS TOWARD A RISE IN A CURRENT PRICE)

Elasticity	Coefficient[a]	Remarks[b]
High	> 1	Buyers expect that future prices will rise by a *larger* percentage than current prices.
Unit	1	Buyers expect that future prices will rise by the *same* percentage as current prices.
Low	$< 1 > 0$	Buyers expect that future prices will rise by a *smaller* percentage than current prices.
Zero	0	Buyers expect current rise to have no effect on future prices.
Negative	< 0	Buyers expect that current rise will be followed by a *fall* in future prices.

[a] Let future prices be F, and current prices be C. Then the coefficient of the elasticity of price expectations is $\dfrac{\Delta F}{F} \Big/ \dfrac{\Delta C}{C}$.

[b] Buyers normally have different elasticities of price expectations. The remarks are all based on the simplifying assumption that the buyers in a market have the same elasticities.

being currently paid has no effect at all on the current demand. If, for example, a rise of 10 per cent in the current price causes buyers to revise their original estimates of future price by plus 10 per cent, the *ratio* of current and future prices remains constant. Thus there is no reason to alter the distribution of purchases through time.

Producers too must think what to do when they see a rise in current prices. If their elasticity of price expectations is high, producers believe that future prices will advance by a larger percentage than current prices. Producers will, if they can, hold their products back from the current market so that they will enjoy the higher expected future prices. Thus their current supply curves shift to the left. But if producers' elasticities are low or negative, their supply curves would shift to the right, because they would want to sell more now so as to avoid the expected lower future prices.

It seems that the extremely high beef prices prevailing at times in the early 1970s reflected, at least in part, high elasticities of price expectations in the minds of both consumers and producers. Both thought beef prices would be still higher in the future. So families bought more beef, stocking up their freezers. Producers curtailed the amount of beef they put on the market. Thus the soaring beef prices came as the result of the rightward shift of the demand curve and the leftward shift of the supply curve.

ELASTICITY OF SUPPLY

Elasticity of supply is just as important as elasticity of demand and has the same meaning. Let E_s be the symbol for elasticity of supply.

The definition is

$$E_s = \frac{\Delta Q}{Q} \Big/ \frac{\Delta P}{P} = \frac{\Delta Q}{\Delta P} \frac{P}{Q}.$$

E_s is also the coefficient of elasticity of supply. Since, in general, both price and quantity go up and go down together, E_s has a positive sign.

When supply is elastic, the responsiveness of sellers (or producers, depending on the context) to small changes in price is relatively great. If price changes by 10 per cent, the amount changes by more than 10 per cent. Inelasticity of supply, of course, signifies a relatively small response of sellers or producers. The amount supplied changes by a smaller percentage than does the price.

Elasticity of supply can vary from one price range to another. Figure 4–2 shows a supply curve whose different shapes are probably typical of many supply curves in the short run. The different elasticities of the one curve are indicated in the figure. As is true of a demand curve, a supply curve is perfectly elastic when it is horizontal and perfectly inelastic when it is vertical. Over the arc AB, supply is elastic, but in the arc BC, it is inelastic. An economic interpretation of the supply curve in Figure 4–2 is this: Below some price, namely OP, nothing at all is sold by the sellers. But if the price is in fact OP, they will sell any amount up to OQ_1 without having to get a higher price. For amounts larger than OQ_1, however, the price must be higher. Finally, the sellers cannot or will not sell any amount larger than OQ_2, no matter how high the price might be.

The geometry of the elasticity of supply is a little different from that of the elasticity of demand. The supply curve in Figure 4–2 has unit elasticity at point B, where the curve is tangent to a straight line drawn from the origin. When it is a straight line through the origin, a supply curve has unit elasticity over its whole length, no matter what its slope. If the straight line cuts the price axis, supply is elastic. And if the line cuts the quantity axis, supply is inelastic.

FIGURE 4–2   **DIFFERING ELASTICITIES OF SUPPLY**

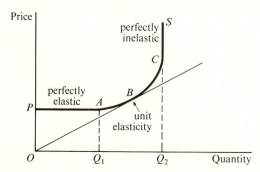

FIGURE 4-3

ELASTICITY OF SUPPLY

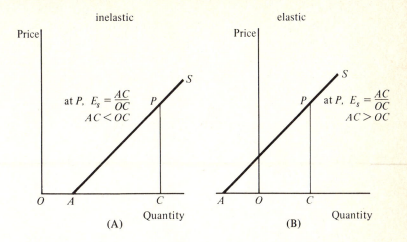

In Figure 4-3A, the elasticity of supply at point P is exactly $\frac{AC}{OC}$.[3]
Because $AC < OC$, supply is inelastic. For a supply curve intersecting the price axis, point A lies to the left of the origin O. This
is shown in Figure 4-3B. Therefore, $AC > OC$, and $\frac{AC}{OC} > 1$; thus
supply is elastic. For supply curves coming from the origin, point A
is at the origin and $\frac{AC}{OC} = 1$.

If the supply curve is a curved line, its elasticity at any point can
be measured by drawing a line tangent at that point. The same rules
hold: If the tangent cuts the quantity axis, supply is inelastic at the
point of tangency, and so on.

Time and
Elasticity of
Supply

Time is even more important for the elasticity of supply than it is for
the elasticity of demand. The longer the period of time, the more
elastic is supply likely to be.

Figure 4-4 has three supply curves pivoted around the price P.
The curve S_1 is perfectly inelastic, representing supply in a very
short period of time. A rise in price cannot call forth a larger
amount. The curve S_2 is the supply of the same commodity over a
longer period of time. Here a rise in price does call forth a larger
amount. The curve S_3, let it be supposed, is supply when time is long
enough for the fullest adjustment, as in the long run. The same rise
in price results in a still larger amount.

[3] The proof is symmetrical with that for point elasticity of demand on page 40.

$$E_s = \frac{P}{Q}\frac{\Delta Q}{\Delta P} = \frac{PC}{OC}\frac{AC}{PC} = \frac{AC}{OC}.$$

FIGURE 4-4   **TIME AND ELASTICITY OF SUPPLY**

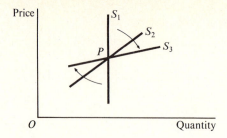

Perfect Elasticity of Demand and Supply

Now that the price elasticities of demand and of supply have been introduced, we can take another look at the market with the large number of buyers and sellers. In such markets, the elasticity of demand for any one seller is infinite; so is the elasticity of supply for any one buyer. Figure 4-5 illustrates this point. For the entire market, demand, supply, and price are shown in the panel on the left. Notice that the quantity scale for the entire market is in millions (of bushels, for example), and that the scales for the one seller and the one buyer are in thousands. At the equilibrium price *P*, any *one* seller can sell a larger or a smaller amount without any effect on price. That is the meaning of the horizontal—or perfectly elastic— demand curve, *d*, as it appears to one seller. Of course, the seller doesn't have to think of it this way; if it is known that 10,000 bushels could be sold today at the same price as 5,000 bushels could be sold, then the seller would act *as if* a perfectly elastic demand curve existed.

Similarly with any one buyer, to whom the supply curve, *s*, is horizontal, i.e., supply is perfectly elastic. Again, the common sense is simple—any one buyer can buy more and can buy less, without affecting price. One buyer can shift his or her demand curve, *d*, along the supply curve, *s*. Likewise, one seller can shift his or her *s* curve along the demand curve, *d*. However, if *many* buyers or sellers, or both, change their minds, the *D* and *S* curves in the entire market shift, bringing about a new equilibrium price and therefore new *d* and *s* curves for individual sellers and buyers.

FIGURE 4-5   **ELASTICITIES TO INDIVIDUAL SELLERS AND BUYERS**

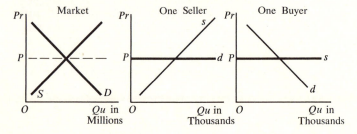

This point is brought up because in chapters to follow there will be frequent use of the concepts of perfectly elastic demand and supply for individual buyers and sellers.

SUMMARY

Income elasticity differs much from one commodity to another. *Income sensitivity* of demand is a rough measure of the relation between percentage changes in expenditures on a commodity and percentage changes in disposable income. *Cross elasticity* of demand relates percentage changes in the quantity demanded of one commodity to percentage changes in the price of another commodity. Low cross elasticities of demand between a commodity and its substitutes could be an indication that the commodity is monopolized. The demands for commodities undergo continual changes. The *elasticity of price expectations* can have a strong influence on current demands. *Elasticity of supply* is the ratio of a percentage change in quantity supplied to a percentage change in price. In a market with many buyers and sellers, supply is perfectly elastic to any one buyer and demand is perfectly elastic to any one seller.

SELECTED REFERENCES

General references on the topics covered in this chapter are George J. Stigler, *The Theory of Price,* 3d ed. (Macmillan, New York, 1966), chap. 3; W. Warren Haynes and William R. Henry, *Managerial Economics: Analysis and Cases,* 3d ed. (Business Publications, Dallas, 1974), chap. 3.

On the use of the cross elasticity concept in antitrust analysis: George W. Stocking and Willard F. Mueller, "The Cellophane Case and the New Competition," *American Economic Review,* 45 (March 1955), 29–63; reprinted in American Economic Association, *Readings in Industrial Organization and Public Policy* (Irwin, Homewood, 1958).

On the elasticity of price expectations: J. R. Hicks, *Value and Capital,* 2d ed. (Oxford, London, 1946), pp. 203–206.

On shifts in demand over time: Henry Schultz, *The Theory and Measurement of Demand* (University of Chicago Press, Chicago, 1938).

EXERCISES AND PROBLEMS

1. The lines in Figure 4–1 on page 53 are straight. Shouldn't they be curved? Why?
2. If a commodity has a low price elasticity, why is it also likely to have a low income elasticity?

3. Speculate on the cross elasticities of demand between air and bus transportation, gas and electric stoves, ham and eggs, coffee and tea.

4. Describe the effect on the current demand for a commodity when its future prices are expected to *fall*. Do this for different elasticities of expectations.

5. Explain what might happen to the price of gold if the coefficient of price expectations of buyers were low and that of sellers high. What might happen if the reverse were true? What might happen if they were both high? Or if they were both low?

6. Explain why the following goods or services could have high, low, zero, or negative coefficients of income elasticity for different groups of purchasers: commercial air transportation, membership in a community swim club, Lincoln Continentals, and motorcycles.

7. Of the goods and services you now buy, some with currently high coefficients of income elasticity for you will in all likelihood come to have low coefficients sometime during the next 5 to 15 years. Make a list of those goods and services. Which will probably carry the lowest coefficients for you in the future? Why?

8. Explain why the coefficients of price elasticity, income elasticity, and cross elasticity of demand can all play a role in the amount of crowding at a public camping ground. Using these elasticity concepts, explain why some camping grounds are less crowded than others.

9. What impact can a successful advertising campaign have on the coefficients of price, income, and cross elasticity of demand?

10. Many private colleges have had to close because of their inability to raise tuition fees high enough. Use the different concepts of elasticity to explain this.

11. Speculate on the sizes of the coefficients of price, income, and cross elasticities for marijuana. Would the coefficients differ by age group and by socioeconomic status? Why? Would the coefficients of elasticity for marijuana differ from those for alcoholic beverages? Why?

12. The astronauts, as part of their mission, brought moon rocks to the earth. What can be said about the elasticity of demand for and the elasticity of supply of these moon rocks? Assume that the federal government offered one-third of its supply of moon rocks for sale. Draw hypothetical demand and supply curves that show the price of moon rocks. What would happen to the demand and supply curves (elasticity and position) if the government sold all of its moon rocks?

5
Cardinal Utility
AND CONSUMER DEMAND

The demand curves for consumer goods described in Chapters 2 and 3 are market, or aggregate, demand curves. They are composed of the demand curves of many individual consumers. The behavior of the individual consumer is the subject of this chapter and of the next two. This chapter confines itself to *cardinal utility* as the leading idea in the analysis of consumer demand. The concept of cardinal utility, which will be defined shortly, was employed by the classical economists of the late eighteenth and nineteenth centuries. The twentieth-century version of the concept is the *neoclassical*. Another form of cardinal utility is the leading idea in the theory of making choices when there are risks. This is modern cardinal utility theory, presented in Chapter 7.

The words *consumer* and *individual* need a brief explanation. These words will be used here to mean a consuming (or spending) unit with a budget. The unit can consist of one person or of the two or more persons in a family. The one budget for the unit is the essential thing for the purposes of the theory of consumer demand, or *theory of consumption*, as it is also called. How the members of a family come to their joint decisions on the family budget is, fortunately, a matter that does not have to be gone into here. Consuming units are also referred to as households. Simple models of an enterprise economy can be built on the assumption that the economy consists of households and firms—consuming units and producing units. Just as the household is imagined as having one decision maker, who is *the* consumer, so the firm is imagined as being guided by one decision maker, the entrepreneur.

THE MEANING OF UTILITY

With given prices of commodities and services, and with a given income, purchases are made according to the consumer's tastes (or desires, or preferences, or wants—these words are synonyms in this context). A consumer desires a unit of commodity *A* more than a unit of commodity *B* because commodity *A* has more utility. *Utility* means want-satisfying power. It is some property common to all commodities wanted by a person. Utility resides in the mind of the consumer. The consumer knows it by introspection. Utility is subjective, not objective. A commodity does not have to be useful in the ordinary sense of that word; the commodity might satisfy a frivolous desire or even one that some people would consider immoral. The concept is ethically neutral.

This chapter is devoted to the utility of goods and services to consumers. The concept of utility does indeed have other applications, which can be mentioned briefly here. Current wealth has utility to an investor, and so do expected capital gains. To one business executive, profits alone have utility; to another, both profits and rapid growth possess utility. Nowadays the utility concept appears in analyses of economic policy decisions in government. If, for example, policy makers decide that full employment yields more utility than price stability, they will manipulate their controls (such as they are) accordingly. These topics will be taken up in later chapters. They are mentioned now because some of the formal properties of utility are the same regardless of its field of application.

Cardinal and Ordinal Utility

Neoclassical utility and the ideas treated in Chapter 7 are concepts of *cardinal* utility, whereas Chapter 6 discusses *ordinal* utility. The terms *cardinal* and *ordinal* are borrowed from the vocabulary of mathematics. The numbers 1, 2, 3, etc., are cardinal numbers. The number 2, for example, is twice the size of number 1. In contrast, the numbers 1st, 2nd, 3rd, etc., are ordinal numbers. Such numbers are ordered, or ranked, and there is no way of knowing, just from the ranking, what is the size relation of the numbers. The second one might or might not be twice as big as the first one. The ordinal numbers 1st, 2nd, and 3rd *could* be 10, 20, and 30, or they *could* be 10, 11, and 40. All we can know of ordinal numbers is that the second number is greater than the first, that the third is greater than the second, etc.

To use the concept of cardinal utility is to assume that quantities of utility are meaningful, that it makes sense to say, for example, that you get twice as much satisfaction from a cup of coffee as from a glass of milk. On the other hand, the concept of ordinal utility permits you to say only that you *prefer* a cup of coffee to a glass of milk. But ordinal utility does not let you compare quantities of satisfaction or utility.

Why not? Economists who insist on using the concept of ordinal utility maintain that quantities of utility are inherently immeasurable, theoretically and conceptually, as well as practically. The same economists also maintain that many aspects of the theory of consumer behavior can be explained without the idea of measurable utility.

Neoclassical cardinal utility carries with it the assumption of measurability. The units of measurement are arbitrary; they are called *utils*. Thus, under some given conditions, someone thinks of an apple as having four utils and an orange as having two utils. This is just another way of saying that one apple has twice as much utility as one orange.

Rational Behavior

To say that the consumer behaves rationally means that the consumer calculates deliberately, chooses consistently, and maximizes utility. Consistent choice rules out vacillating and erratic behavior. If a person prefers A to B, and B to C, then consistency compels that person to prefer A to C. The maximization of utility means that the consumer makes those choices that will result in the greatest possible amount of utility—given the individual's circumstances.

Rational behavior also can be described as behavior that results in an optimum decision. For the consumer, the optimum is the maximum attainable utility. The consumer achieves the optimum by using the best method and by making precise calculations. The rational consumer is not the only decision maker who seeks an optimum. The executive in a business corporation, or in a government agency, or in a nonprofit organization, can also be thought of as searching for optimum decisions through rational behavior.

True enough, the consumer is often ignorant about the best way to satisfy his or her own wants. More important than that is the insufficient and imperfect knowledge that most consumers have about many of the products they buy. Then too, it is a common experience to be disappointed by a purchase—to find that the utility enjoyed is less than the utility that had been anticipated. But ignorance, imperfect knowledge, and the gap between expectations and fulfillment are also set aside in the theory of consumer behavior, again for the sake of simplicity.

TOTAL UTILITY AND MARGINAL UTILITY

The next step is to examine the relation between utility and quantity. Consider a consumer and one of the commodities he or she wants. Imagine that the consumer contemplates 1, 2, 3, etc., units of the commodity. The consumer does not do this in a time sequence but, instead, thinks what it would be like to have 1 unit, *or* 2, *or* 3, *or* etc. Hence the different quantities are simultaneously existing possibilities.

One unit of the commodity yields some amount of utility to the consumer. Two units yield more, 3 units still more, and so on. As quantity increases, total utility increases. But total utility increases at a *diminishing* rate. Why this is so will be demonstrated shortly. To increase at a diminishing rate means that the successive increases, or increments, become smaller and smaller. Thus, 3 units have more utility than 2, and 4 have more than 3; but the gain in utility from acquiring the fourth unit is less than the gain from acquiring the third. The *marginal utility*[1] of 3 units is the utility of any one of the 3 units—it is the gain, or increment, from having 3 units instead of 2. To generalize: The marginal utility (MU) of any quantity n is the total utility (TU) of that quantity minus the total utility of one less. Thus: MU of $n = TU$ of $n - TU$ of $(n - 1)$.

Figure 5–1 shows the relations between total utility and marginal utility. In the upper part of the figure, the three bars show increasing total utility. Then the curve takes over and indicates how total utility continues to grow as more units are added. The lower part of the figure displays only the *increases* in total utility, i.e., the marginal utilities of different quantities of the commodity.

Slope of Total Utility Curve

The marginal utility of any quantity can also be stated as the *slope* of the total utility curve for the same quantity. The slope of the total curve at a point is the gain of utility at that point and is equal to the height of the marginal utility curve at the corresponding quantity. In Figure 5–1, the slope of the total utility curve TU steadily diminishes as quantity increases. Imagine a series of tangent lines at successive points on the curve TU. The tangent lines would come closer and closer to being flat. At the peak of the curve TU, the tangent line is indeed flat, as Figure 5–1 shows.

When the total utility curve reaches its maximum, its slope, then, is zero, as shown by the horizontal line that is tangent at the maximum point. Marginal utility is zero when total utility is a maximum; when the total is a maximum it is neither increasing nor decreasing, and since marginal utility is the increase or decrease, it has to be zero. Finally, when total utility is declining, its increases are negative, which is the same thing as saying that marginal utility is negative.

The economic meaning of zero marginal utility is that you have all you want of the commodity in question. You don't want another unit or two of it because you have all you want; nor do you care if you

[1] A note on the word *marginal*: This word has been used in economic theory for many decades, always with the same meaning, which is the rate of change of a total. The total can be utility as above, or cost, revenue, product, etc. Quite another meaning of *marginal* has come into common usage, i.e., marginal as signifying inferior or poor or doubtful. Even economists sometimes use the word in this other sense in ordinary conversation.

FIGURE 5-1 **TOTAL UTILITY AND MARGINAL UTILITY**

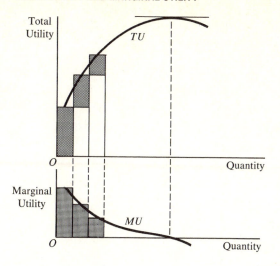

lose a unit because you have so many. Negative marginal utility means that you have so many units of something that you'd rather have fewer; cats, for example.

For someone who likes them, 2 cats can be a joy, whereas 12 are a nuisance. It is a question of how many, of numbers in some context. But if, at some number, the cry rings out, "That's enough," then for any larger number, marginal utility is negative. The modern physical environment offers, however, all the examples one could want of things with negative marginal utilities for any quantities, even for the smallest. Trash of course is one of the examples. A diagram for trash would have disutility, instead of utility, on the vertical axis. The curve of total disutility would increase at an increasing rate and the curve of marginal disutility would rise.

An important property of any marginal utility curve is that, for any quantity, the area under the marginal utility curve is equal to the total utility of the same quantity. This property can be seen in Figure 5-1. For 3 units of the commodity, the area under the *MU* curve is the sum of the 3 shaded bars. This sum is also equal to the total utility of 3 units, as can be seen in the upper panel of the diagram. For 2 units, the area under the *MU* curve is the sum of the first 2 bars, which is equal to the total utility of 2 units of the commodity.

Total utility and marginal utility are just one pair of total-marginal relations. Others will come along in later chapters. The relations

69   *Cardinal Utility and Consumer Demand*

TABLE 5-1   **RELATIONS BETWEEN TOTAL QUANTITIES AND MARGINAL QUANTITIES**

When Total Is	Then Marginal Is
Increasing at a constant rate	Constant
Increasing at an increasing rate	Increasing
Increasing at a decreasing rate	Decreasing
At a maximum	Zero
Decreasing	Negative

between any total and its marginal are the same. The relations are summarized in Table 5–1.

Diminishing Marginal Utility

Imagine the consumer contemplating all of the commodities he or she wants and thinking of different quantities of each. For each commodity, diminishing marginal utility prevails. The more you have of anything, the less important to you is any *one* unit of it. So certain is this generalization, because it expresses a universal human experience, that it too is often referred to as a law, the *law of diminishing marginal utility*.

For the law of diminishing marginal utility to hold, certain conditions must exist. The units of the commodity must be relevantly defined. The law holds for pairs of shoes, but not for a single shoe. If the units of a vacation are defined as days, it might be that the second day of a vacation would have more utility than the first. Hence there would be increasing marginal utility for the second and perhaps the third day. But from the fourth day on, additional days would be less and less satisfying. The law holds for individual commodities desired by individual consumers with given tastes. If a consumer's tastes change, so that he or she likes a commodity more, then the marginal utility of any quantity of that commodity rises.

The diminishing marginal utility of larger quantities of a commodity is clear when the commodity is bought in small units, such as oranges per week, pounds of steak per month, and so on. Such commodities are said to be divisible. But what about the commodities that are bought one at a time at long intervals? Such commodities are indivisible goods—automobiles, television sets, overcoats, etc. And what of the commodities that are bought once (usually) in a lifetime, such as wedding cakes?[2] Most indivisible commodities are, however, durable consumer goods, which yield

---

[2]Someone, however, is bound to insist that the law of diminishing marginal utility does indeed apply to a wedding cake, because the bride-to-be and her mother have to decide, among other things, how big the cake should be. The bigger the cake, the more pieces can be served; the more pieces, at least after some number, the less the utility per piece.

units of service over periods of time—the miles of an automobile, the hours of a radio or television set, the degrees of warmth of a furnace, and so on. The mind of the rationally behaving consumer concentrates on the marginal utilities of the miles per year, of the hours per year, etc., of the so-called indivisible goods. Besides, such goods are typically paid for in installments; the payments stretch out over time, just as do the units of service. Then too, cars and TV sets, to mention just two examples, can be rented by persons who want just a few units of service.

Why does marginal utility diminish? Several kinds of explanations are possible. Some of these are physiological and psychological—too many units of a commodity bring physical satiation, or, the response to a repeated stimulus diminishes. Even though they have been relied on by economists, such explanations lack generality and anyway are not needed. Another explanation is this: If a consumer could have everything he or she wants without having to pay anything, the consumer would choose those quantities of each good that would make the marginal utility of each one zero; i.e., the consumer would maximize total utility for each good. Marginal utility would therefore have to diminish to get to zero. If this were not so, the consumer who could have everything free would take infinite quantities of everything. The best explanation, however, is to visualize each commodity as having several uses and to assume that each consumer ranks the uses. One unit of a commodity is put to its most important use. If the consumer has two units, one of them is put to the next most important use, and so on. Marginal utility diminishes because of the successively less important uses of additional quantities of a commodity.

THE EQUIMARGINAL PRINCIPLE   Usually, more than one unit of a commodity can be put to each of its uses. If a consumer possesses some quantity of a commodity, the consumer allocates the units among the several uses of the commodity in such a way as to contribute most to his or her well-being. The best, or the optimum, allocation is one that causes the marginal utilities in *each* use to be equal. For if this were not so, the consumer could improve his or her well-being by cutting back in one use and expanding in another. Suppose that a drought causes a farmer's well to yield very little water and that careful thought has to be given to how to use what water there is. In the farmhouse, water is used for drinking, cooking, washing, and for other purposes; elsewhere on the farm, water is given to the animals and is used for cleaning. With very little water, the farmer must be careful with each pint. The farmer's final decisions on the allocation of water are such that matters could not be improved by switching a pint from one use to another. The utility of the last pint in each use is equal.

FIGURE 5-2

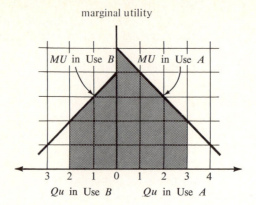

A simple illustration of the equimarginal principle is given in Figure 5-2. Here are two uses for a commodity, use *A* and use *B*. The figure is a Janus diagram: It has two faces that look in opposite directions—use *A* is on the right side, and use *B* is on the left. The curves of marginal utility for each use are shown. The *A* curve is farther from the vertical axis than the *B* curve. Curve *A* also intersects the vertical axis at a higher point than curve *B*. This indicates that the desire for use *A* is stronger—the marginal utility of any quantity of the commodity in use *A* is greater than that of the same quantity in use *B*.

Suppose that the consumer has 5 units of the commodity. Given the *MU* curves in Figure 5-2, the best allocation is 3 units in use *A* and 2 units in use *B*, because with these quantities the marginal utilities are equal. Why is this the best allocation? To see that it is, try another one. Let 4 units of the commodity be devoted to use *A* and 1 unit to use *B*. There would indeed be a gain here—the area between 3 and 4 under the *MU* curve in use *A*. But there would also be a loss—the area between 2 and 1 under the *MU* curve in use *B*. Clearly, the loss is greater than the gain. Any other change from the allocation of 3 to *A* and 2 to *B* would give the same result, a loss of utility greater than the gain of utility.

Another way to see the optimality of the allocation that equalizes marginal utilities is to look at total utility. Remember that the total utility of any quantity is always the area under the marginal utility curve. When marginal utilities in the two uses are equal, total utility—the entire shaded area in Figure 5-2—is at a maximum. Once again, imagine any change in the allocation of 5 units; any change can only reduce total utility.

The equimarginal principle can be generalized. Any decision maker can obtain the maximum return (or gain, or benefit, etc.) from a given quantity of a resource that has two or more uses if the individual allocates units of the resource in such a way that the marginal returns in each use are equal. For this principle to hold, marginal returns must diminish as more and more units of a resource are applied to any one of its uses.

<table>
<tr><td>THE MARGINAL UTILITY OF MONEY INCOME</td><td>The law of diminishing marginal utility applies to money income as well as to goods and services. It is better of course to have $20,000 a year than $10,000. But is $1 as important when a consumer has $20,000 as when he or she has $10,000? The marginal utility of money is the utility of $1; for some purposes, however, it is convenient to think of money in larger units, such as $100. Because a consumer with given tastes in a given period of time applies any additional dollars he or she gets to less and less important uses, the law must hold. Still, the concept of the marginal utility of money is surrounded with difficulties. They will be discussed later; meanwhile, let the diminution be assumed.</td></tr>
</table>

Thus far, the consumer's wants have been discussed. Now the consumer's income is brought in. If he or she has $10,000 a year, the marginal utility of money is higher than if instead, and in the same time period, he or she had $20,000 a year. With $10,000, the consumer is more careful with a dollar and therefore might take a taxi only in a heavy rain, whereas with $20,000, the consumer might use taxis several times a month. In other words, one *additional* dollar *spent* yields more utility or satisfaction if income is low than if it is high.

Assume now that the utility of $1 to a consumer is 20 "utils." The choice of the number 20 is quite arbitrary; any positive number will do. The only requirement is that if 20 utils per dollar applies to a consumer with an income of $10,000, a number less than 20 must apply to an income of $20,000 for the same consumer in the same period of time. The larger the income, the smaller the number of utils per dollar. To assign 20 utils to $1 of income of our consumer is therefore to fix the utility significance of money prices to the consumer. Thus if the person pays $1 for something, 20 utils are given up; if $5, 100 utils are sacrificed; and so on. In what follows, it will be assumed that the number of utils per dollar remains constant as the consumer makes purchases.

<table>
<tr><td>EQUILIBRIUM OF THE CONSUMER</td><td>The consumer's desire for different quantities of a commodity is represented by the diminishing marginal utility of the commodity to the consumer. The size of the person's money income determines the utility of a dollar to the consumer. With this information, then, the demand curve of a consumer for particular commodity can be constructed.</td></tr>
</table>

A consumer's demand curve looks like those described in Chapters 2 and 3. The quantity bought, at any price, by one consumer is of course relatively small. Diminishing marginal utility is the cause of the downward slope of the demand curve of a consumer.

The market demand curve described in Chapter 2 is simply the sum of the demand curves of the individuals who are actual or potential consumers in a market. The individual demand curves are added horizontally, that is, the amounts bought in the market at each possible price are the sums of the amounts the consumers buy at that price. At high prices, some consumers do not buy at all because the high prices lie above any points on their individual demand curves. At successively lower prices, more and more is bought for two reasons. One is that each consumer buys more at lower prices; the other is that each lower price brings in new buyers whose tastes or incomes did not permit them to buy at higher prices.

The law of demand, therefore, rests firmly upon the principle of diminishing marginal utility as well as upon differences in tastes among consumers and upon differences in their incomes.

Figure 5-3 shows the demand curve of a consumer for, say, shirts. The price of a shirt is $6. The horizontal line from $6 signifies that the price to the consumer is the same no matter how many shirts are bought; the supply of shirts to that consumer is perfectly elastic (see page 62). The vertical axis in Figure 5-3 is price in dollars. Because cardinal theory follows the assumption that utility can be measured, the demand curve, *D*, can relate utils and dollars to quantities of shirts. With the consumer deriving 20 utils from $1, the vertical axis could be calibrated in utils—80 utils for $4, 120 utils for $6, etc.

The consumer buys 5 shirts. Why this number? The fifth shirt yields 120 utils; the $6 sacrificed for it also yields 120 utils. Thus the fifth shirt is just barely worth buying. A sixth shirt would have a marginal utility less than that of $6, which sum of money can always be spent on something else that would yield at least 120 utils. And on the other hand, if our consumer bought only 4 shirts, he or she

FIGURE 5-3   **EQUILIBRIUM OF THE CONSUMER**

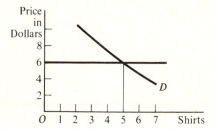

would not be taking advantage of the opportunity of buying something affording more utility than that yielded by $6.

For a consumer's purchase of the optimum quantity of any one
commodity, then,

$$MU = \lambda P.$$

Here MU is of course marginal utility, P is price and λ (lambda) is
the usual symbol for the marginal utility of money income. With the
shirt example, the equation states that 120 utils equals 20 utils per
dollar times 6. The generalization of the equation is that marginal
utility is proportional to price, λ being the factor of proportionality.
Another way of expressing this idea is that λ is the conversion factor
between money price and the marginal utility of the optimum quantity. A dollar's worth of utility is λ, and therefore marginal utility
divided by price is also a dollar's worth of utility.

With MU proportional to price, the consumer is in equilibrium.
The quantity he buys is the *equilibrium quantity*.[3] Purchase of this
quantity maximizes the utility the consumer can gain from the commodity. Maximization is not a state of bliss; maximization means
only the most satisfaction that is compatible with price and with the
person's limited income.

Equilibrium has the general meaning of a balance of opposing
forces. The consumer's force is desire, which is limited by income.
The opposing force is price, the sign and condition of the availability
of a commodity. If price rises, the consumer buys less; if it falls, the
consumer buys more. If the consumer's desire becomes stronger, he
or she buys more; if weaker, less. If both price and desire change,
the new equilibrium reflects the strengths of the two forces.

*The Optimum
Budget*

So far a consumer's purchase of just one commodity has been
analyzed. Consider next the consumer's budget, or purchase plan
for many commodities. Everyone seems to agree that there is indeed
such a thing as a best, or optimum, budget. The question now is the
properties of that optimum.

First of all, take two commodities, A and B, that the consumer
buys. Their prices are P_A and P_B. The marginal utility of money
income to the consumer is λ. Then as we know,

(5-1) $MU_A = \lambda P_A$ and
(5-2) $MU_B = \lambda P_B.$

---

[3] A logically complete statement of the equilibrium of the consumer must repeat that
marginal utility is diminishing. For, if marginal utility were increasing, as it could
over some range of quantity and under unusual circumstances, the consumer would
want to buy more than the quantity corresponding to the intersection of the demand
curve and the price line.

Now divide the first equation by the second. The result is

$$(5\text{-}3) \qquad \frac{MU_A}{MU_B} = \frac{P_A}{P_B}.$$

Equation (5-3) says that if the price of A is twice that of B, MU_A has to be twice MU_B. The consumer adjusts the quantities bought to achieve this result. Equation (5-3) gives another view of the proportionality of marginal utilities and prices.

The foregoing equations can also be put in this form

$$(5\text{-}4) \qquad \frac{MU_A}{P_A} = \frac{MU_B}{P_B} = \lambda.$$

Equation (5-4) is equivalent to saying that the last dollar spent on A yields the same marginal utility (λ) as the last dollar spent on B. Here again is the equimarginal principle. The consumer has just so many dollars (per month or whatever the budget period happens to be). In the consumer's optimum budget dollars are allocated so that the marginal utilities yielded by the last dollars spent on each commodity are equal. This does not mean equal amounts of money for each commodity. Not at all. It does mean equal *marginal* utilities for all of the commodities in the consumer's budget. It also means that the marginal utilities of all these commodities are proportional to prices. To illustrate: Suppose the fiftieth dollar spent on A gives 30 utils and the tenth dollar spent on B gives 15 utils. This is not an optimum allocation because it can be improved. The improvement, i.e., more utility, comes by spending, say, $55 on A and $5 on B. If this adjustment equalizes the marginal utilities of dollars spent on A and B, no further improvement is possible.

The generalization for the many commodities in a consumer's budget is straightforward

$$(5\text{-}5) \qquad \frac{MU_A}{P_A} = \frac{MU_B}{P_B} = \frac{MU_C}{P_C} = \cdots = \lambda.$$

All of this is very formal. How many consumers have ever heard of λ or even of marginal utility? But if consumers behave with consistent calculations they act *as if* they know about the formal theory. The common sense of Equation (5-5) is simply that of a person who has put a budget on a piece of paper and who after making some changes finally gets the budget into a shape that cannot be improved.

CONSUMER'S SURPLUS

In modern societies, a consumer is able to buy a multitude of commodities for any one of which, taken by itself, the consumer would be willing to pay much more than he or she does in fact have to pay. The difference between the amount a consumer *would* pay for the quantity of a commodity bought and the amount the consumer *does* pay is called *consumer's surplus*.

The doctrine of consumer's surplus has had much attention from economic theorists, with the inevitable result that thought stimulated by controversy has caused the doctrine to assume several highly complicated forms. But the original and simple form of the doctrine, as first stated by Alfred Marshall, will be presented here. Marshall's doctrine remains sturdy, mainly because of its simplicity and because, in some analyses, it is hard to get along without it. His doctrine has been used, for example, in empirical studies of the effects of monopoly, of the benefits from the introduction of hybrid corn, and of the effects of different methods for the pricing of electricity.

As an example, consider the consumer's surplus that a consumer gets from the weekly purchases of steak. Table 5–2 gives hypothetical data. For this consumer, let $\lambda = 20$; that is, $1 yields 20 utils. The choice of a number for λ is of course arbitrary. It is also assumed here that λ is constant at each price because changes in price cause such small changes in the marginal utility of money that they can be disregarded.

The first two columns are a demand schedule, giving pounds per week that would be purchased at the various prices. Column (3) is the consumer's total money expenditure at each of the possible prices. Column (4) is marginal utility in utils. Column (5) is total utility in utils. This column is constructed from Column (4) by adding the utils obtained from the purchase of successive pounds of steak.

Column (6) gives the utility of the expenditure on steak, which is marginal utility times the number of pounds purchased. The utility of expenditure measures the consumer's sacrifice for any quantity bought, i.e., the utility of the money the consumer has to pay.

TABLE 5–2

THE CALCULATION OF CONSUMER'S SURPLUS

Price	Quantity Bought	Total Expenditure	Marginal Utility[a]	Total Utility[a]	Utility of Expenditure[a]	Consumer's Surplus[a]	
(1)	(2)	(3)	(4)	(5)	(6)	(7)	(8)
$2.50	1 lb.	$2.50	50 utils	50 utils	50 utils	—	—
2.25	2	4.50	45	95	90	5 utils	$0.25
2.10	3	6.30	42	137	126	11	0.55
2.00	4	8.00	40	177	160	17	0.85

[a] By assumption, the utility of $1 ($\lambda$) is 20 utils and is constant.

Consumer's surplus, then, is obtained in Column (7) by subtracting the utility of expenditure from total utility. Column (8) gives consumer's surplus in money, with $1 = 20$ utils as the conversion factor.

If the actual price is $2.00 per pound, the consumer buys 4 pounds of steak a week. Because we assume we know what this consumer's λ is, we can say that his or her consumer's surplus is 17 utils, or we can point to its money equivalent, the $0.85. If we did not know λ but only the quantities the consumer would buy at different prices, we would still have the $0.85 as the measure of consumer's surplus in this example. We obtain the $0.85 consumer's surplus by adding the prices and by subtracting from their total the total expenditure. Consumer's surplus, then, is utility measured as an amount of money.

Figure 5–4 displays diagrams for consumer's surplus. The diagram on the left shows the numbers contained in Table 5–2. The stippled area is consumer's surplus. Total utility is the area under the demand curve. The striped area is the sacrificed utility of the money spent for 4 pounds of steak.

If the price of a commodity or a service goes up, the consumer is said to be injured, particularly if the price is that of a public utility service or of something else looked upon as important. Similarly, if a price goes down, the consumer benefits. What does the injury or benefit consist of? The answer is—a loss or a gain of consumer's surplus. This is illustrated in the diagram on the right in Figure 5–4. Let the initial price be P_0. At this price consumer's surplus is the sum of the areas A and B. When price goes up to P_1, consumer's

FIGURE 5–4   **CONSUMER'S SURPLUS**

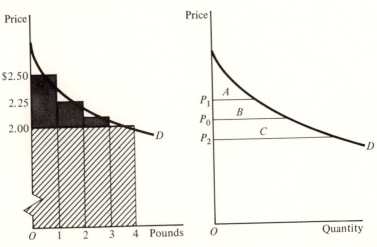

surplus shrinks to the area A; thus area B is the loss of consumer's surplus from the price increase. Similarly, a fall in price from P_0 to P_2 brings a gain of consumer's surplus equal to area C. The sizes of the gains and losses depend on how large are the price changes, as well as upon elasticity of demand. (Note 6 in the Appendix to Part 1 is on consumer's surplus.)

Consumers'
Surplus
in a Market

The concept of the loss or the gain from a higher or a lower price can be extended from the individual buyer to the total of the consumers of a commodity or a service. Suppose the telephone company is permitted to raise the rates it charges residential subscribers. The higher rates, i.e., the higher average price for a unit of service, bring a gain to the telephone company and a loss to the consumers. (Assume that the quality of the service remains unchanged.) The gain to the telephone company is so many million dollars of additional revenue, the demand for telephone service being inelastic. The loss to the consumers is the loss of consumers' surplus, which is also an amount of so many million dollars.

Figure 5-5 has a market demand curve; the original price was P_0 and the new price is P_1. At the original price, the consumers spent and the telephone company received an amount in millions of dollars equal to area J plus area K. At the new price, the expenditure/revenue is area J plus area M. Area M is greater than area K because demand is inelastic. The loss of consumers' surplus is the area M *plus* area L.

For a commodity or service with an elastic demand, consumer expenditures would be smaller at a higher price. But there still would be a loss of consumers' surplus.

In practice, demand curves often can be statistically estimated. When this is done, a loss or a gain of consumers' surplus can be

FIGURE 5-5   CONSUMERS' SURPLUS IN A MARKET

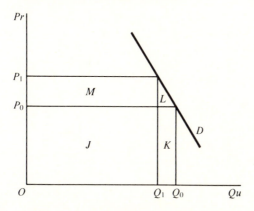

calculated as an amount in millions of dollars. Such an amount is proportional to the loss or gain of utility to the consumers.

For the thousands of consumers in a market, the demand curve is the sum of their individual demand curves. So too, a loss or gain of consumers' surplus is a summation over the individual consumers. The surplus is measured or measurable in dollars that stand for the sum of utility lost or gained by the consumers. For this sum or aggregate of utility to be meaningful, two assumptions are needed. One was mentioned before, namely, the assumption that changes in prices have negligibly small effects on the marginal utility of money, i.e., on λ. The other assumption is that λ is the same for all consumers; this principally means that the effects of differences in income are overlooked.

Many economists maintain, however, that it is not possible, even in principle, to compare the utility enjoyed by one person with the utility enjoyed by another person. And if the two utilities cannot be compared, they cannot be added. This point of view is the doctrine of "the invalidity of interpersonal comparisons of utility." It denies the possibility of adding individual consumers' surpluses to get the consumers' surplus for a whole market. The denial is not just a practical objection. It is made, to repeat, on grounds of principle.

But this view is too strict. Anyone who would try to adhere to it would simply have to eliminate serious thought about great political, social, and economic issues, as well as about injuries and benefits to groups of consumers. It is impossible to think about such issues without assuming that, for the purpose at hand, people are pretty much alike, and alike too, in their capacities for receiving satisfactions from consumption. Certainly the cardinal utility concept implies comparison and addition. The lesson taught by doubts of the validity of interpersonal comparisons is that when they are made, such comparisons should be made carefully in the knowledge that at best they can only be rough. Even if people are for many purposes pretty much alike, they are not identical.

There are ways to evade the taboo on interpersonal comparison. One is through the device of "the representative consumer," who turns up from time to time in economic literature. But to put him on display is simply to make the adding of utilities implicit rather than explicit. And in spite of the taboo, which in any case is becoming weaker, economists more and more find it useful to employ the concept of consumers' surplus in dealing with certain kinds of problems. Some of these will be discussed in later chapters.

APPLICATIONS   The concepts of total utility and marginal utility are aids to clear thinking. The total utility of water is incalculably high, yet its marginal utility—the utility of the last gallon—is normally so low that most people cheerfully "waste" many gallons a day. The total utility of a bridge can also be high; but if there is no toll, people cross it as much as they please, the marginal utility of a crossing being zero. On the other hand, the marginal utility of champagne, for example, is high, whereas its total utility to most people who buy it is probably low.

Ever since the early 1930s surplus foodstuffs have been distributed under various programs to needy families. On one occasion when the surplus food was oranges, the good citizens in a community were shocked and indignant to see children of destitute families playing ball with some of the oranges. The indignation was, however, misdirected. It should have gone to the administrators who apparently gave "too many" oranges to families in the one community, so many in fact that marginal utility approached zero. What could be more rational than to allocate the last oranges to their best last use—as makeshift balls?

The Redistribution of Income

In the United States, government imposes progressive income taxes and provides social services. Income is thus transferred from the high-income groups to low-income groups. Does the transfer of income from rich to poor increase the nation's economic welfare?

Let it be assumed, for the purpose of this discussion, that the transfer of income has no effect on incentives to produce. The question, then, is the effect of the transfer upon economic welfare as the satisfaction from consumption. Assume next that all persons have the same capacity for enjoying consumer goods and services, and therefore that the *same* curve of the diminishing marginal utility of income can be drawn for every person.

Figure 5-6 shows such a curve. In the figure, *OL* is a poor family's income and *OH* is a rich family's income. Let the rich family's income be reduced by *HH'*, and let the same amount of money income be transferred to the poor family, so that its income

FIGURE 5-6   WELFARE AND THE REDISTRIBUTION OF INCOME

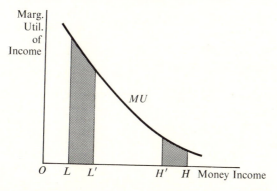

rises by LL'. It is clear from the figure that the gain in utility—the shaded area above LL'—to the poor family exceeds the loss of the rich family—the shaded area above HH'. Hence the total utility—economic welfare—of both together is larger. With reasoning like this, some economists have actually advocated that government redistribute income.

Is the reasoning correct? Most economists say that it is not, because people differ, and no one knows the shapes of the curves. Nevertheless, remember that income is in fact redistributed. What is the effect on economic welfare? The question remains open.[4]

Progressive Income Taxation

Continuous controversy has long surrounded the subject of progressive income taxation. Apart from the disputes over the soundness of actual tax systems, such as the existing federal personal income tax in the United States, controversy and honest doubt still attach to the *principle* of progressive income taxation. The principle can be explained and justified because of the need for revenue, because the income tax is one of the stabilizers of national income, because the tax reduces the inequalities of personal income, and because it achieves an equitable distribution of the burden of taxation. Discussion here will confine itself to the last point—equity—and its connection with the concepts of utility and marginal utility. Is the income tax, in principle, the fairest of all taxes?

It has long since been generally agreed that equity in taxation means taxing according to ability to pay and that ability to pay is a function of income. The development of utility theory in the second half of the nineteenth century led to agreement that, ideally, taxpayers should make equal sacrifices in paying taxes out of their incomes. Now what does equal sacrifice mean? It does not mean the payment of equal amounts of money to government. No, equal sacrifice means equal *subjective* sacrifice, i.e., equal loss of utility by taxpayers. What about progression? Does the doctrine of equal subjective sacrifice call for progressive rates of taxation on personal incomes? No, not necessarily, for the answer depends on how fast the marginal utility of income diminishes. But no one knows or can probably ever know just how fast this is. It should not be blandly taken for granted that progressive income taxation means fairness or equity in sharing the burden of taxes, if equity means equality (or an attempt at it) of subjective sacrifice.

There is more to be said. Proportional taxation would be called for if marginal utility declined in accordance with Bernoulli's

[4] Some theorists, however, evade the prohibition of interpersonal comparisons of utilities by pretending that "policy makers" assign different "distributional weights" to different classes of persons. With a transfer of income, the "weight" assigned to the rich family's loss is smaller than the "weight" of the poor family's gain. Here, then, is another way of justifying some redistribution of income.

FIGURE 5-7

HOW FAST DOES THE MU OF MONEY DECLINE?

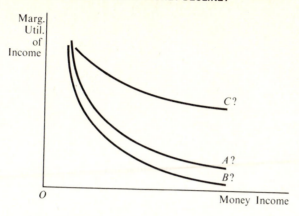

hypothesis. Daniel Bernoulli (1700–1782), the Swiss mathematician, said, approximately, that after some minimum income is attained, the marginal utility of income declines by a rate equal to the relative (i.e., percentage) increase in income.[5] Such a curve of the diminishing marginal utility of income is like curve A in Figure 5-7. Curve A is a rectangular hyperbola; it has the same properties as a demand curve with unitary elasticity throughout. Under this hypothesis, a person with an income of $20,000 who pays a $4,000 tax makes the same sacrifice as a person with $10,000 who pays $2,000. The subjective sacrifice is the same (both absolutely and proportionally) because the marginal utility of a $20,000 income is half that of a $10,000 income. That is, $4,000 times ½ equals $2,000 times 1. Only if the marginal utility of incomes declines *faster* than in Bernoulli's hypothesis is progressive taxation justified on grounds of equity. The curve has to look like curve B in Figure 5-7. With the faster decline, the $20,000 income would have less than half the marginal utility of the $10,000 income, and the tax would therefore have to be more than $4,000 to match, subjectively, the $10,000-a-year person's $2,000 tax sacrifice. And if marginal utility should decline as in curve C, equity would call for regressive, not progressive, rates of personal income taxation. It follows that the progressive income tax rests upon an uncertain foundation of logic, at least so far as equality of sacrifice is concerned.

SUMMARY

The neoclassical theory of consumer behavior rests on the concept of utility, which is subjective want-satisfying power, a property

[5] See Note 6 in the Appendix to Part 1.

common to commodities. *Cardinal utility* is utility assumed to be measurable in principle. *Rational behiavor* by consumers is the making of deliberate, calculating, and consistent choices aimed at maximizing utility. As a consumer acquires, in fact or in contemplation, more units of a commodity, their *total utility* increases, but at a diminishing rate. This is equivalent to *diminishing marginal utility*. The utility added by the last unit of a quantity of a commodity is the marginal utility of the commodity. When total utility is maximum, marginal utility is zero. Marginal utility diminishes because additional units of a commodity are put to less and less important uses. A consumer allocates units of a commodity among different uses in such a way that marginal utilities in each use are equal—*the equimarginal principle*. The size of a consumer's income determines *the marginal utility of money* to that consumer and, therefore, the marginal utilities represented by the prices of commodities. A consumer's demand curve for a commodity slopes downward because of diminishing marginal utility. Market demand curves are the sums of the demand curves of individual consumers. The consumer is in *equilibrium* when the consumer buys that quantity of a commodity whose marginal utility is proportional to its price; in equilibrium, the consumer maximizes his or her satisfaction. In the *optimum budget*, the consumer buys *all* commodities in such amounts that $MU = \lambda P$, λ being the marginal utility of money income. The last dollar spent on each commodity yields the same increment of satisfaction. *Consumer's surplus* is the excess of total utility measured in dollars over the expenditure for a commodity. Some economists have advocated the redistribution of income by government because, they argue, dollars of income transferred from the rich to the poor would increase the *economic welfare* enjoyed by both together, owing to the diminishing marginal utility of money income. Other economists disagree, either because they deny the validity of *interpersonal comparisons of utility* or because they contend that the marginal utility of income diminishes in different unknown ways for different persons. Because no one knows how fast the marginal utility of money income diminishes, *the equity of the principle of progressive income taxation* rests on an uncertain logical foundation.

SELECTED REFERENCES

Alfred Marshall, *Principles of Economics,* 8th ed. (Macmillan, London, 1920), III. An advanced discussion is in J. R. Hicks, *A Revision of Demand Theory* (Oxford, London, 1956).

   On the utilities of indivisible goods: Philip H. Wicksteed, *The Common Sense of Political Economy* (London, 1910; reprinted and edited by Lionel Robbins, Routledge, London, 1933), chap. 3.

On decisions on consumer spending, including joint decisions by husbands and wives: R. A. Ferber and F. M. Nicosia, "Newly Married Couples and Their Asset Accumulation Decisions," in *Human Behavior in Economic Affairs: Essays in Honor of George Katona* (New Holland Publishing Company, Amsterdam, 1972).

On the redistribution of income: A. C. Pigou, *The Economics of Welfare*, 4th ed. (Macmillan, London, 1932), part I, chap. 8, part 4; Appendix II in the reprint of 1952 contains Pigou's defense of the validity of the comparability of utilities. An extreme position is taken by Abba P. Lerner, *The Economics of Control* (Macmillan, New York, 1944), chap. 3. A clear exposition is in Howard R. Bowen, *Toward Social Economy* (Rhinehart, New York, 1948), chap. 19.

On progressive income taxation: Richard A. Musgrave and Peggy B. Musgrave, *Public Finance in Theory and Practice* (McGraw-Hill, New York, 1973), pp. 199–204. A less technical but fuller discussion is contained in Walter J. Blum and Harry Kalven, Jr., *The Uneasy Case for Progressive Taxation* (University of Chicago Press, Chicago, 1953).

EXERCISES AND PROBLEMS

1. For a rich family and a poor family, draw curves of the marginal utility of income in such a way as to increase their joint welfare by a transfer of income from the poor to the rich family.
2. In the eighteenth century, the "diamonds and water paradox" was discussed. The paradox was this: Why are diamonds, which are useless baubles, so valuable when water, which is essential to life, is so cheap? Resolve the paradox with the concept of marginal utility.
3. Draw diagrams to show different positions of equilibrium of a consumer for the purchase of one commodity. For example, show the consumer buying *more* at a higher price because a change in desire more than offsets the higher price.
4. What is the marginal utility of the services of the public library to an avid reader who lives nearby? The total utility? The consumer's surplus?
5. Show how a sensible ("rational") student would allocate 20 hours of time to preparation for three examinations in accordance with the equimarginal principle.
6. From the dozens of different goods and services you currently buy, compile a list of those whose marginal utility declines rapidly. Compile another list of items whose marginal utility declines less rapidly. Why do you put items on one list rather than on the other? Can you think of anything you buy that yields increasing marginal utility?

7.   Use the concept of marginal utility to explain why some services are provided by government (federal, state, and local), while other goods and services are provided by the private market.

8.   Why does a flat-rate water pricing policy, i.e., a fixed sum regardless of the quantity of water used, give no incentive to reduce the consumption of water?

9.   Explain why a fee schedule for a toll bridge connecting a central business district with a residential area might be as follows: No charge between 8 P.M. and 6 A.M.; $2 between 6 A.M. and 10 A.M. and between 4 P.M. and 8 P.M.; and $1 during the rest of the day.

10.   Speculate, by drawing diagrams, on the marginal utility of money to you five years ago, today, and five years from now.

11.   Using hypothetical data, calculate the consumers' surplus in the market for pocket electronic calculators when they first came on the market (about 1972) and compare it with the consumers' surplus that probably exists today.

12.   Draw a diagram that reflects the change occurring in your welfare as a result of rising gasoline prices. Draw a similar diagram for a person richer than you and one for a person poorer than you. What are your assumptions about price elasticity of demand?

13.   Assume that the utility of $1 is 30 utils, and is constant. Using hypothetical data, construct a table showing the consumer's surplus for beer. In your table, include the following: price, quantity, total expenditure, marginal utility, total utility, utility of the expenditure, and consumer's surplus.

14.   Draw demand curves showing how different price elasticities of demand influence changes in the size of consumers' surplus when a seller lowers the price.

6

ORDINAL UTILITY AND
Indifference Curves

The attacks on the neoclassical cardinal utility concept early in the twentieth century were skirmishes on the outposts. But in the 1930s, heavy artillery was brought up and fired with apparently devastating results. Ordinal utility was set on a throne consisting of a box of tools containing *indifference curves*.

The indifference curve, to be explained shortly, was not new. Invented late in the nineteenth century by the English economist F. Y. Edgeworth, the indifference curve was carried to the continent of Europe where the Italian economist, Vilfredo Pareto, put the indifference curve to extensive use. Not until the 1930s did it return to the English-speaking world. Two English economists, R. G. D. Allen and J. R. Hicks, fired the heavy shells at cardinal utility. They urged that the theory of consumer behavior be built anew on the basis of ordinal utility. Their views prevailed. The indifference curve replaced the curve of diminishing marginal utility.

So it seemed for a while. But the ordinal attack turned out to have no more effect than to tone down some of the claims for cardinal utility. It has also been found that ordinal utility has its own shortcomings. Thus, both kinds of utility coexist in economic theory, and peacefully at that.

**PREFERENCE
AND
INDIFFERENCE**

Ordinal utility means that the consumer is assumed to order, or rank, the subjective utilities of goods. That is all. There is no need to assume that the consumer knows quantities of utilities. Suppose the consumer prefers a unit of commodity A to a unit of commodity B, and also prefers A to C. But suppose also that the consumer has no preference between B and C. If offered a choice between a unit of B and one of C, the consumer is indifferent, not caring which one is chosen.

The tastes of the consumer can therefore be described with the ideas of preference and indifference. If the consumer can choose between two goods or collections of goods, he or she always prefers one to the other or else is indifferent. Observe that the only assumption is *that* the consumer prefers or is indifferent. *Why* the person prefers can be left out of it. And so can *by how much* the consumer prefers. This last is the assumption omitted in the indifference curve analysis of consumer demand; the assumption is not needed. The neoclassical cardinal utility analysis of Chapter 5 says that A is preferred to B because A has a larger quantity of utility.[1]

INDIFFERENCE SCHEDULES

The ordinal utility theory of behavior is usually called the *indifference curve analysis* because indifference curves are its main analytical tool. To understand indifference curves, it is best to begin with *indifference schedules*.

An indifference schedule is a list of combinations of two commodities, the list being so arranged that a consumer is indifferent to the combinations, preferring none of them to any of the others. Table 6-1 contains two indifference schedules. Consider schedule A. There are two commodities, which are X and Y. The reason for having two commodities is that the analysis is two-variable and, hence, can be put on a two-dimensional diagram; the analysis of more than two commodities requires advanced mathematics. The consumer is imagined as contemplating various combinations of units of X and of Y. In schedule A, these combinations are 10 units of X and 0 units of Y, 7 of X and 1 of Y, and so on. The consumer desires both commodities, but the question here is the relation between the consumer's desires and the *quantities* of the commodities. In schedule A, the quantities of X and Y are so arranged

TABLE 6-1

TWO INDIFFERENCE SCHEDULES

Schedule A		Schedule B	
X	Y	X	Y
10 units	0 units	12 units	0 units
7	1	10	1
5	2	8	2
4	4	6	4

[1] In the 1930s, Hicks and others made much of the difference between ordinal and cardinal utility. Later thinking narrows the gap. For example, consumers often experience difficulty in making choices. Suppose that the consumer prefers A to B and B to C, but that it is harder to make the choice of A over B than of B over C. It then can be hypothesized that the difference of (cardinal) utility between A and B is less than between B and C. Consumers are also sometimes inconsistent. Suppose a consumer chooses A over B 70 per cent of the time, and B over C 90 per cent of the time. Here again it can be argued that the difference of (cardinal) utility between A and B is less than between B and C.

that the consumer is indifferent among the combinations. Each one is equally desirable; the consumer feels equally well off in having any one of the combinations as in having any other.

Similarly, each one of the combinations in schedule B is as desirable as any of the others in the same schedule. But schedule B begins with 12 of X and none of Y. On the assumption that more of a commodity is preferable to less, *any* combination in B is preferred to *any* combination in A.

To extend all this: Imagine a consumer who likes two commodities. Take at random a combination of so many units of the one commodity and so many units of the other. Given this combination, there must be others to which the consumer is indifferent. Given the combination, there are others less and others more desirable. Look again at Table 6-1. The table has only two indifference schedules. Imagine it as having many more, stretching far to the right— schedules C, D, E, F, etc. Moreover, the schedules in the table show only four combinations of X and Y. Imagine them stretching farther down until the X columns show the number zero.

INDIFFERENCE CURVES

The next step is to go from indifference schedules to indifference curves. Here too is another move from arithmetic to geometry, a move that achieves the convenience of smooth curves and leaves behind the awkwardness of jumping from one number to another. Here too the smooth curve means that the commodities in question are assumed to be divisible into very small units.

Figure 6-1 is an indifference diagram; on it is an indifference curve. The diagram itself is unlike those appearing in earlier chapters; those diagrams have quantity on the horizontal axis and either price or utility on the vertical axis. But the indifference diagram has quantity on *both* axes. The horizontal axis measures physical units of a commodity X, and the vertical axis measures physical units of a commodity Y. Any point in the field, therefore, represents one combination of quantities of X and of Y. Take any point such as A in

FIGURE 6-1   **AN INDIFFERENCE CURVE**

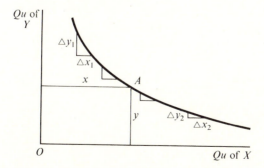

Figure 6-1. At the point A, the number of units of X and of Y is shown by the lengths of the lines x and y. Through point A an indifference curve is drawn and drawn in such a way that any other point on the curve shows quantities of X and of Y that are equally desirable to the consumer. If the consumer could choose among all the combinations of X and Y on the curve, the consumer would be indifferent because, to repeat, all of the combinations provide the same level of satisfaction. Think of the consumer as sliding up and down the indifference curve; there being no law of gravity here, the consumer can slide up as easily as down. No matter where the person is, he or she is equally well off—as an actual or potential consumer of X and Y.

Why is the indifference curve shaped the way it is in Figure 6-1? The curve bends so that it is relatively steep at the top and relatively flat at the boom; the curve is *convex* to the origin. The explanation is this: Imagine the consumer sliding down the curve in Figure 6-1. In doing so, the consumer is giving up—only in his or her mind, of course—Y for X. Moving down the curve, the consumer is trading off units of Y for units of X, subject always to the condition that each new combination is subjectively no better and no worse.

At the top of the curve, the consumer gives up Δy_1 of Y for Δx_1 of X as he or she slides down the curve. Here the consumer has lots of Y and not much of X, and hence, is willing to trade Δy_1 units of Y to get Δx_1 of X. Thus the length Δy_1 is greater than the length Δx_1—at the top of the curve. But as the consumer slides down the curve, the relative quantities of X and Y change. In Figure 6-1, the length Δx is uniform. That is, the increments of X are equal. The lengths of the lines Δy become shorter and shorter as the consumer slides down the curve. This signifies that when the consumer has lots of X and not much Y, the consumer will trade off just a little of Y to get the same number of units of X. Notice how short the length of Δy_2 is at the bottom of the curve.

The rate at which the consumer trades off Y for X is called the *marginal rate of substitution*. Sliding down the curve, the consumer is willing to give up less and less Y for a given gain in X, and therefore the marginal rate of substitution diminishes. It diminishes in the other direction too, because if the consumer slides *up* the curve, he or she is willing to trade diminishing amounts of X for equal increments of Y. You can see this by drawing an indifference curve like that in Figure 6-1 and by making the Δy's equal in length. The Δx's become shorter as you go up the curve from right to left.

So far, only one indifference curve has been described. A complete description of a consumer's tastes for two commodities appears in the *indifference map* which corresponds to an entire system of indifference curves. Since the field in the diagram contains an

FIGURE 6-2

AN INDIFFERENCE MAP

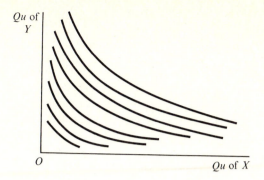

Qu of Y

O

Qu of X

infinite number of points and since an indifference curve passes through every point, it follows that the number of indifference curves is infinite. Figure 6-2 shows several indifference curves. Taken together, they comprise the indifference map of the consumer. Each curve shows X and Y combinations that are equally good to the consumer—they yield the same utility. Any curve that lies to the right of another is said to be higher—it yields more utility. Any of the combinations on a higher indifference curve is preferable to any of those on a lower curve. Indifference, therefore, means sliding back and forth on any one curve, and preference means moving northeast to higher levels of utility.

Indifference curves do not intersect or touch one another. If they did, a consumer's preferences would not be consistent, or to use the proper technical term, *transitive*. Transitivity means that if the consumer prefers A to B and B to C, he or she also prefers A to C. Or, if the consumer is indifferent between A and B, and between B and C, the consumer must also be indifferent between A and C. Figure 6-3 has two intersecting indifference curves. They cross at

FIGURE 6-3

INTERSECTING INDIFFERENCE CURVES

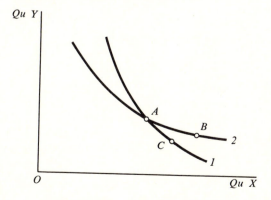

Qu Y

A

B

C

2

1

O

Qu X

91   *Ordinal Utility and Indifference Curves*

point A, which is a bundle of X and Y. On curve *1*, A and C yield the same utility. On curve *2*, A and B do. But bundle B is clearly preferable to C, because B contains more units of both X and Y. Bundle B cannot simultaneously have more utility than C and the same utility as C.

Resembling a snapshot, a consumer's indifference curves exist at a point of time. Therefore, Figure 6–3 could represent rational choices if the two curves are imagined as existing at two points of time, between which the consumer's pattern of preferences undergoes a shift. The change from curve *1* to curve *2* means that the desire for Y has become stronger. The slope of curve *2* is less. The consumer is willing, at the second point of time, to trade off less Y than before, to acquire more units of X.

Although consumers' tastes do of course change, they are not always in perpetual motion. Fads for this and that come and go, but broad patterns of consumption are fairly stable. When a consumer's tastes remain constant for a period of time, the indifference map for any two of the commodities the consumer likes also holds steady for the same period of time.

The Shapes of Indifference Curves

If nothing more is said about it, the only requirement for the shape of a demand curve is that it slope downward to the right. Similarly, the only requirement for an indifference curve is that it be convex to the origin. The diminishing marginal rate of substitution of Y for X and of X for Y makes the curve convex. Within this limitation, however, many variations of shapes are possible. The variations reflect differences in taste. The tastes of any one consumer for pairs of different commodities vary from one pair to another; for the same two commodities, each consumer has different tastes.

Take two commodities that are very close substitutes. An example is nickels and dimes. For many purposes, they are perfect substitutes at the constant ratio of two to one. But consider a person who frequently uses parking meters that take dimes and who, therefore, wants to be sure to have a dime or two in small change. For such a person, nickels and dimes are not perfect substitutes. This person's indifference curves for nickels and dimes would have a slope of roughly two to one, and would be bent just slightly.

If two commodities have a rigid one-to-one complementary relation in the mind of the consumer, the indifference curves are right angles. An example is right shoes and left shoes; the consumer is no better off in having two or more right shoes if he or she has only one left shoe; and vice versa. But the consumer is better off if he or she has more pairs of shoes; that is, the consumer moves due northeast on the indifference map.

Provided that they are convex to the origin, indifference curves can take any shape between the extremes of the straight line and the right angle. Indifference maps are often drawn so that the curves appear to be parallel to one another. Parallelism, however, is almost devoid of economic significance.[2] An indifference curve can change its general shape in different regions of the field. A move to the northeast is a move to combinations successively preferred. It is also a move to larger quantities of both commodities. Larger quantities of anything are put to more and more uses. If X and Y are, say, apples and pears, larger quantities of both mean that the extra apples are turned into applesauce and the extra pears into gifts. Hence, the apple-pear relation can be different for large quantities than for small.

UTILITY AND DISUTILITY

For most purposes the theory of consumer behavior operates with indifference curves shaped like those in Figures 6-2 and 6-3. The usual diagram for the family of convex indifference curves does not show maximum utility. It implies only that more of X and of Y results in more utility. Nor does the diagram show *disutility*, i.e., negative marginal utility, which means that more of something brings *less* total utility.

It will be well to make a short excursion into the domain of disutility. For convenience and brevity of language, let a commodity with positive marginal utility be called "a utility," and a commodity with negative marginal utility "a disutility." A consumer, of course, wants to have more of a utility and less of a disutility.

Figure 6-4 displays utilities and disutilities. Imagine a cone projecting perpendicularly from the page of this book. The center of the circles is the apex of the cone, which, for the sake of simplicity, is a right circular cone, a solid generated by the rotation of the right triangle about one of its legs as axis. Hence the circles in Figure 6-4. (If the cone were irregularly shaped, the circles would be replaced by irregular curves.) The altitude of the cone—the third dimension provided by the reader's imagination—is utility. The apex of the cone is maximum utility. The circles are levels of utility, the outer circles showing lower levels.

Figure 6-4 is divided by the dashed lines into four segments. In the SW segment there are "small" (as we can call them) quantities of both X and Y. In the NW segment, the quantities of X are "small," but the quantities of Y are "large." The opposite holds in the SE segment. And in the NE segment, both X and Y exist in "large" quantities.

Consider now the SW segment of the diagram. The parts of the

---

[2] Except that, if indifference curves are parallel in a due north-south direction, the income effect is exactly zero. See below.

FIGURE 6-4   UTILITY AND DISUTILITY

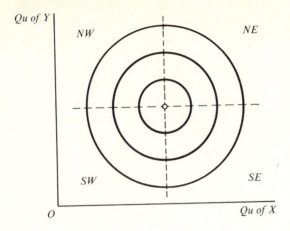

circles within this segment are indifference curves for X and Y, both of them being utilities for the quantities shown. Here the indifference curves have negative slopes and are convex. Any movement horizontally (more X), or vertically (more Y), or up and to the right (more of both X and Y) is a movement to an inner circle, and thus to a higher level of utility.

Next, take the NW segment. The parts of the circles here are still indifference curves, but they have positive slopes. The quantities of Y are "large." In fact, there's "too much" Y, so that less of it means more utility. Thus in the NW segment, Y is a disutility, though X is a utility.

Similarly, in the SE segment there is "too much" of X. Hence X is a disutility and Y is a utility.

In the NE segment, both X and Y are disutilities. Less of both of them results in higher levels of utility. Notice that although the NE indifference curves have negative slopes, they are concave, not convex.

Examples and applications of these concepts will come later. Chapter 7 will present indifference curve analyses dealing with choices between two disutilities and between a utility and a disutility. In the meantime, the theory to follow will be confined to indifference curves like those in the SW segment of Figure 6-4. This means simply that more of both goods is preferable to less.

PRICES AND BUDGETS

The next step is to introduce the prices of commodities and the consumer's budget. A consumer's purchases can be determined once prices and the consumer's budget and tastes are known. An

FIGURE 6-5

PRICES AND THE BUDGET

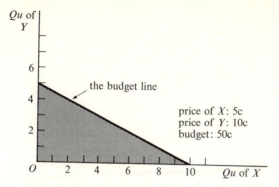

advantage of the indifference curve diagram is that all three variables can be represented at once.

Figure 6-5 shows how prices and the consumer's budget are put on the diagram. Let the price of X be 5¢ a unit and the price of Y 10¢. Let the consumer's budget be 50¢ a time period. Then 10 units of X could be bought if the consumer spent the whole budget on X, and 5 units of Y could be bought if the consumer spent the 50¢ on it. A straight line between $10X$ and $5Y$ shows every possibility of spending the budget on the two commodities at their given prices. The straight line is the *budget line*.[3] A glance at Figure 6-5 shows this: The consumer can buy $10X$ and $0Y$, or $8X$ and $1Y$, or $4X$ and $3Y$, etc. And for that matter, the consumer can also buy any quantity *inside* the shaded area; but if the consumer does this, he or she is not spending all of the 50¢. Remember that the diagram shows only physical quantities of X and Y. Prices and the budget are represented indirectly by the physical quantities. The budget line can be thought of as the boundary to the consumer's opportunities for acquiring X and Y.

The *slope* of the budget line is the ratio of the prices of the two commodities. The ratio is $\dfrac{P_X}{P_Y}$, the price of X divided by the price of Y. At first sight the ratio might seem puzzling, because slope is vertical divided by horizontal. But remember, X and Y are physical quantities. Thus for any budget line,

$$\text{slope} = \frac{\text{quantity of } Y}{\text{quantity of } X} = \frac{\text{budget}}{P_Y} \Big/ \frac{\text{budget}}{P_X} = \frac{P_X}{P_Y}.$$

[3] Terminology for this line is not standardized. Other names in the literature for the budget line are: *budget restraint, consumption possibility line, expenditure line, outlay line, price line,* and *price-income line.*

To use the numbers from the simple example above,

$$\text{slope} = \frac{5}{10} = \frac{50}{10} \bigg/ \frac{50}{5} = \frac{5}{10}.$$

If both prices were equal, a budget would buy equal quantities of the two commodities; the slope of the budget line would be unity. If the slope is less than unity, X has the lower price; if it is more, Y has the lower price.

The *position* of the budget line depends on the size of the budget. If the budget increases, the line would be farther to the right. Changes in prices and the size of the budget are shown by changing the slope and the position of the budget line.

For many purposes, it is convenient to let the horizontal axis represent amounts of a commodity and the vertical axis an amount of money income per time period. Then X is a commodity, and Y is money income. To do this is really to say that Y stands for other commodities. One commodity, X, is then compared with all other commodities which are represented by money income.

EQUILIBRIUM OF THE CONSUMER

How much of X and of Y does the consumer buy? The consumer buys those amounts of the two commodities that make him or her most satisfied according to his or her own notions of being well off. The consumer has no reason to change the purchases, and is, therefore, in equilibrium.

In Figure 6–6, the straight line is the budget line, its slope showing the ratio of the prices, and its position the size of the consumer's budget. The three curves are three of the indifference curves selected from those comprising the consumer's indifference map. The consumer is in equilibrium at point A, which is on the budget line, and also on indifference curve 1, which just touches—is tangent to—the budget line. The opportunities open to the consumer are those anywhere on the budget line or, for that matter, anywhere

FIGURE 6–6   **EQUILIBRIUM OF THE CONSUMER**

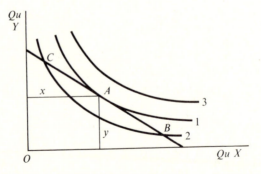

below it. The consumer wants to be on the highest attainable indifference curve. This is curve *1*, tangent to the budget line. The combination of *x* and *y* at *A* is thus preferred to all others attainable. If the consumer were to buy less *X* and more *Y*, moving up to *C*, the consumer would be on a lower indifference curve, curve *2*. If the consumer did the opposite and moved down to *B*, he or she would also be on the lower curve *2*. The consumer of course would like to be on a still higher indifference curve such as *3*. But that cannot be done because the consumer's budget is too low, or the prices are too high, or because of some combination of these.

At point *A* in Figure 6-6, the consumer achieves a maximum of utility. This, however, is a *constrained maximum*, constrained by the consumer's limited budget and by the prices that have to be paid.

When the consumer is in equilibrium, the highest attainable indifference curve is tangent to the budget line. The slopes of the curve and of the line are therefore equal. Has this equality of slopes any economic meaning?

Yes it has. The slope[4] of the indifference curve is $\frac{\Delta Y}{\Delta X}$, which means a change in *Y* divided by a change in *X*. This is the *marginal rate of substitution—MRS*. Suppose the change is a small movement *down* the indifference curve. Then $\frac{\Delta Y}{\Delta X}$, or *MRS*, means a small loss of *Y* divided by a small gain in *X*. But the *utility* of the loss is equal to that of the gain by definition of the indifference curve. Therefore

$$\Delta Y \times MU_Y = \Delta X \times MU_X.$$

That is, the loss of *Y* times the marginal utility of *Y* is equal to the gain of *X* times the marginal utility of *X*. By transposing,

$$\frac{\Delta Y}{\Delta X} = \frac{MU_X}{MU_Y}.$$

That is, the slope of the curve is equal to the ratio of the marginal utilities.[5]

To see just why $MRS = \frac{\Delta Y}{\Delta X} = \frac{MU_X}{MU_Y}$, look at Figure 6-7. At point *A*, the slope of indifference curve *1* is (approximately) $\frac{\Delta Y}{\Delta X} = \frac{1Y}{2X}$.

If the consumer is at point *A* and gives up 1 unit of *Y* he then moves down to point *B* on indifference curve *2*. But curve *2* is lower, and the move from *A* to *B* would be a loss of utility. The loss is offset

[4] The absolute value of the slope is taken here. That is, the minus sign for the slope of the indifference curve is ignored. To do so is usual.
[5] It would be more precise to say that the slope is equal to the reciprocal of the ratio of the respective marginal utilities.

FIGURE 6–7   **SLOPE OF AN INDIFFERENCE CURVE**

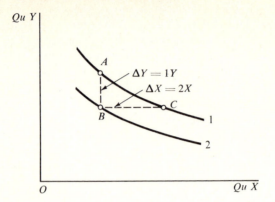

when the consumer gains 2 units of X in moving to point C on curve 1. That is to say, the utility lost by giving up 1 unit of Y is restored with the acquisition of 2 units of X. Therefore,

$$MU \text{ of } 2X = MU \text{ of } 1Y, \text{ or,}$$
$$MU \text{ of } 1X = \tfrac{1}{2}MU \text{ of } 1Y, \text{ or,}$$
$$\frac{MU_X}{MU_Y} = \frac{1}{2}.$$

If, then, the consumer needs 2 units of X to compensate for 1 unit of Y, the marginal utility of a unit of X must be half the marginal utility of a unit of Y.

The slope of the budget line is $\dfrac{P_X}{P_Y}$. At the point of equilibrium, accordingly,

$$MRS = \frac{\Delta Y}{\Delta X} = \frac{MU_X}{MU_Y} = \frac{P_X}{P_Y}.$$

It therefore follows that

$$\frac{MU_X}{P_X} = \frac{MU_Y}{P_Y}.$$

All of which means that when the consumer is in equilibrium, the marginal rate of substitution is equal to the ratio of the prices of the two commodities. Equivalently, the last equation says that the marginal utilities derived from the last dollar spent on each good are equal. (See Note 8 in the Appendix to Part 1.) This last statement is of course identical with one of the propositions, or theorems, of neoclassical cardinal analysis (see pages 75 and 76).

Consider next what happens with a change in the income of the consumer, with prices and the consumer's tastes remaining constant.

From now on attention will center on the consumer's purchase of just one good, the commodity X. Up to now the consumer was considering the utilities of both X and Y, dividing his or her budget between the two goods. Henceforth, the vertical axis will measure money income during a period of time; the horizontal axis will continue to measure quantities of the commodity X during the same period of time. The indifference curves will show the trade-offs between various quantities of X and amounts of money. Because money can be exchanged for other goods, the indifference curves, accordingly, show preference and indifference for various combinations of X and other goods. The budget line is constructed by taking a point on the vertical axis that measures the dollar amount of income, because budget and income are assumed to be identical; on the horizontal axis the point is obtained by dividing income by the price of X; and a line joining the two points gives us the budget line.

In general, the higher a consumer's income the more of a commodity the person will buy. Commodities bought in larger quantities when income rises are sometimes called *normal goods*. This is shown in Figure 6–8. Here are three budget lines. They are parallel, which signifies that the price of X is held constant; the "price" of money income, which is unity, is of course also constant. The lowest budget line, line *1*, shows the lowest income. Shifts of the budget line up and to the right signify higher incomes. In Figure 6–8

FIGURE 6–8　　　**EFFECTS OF CHANGES IN INCOME**

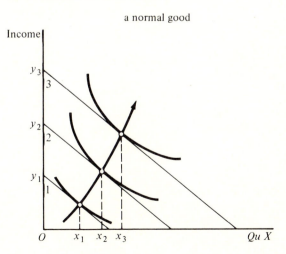

a normal good

there is one set of indifference curves. They remain constant because preferences are assumed to be unchanged. The figure shows only those indifference curves that are tangent to the budget lines.

At higher incomes, higher indifference curves become tangent to the budget lines. Through the successive points of tangency a line is drawn. This line is the *income-consumption curve*; the heavy line with the arrow head traces out the path of the changes in the consumption of the commodity X as income varies. With budget line *1*, the consumer buys Ox_1 units of X. With budget line *2*, the consumer buys Ox_2 units, and so on.

In Figure 6–9, the income-consumption curve first moves northeast, then curls around and moves northwest, signifying that after the consumer's income reaches a certain level, *less* of X is consumed. Commodities of which this is true are called *inferior goods*. Potatoes are a standard example. Another, at least for many consumers, is hamburger meat. A generation or two ago, margarine was the commonly cited example of an inferior good.

An inferior good is one that consumers buy less of when their incomes go up and more of when their incomes go down.

Though this technical definition of *inferior good* is well established in economic literature, some of the connotations of the expression might be misleading. One connotation is that in the long list of the commodities produced in a modern society, a few can be found that are inferior, that is, deficient in some respect. Another connotation seems to be that inferior goods are poor people's goods. When income rises and poverty is left behind, consumption of the inferior goods declines. Actually, however, to consume less of a commodity at higher incomes is a form of behavior much more common than might at first be supposed. If their social environment causes movie actors to buy Cadillacs when their incomes are high and to buy Rolls Royces when their incomes are still higher then, for these people, Cadillacs are an inferior good. They are not inferior automobiles, let it be noted, but are an inferior good to *some* buyers.

FIGURE 6–9   **EFFECTS OF CHANGES IN INCOME AN INFERIOR GOOD**

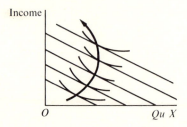

To generalize: When commodities are defined as specific grades or qualities of goods and services, and if there are several grades or qualities, then almost any commodity so defined can be an inferior good for somebody or some class of persons.

Income Elasticity

Income elasticity is discussed in Chapter 4, along with the other elasticity concepts. The earlier discussion of income elasticity has to do with the behavior of many buyers. Here we can turn our attention to the income elasticity of a commodity to the individual consumer. The definition is the same, namely,

$$E_y = \frac{\Delta Q}{Q} \bigg/ \frac{\Delta Y}{Y} = \frac{Y}{Q} \frac{\Delta Q}{\Delta Y},$$

with E_y the coefficient, Q the quantity purchased by the consumer, and Y the consumer's income.

In Figure 6–8, the consumer's income elasticity for the commodity is low, the coefficient being less than 1. Another look at Figure 6–8 will show that the *relative* increase in quantity is less than the *relative* increase in income. The income-consumption curve rises steeply upward. For a high income elasticity, with E_y greater than 1, the curve would rise gently to the right, the relative increases in quantity being greater than those of income.[6]

The income-consumption curve in Figure 6–9 has both positive and negative income elasticities. At the lower left of the curve E_y is positive, but where the curve goes northwest, E_y is negative. Inferior goods, then, have negative income elasticities.

Engel Curves

Income-consumption curves for groups of consumers are called *Engel curves*. The name comes from the German statistician Ernst Engel, who in the nineteenth century was a pioneer in the study of family budgets. Engel curves show the relations between consumer incomes and purchases of commodities or services. Usually, these curves relate incomes and dollar expenditures. When they do this, Engel curves are not exactly identical with income-consumption curves, which relate incomes and physical units purchased. In practice, too, economists who construct Engel curves have to swallow hard as they make the assumption that prices and consumers' tastes remain constant.

Figure 6–10 displays two Engel curves, one for food and one for housing. The vertical axis, income, signifies average family income for a year. The horizontal axis, expenditure, measures dollar expenditures per year. The figure shows that families with low incomes spend more on food than on housing and that the opposite holds for

---

[6]Remember that slope alone does not measure elasticity. E_y is not $\frac{\Delta Y}{\Delta Q}$, but $\frac{Y}{Q} \frac{\Delta Q}{\Delta Y}$.

FIGURE 6-10

ENGEL CURVES

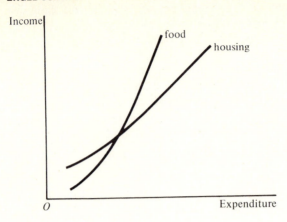

families with higher incomes. Figure 6–10 also shows that although both are larger for higher incomes, food expenditures increase less than proportionately, whereas housing expenditures increase more than proportionately. In other words, the income elasticity of food is less than unity and housing's is greater than unity.

EFFECTS OF CHANGES IN PRICES

The indifference curve analysis has, to repeat, three explicit variables. Two can be held constant while the third is made to change. When the price of a commodity changes, the consumer alters purchases, provided of course that the consumer's tastes and income remain constant.

The effects of changes in price are shown in the upper part of Figure 6–11. In this figure, X is a commodity and Y is money income. First of all, let the consumer be in equilibrium at A. The budget line is Y_1X_1, which is touched at A by the indifference curve shown in the diagram. Suppose the price of X falls. To represent this, the foot of the budget line is moved to the *right* by a distance proportionate to the fall in price. The amount OX_1 is the quantity of X that *could* be bought at the initial price if the *entire* budget were spent on X. With a fall in price, the consumer could buy more with the entire budget, namely, the amount OX_2. With another reduction in price, the consumer *could* buy still more, say, OX_3. Each fall in price establishes a new budget line—Y_1X_2, Y_1X_3, etc. To each, an indifference curve is tangent—at point B, point C, etc. The line drawn through the points of tangency is the *price-consumption curve*. The line shows how the consumption, or purchase, of X varies as its price varies.

FIGURE 6-11

EFFECTS OF CHANGES IN PRICES

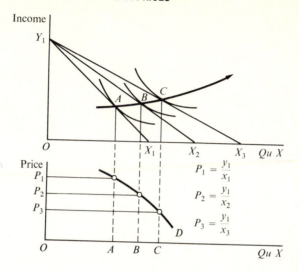

The price-consumption curve shows the quantities of X the consumer buys at each price. The curve, therefore, contains the information from which the consumer's demand curve can be constructed. The lower part of Figure 6–11 shows how this can be done. In the lower diagram, the horizontal axis is quantity. The quantities A, B, and C are marked off. The vertical axis is price. The prices are found from the upper part by dividing money income by the maximum quantity of X that can be bought. This gives the three prices P_1, P_2, and P_3 in the lower diagram. The three prices and the three quantities A, B, and C give three points on demand curve D.

Price
Elasticity

In Figure 6–11, the price-consumption curve slopes gently upward toward the right. This means that the consumer's demand for X is slightly inelastic. If the curve were horizontal—the consumer's tastes could be such as to cause the indifference curves to be tangent along a horizontal line—demand would have unit elasticity. And if the curve were to slope down toward the right, the consumer's demand for X would be elastic. This is the proof: If he or she is at Y_1, the consumer is buying no X and is keeping his or her money for other things. To buy some X, the consumer must go down a budget line which means trading Y for X. But Y stands for money, and to trade money for units of a commodity is, in plain English, to spend money on it. Therefore, the vertical distance from a line horizontal to Y_1 shows the amount of money spent for any given quantity of X. Finally, to point to the amounts of money spent on a commodity when its price changes is the simplest way of defining price elasticity. This is covered on pages 36 and 37.

when its price changes is the simplest way of defining price elasticity. This is covered on pages 36 and 37.

THE INCOME EFFECT AND THE SUBSTITUTION EFFECT

Suppose that your budget for the school year includes a plan to make 7 airline trips home. The decision is based on the amount of money in your budget, on the satisfactions from the trips home, and on the fare you have to pay for each trip. Imagine now that the air fare is reduced substantially, with the result that you revise your budget. The new plan is to make 10 trips instead of 7. This is hardly surprising, because all that happens is that you will buy more plane tickets at the lower price.

But the effect of the lower price can be divided into two parts. One is called *the income effect*, and the other is called *the substitution effect*. The reduction in the air fare, with no increases in the prices of other goods and services, does make your budget go farther and therefore puts you on a higher level of utility. Then, too, the cut in the fare makes the airline trips cheaper relative to the other goods and services you buy. This by itself causes you to substitute airline trips for other things.

With your new plan calling for 10 trips instead of 7, how much of the increase of 3 trips is due to the income effect and how much to the substitution effect? Take the substitution effect first. Remember that the lower price puts you on a higher level of utility. How much income could be taken from you to put you back on the same level of utility you were on when you made your plans at the old and higher price? Suppose the imagined reduction in income is $100. Now, if you had $100 less in your budget but could buy at the lower price, how many airline trips would you plan to make? Suppose your answer is 8 trips. The one extra trip at the lower price and with the imagined loss of $100 is the substitution effect.

But, in fact, you don't lose $100 and you are indeed better off, enjoying a gain of utility. This gain of utility, or of *real income*, as it is usually called in this context, is responsible for the other 2 of the 3 extra trips. The 2 extra trips attributable alone to the gain of utility are the income effect.

To recapitulate and to generalize (because prices can go up as well as down): The total effect of a change in price consists of the income effect and the substitution effect. The income effect is that part of the change in the quantity purchased attributable solely to the gain or loss of utility. The substitution effect is the other part of the change in quantity purchased attributable to the change in price, independently of the gain or loss of utility.

Figure 6–12 illustrates the substitution effect and the income effect of a decline in price. Let the consumer first be in equilibrium at point *A*, where indifference curve *I* is tangent to the budget line

FIGURE 6–12   **THE INCOME EFFECT AND THE SUBSTITUTION EFFECT**

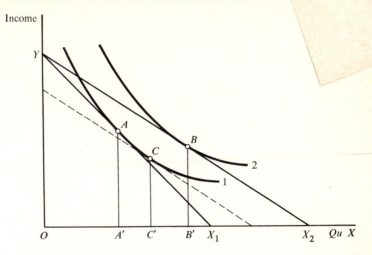

YX_1. At point A on indifference curve 1, the consumer is on some level of well-being or utility; in this context the expression *real income* has the same meaning. Now let the price of X fall, the new budget line being YX_2. The consumer then moves to a new equilibrium at point B on indifference curve 2.

The fall in price causes the consumer to buy more of the commodity X. The additional amount on the horizontal axis is $A'B'$, which is identical with the horizontal distance between points A and B. The amount $A'B'$ is *the total effect* of the change in price. The substitution effect is $A'C'$, and the income effect is $C'B'$.

The substitution effect is found from the dashed line, which is parallel to the budget line YX_2. Reflecting the new and lower price of X, the dashed line represents an imaginary movement of the budget line YX_2, down and to the left. Thus the dashed line stands for an imaginary reduction in income, a reduction of such size as to nullify the gain in real income that comes with the fall in price. The dashed line is tangent at point C to indifference curve 1. Accordingly, point C on the dashed line shows how much more X the consumer would buy, independently of the gain in his real income.

The income effect is, then, the other part of the total effect. Imagine that the dashed line moves to the right, becoming identical with the new budget line YX_2. The vertical distance between the dashed line and the new budget line is a measure of the gain in real income. By itself, it causes the increased purchase of $C'B'$ of the commodity.

The substitution effect is said to be negative, because a decrease in price always accompanies an increase in quantity, and vice versa.

That is, either the change in price or the change in quantity has a minus sign; thus the ratio, $\dfrac{\Delta Q}{\Delta P}$, always has a minus sign. The income effect is normally positive, the gain in real income causing the purchase of a larger quantity. Still another look at Figure 6–12 will show that the position of point B depends on the shape of indifference curve 2. With a little imagination the reader can see that other shapes of indifference curve 2 could establish point B at other positions.

Four combinations of substitution and income effects can be distinguished:

1. The normal effects are those already mentioned: Point B lies to the right of point C. The negative substitution effect and the positive income effect work in the same direction to increase the purchase of X with a fall in its price.

2. The income effect can be zero. If it is, point B lies vertically above point C. The two indifference curves would be parallel and have the same slopes at the two points. Only the substitution effect causes the change in the purchase of X.

3. The income effect can be negative but have a smaller force than that of the substitution effect. Indifference curve 2 would be shaped so as to put point B between A and C. The total effect is still an increase in the purchase of X with a fall in its price. Commodities with negative income effects are the inferior goods described earlier.

4. The income effect can be negative and large enough to over-power the substitution effect. Point B then lies to the left of point A. This result is known as the *Giffen effect*, which is also mentioned in Chapter 2 (page 21). The Giffen effect, also sometimes called the *Giffen paradox*, means that a lower price of a commodity results in *less* being bought, not more. Such a commodity is a *Giffen good*.

Could there ever be such a thing as a Giffen good? There could, perhaps, in circumstances where consumers are so poor that they live mainly on bread. A large fall in the price of bread frees income to buy other foods such as meat, thus causing the consumer to buy less bread.

All Giffen goods are inferior goods, but not all inferior goods are Giffen goods. The demand curve for a Giffen good has a positive slope—less is bought at a lower price and more at a higher price. The key to the concept of the Giffen good is this paradoxical effect of a change in *price*. In contrast, the inferior good that is not a Giffen good—item 3 above—has a demand curve with a negative slope. The key to the concept of the inferior good that is not a Giffen good is the effect of a change in *income*. An increase in income shifts the demand curve to the left, with the result that less is bought at an unchanged price. But when there is only a fall in price, more is

TABLE 6–2

POSSIBLE COMBINATIONS OF INCOME AND SUBSTITUTION EFFECTS OF A FALL IN PRICE

	1	2	3	4
Substitution Effect	negative	negative	negative	negative
Income Effect	positive	zero	negative, but *smaller* than substitution effect	negative, but *larger* than substitution effect
Total Effect	increase	increase	increase	*decrease*
Kind of Commodity	normal	normal	inferior	Giffen

bought, the substitution effect overpowering the negative income effect.

The possible combinations of income and substitution effects are summarized in Table 6–2.

Importance of the Income Effect

The income effects of changes in the prices paid by consumers are normally so small that for most purposes they can be disregarded. If the price of a bottle of pop goes up by five cents, you are not going to jump up and down in rage and revise your entire budget. This is the same thing as saying that price changes have only a negligible effect on the marginal utility of income for the consumer. The usual indifference curve diagrams, those in this chapter being no exception, contain a gross exaggeration. They show, as J. R. Hicks himself says,[7] the consumer spending a preposterously large part of income on the one commodity X. It was explained earlier that the amount spent is the distance down from the left end of the budget line. This amount is made large in the diagrams for no other reason than to make them clear. The same reason also calls for large changes in price in the diagrams. The two exaggerations in the diagrams make the income effect look more important than it is.

With the exception of housing, the commodities bought by consumers in the United States account each for a tiny fraction of income. However, if the prices of most kinds of food were to go up while the prices of other goods and services stayed the same, or nearly so, the income effect of the higher food prices could be large.

APPLICATIONS

The indifference curves of consumers have not yet been measured and portrayed in actual numbers. Attempts to derive numbers from experiments have so far been nearly fruitless. Nevertheless, the

[7] *A Revision of Demand Theory*, Oxford, London, 1956, p. 60n.

indifference curve technique of analysis is a means of clear thinking on problems with important practical aspects.

Subsidies to Consumers

One application of the indifference curve analysis is to the effects of subsidies to persons with low incomes. Suppose that the government makes certain commodities available at lower prices to certain low-income groups. To do this is a normal activity of the modern social service state. As an illustration, take public housing. Assume that the tenants in public housing projects pay about half the rent that would normally be charged for similar accommodations and that the other half of the rent is a subsidy. (This assumption, by the way, is quite realistic.) Is the benefit to the tenants as great as the cost of the subsidy?

Figure 6–13 furnishes the answer to this question. In the figure, the position of one family is portrayed. Income is on the vertical axis and housing—measured in square feet of floor space—is on the horizontal. Let the family's income be OY. If it rented unsubsidized housing and spent all of its income on it, the family could rent OH_1 square feet. Hence YH_1 is the budget line without subsidy. The subsidy is given by reducing rents one-half. So the budget line with subsidy is YH_2; this is the same as a reduction in price by one-half, i.e., OH_2 is twice OH_1. The family is in equilibrium when it rents OA square feet of housing. The family is at point J on the indifference curve, which is tangent to the budget line with subsidy, i.e., the line YH_2. The indifference curve reflects the higher level of utility that the housing subsidy lifts the family to.

Now the next step. The amount of the subsidy is BC dollars. This is explained as follows: In equilibrium, the family spends YB on housing. Without subsidy and renting the same amount, it would have to spend YC. Hence the cost to the government of the subsidy is BC, the vertical distance between the two budget lines. But to the

FIGURE 6–13   SUBSIDIES TO CONSUMERS

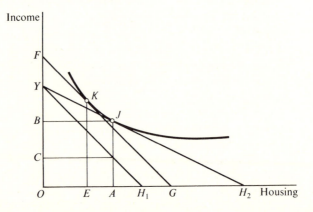

family, the subsidy is not cash but more housing. What is the money equivalent to the subsidy to the family? That is, how much money will make the family as well off—lift it to the same indifference curve—as the housing subsidy does? In Figure 6-13, it is *FY* dollars. The budget line without subsidy is moved to the right just far enough to become tangent to the indifference curve at point *K*. This is the line *FG*, whose meaning is the increase in *money* income that makes the family just as well off as the subsidy.

Clearly, *FY* is less than *BC*. In fact it will always be, whatever the subsidy and whatever the preferences of consumers, so long as only the indifference curves remain convex and smooth. Thus the cost of giving subsidies to consumers is always greater than the money equivalent of the subjective gain to the consumers. Here, of course, is a special case of the general principle that, if you brush aside etiquette and sentiment, you can make people happier if you give them cash instead of units of one commodity, even a commodity they want.

But the validity of the principle does not by itself condemn public housing programs. They must be judged by criteria going beyond the subjective benefits to the tenants. Another glance at Figure 6-13 shows that with the subsidy, the family chooses *OA* housing. But if it got the equivalent cash subsidy, the family would choose *OE* housing, which is less. Accordingly, the subsidy induces the family to rent more (square feet of) housing. This, too, is one of the goals of a public housing program.

A little more should be said on this last point. The theory of the consumer implicitly embodies the doctrine of consumer sovereignty, i.e., that each consumer is the best judge of his or her own interest, that the consumer alone is capable of maximizing his or her own utility, and that the maximization of subjective utility is the sole criterion of decision. Applications of the theory of the consumer often reach conclusions at odds with deliberate *social* judgments based on other criteria. Besides public housing, another similar example is the provision of meals, even breakfasts, to school children who live in neighborhoods with low incomes. If it is granted that something should be done for such children, who would stand up and argue that the children would be better off with cash instead? The criterion of consumer sovereignty is important, but modern governments apply other criteria in carrying out some social policies.

SUMMARY

The indifference curve analysis of consumer demand is based on the concept of *ordinal utility*. Having a choice between two combinations of goods, the consumer either prefers one combination or is indifferent. The *indifference curve* shows all combinations of two commodities that give the same satisfaction to a consumer. The indifference curve is convex; there is a *diminishing marginal rate of substitution* between the two commodities. A complete description of a consumer's tastes for two commodities is provided by the *indifference map*. The consumer's budget and the prices of the two commodities are represented by the *budget line*. The slope of the budget line is the ratio of the price of X to the price of Y. The position of the line reflects the size of the budget. The consumer is in *equilibrium* when buying the two commodities in the quantities defined by the tangency of an indifference curve to the budget line. In equilibrium, the ratio of the prices is equal to the marginal rate of substitution.

If income increases, the budget line moves to the right. The *income-consumption curve* goes through the points of tangency of indifference curves with parallel budget lines. If the income-consumption curve has a positive slope, the commodity is *normal*. But if the curve has a negative slope, the commodity is called an *inferior good*. When the Y-axis (vertical axis) measures money income and the X-axis (horizontal axis) physical quantities of a commodity, the slope of the income-consumption curve gives an indication of *income elasticity of demand*, which is the percentage change in quantity demanded divided by the percentage change in income.

If the price of commodity X changes, the budget line changes its slope. The *price-consumption curve* goes through the points of tangency of indifference curves with budget lines of different slopes. The *income effect* of a change in price is the change in quantity demanded attributable to the ensuing change in real income, whereas the *substitution effect* is the change in quantity demanded that is independent of the change in real income. Generally, the income and the substitution effects of a fall in price work together in leading to an increase in the quantity demanded. In the *Giffen effect*, however, the income effect is negative, and it is strong enough to offset the substitution effect. The income effect, however, is nearly always very small.

SELECTED REFERENCES

J. R. Hicks, *Value and Capital,* 2d ed. (Oxford, London, 1946). Also by Hicks, *A Revision of Demand Theory* (Oxford, London, 1956).

A good commentary on the cardinal-ordinal controversy is in D. H. (Sir Dennis) Robertson, *Utility and All That* (Macmillan, New York, 1952), chap. 1.

An attempt to give empirical content to indifference analysis:

John H. Kagel, Raymond C. Battalio, Howard Rachlin, Leonard Green, Robert L. Basmann, and W. R. Klemm, "Experimental Studies of Consumer Demand Behavior Using Laboratory Animals," *Economic Inquiry*, 13 (March 1975), 22–38.

Some good applications of indifference curve analysis are in George J. Stigler, *The Theory of Price*, 3d ed. (Macmillan, New York, 1966), chap. 4.

The housing application is adapted and modified from a food-stamp application in Tibor Scitovsky, *Welfare and Competition* (Irwin, Homewood, 1951), pp. 65–67.

EXERCISES AND PROBLEMS

1. Instead of a diminishing marginal rate of substitution, some economists write about an *increasing marginal rate of substitution*, even though they refer to convex indifference curves. Draw a diagram like Figure 6–1 on page 89 and change the increments of X and Y so as to get an increasing marginal rate of substitution.

2. Draw indifference curves to show commodity Y as a nuisance over some range of quantity. Do the same for X.

3. Draw a diagram with the consumer in equilibrium. Then change both income and P_X by moving and changing the slope of the budget line. Show the new equilibrium.

4. If the consumer's income doubles and if the prices of X and Y double, what does the consumer do?

5. Prove that if indifference curves were straight lines or were concave, the consumer would always buy just one of the commodities, not both. The result here is often called a *corner solution*, because the consumer maximizes utility by going to either the upper left or the lower right corner of the triangle formed by the axes and the budget line. What makes the consumer go to one corner rather than the other?

6. Draw a diagram that makes Y the inferior good. (Do not change the axes!)

7. Draw a price-consumption curve for three prices of Y, holding the price of X constant.

8. Draw a diagram showing the income and substitution effects of an *increase* in the price of X. Suppose the higher price of X results from a sales tax. For a 5 per cent sales tax, use a ruler to raise the price of X by 5 per cent. See if you can distinguish the income and substitution effects. Then try a 50 per cent sales tax.

9. Draw a diagram for the Giffen effect, where price rises.

10. Prove that a member of the armed forces would be better off receiving an income supplement equal in amount to what would be saved by buying things at lower prices at post exchange stores.

11. Use the income and substitution effects to explain the downward sloping demand curve.

12. Tariffs, like sales taxes, can change relative prices. Using a two-commodity model, one a domestic good and the other an imported good, show how a reduction in the size of a tariff encourages imports. What, if anything, happens to your analysis if you assume that the imported item is an inferior good?

13. Why *must* the marginal rate of substitution diminish if the consumer buys a unique and utility-maximizing combination of the two commodities?

14. What is the equilibrium position of a miser?

15. Show the new equilibrium of a consumer who will receive both an income supplement for rent and also a cash income supplement. Show the new equilibrium of the taxpayer who will finance the two subsidies.

7

CARDINAL UTILITY AND

Risk

The principal subject of this chapter is a theory of the utility of money to a person. Though it is a product of the postwar period, the theory is sometimes called Bernoullian utility theory, after Daniel Bernoulli, an eighteenth century Swiss mathematician. The modern theory establishes a method of measuring utility under certain conditions, shows the possibility of the *increasing* marginal utility of money, and creates a logical foundation for making certain kinds of rational decisions.

This chapter presents some of the applications of the utility concept in fields other than the theory of the household as a purchaser of consumer goods. Since the 1960s the utility concept has had ever wider application in the fields of decision making in business and government.

The neoclassical theory of utility reviewed in Chapter 5 stands firmly on the principle of diminishing marginal utility and on the rule that consumers maximize their total utilities. The neoclassical theory can also be called one of consumer behavior where all of the choices are made among *riskless* alternatives. Here stands the consumer in the supermarket: These and those goods are available; all have price tags; the consumer has such-and-such an income; and he or she has some given kind of tastes. The consumer faces no uncertainties about the availabilities of commodities and no uncertainties about their prices. Nor is the consumer uncertain about how much income there is to spend. Knowing these things exactly, the consumer of the neoclassical theory calmly makes choices, maximizing utility by equating the marginal utility of each commodity to the utility that is yielded by its price.

The marginal utility of money income also diminishes for the consumer of the neoclassical theory. For this reason, the rational consumer would never buy a lottery ticket or take part in any other kind of gambling, even fair gambling. Why not?

At one point in his career, Bernoulli became interested in a problem called the "St. Petersburg paradox." The problem is why people are unwilling to make bets at better than 50-50 odds when their mathematical expectations of winning money, in a particular kind of gamble, are greater the more money they bet. (See Note 6 in the Appendix to Part 1.) Bernoulli's solution to the paradox was to say in effect that the marginal utility of money diminishes as money income increases. If you have $1,000 and can make a fair bet, i.e., at even odds, of winning or losing $100 you will not do it if you make a rational decision. If you win, you will have $1,100 and the gain of utility from $100 added to $1,000. If you lose, you will have $900 and the loss of utility from $100 subtracted from $1,000. Diminishing marginal utility means that the gain of utility is smaller than the loss, even though the amounts of money are equal.

This proposition is demonstrated in Figure 7-1. The horizontal axis is marked in hundreds of dollars. The distances between 9 and 10 and between 10 and 11 are equal. The loss and the gain in utility are shown as the areas under the curve of marginal utility. The loss of utility is always greater than the gain; how much greater of course depends on how fast or how slowly marginal utility diminishes.

The marginal utility of money here, and in the rest of this chapter, is the marginal utility of money as a stock of wealth. The λ described in Chapter 5 is the marginal utility of current money income spent for consumer goods.

A rational person would be unwilling to gamble even at favorable odds, if the marginal utility of money falls fast enough. Suppose a rich relative would let you toss a coin with a prize of $200 if heads comes up and a loss of $100 if tails comes up. In a diagram like Figure 7-1, the gain area would be broader at the base, but if the *MU* curve were very steep, the whole gain area could still be smaller than the loss area.

FIGURE 7-1   **UTILITY OF GAINS AND LOSSES OF MONEY**

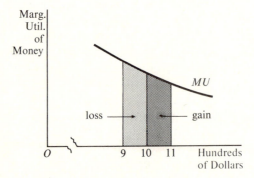

This discussion ignores the pleasures of gambling, such as they are. Among the many who have censured these pleasures is Alfred Marshall, who said they are likely to make people restless and feverish and to develop personalities as incapable of steady work as they are of enjoying the higher and more solid things of life. However this might be, the utility flowing from the excitement of gambling will be set aside here.

CHOICES UNDER RISK

Gambling has just been mentioned and will be returned to a little later. Gambling gets attention from economic theorists and from mathematicians, not for its own sake, but because in most gambling the odds, or probabilities, are exact and can therefore be put to exact analysis. The importance of the analysis of gambling is the light it throws upon choices that are accompanied by risk.[1]

Any person must make a wide range of choices subject to varying degrees of risk. Many kinds of insurance are available. The individual decides which kinds to buy and the amounts of each kind. He or she must choose what to do with liquid assets—to hold them in the form of money or to convert them into a savings account, or government bonds, or blue chip stocks, or into some highly speculative investment. Here are degrees of risk. The individual must also choose an occupation; perhaps the decision is to change from one occupation to another. Some occupations, such as government employment and school teaching, offer the prospects of security along with incomes that remain within more-or-less well-defined limits. Other occupations, such as the practice of law, offer the possibilities of higher incomes along with less security, i.e., greater risk. Still other occupations, such as playing professional golf and prospecting for oil, offer great prizes along with extreme risks.

It should be plain that the discussion here is drifting from the behavior of people as consumers to their behavior as investors and workers. The drift is intentional, because modern utility theory offers explanations of choices under risk for *both* kinds of behavior—in spending income and in earning it.

THE NEUMANN-MORGENSTERN METHOD OF MEASURING UTILITY

One of the accomplishments of modern utility theory is a method of measuring utility. The measurement is theoretical, or conceptual. It does not make possible an instrument that will allow you to find out how much the bride *really* enjoyed the present you gave her. In the modern theory, measurement is confined to the *expected* utilities that determine choices when there are risks. The measurement is also practical in the sense that it can be tested by controlled experiments of behavior and in the further sense that it can be built into a

[1] In this chapter, risk and uncertainty are not distinguished. They are, however, in Chapter 8.

way of thinking about how to make rational decisions where there are measurable risks.

Although others had tackled the problem before, the credit for the method of measuring utility goes to John von Neumann and Oskar Morgenstern who developed it in their well-known *Theory of Games and Economic Behavior*.[2] Many others have extended and refined the method, which amounts to an extension of Bernoulli's idea that in taking risks, people look to expected utility, not expected money.

When put in the simplest way, the essence of the method is to convert the betting odds a rational individual would insist on having into an index of the utility of money. Take again the example of the person who has $1,000 and is offered bets or lottery tickets with the opportunity to win or lose $100. Remember that the individual wants, not the maximum expected payoff in money, but the maximum expected *utility*. What the money means, rather than its amount, is what counts.

Which would you rather have, a tax-free gift of $1,000 or an opportunity to toss a coin for a tax-free $2,000—heads you get the $2,000 and tails you don't? Most people, it seems, would choose the certain $1,000 rather than the uncertain $2,000. To carry this example one step farther: Suppose you were asked to choose between the 50–50 chance of $2,000 and the least amount of money that would be equivalent to you, given your circumstances, temperament, and scale of preferences. Imagine that this is your answer: "I'd rather have the $1,000, of course, but if I were offered $800 in cash, I'm not sure which I would choose, that much cash or the chance to toss a coin for $2,000."

This little example contains the tools that can be used to construct a numerical index of the utility of money to an individual. The tools are the numerical probabilities of the uncertain prospects of acquiring money and the *certainty equivalent*. In the preceding paragraph, $800 is the certainty equivalent, the amount of money that makes you indifferent between it and the gamble.

Besides the tools, some assumptions are needed to construct a Neumann-Morgenstern index of utility. One assumption is that the person has a system of preferences that is all-embracing and complete. This is the same kind of assumption that underlies the use of indifference curves for the analysis of the behavior of consumers. The question now is not choices of combinations of consumer goods but choices of "events." The events here are amounts of money, some of them certain (i.e., sure-thing) amounts and others, amounts with probabilities attached to them. Between any two

[2] 2d ed., Princeton University Press, Princeton, 1947.

alternative events, the person can always tell which one is preferable, or whether he or she is indifferent. This means that the person can make probability calculations and can compare one with another. That is, the person can compare the event of receiving $1,000 for sure with the event of receiving $2,000 with a 50-50, or any other, probability. The person can also compare two events, each with a probability. Having compared the events, the person prefers one or is indifferent between them. Finally, let it also be assumed that choices are consistent, that a higher probability of success is preferable to a lower, and that more utility is preferable to less.

There are various ways to illustrate the construction of a utility index. It will be simplest to continue with an individual's attitude toward gambles. To make matters a little more interesting let the sum of money be raised now to $10,000. Somebody, call him Mr. X, is now going to bare his mind to us. Imagine his being interrogated; experiments in the construction of utility indexes have indeed been performed many times. The questions directed to Mr. X can be intended to find the certainty equivalent of a gamble, and they can be couched so as to find the probabilities that make Mr. X indifferent between a gamble and any sure sum of money. It will turn out that Mr. X's answers will show that for him the marginal utility of money diminishes.

The first step is to assign a utility number to $10,000. At the start any number will do; the choice is quite arbitrary. Let the number be 10. So then, $10,000 is assigned 10 units of utility, or 10 *utils*. Next, let $0 have 0 utils, surely a plausible thing to say. But 0 utils for $0 is also arbitrary, though not quite so much so. In fact, the number of utils assigned to $0 *must* be less than 10, because of the assumption that more is preferred to less. Thus the assignment of 0 utils to $0 is "almost" arbitrary.

Next, our subject, Mr. X, is asked to contemplate a gamble with a probability (p) of $\frac{1}{2}$ of winning $10,000, and the p of $\frac{1}{2}$ of winning nothing. The *mathematical expectation* of this gamble is $5,000, i.e., $\frac{1}{2} \times \$10,000$ plus $\frac{1}{2} \times \$0 = \$5,000$. The *expected utility* of the gamble is 5 utils, i.e., $\frac{1}{2} \times 10$ utils plus $\frac{1}{2} \times 0$ utils = 5 utils.

How much money would Mr. X be willing to offer for this gamble? Clearly, in his right mind he would not offer more than $5,000. Would this gamble be worth $1,000 to him? He tells us, yes, it would. He gives us the same answer for $2,000 and $3,000. But when we ask him about $4,000, he hesitates, telling us that $4,000 in cash is just about as good as the prospect of winning $10,000 with a p of $\frac{1}{2}$. Thus we can say that he is indifferent between this prospect and the $4,000 in cash. Since the gambling prospect has 5 utils, the $4,000 in cash must also have 5 utils for Mr. X. He is indifferent because he would lose 5 utils by paying $4,000 for the gamble and he would gain 5 utils by accepting it.

Given the assigned utilities of $u(\$10,000) = 10$ utils, $u(\$0) = 0$ utils, and the information that $u(\$4,000) = 5$ utils, we find three points on Mr. X's utility index. If we keep up the questioning, we can get two more points, for, say, $u(\$20,000)$ and $u(\$50,000)$. We can tie into our reference points and question Mr. X until he tells us what probability of winning $20,000 is as good as but no better than the certainty of having $4,000 in cash. We already know that $u(\$4,000) = 5$ utils.

Given the assumptions that marginal utility diminishes and that more is preferred to less, the probability of winning $20,000 must lie between $\frac{1}{4}$ and $\frac{1}{2}$. If p were $\frac{1}{4}$, then $u(\$20,000)$ would be 20 utils, which contradicts diminishing marginal utility. Similarly, if p were $\frac{1}{2}$, then $u(\$20,000)$ would be 10 utils, which defies the axiom that more is preferred to less.

Suppose that p is $\frac{1}{3}$ for the gamble of $20,000. Then, because $u(\$4,000) = 5$ utils and Mr. X is indifferent between a certain $4,000 and the gamble of $20,000, we get a fourth point on his utility index,

$\frac{1}{3}u(\$20,000) = 5$ utils, and
$u(\$20,000) = 15$ utils.

Remember too the assumption that Mr. X can make consistent choices. He also would be indifferent between $10,000 and a $\frac{2}{3}p$ of winning $20,000. Therefore,

$\frac{2}{3}u(\$20,000) = 10$ utils, and
$u(\$20,000) = 15$ utils.

To find the number of utils for $50,000 for Mr. X, we proceed in the same way. Suppose the answer comes out as 20 utils. We can get this in one of three ways,

$\frac{1}{4}u(\$50,000) = 5$ utils, and
$u(\$50,000) = 20$ utils; or
$\frac{1}{2}u(\$50,000) = 10$ utils, and
$u(\$50,000) = 20$ utils; or
$\frac{3}{4}u(\$50,000) = 15$ utils, and
$u(\$50,000) = 20$ utils.

Mr. X is indeed consistent, and we must be glad he keeps the arithmetic simple for us.

Table 7-1 gives a summary of the procedure for constructing the utility index for Mr. X.

The results of the calculations based on Mr. X's responses are given in Figure 7-2. The total utility curve is drawn through points relating dollars and utils. Figure 7-2 is perhaps a little too pat,

TABLE 7–1

DERIVATION OF A UTILITY INDEX

Amount of Money	Utils	Explanation
$ 0	0	Almost arbitrary
4,000	5	Indifferent between $4,000 and ($p = \frac{1}{2}$) of $10,000
10,000	10	Arbitrary starting point
20,000	15	Indifferent between $4,000 and ($p = \frac{1}{3}$) of $20,000 and $10,000 and ($p = \frac{2}{3}$) of $20,000
50,000	20	Indifferent between $4,000 and ($p = \frac{1}{4}$) of $50,000 and $10,000 and ($p = \frac{1}{2}$) of $50,000 and $20,000 and ($p = \frac{3}{4}$) of $50,000

FIGURE 7–2

A UTILITY INDEX

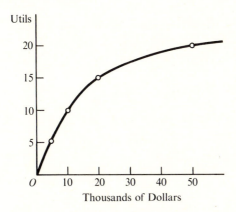

Thousands of Dollars

because all the points lie on the one smooth "well-behaved" curve. But some experiments have shown that the points often lie fairly close to smooth curves.[3]

The numbers in a Neumann-Morgenstern utility index must be interpreted with caution. These numbers are not like measures of length or weight. It is meaningful to say that 1 piece of lumber is 3 times as long as another. But for Mr. *X* we cannot say that $50,000 (20 utils) has 4 times the utility of $4,000 (5 utils). Analogously we cannot say that 100° Fahrenheit is twice as hot as 50° F; in the Centigrade scale, the same temperatures are 38° C and 10° C. What

[3] The results of experiments in finding the utility functions of business executives are described by Ralph O. Swalm, "Utility Theory—Insights into Risk Taking," *Harvard Business Review* (Nov.-Dec. 1966), 123–136. This article displays utility curves for a dozen or so business executives.

counts, in utility indexes, are the *differences* between the numbers. If Mr. X's index had been calculated from another pair of arbitrary numbers, the index would consist of other numbers. But the relative magnitude of the differences from one number to another would still be the same. One more caution: Utility indexes are personal and subjective. No comparisons from one person to another can be made.

The total utility curve in Figure 7-2 rises at a diminishing rate, i.e., the marginal utility of money diminishes. For some people the curve could conceivably be a straight line; anyone with a linear utility function would come to the same decisions in maximizing expected utility as in maximizing expected monetary value, simply because in a linear function, money and utility are exactly proportional. An economist who studied a 10-year record of racing results at four New York race tracks was able to arrive at a measurement of the utility of money for the average man at the race track. This utility curve for the range $5-$600 increases at an increasing rate, though after $500 the rate of increase is exceedingly small.[4]

The Neumann-Morgenstern method, therefore, yields measures of cardinal utility, either conceptually or as the outcomes of actual experiments. The method has indeed been substantiated by controlled experiments. The Neumann-Morgenstern cardinal utility is not, however, identical with the older neoclassical cardinal utility. The Neumann-Morgenstern method does not measure the strength of feelings toward goods and services. All that the Neumann-Morgenstern method can do is to illuminate the actions of a person making choices in the face of risk. But by opening up new possibilities of measurement, Neumann and Morgenstern have given new strength to the older idea of neoclassical cardinal utility.

THE FRIEDMAN-SAVAGE HYPOTHESIS

Does the marginal utility of money always diminish? If it does, how can the widespread practice of gambling be explained? More than that, why do some persons actually prefer to make choices among alternatives with high degrees of risk? To point to the entertainment and pleasure that many people find in gambling is not enough, nor does it suffice to dismiss gambling and other decisions under risk as "irrational." Though the world abounds with people who are thoughtless and scatterbrained in their decisions, much gambling is done with cold and careful calculations. Remember, too, that gambling has flourished for centuries and in many cultures. Whatever its morals and legality might be, gambling is not an aberration in the behavior of a part of the population.

Anyone who buys ordinary insurance behaves as if the marginal

[4] Martin Weitzman, "Utility Analysis and Group Behavior: An Empirical Study," *Journal of Political Economy,* 73 (February 1965), 18-26.

utility of income were diminishing. The payment of insurance premiums is a sacrifice of money and thus a loss of utility. Though this loss is certain, it is also relatively small and is much less than the expected loss of utility in the uncertain event that the house would burn down, the jewelry be stolen, etc. To buy insurance is therefore to *avoid* risk.

Consider an example with the following simple numbers: You have $100 and face a risk of losing $10 with a probability of $\frac{1}{10}$. You can buy insurance against the risk for $1. If you do buy the insurance, you lose the dollar, your wealth being reduced to $99. If you do not insure, the expected value of your wealth is also $99, because the probability of losing $10 is $\frac{1}{10}$ and of not losing it is $\frac{9}{10}$. Thus, $90 \times \frac{1}{10} + \$100 \times \frac{9}{10} = \$99$. Thus the dollar outcome of "insure" or "not insure" is the same. Should you therefore be indifferent? Not if the marginal utility of money is diminishing.

The numerical example is illustrated in Figure 7–3. The numbers for the dollars are on the horizontal axis. The stippled and striped areas under the marginal utility curve are losses of utility. The stippled area in the interval $90 to $100 is the possible loss of utility from the risk. The thin striped area centered at $95 is the expected loss of utility, taking into account the $\frac{1}{10}$ probability.[5] The thin striped area in the interval $99 to $100 is the certain loss of utility with the purchase of insurance. Clearly, the certain loss is less than the expected loss. The utility outcome of "insure" or "not insure"

FIGURE 7–3   PURCHASE OF INSURANCE

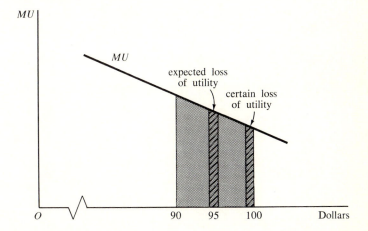

[5] Marginal utility at $95 is the average of the marginal utilities of $90 and $100 and thus the expected loss of utility can be centered at $95. This is accurate only for linear marginal utility functions. But they are derived from quadratic total utility functions, which are very popular.

is not the same. A rational person would buy insurance. The insurance premium in this example is in fact a bargain, there being no allowance for the insurer's costs and profits. When they are added to the price of the insurance, the certain loss of utility becomes larger. But as long as the certain loss is less than the expected loss, the purchase of insurance is rational.

In a well-known article published in 1948, Milton Friedman and L. J. Savage advance a hypothesis that explains why the same groups of people both buy insurance and engage in gambling, why they both avoid and choose risks. Stated briefly and without regard for its refinements, the Friedman-Savage hypothesis is that for most people, the marginal utility of income diminishes when incomes are below some level, increases for incomes between that level and some higher level, and diminishes again when incomes are above the high level.

The Friedman-Savage hypothesis is illustrated in Figure 7-4. The roller-coaster curve[6] has three segments indicating from left to right, diminishing, increasing, and then again diminishing marginal utility of income. The dashed vertical lines in Figure 7-4 separate the three segments. Suppose a person has an income OA which is still in the first diminishing segment. This person buys insurance because the payment is small when compared with the large loss of utility, even though the probability is low that she or he would suffer the loss without insurance. The loss of utility is large because the person looks up the curve to the left where L is. The same person also buys long-shot lottery tickets or makes similar gambles. Here though the payment is small, the probability of winning is also small. The expected utility of the gamble would be negative were it not for the rising marginal utility of the possible gain in income shown on the rising part of the curve where M is.

FIGURE 7–4   FRIEDMAN-SAVAGE HYPOTHESIS

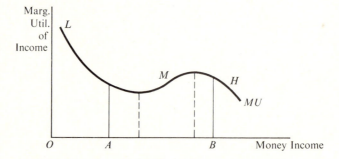

[6] Friedman and Savage draw total utility curves, like the one in Figure 7-2. The curve in Figure 7-4 is consistent with their curves.

A person with an income *OB* in Figure 7–4 has a high income; because of this, that person has no preference for risk and is unwilling to gamble or to undertake risky investments except, of course, at favorable odds.

Friedman and Savage tentatively believe that the three segments of the curve in Figure 7–4 are descriptive of the attitudes of people in different socioeconomic groups. They recognize the multitude of differences from one person to another even in the same socio-economic group; some persons are inveterate gamblers, others avoid all possible risks. Still, Friedman and Savage think that the curve describes the propensities of broad classes. The middle group with the increasing marginal utility of money are those, they argue, who are eager to take risks to improve themselves. The expectation of more money means much to this group of persons; if their efforts succeed, they lift themselves into the next socioeconomic class. These persons want not just more consumer goods; they look up in the social scale. They want to rise, to change the patterns of their lives. No wonder that marginal utility increases for them.

However that might be, the dominant belief of analysts who work with Neumann-Morgenstern utility is that most people make their financial decisions in such ways that the marginal utility of money (or wealth) clearly diminishes. Most people, then, seem to have a strong aversion to risk, not a preference for it.

APPLICATIONS

Since the end of World War II, much work has gone into expanding and refining the concepts of modern utility theory. Part of the research effort has devoted itself to the task of finding formal techniques for making rational decisions.

The thrifty homemaker needs no advice derived from the formal theory of economic behavior. Rather, the problem is technical—the accuracy and completeness of the information on, for example, new fabrics. Over the centuries, gamblers have often run for help to mathematicians who then found new stimulus to advance knowledge. Apart from this, superstition seems to dominate gambling. But to many kinds of business decisions, formal theory is being increasingly applied.

To make a rational decision on a risky investment, for example, two pieces of information must be obtained or estimated as well as possible. One is the numerical probabilities of successes or failures, of probable money gains and probable money losses. The other is the utility function of the decision maker.

An index of the utility function can be constructed after the method of von Neumann and Morgenstern by careful and deliberate introspection. To do this is perhaps like making your own thermometer without instruments or external guides, relying solely on your own feelings of hot and cold. Still, careful introspection is better than a hasty guess. For many purposes, deliberate reflection need not be made to yield an actual numerical index; it may suffice to have a clear conception of how strong or how weak is an aversion to risk.

In the rational decision, the probabilities of success and failure are joined with the index of utility: Go ahead with the investment or project if the expected gain in utility exceeds the expected loss; decline, if it is the other way around.

Does this apply to a corporation, which certainly has no soul and not always a definite collective mind? The *neoclassical* cardinal utility concept never did have any meaning for a corporation, which can hardly be said to have subjective feelings toward individual goods and services. Though the literature on utility as a basis for decision making refers mainly to individual businessmen, it should be possible to construct an index of the utility of money for a corporation when certain conditions are taken into account. The conditions are the ease or difficulty of financing. If a corporation can acquire new funds in any amount at any time and at the same cost, then the marginal utility of money is constant. This being so, utility can be disregarded, because expected money and expected utility are then identical. If, however, a corporation faces difficulty or perhaps an impossibility of acquiring new funds, a loss on a risky venture might be a grave matter. The utility index would show a decline in marginal utility. The odds favoring the risky venture would have to be high to justify it. Just how high is to be determined by calculations which include the construction of a numerical index of utility. The index might adequately, if crudely, reflect the consensus of the executives who make the decision.

Choosing a Portfolio

There are many kinds of personal investment decisions—to buy real estate, to put money into savings accounts, to buy shares in mutual funds, to buy stocks or bonds, and so forth. A common investment decision is to select a portfolio of securities, i.e., a list of stocks and bonds. Many thousands of different stocks and bonds can be bought; they can be arranged in portfolios in countless ways. Any portfolio will have an expected reward, or return, and an expected risk. The expected reward consists of expected dividends (if any) from stocks and interest from bonds, plus expected appreciation in value. Thus, for example, a portfolio might have an expected reward of, say, 12 per cent for the next year, the 12 per cent consisting of dividends and interest plus increases in the market values of the securities. The risk that goes with any portfolio can be thought of and measured in different ways. A common method is to define risk as the expected variability of the return and to measure it by the standard deviation of the return. Thus risk is also a percentage.

Consider an investor who is going to choose a portfolio of securities at some point of time when she or he thinks the general investment outlook is favorable. Each of the portfolios that could be selected has an expected reward and an expected risk. In Figure 7-5, reward is on the vertical and risk is on the horizontal axis. The shaded area shows all the combinations of reward and risk in portfolios available to the investor. The heavy line E is the locus of "efficient" portfolios. An efficient portfolio has the highest reward for a given risk, or the least risk for a given reward. Take point J in the diagram. It is as high as it can be, given its horizontal position; likewise, point J is as far to the left as it can be, given its vertical position. In contrast, point K represents an "inefficient" portfolio; it has the same risk as J, but offers a smaller reward. Again in contrast, point L is one of the portfolios that does not exist in the investment climate where the decision is to be made.

If an investor has a utility index for money, or wealth, with the property of diminishing marginal utility, she or he is said to be *risk-averse*. And, if so, the risk-averse investor will act as if he or she had a utility index with diminishing marginal utility. The modern theory of finance does indeed focus most of its attention on the decisions of risk-averse investors. We can pass now from the utility-of-money curve in Figure 7-2 to the family of indifference curves in Figure 7-5.

Reward is of course expected utility and risk is expected disutility. The utility function of the risk-averse investor can be portrayed by a family of indifference curves, like those in the SE segment of

FIGURE 7-5   CHOICE OF OPTIMUM PORTFOLIO OF SECURITIES

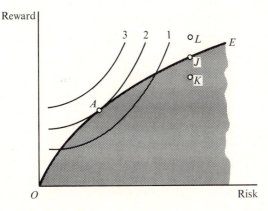

Figure 6–4 on page 94, where more of Y and less of X bring an increase of the total utility from both. Maximum utility means getting as far up and to the *left* as possible. Figure 7–5 has three of the investor's indifference curves. The highest that can be reached gives maximum expected utility. This is at point A, where indifference curve 2 is tangent to the curve E, the curve of efficient portfolios. Thus the investor chooses an optimum portfolio with the combination of reward and risk stated by point A.

Another investor with a greater aversion to risk would have steeper indifference curves. This investor's optimum would be down and to the left from point A.

The next chapter has a further discussion of utility functions of business people.

UTILITY IN POLICY ANALYSIS

Let us turn away from the Neumann-Morgenstern index of the utility of money for a brief glance at how the concept of utility is used in the theory of economic policy.

The decisions made in and for government agencies have always, of course, employed some concept of utility, either implicitly or under some other name. Since the 1960s the utility concept in open and explicit form has been incorporated increasingly in analytical studies of individual government programs. The utility concept has appeared also in discussions of macroeconomic policy problems. Here, *social welfare* and *utility* are often interchangeable expressions. Mathematical models show how to maximize this macro utility by, for example, choosing the correct volume of expenditures by the federal government. In models of decision making for local government, an ordinal utility function, similar in form to that of the consumer, can be specified. Utility here goes under the name of the "ordinal collective welfare" of a community; utility is a function of public and private expenditures and is subject to the constraint of a budget.

To show one of the bridges between the micro and macro worlds, there now follows a simple example of utility analysis in a problem of economic policy.

Minimizing Disutility

The problem is to minimize a combination of two disutilities. Indifference curves displaying two disutilities are illustrated in Figure 6–4 on page 94.

One of the issues of national economic policy that became serious more than once during the years after the end of World War II is the problem of choosing the least undesirable mixture of the evils of inflation and unemployment. Policy makers in the federal government can be imagined as thinking of inflation and unemployment as disutilities and of trade-offs between them. Thus the policy makers can be said to have a family of indifference curves expressing their views of trade-offs along a constant level of disutility. Accordingly, a 1 percentage point increase in the annual rate of inflation would be acceptable if it could be accompanied by a reduction of so many percentage points of unemployment. And of course it would be better—less disutility—if both inflation and unemployment could be reduced. Less disutility means a lower indifference curve.

In Figure 7–6 the indifference curves A, B, and C are from one possible family of curves. Along curve A, for example, are equally undesirable combinations of inflation and unemployment. Curves B and C show lower levels of disutility.

The indifference curves A, B, and C in Figure 7–6 are fairly steep. This means that the policy makers are willing to accept a large increase in inflation for a given reduction in unemployment. Since normally there is disagreement among policy makers in high places in the federal government, it is easy to imagine another group of policy makers who would have another disutility function. Their indifference curves are the dotted curves E, F, and G. Because these curves are not nearly so steep, the trade-offs here are such that only small increases in inflation are acceptable for given reductions in unemployment.

Just as a budget line shows the limits imposed on a consumer, so too there is an opportunity line to indicate what is attainable in controlling inflation and unemployment. This line is the *Phillips*

FIGURE 7–6   **MINIMIZING DISUTILITY**

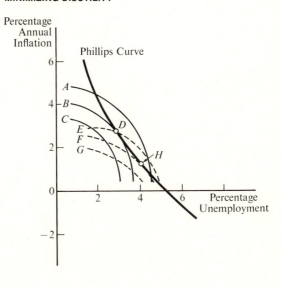

curve, which shows what can be done, given the condition of the economy in some period of time and the efficiency of the monetary and fiscal controls. Points on the Phillips curve are, then, possible "targets" for the policy makers. The optimum target would be at point *D* for the policy makers with indifference curves *A*, *B*, and *C*. But the optimum would be at point *H* for the other group of policy makers.

SUMMARY

Modern utility theory deals with *choices subject to risk*. Rational decisions look to *expected utility,* not expected money value, when risks are present. The *Neumann-Morgenstern method* of measuring the utility of money to a person is to find the odds, or probabilities, the person will accept in deciding whether to put a sum of money to risk, as in a gamble. If the person insists on favorable odds, then for this person the marginal utility of money diminishes. If even odds are accepted, the marginal utility of money is constant, at least over some range. And if a person willingly accepts unfavorable odds, the marginal utility of money increases, over some range. The *Friedman-Savage hypothesis* holds that the marginal utility of money to many persons does indeed increase over some range of income, for otherwise much behavior could not be explained. Modern utility theory is being increasingly applied in methods of formal decision making for use by business enterprises. The utility concept is also being used more and more in the analysis of policy decisions in government.

SELECTED REFERENCES

An excellent treatment with a full bibliography is contained in Ernest W. Adams, "Survey of Bernoullian Utility Theory," in *Mathematical Thinking in the Measurement of Behavior,* ed. Herbert Solomon (Free Press, Glencoe, 1960). A rigorous but non-mathematical discussion is by Armen A. Alchian, "The Meaning of Utility Measurement," *American Economic Review*, 43 (March 1953), 26–50. A good exposition is contained in William J. Baumol, *Economic Theory and Operations Analysis*. 3d ed. (Prentice-Hall, Englewood Cliffs, 1972), chap. 22.

Milton Friedman and L. J. Savage, "The Utility Analysis of Choices Involving Risk," *Journal of Political Economy,* 51 (1948), 279–304 [reprinted in *Readings in Price Theory,* ed. George J. Stigler and Kenneth E. Boulding, American Economic Association (Irwin, Homewood, 1952)], chap. 3.

William Fellner, *Probability and Profit* (Irwin, Homewood, 1965); Alfred N. Page, *Utility Theory: A Book of Readings* (Wiley, New York, 1968).

On the selection of a portfolio: H. A. John Green, *Consumer Theory* (Penguin Modern Economics Texts, Baltimore, 1971), pp. 249-273; Gary S. Becker, *Economic Theory* (Knopf, New York, 1971), pp. 57-66.

EXERCISES AND PROBLEMS

1.   After making appropriate assumptions, construct indexes of the utility of money for: (a) a college student, (b) an elderly widow with real estate and securities, (c) a speculator in oil lands, and (d) a young woman with her own business.

2.   Suppose a successful businessman is thinking of running for a political office. He knows he will have to spend much money in political life. Speculate on the marginal utility of money to him.

3.   If the utility of a person's wealth increases at a diminishing rate, must it not reach a maximum? What does this maximum mean? And would still more wealth have negative marginal utility?

4.   If buying insurance is rational, why don't more people have more insurance?

5.   Derive a utility index for a woman with $20,000 who is considering two speculations. One promises to double her money with a probability of success of $\frac{8}{10}$; the other speculation promises to quadruple her money with a probability of $\frac{7}{10}$. Assume that the woman finds it hard to decide whether to keep her money or to venture on either one of the speculations. This utility index will have three points, one of them the arbitrary starting point.

6.   Jobs versus pollution: Suppose that a community can control pollution, but only at the expense of employment. Assume that there is an ascertainable relation between the degree or amount of pollution and the number of jobs in the community. Draw a diagram to show a decision maximizing the collective utility of the community. Hint: Pattern your diagram after Figure 7-5.

7.   Explain why a family of indifference curves describing the trade-off between working and going to school could be convex for some persons and concave for others. Explain also why the set of curves could change from convex to concave, or vice versa.

8.   Draw disutility curves for the trade-off between inflation and unemployment that could reflect the views of: (a) a student majoring in economics, (b) a college student who has had no economic theory, (c) a senator from Michigan, (d) a Wall Street banker, and (e) a retired professor.

Appendix

TO PART 1

MATHEMATICAL NOTES

This appendix and the others in this book contain brief mathematical notes whose purpose is to extend and to give greater precision to some of the ideas contained in the text. The notes are incomplete and elementary; they are intended only to convey a little of the flavor of mathematical economics to readers who remember some algebra and the elements of the calculus.

The symbols used in this appendix include the following.

p = price
q = quantity
y = income
p_r = price of related good r
w = wants or tastes
E = price elasticity
E_y = income elasticity
E_r = cross elasticity with respect to price of related good r

U = utility
MU = marginal utility
Δp = change in p
Δq = change in q

The letters a, b, c, etc., are used as coefficients or exponents of economic variables to denote the parameters of a function.

NOTE 1.
THE DEMAND
FUNCTION

In general, the *demand function* for a commodity can be written as

$$q = f(p, y, p_r, w),$$

where quantity demanded (q) is a function of price (p), income (y), price of related good (p_r), and taste (w). The exact form of such a function is an empirical question and depends on how consumers respond to changes in the value of each of the independent factors—price, income, price of related commodities, and taste.

If income, the prices of related commodities, and taste are all assumed to be constant, the demand function can be expressed in the simple form, $q = f(p)$. But when the other determinants are not constant or when structural changes occur in time, a dynamic function must be used to allow for all changes. *Econometrics* is the discipline that combines economic and statistical theory for the purpose of measuring actual economic relations. Mathematical models are established on the basis of economic theory. Statistical procedures are utilized to estimate the values of model parameters from empirical data.

NOTE 2.

DEMAND, SUPPLY,

AND PRICE

When income, price of related goods, tastes, and other determinants are held constant, the demand function takes the simple form, $q = f(p)$. The form of the function can vary considerably. The curve should always be downward sloping, with quantity varying inversely with price. An example of a demand function with this property is the curve, $q = ap^{-b}$ ($a > 0$, $b > 0$). The elasticity of demand for this function is b throughout the range of relevant values.

In this book, the linear demand function plays a prominent role. Its behavior is described by the function

$$q = a - bp, \qquad a > 0 \text{ and } b > 0.$$

The value of a represents the quantity demanded when price is zero, i.e., the intercept on the quantity axis. For a fixed value of b, the entire curve shifts parallel to an initial position with a change in the value of a. The value of b is the change in quantity associated with a change of one unit in p. When taken with the minus sign ($-b$), this value represents the slope of the demand function. (In the text of this book, as in economic literature generally, the term *slope* is used for the ratio of the vertical change to the horizontal change.)

A commonly used curvilinear form is the rectangular hyperbola with unitary elasticity: $q = ap^{-1}$. Here, a represents the quantity associated with a price of 1.

Supply functions can take many forms. Discussion here is confined to a simple linear form. Let the supply function be

$$q = bp + a, \qquad b > 0,$$

where q is the quantity supplied, p is price, a is a constant, and b is a positive constant. The intercept on the quantity axis is a, and b is the slope of the supply curve. The existence of normal, i.e., positively sloped, supply curves is assumed here, as indicated by positive b. But $a \gtreqless 0$. If $a = 0$, the supply curve begins at the origin, which means that at price zero, the quantity supplied is zero. If $a < 0$, then the supply curve begins at some point on the p axis; that is, at some finite price, the quantity supplied is zero. If $a > 0$, the supply curve begins at some point on the quantity axis; literally, this means that some amount will be supplied, even at price zero.

The coefficient of *price elasticity of demand*, when $q = f(p)$, is defined as follows

$$E = -\frac{dq}{dp}\frac{p}{q}.$$

This expression can be used to determine the price elasticity of demand.

For the straight-line demand curve ($q = a - bp$), the derivative $\frac{dq}{dp}$ is equal to $-b$ and the value of the coefficient of elasticity becomes

$$E = -b\frac{p}{q}.$$

Since $\frac{dq}{dp} = \frac{\Delta q}{\Delta p}$ when the relationship between q and p is linear, the definition of coefficient of elasticity can also be stated as -1 times the ratio of the percentage change in quantity to the percentage change in price.

$$E = -\frac{\Delta q}{\Delta p}\frac{p}{q} = -\frac{\Delta q}{q}\bigg/\frac{\Delta p}{p}.$$

This last definition is correct only for the straight line.

For the constant elastic curve $q = ap^{-b}$, the derivative $\frac{dq}{dp}$ becomes $-abp^{-b-1}$. Then

$$E = -ab\,p^{-b-1}\frac{p}{q} = \frac{-ab\,p^{-b}}{q} = -b \quad \text{since} \quad q = ap^{-b}.$$

The exponent of the price variable in this nonlinear demand function is therefore the coefficient of price elasticity of demand.

For the same linear supply function as in Note 2, *elasticity of supply* is

$$E_s = \frac{p}{q}\frac{dq}{dp} = b\frac{p}{q}.$$

Page 61 describes the elasticity of a linear supply curve and also the elasticity of a tangent line to a curvilinear supply curve at the point of tangency, i.e., point elasticity. The geometric proof on page 61 can now be supplemented.

$$E_s = b\frac{p}{q} = \frac{bp}{bp + a}.$$

Therefore, if $a = 0$, $E_s = 1$. The supply curve beginning at the origin has an elasticity of unity regardless of the value of b, i.e., regardless of the slope of the curve. If $a > 0$, $E_s < 1$. That is, if the supply curve cuts the quantity axis, elasticity is less than unity, again regardless of the slope. And if $a < 0$, $E_s > 1$. If the supply curve cuts the price axis, elasticity is greater than unity. Where $a \neq 0$, the value of the coefficient of elasticity is dependent on price.

Income elasticity of demand is the rate of change of quantity with respect to changes in income, other determinants remaining constant. With constant price and variable income, the linear income-demand function can be written

$$q = a + cy, \quad c > 0.$$

Then since the derivative $\dfrac{dq}{dy}$ is equal to c, the coefficient of elasticity can be written

$$E_y = c\frac{y}{q}.$$

A curvilinear income-demand function with constant elasticity can be written $q = ay^c$. The value of E_y is then c.

Cross elasticity of demand is the rate of change in quantity of a given good, say, good A, associated with a change in the price of a related good, p_B. The coefficient of cross elasticity of good A with respect to a change in the price of B, $E_A p_B$, is defined as $\dfrac{dq_A}{dp_B}\dfrac{p_B}{q_A}$.

Consider linear demand functions for the commodities A and B.

$$q_A = a_1 + b_1 p_A + c_1 p_B, \text{ and}$$

$$q_B = a_2 + b_2 p_A + c_2 p_B.$$

These functions show that the quantity demanded of each commodity depends on that commodity's price and also on the price of the other commodity. For these functions, the derivatives with respect to related price are

$$\frac{dq_A}{dp_B} = b_1 \frac{dp_A}{dp_B} + c_1, \quad \text{and}$$

$$\frac{dq_B}{dp_A} = b_2 + c_2 \frac{dp_B}{dp_A}.$$

If the price of A is not changed when the price of B is changed, then $\dfrac{dp_A}{dp_B} = 0$; similarly, $\dfrac{dp_B}{dp_A} = 0$. In this case, the cross elasticity of demand for each good with respect to a change in the price of the related good is

$$E_A p_B = c_1 \frac{p_B}{q_A}, \quad \text{and}$$

$$E_B p_A = b_2 \frac{p_A}{q_B}.$$

With all other things held constant, a positive value of $E_A p_B$ implies that A and B are substitutes, a negative value that they are complements.

In general, $E_A p_B$ is not equal to $E_B p_A$. If they are to be equal in the demand functions specified here, it is necessary that the ratio of the slopes, c_1/b_2, be equal to the ratio of expenditures at the initial point (p_A, q_A, p_B, q_B). That is, if

$$E_A p_B = E_B p_A,$$

then

$$c_1 \frac{p_B}{q_A} = b_2 \frac{p_A}{q_B},$$

which implies that $\dfrac{c_1}{b_2} = \dfrac{p_A q_A}{p_B q_B} =$ ratio of initial expenditures.

NOTE 4.
LOG SCALE FOR
CONSTANT
ELASTICITY

If $q = ap^{-b}$, then $\log q = \log a - b \log p$. In this form, the logarithms follow a straight-line pattern, and the slope $(-b)$ of the logarithmic equation is the coefficient of elasticity of the original function. Therefore, if price and quantity are plotted on graph paper with both scales logarithmic, the slope of the resulting line is the coefficient of elasticity for that function possessing constant elasticity. If the line slopes downward to the right at a 45-degree angle, the curve is unit elastic; if less steep than 45 degress, it is elastic; otherwise, it is inelastic.

NOTE 5.
CONSUMER'S
SURPLUS

Consumer's surplus is the difference between the total area under a demand curve and the area representing expenditure by the consumer. Thus for any given price (p_1) and its associated quantity (q_1),

$$\text{consumer's surplus} = \int_0^{q_1} g(q)dq - p_1 q_1,$$

where g is the inverse function of f and the integral sign $(\int)$ represents the process of calculating the area under $p = g(q)$—in this case from zero quantity to given quantity (q_1).

A way of expressing Δc, the difference in consumer's surplus for two different prices, is in terms of the quantity change, which becomes

$$\Delta c = \int_{q_2}^{q_1} g(q)dq - (p_1 q_1 - p_2 q_2)$$

$$= \int_{q_2}^{q_1} g(q)dq - (\text{change in expenditure}).$$

NOTE 6.
THE ST. PETERS-
BURG PARADOX

Bernoulli thought that the marginal utility of money declines in a particular way as additional increments of money are received. His hypothesis states that the marginal utility of money is inversely proportional to the amount already possessed. With U standing for utility and M the initial amount of money, the hypothesis can be stated as

$$\frac{dU}{dM} = \frac{k}{M},$$

where k is some positive constant. Then

$$U = k(\log M + \log C) = \log (CM)^k,$$

where C is another constant. It was Bernoulli's contention that rational decisions under circumstances of risk would be made on the basis of expected utility rather than expected monetary value. The game in the St. Petersburg paradox is one that calls for the tossing of a coin until it falls heads up; then a payment equal to 2^x is made— where x is the number of tosses required to obtain a head. Since mathematical expectation, i.e., expected monetary value, is equal to the sum of the products formed by multiplying a given sum of money by its probability of payment, the mathematical expectation is

$$Exp \ (M) = \tfrac{1}{2}(2) + \tfrac{1}{4}(4) + \tfrac{1}{8}(8) + \cdots$$

$$= 1 + 1 + 1 + \cdots = \text{infinite sum.}$$

Although the expected monetary value is infinite, no rational person would want to play the game. This was the St. Petersburg paradox, which is resolved by the concept of the diminishing marginal utility of money.

The expected gain in *utility* is

$$\sum_{1}^{\infty} \frac{k}{2^x} \left\{ \log (M + 2^x) - \log M \right\}.$$

Without loss in generality, M may be assumed to equal 2^n. Then it can be shown that the expected gain in utility $E(\Delta U)$ decreases as the value of M increases and approaches zero as the initial amount of money approaches infinity. With $M = 2^x$,

$$E(\Delta U) = \sum_{1}^{\infty} \frac{k}{2^x} \left\{ \log (2^n + 2^x) - \log 2^n \right\}.$$

The sum indicated here is less than $k/3 \times 2^n \ (3 \log_e 2 + 3n + 1)$. Since k is a positive constant, it is obvious that this function of n decreases rapidly as n increases. When $n = 3$, the value is $.5k$ and when $n = 10$ it is approximately $.01k$. Consequently, the ratio of the utility of the expected winnings to the utility of the initial amount of money decreases still more rapidly as M is increased.

NOTE 7.
UTILITY
FUNCTIONS
FOR MONEY

Note 6 mentions Bernoulli's logarithmic function for the utility of money, or of wealth. Several other forms of utility functions have been put forward. The logarithmic utility function, however, still turns up from time to time in the modern literature. A commonly used form is the quadratic utility function, which plays a role in the theory of the selection of portfolios of securities.

A quadratic utility function can be written

$$U = aM - bM^2, \qquad a > 0 \quad \text{and} \quad b > 0,$$

where U again is utility, M is money, and a and b are positive constants. When graphed, the function is concave from below. For an investor, the function describes a conservative attitude. The marginal utility of money, $\dfrac{dU}{dM}$, or U', diminishes. The second derivative, U'', is negative.

One property of the quadratic utility function makes no economic sense. Utility reaches a maximum and then declines. It is therefore necessary to bound the function, that is, the function holds for $M \le \dfrac{a}{2b}$.

Anyone who handles money conservatively is averse to risk. An index of *absolute risk aversion* at wealth level M is

$$I = \frac{-U''(M)}{U'(M)} \, ,$$

which means that as M increases, I increases monotonically. For some purposes an index of relative risk aversion is used,

$$I' = \frac{-MU''(M)}{U'(M)} \, ,$$

which also means that as M increases, I' increases monotonically. The growth of risk aversion with wealth is another property of the quadratic function.

NOTE 8.
THE
INDIFFERENCE
CURVE
ANALYSIS OF
DEMAND

The system of indifference maps of a consumer's preferences for two goods is a family of curves, having the property that one and only one curve of the system passes through each point in the positive quadrant of the xy plane, when x and y represent quantities of the two goods. Indifference curves are generally somewhat similar to hyperbolic functions and are negatively inclined to each axis. Symbolically, the equation for any given indifference curve which possesses constant utility (U_o) can be written

$$U_o = \phi(x,y).$$

Allowing U to vary, this relation then describes the utility surface with each indifference curve being the intersection of that utility surface and a plane parallel to and U units from the xy plane. Changes in a consumer's relative tastes for the two goods alter the function ϕ.

Many functional relations might be used to describe the relative tastes of a consumer. One such relation is

$$U = x + y + \sqrt{2xy}.$$

Now with the consumer's income represented by M, and the prices of x and y by p_x and p_y, respectively, the maximum consumer's budget for (or expenditure on) these two commodities is represented by the following relationship

$$M = xp_x + yp_y.$$

Hence, the basic problem is to find values for x and y that will maximize U and that can be purchased with M.

One method for determining the maximum value of a function of two or more variables subject to functional constraints employs the *Lagrange multiplier technique*. Assume that $U = \phi(x,y)$ is to be maximized subject to a constraint relationship, $f(x,y) = 0$. From these two functions, form a third function

$$G(x,y) = \phi(x,y) + \lambda f(x,y)$$

where λ is the Lagrange multiplier. Conditions necessary for maximizing U are

$$\frac{\partial G}{\partial x} = \frac{\partial \phi}{\partial x} + \lambda \frac{\partial f}{\partial x} = 0$$

$$\frac{\partial G}{\partial y} = \frac{\partial \phi}{\partial y} + \lambda \frac{\partial f}{\partial y} = 0.$$

Then

$$\frac{\partial \phi}{\partial x} = -\lambda \frac{\partial f}{\partial x}$$

$$\frac{\partial \phi}{\partial y} = -\lambda \frac{\partial f}{\partial y} \; ;$$

$$xp_x + yp_y - M = 0$$

$$\frac{\partial f}{\partial x} = p_x, \quad \frac{\partial f}{\partial y} = p_y,$$

and

$$\frac{\dfrac{\partial \phi}{\partial x}}{\dfrac{\partial \phi}{\partial y}} = \frac{-\lambda p_x}{-\lambda p_y} = \frac{p_x}{p_y}.$$

This demonstrates that total utility is maximized when the ratio of the marginal utilities is equal to the ratio of the prices.

2
THE THEORY OF
THE FIRM

8
The Firm
AND ITS DECISIONS

In the market economy, the units are households and firms whose activities as consumers and as producers are linked together by the network of prices. This chapter and the four to follow contain the essentials of the theory of the firm. Many million firms produce commodities and services in the United States. The word *firm* is broader than the expression *business enterprise*, because firms also include farming enterprises as well as professional, technical, and service activities operated as independent income-producing units. Hence, to speak of *the* firm is to use the same kind of abstraction as *the* consumer. The many differences among firms are ignored so that the characteristics common to all of them can be described.

THE FIRM AND THE ENTREPRENEUR

The firm is a unit engaged in production for a sale at a profit and with the objective of maximizing the profit. Though it can be an individual proprietorship, or a partnership, or a corporation, the form of organization of a firm is not important in price theory. The essence of the idea of the firm is the profit-maximizing unit. If the several divisions or branches of a large corporation are required by top management to earn profits, each independently of the others and subject only to broad policy direction from on high, then for some purposes each of the divisions or branches can be regarded as a separate firm.

The firm is personified in the entrepreneur,[1] who exercises ultimate and decisive control over the activities of the firm. Although in real life an entrepreneur can be either a man or a woman, the entrepreneur in economic analysis is an abstraction, i.e., a rational,

[1] Following the example of Joseph Schumpeter, some economists prefer to limit the concept of the entrepreneur to the innovator, i.e., to the person who puts into use new methods of production, marketing, etc.

140

maximizing calculator. The entrepreneur brings the firm into existence and takes it out, should there be a need to do so. The entrepreneur decides to expand or to contract output. If possible, the entrepreneur sets prices. As a pure type, the entrepreneur performs no routine work in the firm; others do it. But the entrepreneur makes the decisions. The entrepreneur need own only enough of the firm to have control of it. In the United States, of course, millions of small business owners and farmers combine in their own persons the roles of owners, managers, and entrepreneurs. In many contexts, management and the entrepreneurial function are nearly synonymous terms. If, however, management connotes day-by-day supervision and the execution of delegated tasks, then managers are not entrepreneurs. They are hired help, not the makers of the decisions that are analyzed in price theory. In principle, and sometimes in fact, the entrepreneur need never visit the firm; a few phone calls a year are enough.

In large corporations, however, it is often difficult to identify the entrepreneur or even to be sure who performs this function. Final decisions in the large corporation are often made by the group of people usually called the top management. Multiple goals are likely to be more important in large firms than in small firms. The possible kinds of compromises among multiple goals in large corporations managed by committees defy simple analysis. This matter will be returned to later.

THE FIRM'S COSTS

The firm always acts so as to maximize its profits, which are its revenues minus its costs. The assumption of profit maximization for firms is symmetrical with the assumption of utility maximization for consumers. Some of the problems surrounding the assumption of profit maximization will be discussed later in this chapter. It is necessary first of all to assign clear meanings to the terms *costs* and *profits*. The word *revenue* poses no difficulties. The revenue of a firm is simply its selling price multiplied by the number of units it sells; alternative expressions are *gross receipts* and *gross income*.

Cost Concepts

The fundamental concept of cost is *alternative cost,* which means that the cost of anything is the value of the best alternative, or the opportunity, that is sacrificed. Another name for alternative cost is *opportunity cost.* The alternative cost of producing fuel oil in a refinery is the value of the gasoline that could have been produced from the same crude oil. The alternative cost of being in business for yourself is the sacrifice of the income you could earn by working for somebody else and by investing your capital in other ways. The alternative cost concept has a wide range of applications. Two business examples have just been mentioned. The concept can also be applied to the consumer: Fundamentally, the cost of a vacation in Europe is not so much the money as the foregoing of the enjoyment of the new automobile that could have been bought with the same money. So too, discussion of national problems should look beyond the budgeted billions of dollars and see that the real cost of putting more resources into national defense is the sacrifice of civilian goods. This, of course, is the familiar guns-and-butter problem. Conversely, it can be said that the alternative cost of public works projects constructed during a depression is zero, or close to it. True enough, money has to be spent for the projects, but if the resources going into them would be otherwise idle, then for the nation as a whole, no alternative benefits from the resources are sacrificed.

Business Costs and Full Costs

A firm's *business costs* are its total money expenses as computed by ordinary accounting methods. These expenses include all payments and contractual obligations made by the firm together with the book cost of depreciation on plant and equipment. To define the *full costs* of a firm, two additions to business expenses must be made. They are (1) the alternative or opportunity costs of the firm and (2) *normal profits*. The opportunity costs of the firm include interest on the funds invested in the firm by its owners and the value of the labor services of the entrepreneur, if working in the firm and receiving no salary as a business expense. Normal profits are an additional amount, sufficient, but just sufficient, to induce the entrepreneur to continue to produce the same product, given the uncertainties faced. Why are normal profits a "cost"? They are a cost of a commodity because, unless the entrepreneur expects to receive in the long run a revenue that will cover business expenses, opportunity costs, and some minimum in addition (i.e., normal profits), the commodity in question will not be produced. Another way to see normal profits as a cost is from the perspective of the consumer. To have some commodity available over a long period of time, the consumer must expect to pay prices that cover full costs. Part of those full costs is a minimum inducement to producers. The minimum inducement includes normal profits.

Empirical evidence from industry studies shows that the ratios of prices to costs per unit are typically above unity; the ratios vary much among industries. The minimum excess of revenues over costs that is common to many industries can be taken as an empirical counterpart of normal profits.[2]

The full costs of a firm are conventionally divided into *variable costs* and *fixed costs*. Variable costs vary with output and are the

[2]Norman R. Collins and Lee E. Preston, "Price-Cost Margins and Industry Structure," *Review of Economics and Statistics,* 51 (August 1969), 271.

payments for labor, materials, fuel and power, etc. Fixed costs are those that continue even if, for a while, the firm stops producing. Fixed costs include interest payments, depreciation, certain insurance, certain taxes, some salaries, etc. Although economic theorists are rarely explicit about it, fixed costs also include opportunity costs and normal profits. Fixed costs so defined include, therefore, more than the everyday business notion of overhead expense.

Variable costs are relevant for the short-run decisions of a firm. In the short run, the firm has given plant and equipment, which it cannot alter. Full costs are relevant for the long run when the firm can vary the size of its plant and equipment.

Cost Concepts and Rational Decisions

By their very nature, decisions are made for the future. Whether it is a few minutes away or 50 years away, the future lies ahead. Economic decisions are to buy or to sell, to borrow or to lend, to expand or to contract production, to work more or less, etc.—in the future. Like many others, economic decisions often mean choosing one of several possible courses of action—which size of plant to build, which product to produce, which machine to buy, etc. Each possible course of action has its future revenue and its future cost. Rational decisions mean choosing the optimum combinations of revenue and of cost.

Hence the only costs to be taken into account in rational decision making are future costs. Past costs are bygones, interesting perhaps, but still only bygones. There would be no need to emphasize this point if the truth in it were not so widely ignored. Most people have a mania for loading all they can into a cost calculation for fear of leaving something out.

A simple everyday example of costs and a decision is this: You are going to make a trip; you can drive your own car or ride on a bus, or a plane, or a train. To decide which way to go, you consider comfort and convenience, length of time, and cost. How do you figure the cost of making the trip in your own car? The variable costs are for gas and oil and, for a long trip, the cost of an extra grease job. The overhead costs are depreciation, insurance, annual taxes, and other expenses such as membership in an automobile club. The rational way to calculate the cost of one trip is to look *only* at the variable costs. The overhead costs are ignored. Not that they don't exist; they are real enough, and are normally much larger than the variable costs. But the overhead costs are there whether or not you make that trip. The trip by car is cheaper than by plane, if the gas and oil cost less than the plane ticket. On the other hand, if you are thinking of buying a car to make many long trips in the next two or three years, you will then calculate the total of the overhead and variable costs.

TABLE 8-1   **REVENUES, COSTS, AND PROFITS**

Revenue *minus* business costs	= business profits
Revenue *minus* variable costs	= net revenue
Revenue *minus* full costs	= net profits
Business costs + alternative costs + normal profits	= full costs
Fixed costs + variable costs	= full costs

When the future is the short run, therefore, only the variable costs should be counted. When the future is the long run, full costs should be counted.

NET PROFITS AND NET REVENUE

In this book, *profits* will be the general term. Its meaning should be clear in each context. Profits always mean revenue minus costs. Different contexts require different cost concepts. Revenue minus full costs will be called *net profits*. Full costs belong to the long run, and so do net profits. Some economists refer to net profits as *pure profits* or *economic profits*. Revenue minus business expenses can be called *business profits* because this is the profit concept of the accountant and of the business executive. It must be evident that business profits are always larger than net profits, because business expenses are always less than full costs.

Revenue minus variable costs will be called *net revenue*.[3] Net revenue is the profit concept applicable to the short run.

Table 8-1 presents the definitions of costs and profits in summary form.

THE PROFIT-MAXIMIZING ASSUMPTION

The assumption that entrepreneurs try to make the biggest profits they can is, by and large, a good assumption. It is good, though not perfect. In general, an assumption has to stand one or both of two tests. One test is realism. The profit-maximizing assumption passes this fairly well, because there would be much agreement that most business people most of the time appear to be striving hard for high profits. And if they do not in fact attain literal maximization, it is not for lack of desire or effort, but because they must make their plans and decisions in the midst of constant change and uncertainty. The second test of an assumption is its usefulness in predicting the effects flowing from given causes. Then the question to ask is: Realistic or not, does the assumption work, does it give good results? Most economic theorists argue here that, considering its simplicity, the profit-maximizing assumption scores even better.

Still, the assumption continues to be questioned and debated.

[3] As thus defined, net revenue is very close to what Marshall called quasi rent. Though economists still use the term quasi rent, it seems preferable to employ the simpler and more direct expression.

Almost anyone knows or can observe business people who quite patently do not try to squeeze out the last dollar of profits from their operations. And when making public statements, they hardly ever seem to want more than fair or reasonable profits.

Marginalism   Profit-maximizing behavior is one kind of marginalism, or marginal behavior. Marginal behavior is maximizing behavior, both of the consumer and the entrepreneur. The consumer maximizes satisfaction by adjusting the quantity so that marginal gain equals marginal cost (the price the consumer pays for the last unit bought is, of course, its cost to him or her, and the extra cost of the last unit is marginal cost). So, too, the firm maximizes profits by adjusting the quantity produced and sold so that marginal gain, i.e., marginal revenue, equals marginal cost.

Much controversy, most of it unnecessary, has surrounded the idea of marginalism. Because business people are usually unacquainted with the terms marginal revenues and marginal costs, critics have asked how anyone in his or her right mind can maintain that business people equate the two quantities. In fact, however, marginalism requires business people to do nothing more than to maximize their profits. If they do so, they are behaving marginally whether they know it or not. One hundred business executives might give 100 different kinds of explanations of how they maximize profits. Marginalism is the one general explanation blanketing them all.

Marginal behavior in maximizing profits is illustrated in Figure 8-1. It makes no difference here whether the profits are net profits or net revenue; the same analysis applies to both. The upper part of the figure shows a hypothetical profits curve, the amount of profits being measured as the height of the curve. The vertical axis is total profits in thousands of dollars, not a rate of profit per unit of output. The horizontal axis is quantity of output in physical units. The profits curve says that below some output there are no profits. When output is increased past that point, profits rise to a maximum, which is *AA'*. If output continues to be increased past *OA*, profits begin to fall, becoming zero at some (too) large output.

In the lower part of Figure 8-1, the horizontal axis is the same. The vertical axis measures not total cost and total revenue, but the dollar cost and dollar revenue associated with each single unit of output. The line *MC* is marginal cost, the extra cost of an extra unit. The line *MR* is marginal revenue, the extra revenue from an extra unit. Take the output *OB*. This output is profitable, but the firm can earn more profits by expanding to output *OA*. The additional output *BA* adds to profits. This is evident from the upper part of the figure because *AA'* is longer than *BB'*. The shaded area in the lower part of

FIGURE 8-1   PROFIT MAXIMIZATION

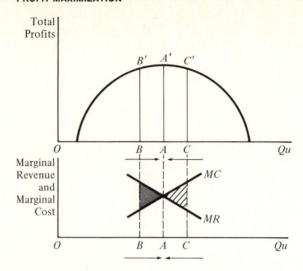

the figure is the excess of extra revenue over extra cost for the output BA. When $MR = MC$, profits are not being added to, nor are they being subtracted from. Therefore, profits must be at a maximum.[4]

Suppose the firm were to produce the output OC. Profits here are good, let it be imagined, but they are not maximum. If the firm cuts back from OC to OA, it adds to profits. The striped area in the lower figure is the reduction of profit by producing OC instead of OA.

Marginalism also means that adjustments are made with pinpoint precision. Usually, however, entrepreneurs have to make their output adjustments in great lumps or chunks. When there are discontinuities, adjustments are said to be incremental. Because they are approximations of marginal adjustments, incremental adjustments differ only in degree, not in kind. Marginal adjustments mean smooth curves; incremental adjustments mean jagged, or kinked, or discontinuous lines.

Satisficing
Behavior

If maximizing were to be denied as a valid premise of business behavior, something else would have to be put in its place. One possibility is the assumption of "satisficing" behavior. Business firms would be thought of as striving for profits that are satisfactory, rather than maximum. A justification for the satisficing assumption would be that motives to action come from drives, and that actions are completed when drives are satisfied. But a major trouble with a

[4]See Note 1 in the Appendix to Part 2.

satisficing assumption would be to find a single clear definition of satisfactory profits. Several "standards" of profits can be mentioned. A company could aim for profits *high* enough to attract outside capital, or to provide for expansion, or to equal the profits of other companies. On the other hand, a company could aim for profits *low* enough to thwart potential competition, to stave off possible government regulation, or to frustrate pressures from the union for higher wages.

Standards such as these can be meaningful in the analysis of one company or industry in one period of time. But they have no use at all in a broad inquiry into the operation of the economy because such standards are vague and shifting. In the theory of oligopoly, however, there is some need to allow for profit behavior other than the maximizing kind.

Uncertainty   The idea of profit maximization implies that the entrepreneur can choose among several sizes of profits. One of them is the maximum; this one of course is the obvious choice. Thus the entrepreneur knows exactly what costs and revenues are and what they will be. The entrepreneur makes decisions under the condition of certainty.

Decisions have to be made for the future; knowledge of the future is necessarily imperfect. Will a fire destroy the buildings this year? The entrepreneur cannot be sure about this, but can buy insurance against the possibility of fire and not worry. Will employees steal from the firm? This worry too can be set aside by buying insurance. All such possible future events can be lumped together as *risks*, which have known and objective probabilities. For present purposes, it suffices to say that anything insurable is a risk. In contrast, those future events that are inherently not insurable and that cannot be foreseen exactly are *uncertainties*. The American economist Frank H. Knight drew the distinction between risk and uncertainty, building a theory of net profits on the concept of uncertainty.

Since revenues are to be received and costs are to be incurred in the future, their amounts are uncertain, even if only to a small degree. In general, the longer the planning period, the more uncertain are the quantities that go into the making of decisions. Rational decision making under conditions of uncertainty must rest on subjective estimates of the probabilities of expected prices and costs and, therefore, on the probabilities of expected profits. Anyone in business will make decisions as if he or she had constructed a Neumann-Morgenstern utility index; thus the decisions are to maximize the expected utility of money profits. Such behavior also of course rests on marginal calculations.

For the sake of simplicity, the chapters to follow will not distinguish between certain and expected prices, costs, and profits. Let the fog of uncertainty be lifted and let decisions be made in the clear if artificial light of certainty.

Multiple
Objectives

Still another of the problems surrounding the assumption of profit maximization is whether maximum profits are the sole objective of a firm. Spokesmen for business draw attention to several other objectives, especially those of large corporations. Here is a partial list: maintaining or increasing market share, growing for the sake of growing, creating or maintaining a desirable public "image," fulfilling social responsibilities, maintaining a desirable financial position, achieving good labor relations, and so on.

The real question is whether such other objectives are distinctly separate from profits or whether they are direct or indirect means of increasing profits, now or in the future. Once more the need for simplicity imposes the further assumption that other objectives of the firm are ancillary to profits.

It seems worthwhile, however, to make a short digression from the theme of profit maximization as the sole objective of a firm and to say a little about the notion of a *utility function*.

Utility
Functions

In Chapter 7, the expression *utility function* has the meaning of a Neumann-Morgenstern index of the utility of money. But in the present context the same expression carries a different meaning. A business executive's utility function now is his or her scale of preferences for profits and for other objectives; they are not instruments for larger profits, because their pursuit is at the expense of profits. Business people maximize utility by achieving the best combination of profits and of the other objectives.

This kind of utility function can be portrayed in a diagram if there is only one other goal besides profits. Then profits can be put on one axis and the other goal on the other axis. The decision maker's scale of preferences can be represented by a family of indifference curves.

One type of utility function for owner-managers is shown in Figure 8-2.

In Figure 8-2, the vertical axis measures profits and the horizontal axis measures output. The curve *EF* is another profits curve. For any output less than *OE* and greater than *OF*, there are no profits. Profits are a maximum when output is *OA*. Clearly, a curve such as *EF* could have many shapes. In the figure, the curve resembles a semicircle simply for convenience. Next, let the horizontal axis also measure both entrepreneurial activity and a subjective attitude toward it. More output requires more activity, more effort. Less output means more leisure. In the figure, the indifference curves *1*, *2*, and *3* show the attitude of one type of entrepreneur, who always

FIGURE 8–2

PROFITS AND ENTREPRENEURIAL ACTIVITY

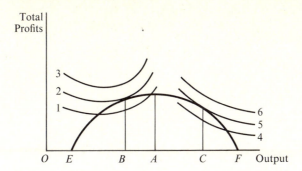

wants more profits and thus wants to be on the highest indifference curve attainable. But he or she is unwilling after some point to put forth more effort unless profits rise sharply; hence the indifference curves turn up, to the right. But they first slope down, meaning that this entrepreneur prefers some range of activity; he or she would rather accept a little less profits than be idle. Thus these indifference curves are *U*-shaped, signifying that the decision maker has a preferred range of output and of activity. Indifference curve *2* is tangent to the profits curve; therefore this entrepreneur would choose to produce the output *OB*, which is less than the profit-maximizing output *OA*. The other indifference curves—those marked *4, 5,* and *6*—apply to a different kind of entrepreneurial behavior. This second entrepreneur likes activity for its own sake. He or she prefers a bigger to a smaller operation and is willing to sacrifice some profits to have a big operation. The indifference curves slope downward to the right. Curve *5* is the highest attainable. And so the choice is for the output *OC*, which of course is larger than *OA*. An entrepreneur who would care about profits *only* would have *horizontal* indifference curves, one of which would be tangent to the profits curve at its top, meaning the choice of the profit-maximizing output *OA*.

There are many types of utility functions for business people. For example, suppose the managers of a large corporation find satisfaction in supervising a large staff of executives in lavish offices. Then a diagram like Figure 8–2 would have dollar expenditure on staff on the horizontal axis. Point *A* would signify the expenditure on staff that is consistent with maximum profits. Point *C* means that staff expenditure is so large that it cuts into profits. But if indifference curves *4, 5,* and *6* denote the managers' preferences, they will choose point *C*, because it maximizes their utility.

Another kind of utility function for managers of large corporations is the essential feature of the so-called sales-maximization model. In this one the managers want both large profits and large dollar volumes of sales.[5] But they cannot simultaneously maximize both. If profits are at their maximum, dollar sales are not; and if sales are at their maximum, profits are not. So the managers must strike a compromise. Figure 8–2 can be put to work once more. The horizontal axis now measures the corporation's dollar volume of sales. The curve *EF* shows the relations between total profits and sales. Because the managers want large sales and profits, they will make a choice somewhere between *A* and *F*. Just where will depend on their preferences, i.e., on their utility (or "preference") function, indicated by indifference curves like the curves *4, 5,* and *6* in Figure 8–2. The point of tangency of, say, curve *5* with the curve *EF* marks the maximization of the utility function.

Many business firms make contributions to various philanthropic causes, despite the complaints that stockholders frequently bring up. A firm's contributions to philanthropy (charity, education, etc.) can be put, along, of course, with profits, into a utility function. The firm's managers maximize utility by selecting an optimum combination of contributions and profits. In Figure 8–3, the line *AB* show the opportunities available to the firm. At the upper left, the line rises at first before declining, signifying that some amount of contributions adds to profits. Whether this could be so is surely debatable, but let it be assumed. By improving relations with the community, with suppliers and customers, and perhaps with employees, some volume of contributions could conceivably make profits a little greater.

FIGURE 8–3   PROFITS AND PHILANTHROPY

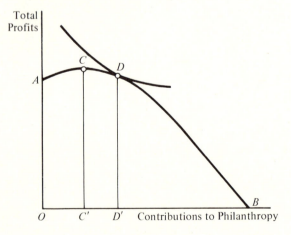

---

[5] William J. Baumol created the model, but he did not explicitly develop a utility function. Chapter 20 has more on this model.

Figure 8–3 displays only one indifference curve from the family of curves that represents the utility function. The tangency of the indifference curve to the opportunity line at point D shows the firm's optimum. If the firm maximized profits alone, the indifference curves would be horizontal and the optimum would be at point C, where profits are at their maximum.[6]

Thus the firm in Figure 8–3 maximizes its utility function by making philanthropic contributions of OD' and having profits of DD'. A firm maximizing profits only would make contributions of OC' and would have profits of CC'.

Before this digression is ended, just two more remarks should be made. To repeat a point made earlier: To maximize a utility function is to behave marginally. And the maximization of a utility function, in contrast to the maximization of profits alone, is a luxury to be indulged in by business people who are not subject to strong competitive pressures. When these are in fact strong, firms that do not seek simple profit maximization do not survive.

With just a few exceptions, the chapters to follow will assume that the firm always aims at the single objective of maximizing its profits.

APPLICATIONS

As Oscar Wilde said, nature imitates art. The theory of the profit-maximizing firm is a theory of rational business behavior. The post-World War II period has seen the growth and proliferation of systematic applications of marginalism to actual business decisions. Though the rough guess and the rule of thumb still prevail, they are beginning to yield to the precision of marginalism. Many new applied disciplines now flourish—managerial economics, operations research, management science, linear programming (Chapter 12). Much of the hard work done in these fields consists of getting quantitative information and of beating and pounding it into the shapes required by theory so that business executives can be provided with the bases for making rational decisions. Much of the applied theory, some of it wholly new, is the extension and complication of the ideas described in this book.

SUMMARY

In the market economy, the producing unit is the *firm*, which is personified in the *entrepreneur* who makes the ultimate decisions. The goal of the firm is to maximize its profits, which are revenues minus costs. The fundamental cost concept is *alternative,* or *oppor-*

[6] Adapted and simplified from Harold L. Johnson, *Graphic Analysis of Multiple-Goal Firms: Development, Current Status and Critique,* Pennsylvania State University Occasional Paper #5, April 1966.

tunity, cost, defined as the value of the alternative sacrificed. A firm's *business costs* are its total money expenses as computed by ordinary accounting methods. A firm's *full costs* are its business costs plus alternative costs plus *normal profits.* Full costs are divided into *variable costs* and *fixed costs.* Rational decisions look only to future costs. Short-run decisions count only variable costs, whereas long-run decisions count full costs. Revenue minus full costs gives *net profits*; revenue minus business costs gives *business profits;* and revenue minus variable costs is *net revenue.* Profit-maximizing behavior is *marginal behavior* because profits are maximum when marginal revenue equals marginal cost. The usefulness of the profit-maximizing assumption has been subject to much debate. Attempts to put in its place an assumption of *satisficing* behavior have not succeeded. Business goals other than profits can be treated as ancillary to profits, or can be incorporated in a utility function, along with profits. The new applied disciplines contribute to the actual spread of marginal behavior in the business world.

SELECTED REFERENCES

General: Frank H. Knight, *Risk, Uncertainty and Profit* (Houghton Mifflin, Boston, 1921); Neil W. Chamberlain, *The Firm: Micro-Economic Planning and Action* (McGraw-Hill, New York, 1962).

On the firm: Fritz Machlup, "Theories of the Firm: Marginalist, Behavioral, Managerial," *American Economic Review,* 57 (March 1967), 1–33; Richard M. Cyert and Charles L. Hedrick, "Theory of the Firm: Past, Present, and Future—an Interpretation," *Journal of Economic Literature,* 10 (June 1972), 398–412.

On profit maximization: Herbert A. Simon, "Theories of Decision-Making in Economics and Behavioral Science," *American Economic Review,* 49 (June 1959), 253–283; Tibor Scitovsky, "A Note on Profit Maximisation and Its Implications," *Review of Economic Studies,* 11 (1943) [reprinted in *Readings in Price Theory,* ed. George J. Stigler and Kenneth E. Boulding (Irwin, Homewood, 1952), chap. 17]; Donald Stevenson Watson, ed., *Price Theory in Action: A Book of Readings,* 3d ed. (Houghton Mifflin, Boston, 1973), chaps. 11–13.

Business applications: Joel Dean, *Managerial Economics* (Prentice-Hall, Englewood Cliffs, 1951), chap. 1; farming applications: Rueben C. Buse and Daniel W. Bromley, *Applied Economics: Resource Allocation in Rural America* (Iowa State University Press, Ames, 1975), chap. 12.

On utility functions: Harold L. Johnson, *Graphic Analysis of Multiple-Goal Firms: Development, Current Status and Critique,* Pennsylvania State University Occasional Paper #5, April 1966.

1. Make up a set of plausible numbers to fit the definitions of net profits, business profits, and net revenue.
2. What is the opportunity cost to a college of a football team?
3. Suppose you are going to sell your car. In deciding whether to accept an offer, how much weight should you give to the cost of the car, i.e., the price you paid for it? Why?
4. What is the difference between maximizing net revenue and maximizing net profits?
5. This chapter does not say that there is something wrong or evil about profits. Is this a serious omission? Why?
6. Those who speak for business continually complain that the public has an exaggerated impression of how large business profits are. The public is supposed to believe that the profits on a $100 sale are somewhere between $25 and $40, whereas, say the business spokespeople, profits are only $5 to $10 in manufacturing and $1 to $2 in some lines of retailing, such as groceries. Can you explain why the different views prevail?
7. In what way are opportunity costs contained in the utility functions of owners of firms who aim at profits and another goal?
8. In the production of petroleum products, what are some of the revenues and costs subject to uncertainty and what are some of the revenues and costs subject to risk?
9. Suppose a retailer buys an article for $5 and then sells it for $10. Is the markup of $5 a business profit or a net profit? How would you analyze it?

9
THE THEORY OF
Production

The theory of production plays two roles in the theory of relative prices. One is to provide a base for the analysis of the relations between cost and volumes of output. Costs influence supplies which, together with demands, determine prices. The other role for the theory of production is to serve as a base for the theory of the demand of firms for factors of production.

Production means the transformation of inputs—the things bought by a firm—into outputs—the things it sells. The word *production*, of course, is not limited to physical changes in matter; the word embraces the rendering of services, such as transporting, financing, wholesaling, and retailing.

A note on terminology: The words *inputs* and *factors of production* are near synonyms and in many contexts are used interchangeably. In general, however, the connotation of inputs is broader. Inputs are *all* the things that firms buy. When the expression *factors of production* takes on a narrower meaning, then factors are labor and capital. (In this book, land is treated as a form of capital.) A synonym for factors of production is *productive services*. The words *output, product,* and *production* are exact synonyms in this book; these words will appear in the contexts where customary usage prescribes them.

THE PRODUCTION FUNCTION

The *production function* is the name of the relation between the physical inputs and the physical outputs of a firm. If a small factory produces 100 wooden chairs per 8-hour shift, then its production function consists of the *minimum* quantities of wood, glue, varnish, labor time, machine time, floor space, electricity, etc., that are required to produce the 100 chairs. Or to put it the other way around: The production function of the same factory consists of the *maximum* number of chairs that can be produced with given quantities of wood, glue, varnish, etc. Like a demand curve, i.e., a demand function, a production function must be specified for a period of time. It is a flow of inputs resulting in a flow of outputs during some period of time. (See Note 2 in the Appendix to Part 2.)

Each firm has a production function whose form is determined by the state of technology. When technology improves, a new production function comes into being. The new one has a greater flow of outputs from the same inputs, or smaller quantities of inputs for the same output. Conversely, a new production function can have less output for given inputs if, for example, they include soil that has suffered physical deterioration.

Besides business firms, other producing units in the economy have production functions. These other producers include nonprofit organizations such as universities, colleges, churches, charitable bodies, as well as farmers' cooperatives, labor unions, and the almost countless units of the federal, state, and local governments. The nonprofit units employ inputs of labor and capital to produce outputs consisting mainly of services. The theory of production of this chapter applies just as much to the nonprofit producers as it does to business firms.

Economists have examined many actual production functions and have employed statistical analyses to measure relations between changes in physical inputs and physical outputs. A famous statistical production function is the Cobb-Douglas[1] production function. In its original form, it applied not to a firm, but to the whole of manufacturing in the United States. In the Cobb-Douglas function, output is manufacturing production. The inputs are labor and capital. Roughly speaking, the Cobb-Douglas formula says that labor contributes about three-quarters of increases in manufacturing production and capital the remaining one-quarter. In the postwar period, economists have shown a heightened interest in the Cobb-Douglas production function because of its simplicity, its many applications, and the good statistical results that it yields.

Knowledge of the details of production functions is necessarily technical or engineering knowledge and is as broad and as complex as the whole of technology. For the most part, economic theory deals with the properties or features shared by all production functions without regard for the multitudinous differences among them.

Economic theory looks to two kinds of input-output relations in production functions. One is the relation where quantities of some, inputs are fixed while quantities of other inputs vary. In the other relation, all of the inputs are variable.

[1] Former Senator Paul H. Douglas, a distinguished economist, and C. W. Cobb, his collaborator. Note 3 in the Appendix to Part 2 shows the mathematical form of the Cobb-Douglas production function.

This chapter discusses only the relations between physical inputs and outputs. The prices that firms pay for their inputs and receive for their outputs are not brought in until the next chapter.

Assume now that a firm's production function consists of fixed quantities of all inputs except one; this one is the variable input. Like a commodity, an input can be defined broadly or narrowly. An input can be one grade of labor or it can be units or crews of workers and equipment. In any event, the problem now is this: The firm can increase output by varying the quantities of just one input. What is the input-output relation?

Suppose that the inputs fixed in amount are plant, equipment, and land, and that the variable input is labor. When the firm expands output by employing more labor, it alters the *proportions* between the fixed and the variable inputs. The *law of variable proportions,* also known as the *law of diminishing returns,* can be stated as follows: When total output, or production, of a commodity is increased by adding units of a variable input while the quantities of other inputs are held constant, the increases in total production become, after some point, smaller and smaller.

Observe that total production increases—it does not diminish. What does diminish is the size of the increases. The law of diminishing (marginal) returns is exactly symmetrical with the law of diminishing (marginal) utility. Both totals increase, but at a diminishing rate. (In everyday conversation, the expression *diminishing returns* usually has a different meaning, namely, that something or other gets worse and worse or becomes fruitless.)

Imagine a farmer who is making plans for the next growing season. The farm has land comprising so many acres, with buildings, fences, and equipment of various sorts. Among the decisions the farmer makes is how many workers to hire for the season. In coming to this decision, the farmer must reflect on the physical productivity of labor on the farm. Table 9–1 contains hypothetical data.

The data in Table 9–1 are to be read as statements of alternatives. *If* the farmer would hire 3 workers for the season, *then* the total product from the farm would be 270 units. If instead the farmer would hire 4 workers, then the total product would be 300 units. And so on. The basic data in the first two columns are the production function. The third and fourth columns are derived from the first two. The average product per worker is obtained by dividing, whereas the numbers in the column headed "marginal product" are obtained by subtracting. With 3 workers, 270 units are produced, i.e., 50 units *more* are produced. Thus the marginal product of the third worker is 50 units and of the fourth worker, 30 units. There is

TABLE 9-1

A PRODUCTION FUNCTION WITH ONE VARIABLE INPUT

Number of Workers	Total Product	Average Product	Marginal Product
		(In physical units)	
1	100	100	100
2	220	110	120
3	270	90	50
4	300	75	30
5	320	64	20
6	330	55	10
7	330	47	0
8	320	40	−10

nothing peculiar or different about the fourth worker that makes his marginal product less than that of the third. The standard assumption here is that the workers, as farm hands, all have equal efficiencies and are therefore interchangeable.

Another note on terminology: In the discussion here, the expression is *marginal product* rather than *marginal physical product*. In this book, the two expressions have exactly the same meaning. The shorter one is used when, as here, the context deals with the physical products only. The longer expression is used for emphasis and clarity, especially to distinguish physical products in tons, yards, bushels, etc., from their dollar values.

There is still more in Table 9-1. Both the average and the marginal products increase at first, and then decline. The marginal product drops off faster than the average. When 6 workers are employed, total product is a maximum. No more is produced with 7 workers; the marginal product of 7 workers is zero. And the marginal product of 8 workers is *minus* 10 units—by getting in each other's way, the 8 workers actually produce less than 6 or 7.

The marginal product of any quantity of the variable input depends on the state of technology and on the amounts and qualities of the fixed inputs. With improved knowledge of methods of production, the numbers in the schedule of marginal product would increase. So they would also if the enterprise had more and better equipment among its fixed inputs. Even with such changes, however, the revised schedules in Table 9-1 would still convey the same message, namely, that after some point, total product would grow at a slower rate, and marginal product would diminish.

The production function with fixed inputs and with one variable input is illustrated in Figure 9-1. Here is the conventional diagram that displays the logical properties of this production function. The

FIGURE 9-1

VARIABLE PROPORTIONS

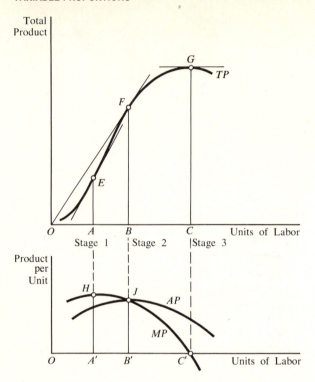

curve of total product (*TP*) rises first at an increasing rate and then at a diminishing rate to its maximum, after which it declines. Figure 9-1 has only one *TP* curve. Imagine now that the quantity of the fixed inputs were increased—more machinery, more land, etc. Then the labor would be more productive. A new and higher *TP* curve would show this. For each possible quantity of the fixed inputs, then, there corresponds a separate *TP* curve.[2]

The slope of the *TP* curve, $\frac{\Delta TP}{\Delta L}$ (where *L* is labor), is marginal product. The slope of the curve continuously varies; at any point, the slope is measured by drawing a tangent line at that point. Figure 9-1 shows three points of tangency. At point *E*, slope is a

---

[2] Different *TP* curves in the production function for oil pipe lines have been worked out by Leslie Cookenboo. The product is "throughput" in thousands of barrels per day; the variable input is thousands of horsepower. For a given diameter of pipe, more horsepower yields more throughput, but at a diminishing rate of increase. The larger the pipe diameter, the greater the throughput per thousand horsepower, but always with a diminishing rate of increase per additional thousand horsepower. See Cookenboo's analysis in Donald Stevenson Watson, ed., *Price Theory in Action: A Book of Readings,* 3d ed., Houghton Mifflin, Boston, 1973, chap. 18.

maximum.[3] In the lower panel of the diagram, point H is the maximum of the curve of marginal product (MP). At point G, the slope of TP is zero; MP is zero at point C' in the lower panel.

At point F, the tangent line is drawn from the origin. The slope of TP at point F is $\frac{FB}{OB}$. But $\frac{FB}{OB}$ is also the average product (AP) of OB workers, i.e., their total product, FB, divided by their number, OB. Point F has still another meaning—here, average product per worker is at a maximum. The steepest line tangent to TP that can be drawn from the origin is the line OF. The equality of MP and AP is shown at point J in the lower panel.

Table 9–2 is intended as a guide to the study of Figure 9–1.

Curves such as those shown in Figure 9–1 are general representations of production functions with fixed and variable inputs. To illustrate particular instances, many thousands of them would be drawn, each different from the others in some way. The stage of increasing marginal product can be absent, or brief, or long. When it

TABLE 9-2
PROPERTIES OF THE CURVES OF TOTAL PRODUCT, MARGINAL PRODUCT, AND AVERAGE PRODUCT

Figure 9–1	Total Product	Marginal Product	Average Product
Stage 1: to point E	first increases at increasing rate	increases	increases
at points E and H	then the rate of increase switches from increasing to diminishing	at a maximum, and begins to diminish	continues to increase
Stage 2: at points F and J	continues to increase at diminishing rate	continues to diminish	at a maximum ($=MP$) and then begins to diminish
at points G and C'	eventually reaches a maximum and begins to diminish	becomes zero	continues to diminish
Stage 3: to right of points G and C'	diminishes	is negative	continues to diminish

[3] Strictly speaking, the line at E should go through the point. Below point E, tangents lie beneath the curve TP and become steeper as they approach E. Above this point, tangents lie above the curve TP and become steadily less steep.

diminishes, marginal product can do so rapidly or slowly. Diminishing marginal product has been demonstated over and over again in such applications as putting different quantities of fertilizer on otherwise identical plots of land.

The production function shown in Figure 9-1 is curvilinear throughout. It is possible, however, for the total product curve to be linear over some range between points F and G in Figure 9-1. The slope of the curve over the linear range would, of course, be constant. And since the slope of the curve is the marginal product, the marginal product curve would be horizontal over the same range.

THE THREE
STAGES When one input is variable, the relations between the input and product are conventionally divided into three *stages*. They are marked on Figure 9-1 and indicated in Table 9-2.

In *Stage 1,* average product per worker increases. Two workers produce more than twice as much as one worker. Where marginal and average products are equal, and where average product is at a maximum, is the boundary of Stage 1.

In *Stage 2,* total product continues to increase, but at a diminishing rate. The right boundary of Stage 2 is at maximum total product and zero marginal product. In Stage 2 also, both average and marginal products are declining. Marginal product, being below the average product, pulls the average down.

In *Stage 3*, total product is declining.

Rational Decisions in Stage 2 There is nothing "wrong" about diminishing returns—the diminishing but still positive marginal products of Stage 2. Nor do diminishing returns mean "inefficiency." Rational producers always choose a volume of production in Stage 2; just which volume cannot be said until prices are introduced, which is done in the next chapter. It must be clear that a rational producer never operates in Stage 3, because he would be producing less, and would be using more units of the variable input. In Stage 3, there is too much labor, in an absolute sense. Even if the labor costs nothing, there is still too much. The boundary between Stages 2 and 3, therefore, marks one limit of the range of rational production decisions. If the labor costs nothing and if production is at all profitable, then the volume of production is maximized at the right boundary of Stage 2.

The other boundary is between Stages 1 and 2. Here, average product is a maximum. Suppose the firm is producing in Stage 1 and that production is profitable.[4] If it is, profits can be increased by

---

[4] It can be shown that there is "too much" of the fixed input in Stage 1. Too much means that marginal product is negative. The numbers in Table 9-1 can be used to illustrate the negative marginal product of the fixed input in Stage 1. For arithmetical convenience, suppose that the fixed input is one acre of land; this is not much land for

160   *The Theory of the Firm*

expansion, because more units of input increase production in greater proportion. Thus the firm always has an incentive to expand through Stage 1 and, in fact, to expand all the way out of it.[5]

The assumption that some inputs are fixed in amount can now be set aside for the time being. The firm, therefore, expands production— expands the *scale* of its operations—by using more of *all* inputs— more labor, more equipment, more space. If the increase in output is proportional to the increase in the quantities of the inputs, *returns to scale* are said to be constant. A doubling or quadrupling of inputs causes a doubling or quadrupling of output. If instead the increase in output is more than proportional, returns to scale are increasing. And if the increase in output is less than proportional, returns to scale are decreasing.

Some words of caution: Everyone is familiar with such phrases as "the economies of large-scale production," or "the advantages of mass production," and others like them. The trouble is that such phrases carry several meanings, some of which are irrelevant here and are therefore possible sources of confusion. The often observably greater efficiency of large producing units, in contrast to small ones, is frequently caused by the fact that the large units use newer and better techniques of production than the older and smaller units. However important they may be, improvements in technology are *not* part of the concept of returns to scale. The concept deals with a given technology.

The concept of returns to scale can be visualized with the help of Figure 9-2. The horizontal axis measures units of labor and capital. Each unit consists of both labor and capital; the units can be imagined as crews or teams of workers and their equipment. The vertical axis measures physical output. The three lines in Figure 9-2 display the three output-input relations for returns to scale. The diagram shows the three kinds of returns as separate; but in expanding its scale, any firm first passes through a phase of increasing returns to scale, then a phase of constant returns, and then a phase of decreasing returns to scale.

---

several workers, but then again imagine that the acre grows special plants requiring much care. Anyway, in Table 9-1, (a) one worker on one acre produces 100 units and (b) two workers 220 units. Two workers work half an acre each. Therefore one worker with half an acre produces 110 units. Now hold the labor input constant at one worker and increase land from half an acre (b) to one acre (a). This increase in the amount of land causes total product to go from 110 to 100 units—a decline, i.e., a negative marginal product for land.

[5] This statement applies to the purely competitive firm, which sells its product and buys its inputs at fixed prices. In monopoly and imperfect competition, the firm might find its most profitable level of output in Stage 1.

FIGURE 9–2   **RETURNS TO SCALE**

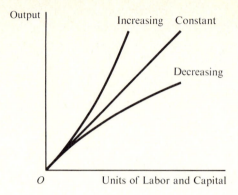

Increasing
Returns
to Scale

Among the causes of increasing returns to scale are purely dimensional relations. If the diameter of a pipe is doubled, the flow
through it is more than doubled. A wooden box that is a 3-foot cube
can contain 27 times as much as a box that is a 1-foot cube, but only
9 times as much wood is needed for the larger box. If the labor and
materials in a motor are doubled, its horsepower is more than
doubled. The carrying capacity of a truck increases faster than its
weight. After some point, however, such increases in dimensional
efficiency come to an end. When they become larger, the pipe and
the box have to be made out of thicker and stronger materials. The
heavier a motor, the more likely it is to need a special foundation.
The size of a truck is limited by the widths of streets, the heights of
overpasses, the capacities of bridges, etc.

A closely related cause of increasing returns to scale is *indivisibility*. In general, indivisibility means that equipment is available only
in minimum sizes or in definite ranges of sizes. As a firm's scale of
operations increases, it can use the minimum sizes and then the
larger sizes of more efficient equipment. But indivisibility is a matter
of degree. Though there cannot be half a typewriter, a typewriter
can be rented half time. Though there cannot be half an accountant,
part-time accounting services can be employed. Indivisibility therefore quickly exhausts itself as a cause of increasing returns to scale.

Still another cause of increasing returns to scale comes from
higher degrees of specialization, as Adam Smith pointed out two
centuries ago. With more labor, the firm can subdivide tasks, with
gains in the efficiency of labor. With more machinery, the firm can
buy special types and also assign special jobs even to standardized
kinds of machinery.

Specialization, however, nearly always means some alteration in
proportions. A change in proportions is not consistent with the strict
and literal meaning of scale—changes in inputs in equal proportions.

162   *The Theory of the Firm*

But again, the seeming inconsistency can be removed by using broad rather than narrow definitions of inputs. A firm can double both its labor and its capital and still alter the proportions in which some of its labor is employed with some of its equipment. And what does doubling of capital mean? The literal meaning is twice as many of each kind of equipment. A looser and more useful meaning is double the dollar outlay on equipment. Then too, to make labor and capital commensurate, dollar outlays have to be used.[6]

Constant Returns to Scale

The phase of increasing returns to scale cannot go on indefinitely. The firm then enters the phase of *constant returns to scale;* doubling all the inputs now simply doubles the output.

The phase of constant returns to scale can be brief, before decreasing returns to scale set in. Empirical evidence suggests, however, that the phase of constant returns is long, that it typically covers a wide range of output. And if after overcoming the inefficiencies of too small a scale, a firm has returns that increase only by the tiniest degrees and if the decreases in decreasing returns are exceedingly small, then it can be *assumed* that returns to scale are constant. Such an assumption has great practical convenience, and it introduces a welcome simplification of theoretical analysis.

Economists often use the language of mathematics in referring to constant returns. A production function exhibiting constant returns to scale is said to be *linearly homogeneous*, or *homogeneous of the first degree*. The Cobb-Douglas production function referred to earlier is linearly homogeneous in the form it is usually written. (The Cobb-Douglas function can, however, be formulated so that production exhibits decreasing or increasing returns to scale.)

Decreasing Returns to Scale

Can a firm keep on indefinitely doubling its inputs and hence always doubling its output? Everyone seems to agree that the answer is no, that eventually there must be decreasing returns to scale. The real problem is to find the clear cause or causes. On this point there is no agreement, even on the theoretical issue. Some economists hold that the entrepreneur is actually a fixed factor—though all other inputs can be increased, he cannot be. He and his decision making are indivisible and incapable of augmentation. In this view, decreasing returns to scale are actually a special case of variable proportions. Other economists believe that decreasing returns to scale arise from the mounting difficulties of coordination and control as scale increases.

Some of the services furnished by city governments are probably

[6] But then the term *returns to scale* ceases to describe a purely technological relationship. The expressions *constant, increasing,* and *decreasing returns to scale* simply become synonyms for *constant, decreasing,* and *increasing average* costs.

subject to decreasing returns to scale. If a city with a million persons requires more police officers per thousand residents than a city with a population of one hundred thousand, then there are decreasing returns to scale—if the quality of the services is the same or about the same. This could be true also of sanitation, fire protection, and the maintenance of streets and highways. Congestion, in its many forms, is no doubt a leading cause.

TWO VARIABLE INPUTS

So far, the firm has been imagined as increasing output either by using more of one input or more of all inputs. Attention is now turned to a firm's expanding its production by using more of two inputs that are substitutes for each other.

In Chapter 5, the behavior of a consumer is illustrated by a curve of diminishing marginal utility, and in Chapter 6 by a set of indifference curves. The theory of production is symmetrical, because the input-output relation can also be portrayed with a single curve of diminishing marginal productivity as well as by a set of curves that look like indifference curves.

The production function can now be conceived as consisting of certain fixed inputs and of two variable inputs. First comes the arithmetical and then the geometrical illustration.

The simple numbers in Table 9–3 illustrate some aspects of the substitution and combination of two variable inputs. The table is to be read from the lower lefthand corner, up and to the right. The machines can be imagined as, say, power saws and the outputs as cords of wood. Two people and 2 saws produce 10 cords a day, 4 people and 4 saws produce 20 cords a day, and so on. Thus the numbers in the table exhibit constant returns to scale—if *both* inputs are doubled, then output is doubled. (Perhaps the reader may wonder how, say, 2 people can use 4 or more saws, or how 2 saws can be used by 4 or more people. But there is more to cutting wood than just using saws; underbrush must be got out of the way, the cut wood has to be piled, the saws have to be tended to and their teeth

TABLE 9–3   **OUTPUTS FROM DIFFERENT COMBINATIONS OF TWO INPUTS**

Number of Machines	Outputs		
6	16	24	30
4	14	20	24
2	10	14	16
	2	4	6
	Number of People		

kept sharp, etc.) If, however, any column is read up or any row read across, it is clear that the increase in output is less than proportional to the increase in input. Except for the diagonal from lower left to upper right, therefore, any other reading of the table discloses diminishing marginal physical productivity. The table, then, gives an illustration of the coexistence of constant returns to scale and diminishing marginal products in the same production function.

In general, a production function with constant returns to scale exhibits diminishing marginal products for increases in one input when the other input is held constant. In the Cobb-Douglas production function, increases of both capital and labor by 10 per cent are accompanied by a gain in output of 10 per cent. But if either capital or labor is increased by 10 per cent, the quantity of the other being held constant, output rises by less than 10 per cent. It is, however, mathematically possible to write the equation for a production function with constant returns to scale in such a way that, at least over some range of output, the marginal product of one input will increase.

Isoquants

A production function with two variable inputs can be represented by a family of isoquants. The word *isoquants* simply means equal quantities; another expression is *isoproduct curves*. Figure 9–3 shows one family of isoquants. The curves in the figure look like indifference curves, which they are not, although still another name sometimes given them is *production indifference curves*. Take the isoquant labeled *100*. The number 100 here means 100 units of output. The curve shows the different combinations of units of labor and capital that can be used to produce 100 units of output. Point *A* on the curve shows that 100 units of output can be produced by *l* units of labor and *c* of capital; point *B* shows that the same output

FIGURE 9–3   **THE PRODUCTION FUNCTION—ISOQUANTS**

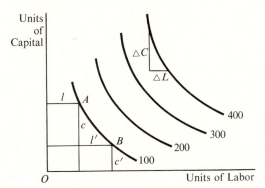

can be produced with l' and c' units. The curves labeled *200, 300,* and *400* show the different possible combinations of labor and capital that can produce 200, 300, and 400 units of output. The reader's imagination can easily see other isoquants for other quantities of output. The shape of the isoquants displays the substitutability of the two inputs. If the inputs were perfect substitutes, the isoquants would be straight lines. If they are good substitutes, the isoquants are slightly curved, as in Figure 9–3. If the inputs are poor substitutes, the isoquants would have a steep curvature. If the inputs can be used only in a fixed ratio, then the isoquants are right angles.[7]

Isoquants do indeed look like indifference curves. Their geometrical properties are similar. The economic analysis is parallel. But one great difference separates them. Indifference curves are subjective. What goes on in the consumer's mind has to be assumed. In contrast, isoquants are objective; they can be measured in practice as well as in principle.

THE SLOPE OF AN ISOQUANT   The slope of an isoquant at a point is the rate of trade-off of one input for another at that point. Here the absolute value of the slope is taken, i.e., the minus sign of the negatively sloped isoquant is disregarded. The formal name for the trade-off rate is *marginal rate of technical substitution (MRTS)*. Consider a small movement down an isoquant, where a small amount of capital is traded off for a small amount of labor. By the definition of an isoquant, output is constant, the gain in output from a little more labor being equal to the loss of output from a little less capital. The gain in output is the extra product of labor, i.e., the marginal product of the additional units of labor ($MP_L \times \Delta L$). The loss of output is the foregone marginal product of the subtracted units of capital ($MP_C \times \Delta C$).

Accordingly,

$$\text{slope} = MRTS = \frac{\Delta C}{\Delta L}$$

$$\text{loss of output} = \text{gain in output}$$
$$\Delta C \times MP_C = \Delta L \times MP_L.$$

Therefore,

$$\frac{\Delta C}{\Delta L} = \frac{MP_L}{MP_C}.$$

[7] Sometimes isoquants are drawn so as to be bent around like hairpins. Toward the *y*-axis, such isoquants curl up and away from the axis; and at the other end, they curl up and away from the *x*-axis. This means that, for example, "too much" labor would have to be accompanied by more, not less capital to hold output at a given level. This corresponds to the Stages 1 and 3 mentioned earlier.

Thus the slope of an isoquant, at any point, is equal to the ratio of the marginal products of labor and capital. To understand this more clearly, the reader might want to turn back to Figure 6-7 on page 98. That diagram shows that the slope of a consumer's indifference curve is equal to the *MU* of *X* divided by the *MU* of *Y*. Here with isoquants, the logic is exactly the same. Figure 6-7 can be read with capital and labor on the axes instead of *X* and *Y*, and with marginal products instead of marginal utilities. (See Note 4 in the Appendix to Part 2.)

The marginal rate of technical substitution is diminishing. Isoquants are convex. Movement down an isoquant means that, for given increment of labor, less and less capital can be traded off if output is to be held at a constant level. Similarly, movement up an isoquant means that less and less labor can be traded off for given increments of capital. The convexity of isoquants is equivalent to diminishing returns. Consider once again a movement down an isoquant. As more labor is used with less capital, the marginal product of labor falls. Two forces are in operation here: The first is that when more labor is used with a fixed amount of capital, the marginal product of labor diminishes. The second is the fact that more labor is being used with *less* capital; this makes the marginal product of labor diminish all the faster.

Diminishing returns also means, to turn things around, that if less of an input is employed, its marginal product increases. Thus, the move down an isoquant signifies that the marginal product of capital is rising—because less of it is being used with more labor.

Scale and Proportion

Isoquant diagrams can also be employed to show and to distinguish between scale and proportion. True enough, scale and proportion were discussed earlier in this chapter. Since they are easily and often confused, it is well to reinforce understanding by using the isoquant technique of analysis.

The isoquants in Figure 9-4 display *constant returns to scale*. The isoquants for 100, 200, etc., units of output intersect the straight lines *OA*, *OB*, and *OC* at equal distances. Thus it requires twice as much of both capital and labor to produce 200 instead of 100 units, 50 per cent more to produce 300 instead of 200, and so on. This is true along the lines *OA*, *OB* and *OC* or along any similar line. These lines, or *rays,* as they are often called in this context, signify particular capital-labor input ratios. The ray *OA* has a slope of 4:3; its slope is the ratio of capital to labor. Moving out along a ray means to increase production always with the same ratio of inputs. The ray *OB* has the slope 2:3.

Increasing returns to scale would be displayed in a diagram like

FIGURE 9-4

SCALE AND PROPORTION

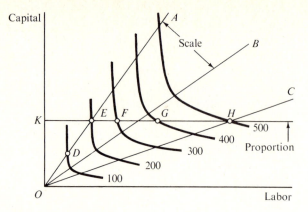

Figure 9-4 if the successive isoquants steadily became closer together. The isoquant for 200 units would be closer to the isoquant for 100 units; doubling the output would require *less* than twice the quantities of inputs. Similarly, the isoquant for 300 units would be closer to that for 200 units.

To show *decreasing returns to scale,* the isoquants for 100, 200, 300, etc., units of output would have to be spaced steadily farther apart.

Proportion in this context means that one input is held constant while production is expanded by increasing the quantity of the other input. In Figure 9-4, capital is held constant at *OK* units. The line *KH* shows how larger quantities of labor can be employed to expand production. Suppose the producer first moves up the ray *OA*, going from point *D* to point *E*. With capital constant at *OK* units, the producer then moves to points *F*, *G*, and *H*.

Notice that the convexity of the isoquants causes *FG* to be longer than *EF*, and *GH* to be longer than *FG*. This means that the 100-unit increases in output can be obtained only by employing successively greater increments of labor. Suppose that *EF* is 10 units of labor and that *FG* is $12\frac{1}{2}$ units. Then from *E* to *F* the output per unit of labor is $100 \div 10 = 10$. From *F* to *G* the output per unit of labor is $100 \div 12\frac{1}{2} = 8$. Thus the marginal product of labor diminishes when output is expanded along the line *KH*.

Thus Figure 9-4 has the same properties as the numbers in Table 9-3 on page 164, namely, constant returns to scale when both inputs are increased in the same ratio, and diminishing marginal returns when one input alone is increased.

AN APPLICATION

The classical economists of the early nineteenth century saw the growth of population as a force dooming mankind to a perpetually low material level of existence. But the steady advance of technology showed how false was the prediction. Per capita real incomes in Western Europe and North America are much higher than they were a century and a half ago. Productivity has grown faster than population.

At the present time, however, the fear of too rapidly growing population has emerged again. In many parts of Africa and Asia, the population explosion threatens, so some observers believe, to wipe out the gains from the new technology being introduced in these areas.

Figure 9–5 contributes to clear thinking on the logical relations between population, technology, and diminishing returns. Imagine a country with given resources and institutions, and with a labor force of given aptitudes and skills. Let the ratio of the labor force to the population be constant, so that population can stand for labor force. In Figure 9–5, curve *1* is a curve of average physical output per capita. The average curve is used here, because average physical output and average real income are the same thing. At the left the curve rises, signifying that when population is very small, more people working on given resources have an increasing average product per capita. This is one way of defining *underpopulation*. Similarly, the number of people corresponding to the highest point on curve *1* (or any of the other curves) can be, and has been, called the *optimum* population. The declining part of the curve is the region of diminishing average returns, of *overpopulation*.

Curves *1, 2, 3,* and *4* in Figure 9–5 stand for successively higher productivities in, say, four successive decades. Improved technology raises the curves, which still, however, decline to the right. Gains in technology and diminishing returns are not logical contradictions, though sometimes they have been viewed as if they

FIGURE 9–5   POPULATION, TECHNOLOGY, AND DIMINISHING RETURNS

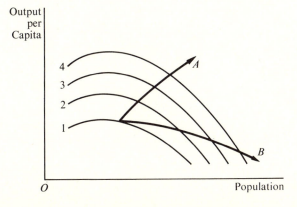

somehow are. Suppose now that population grows while technology advances, as indicated by line *A*. Here technology races ahead of population, with the result that output per capita rises decade by decade. The rising levels of living are indicated by the points of intersection of line *A* with the four successive productivity curves. If, however, population outstrips technology, as shown by line *B*, the country is doomed to a steadily *lower* average income per capita.

SUMMARY

The *production function* of a firm states the relation between its physical inputs and its physical output. When a firm increases output by holding all inputs constant but one, the gains in output are subject to the law of *variable proportions* or of *diminishing returns*. After some point, *marginal product* diminishes. The relations between total product and quantities of a variable input are divided into three stages. Relevant is *Stage 2,* which begins where marginal and average products are equal and ends where marginal product is zero. When a firm increases output by using more of all inputs, the input-output relation is one of scale. *Returns to scale* can be increasing, constant, and decreasing.

A firm can also increase output by using more of one or both of two inputs that are substitutes. The production function can then be represented by a family of *isoquants*. The slope of an isoquant is the *marginal rate of technical substitution* between the inputs and is also the ratio of their marginal productivities. An isoquant diagram can show both proportion and scale.

SELECTED REFERENCES

A standard advanced work: Sune Carlson, *A Study on the Pure Theory of Production,* Stockholm Economic Studies No. 9 (P. S. King, London, 1939).

John M. Cassels, "On the Law of Variable Proportions," in *Explorations in Economics* (McGraw-Hill, New York, 1936) [reprinted in American Economic Association, *Readings in the Theory of Income Distribution* (Blakiston, Philadelphia, 1946)]; Edward H. Chamberlin, *The Theory of Monopolistic Competition,* 7th ed. (Harvard University Press, Cambridge, 1956), app. B; George J. Stigler, *The Theory of Price,* 3d ed. (Macmillan, New York, 1966), chaps. 6 and 7; William J. Baumol, *Economic Theory and Operations Analysis,* 3d ed. (Prentice-Hall, Englewood Cliffs, 1972), chap. 11.

On the Cobb-Douglas production function: Paul H. Douglas, "Are There Laws of Production?" *American Economic Review,* 38

(March 1948); this was Douglas's presidential address to the American Economic Association in 1947.

Use of isoquants: Harold J. Barnett and Chandler Morse, *Growth and Scarcity, The Economics of Natural Resources Availability* (Johns Hopkins Press, Baltimore, 1963), chap. 5.

On the population problem: Harold L. Votey, Jr., "The Optimum Population and Growth: A New Look," *Journal of Economic Theory*, 1 (October 1969), 273-290.

EXERCISES AND PROBLEMS

1. What happens to the curve of the marginal product of labor if the weather turns out to be better than the farmer had expected? If the insects are worse?
2. On an isoquant diagram, draw new isoquants to show the effects: (a) of a labor-saving innovation, (b) of a capital-saving innovation, and (c) of a technological change improving the efficiencies of both labor and capital in equal proportions.
3. On an isoquant diagram, show the diminishing marginal product of capital when the amount of labor is fixed.
4. If total product becomes zero, what is average product? And marginal product?
5. Construct a numerical example of a production function that exhibits both diminishing returns and decreasing returns to scale.
6. Intersecting indifference curves imply irrational, or contradictory, behavior by the consumer. What do intersecting isoquants imply?
7. Speculate on how the output of the following productive activities might be measured: (a) police protection, (b) college administration, (c) research on the common cold, (d) operation of urban mass transportation, and (e) exploration of the moon.
8. For a convex isoquant, what is the relation between the marginal products of labor and capital? Do returns diminish?
9. Using natural resources and labor as inputs and holding technology constant, show how a given amount of natural resources limits the output of a country. Draw the isoquants to show constant and then diminishing returns from the labor input.
10. Draw isoquants that exhibit the following relations between inputs: (a) no possibility of substitution, (b) a constant rate of substitution, and (c) a changing rate of substitution as output increases. Give examples for each.

10
CHOICES OF
Inputs
AND OUTPUTS

Consider the decisions the firm must make in buying its inputs. The firm buys or leases machinery; hires many kinds of labor; buys raw or semifinished materials; buys electrical energy, fuel, and water; buys supplies of many kinds, etc. The physical combination of the firm's inputs has already been described under the name of the production function. The possible physical combinations of the inputs in the production function are determined by technology; they change as technology changes. Each input has a price that the firm must pay. The prices of the inputs, along with the physical productivities of the inputs in the production function, influence the firm's decisions about how much of each to buy.

Assume that the firm wants to minimize the cost of any output it produces. Given the total revenue of a volume of output, the minimization of cost is, of course, the same thing as the maximization of profits. The cost curves of the firm, which will be described in Chapter 11, are drawn on the assumption that *each* point on a cost curve represents the least cost of the corresponding output. The theory of the firm's choices of inputs states the conditions that achieve cost minimization. The theory also develops the basis for the demand of a firm for inputs and, in so doing, creates the demand side of the theory of the determination of incomes (Chapter 21).

In this chapter, it will be assumed that the production function of the firm permits the substitution of one input for another by very small degrees. Chapter 12 will drop this assumption and, instead, will show how the firm makes its decisions on inputs when they are not substitutable or when they are substitutable only within fixed limits. In other words, this chapter assumes, for example, that in employing machine-hours and labor-hours, the firm can produce with more of one and less of the other, and that it is meaningful to substitute one machine-hour for one labor-hour, and vice versa. Chapter 12 will take up the complementary relation between machines and workers, where, for example, the one-machine–one-operator relation is fixed. The two theories do not oppose but, rather, supplement one another. Easy substitution in the production function is the simpler assumption, and being more general, can explain more. This assumption, too, fits the long run, where all is variable. The assumption of rigid input proportions and of limited substitution is appropriate for the short run where much is fixed, and for certain kinds of practical problems.

ONE VARIABLE
INPUT

Consider first the simplest case. Here the firm can produce more or it can produce less by varying the amount of one input. Suppose the input is a certain grade of labor. To solve for the optimum amount of this labor to hire, the firm must fit together three pieces of information—the price to be paid for the labor, the productivity of the labor, and the price of the product sold by the firm.

To maintain simplicity, let it also be assumed for the time being that the firm has no control at all over the price it must pay for the labor and over the price the firm gets for its product. Under these assumptions, the optimum amount of a variable input is the amount whose marginal physical product has a value equal to the price of the input. The last worker hired just pays for himself.

The meaning of marginal product was explained in Chapter 9. The product is measured in such units as bushels, or yards, or tons. The value of marginal product is the marginal product multiplied by the price received by the firm. Suppose the marginal product of 20 workers is 4 tons a day; this means that 20 workers, as opposed to 19, cause output to be 4 tons *larger*. Suppose next that the firm gets $7.50 a ton. The value of the marginal product of 20 workers is then $30.00. If the daily wage (i.e., entire labor cost, including social security taxes, fringe benefits, etc., to the employer) is $30.00, then it will just pay the firm to hire 20 workers. It would not pay to hire more than 20, because the value of the marginal product declines, becoming less than the wage; the marginal product of 21 workers is less than 4 tons even though the price earned per ton is still $7.50. Nor would it pay to hire fewer than 20 workers, because then the firm would not avail itself of the opportunity of buying units of an input that bring in more money than they cost; the marginal product of labor exceeds 4 tons in this range.

Figure 10–1 shows the determination of the optimum quantity of a variable input. The horizontal axis measures quantities of a variable input. The vertical axis measures dollars—the price of the variable input and the dollar value of the marginal product. Let the price of the input be *OP* and the value of the marginal product be the curve *VMP*. The optimum quantity of the variable input is *OA*, the quantity whose *VMP* equals its price. Any larger quantity has a *VMP* less

FIGURE 10-1

OPTIMUM QUANTITY OF AN INPUT

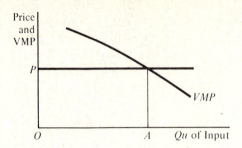

than price, and any smaller quantity a *VMP* greater than price, signifying therefore a missed opportunity. The quantity *OA* can also be called an equilibrium quantity. In the neighborhood of the equilibrium, *VMP* must be declining, for if it were rising or if it were constant and above price, the firm would expand without limit, which is absurd. If the *VMP* curve were everywhere below the price line, the firm would not use this input at all.

Remember that there are three variables here—two prices and physical productivity. If the firm should receive a higher price for its product, the *VMP* curve shifts to the right. So it does too with an improvement in technology. If the price of the input changes, the horizontal input price line shifts up or down. Any of these changes, or a combination of them, results in a new equilibrium, a new optimum quantity of input.

The rule that the optimum quantity of an input is the quantity whose *VMP* equals its price is a rule of *economic efficiency*, a rule with applications extending beyond the business firm. In general, any organization seeking to get the best results from its efforts will use a resource up to the point where the contribution of an additional unit of the resource just equals the sacrifice needed to acquire that last unit.

The main points of the foregoing discussion are summed up in Table 10-1. The numbers in this table can be imagined as part of a larger set; only those in the region of equilibrium—the region of rational decision making—are included. The last column in Table 10-1 gives the marginal cost, i.e., the cost of an additional unit of output. When 20 workers are employed instead of 19, the extra worker costs $30.00 and the extra output is 4 tons. Hence the extra cost of one ton at this level of output is $7.50. Notice that marginal cost equals the price of the output for the equilibrium quantity of input.

Both the meaning and the importance of marginal cost will be gone into more fully in the next and in later chapters. At this point, it

TABLE 10–1

OPTIMUM QUANTITY OF ONE VARIABLE INPUT

Input: Workers	Output: Marginal Product	Prices Price of Input	Prices Price of Output	Value of Marginal Product[a]	Marginal Cost[b]
19	5 tons	$30.00	$7.50	$37.50	$ 6.00
20	4	30.00	7.50	30.00	7.50
21	3	30.00	7.50	22.50	10.00

[a] Marginal product multiplied by price of output.
[b] Price of input divided by marginal product.

suffices to show the relation between the marginal cost of output and the marginal product of a single variable input.

The equilibrium under examination here can be restated this way.

$$\frac{\text{price of input}}{\text{marginal product}} = \text{marginal cost} = \text{price of output.}$$

TWO VARIABLE INPUTS

Suppose next that the firm has two variable inputs, that the firm can expand or contract output by using more or less of one or both of them. The isoquants described in the last chapter can now be put to further use.

Isocost Lines

To choose optimum quantities of two inputs, the firm must take their physical productivities and their prices into account. Productivities are shown by isoquants. The prices of the inputs are represented on the same diagram by *isocost lines*. Figure 10–2 shows three of them. Take the line *BA*: So many units (e.g., hours) of labor, shown by the length *OA*, cost the firm $50. For $50, the firm can also buy *OB* of capital—e.g., machine-hours. In the figure, the length *OA* is twice the length *OB*, which means that the price of a unit of labor is half that of a unit of capital. Thus the slope of the line shows the ratio of the prices. Any point on the line *BA* represents an expenditure of $50 for the corresponding number of units of labor and capital. The

FIGURE 10–2

ISOCOST LINES

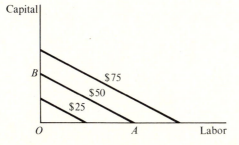

$75 line lies proportionately farther to the right, signifying that more of either or both of labor and capital can be bought at the same prices. The isocost lines are straight, which means that the firm has no control over the prices of the inputs, and that the prices are the same no matter how many units the firm buys.

The slope of an isocost line is $\frac{P_L}{P_C}$, which is the ratio of the price of labor to the price of capital—when labor is on the x-axis and the capital is on the y-axis. For any isocost line,

$$\text{slope} = \frac{\text{quantity of capital}}{\text{quantity of labor}} = \frac{\text{expenditure}}{P_C} \Big/ \frac{\text{expenditure}}{P_L} = \frac{P_L}{P_C}.$$

This property of an isocost line is identical with that of the budget line of the consumer. But there is an important contrast between the two lines. The consumer has only one budget and thus has a single budget line. The firm, however, has a whole family of isocost lines. Figure 10–2 exhibits only three lines. Imagine the existence of many more of them; the firm can expand or contract its level of output and thus can have higher or lower costs. Isocost lines farther to the right reflect higher costs; those farther left reflect lower costs.

The Optimum Combination of Inputs

The firm wants to produce any given volume of output at least cost. The least cost of any output, when it is shown on an isoquant, is given by the point of tangency of the isoquant to an isocost curve. This can be seen in Figure 10–3. Here are two isoquants, each tangent to an isocost line. Any other point on either isoquant would be on an isocost line farther to the right. That is, any other point on an isoquant would represent the same amount of output, but at a higher cost. For example, take the point C on isoquant 1. The labor and capital represented by C produce the same quantity of output as the labor and capital represented by A; but the isocost line for

FIGURE 10–3   OPTIMUM COMBINATION OF INPUTS

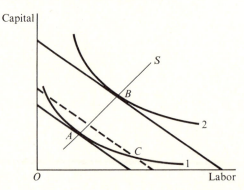

C—the dashed line—lies farther to the right than the isocost line shown for *A*. Tangency therefore means minimum cost.

The line *S* in Figure 10–3 is the expansion line; it connects the points of tangency, i.e., points *A* and *B*, and others not shown. The firm expands output along the line *S*.

The condition for minimum cost is that the firm choose those quantities of the two inputs that correspond to the tangencies of isocost lines and isoquants. At the points of tangency, slopes are equal. The slope of the isocost lines is the ratio of the prices of the inputs. The slope of the isoquants is the ratio of the marginal products of the inputs. The slope is also the marginal rate of technical substitution between the inputs; this was shown on page 166. Let *C* stand for capital and *L* for labor. Therefore,

$$\frac{P_L}{P_C} = \frac{MP_L}{MP_C}, \quad \text{and} \quad \frac{MP_C}{P_C} = \frac{MP_L}{P_L}.$$

That is to say, if a machine-hour costs twice as much as a labor-hour, the marginal product of a machine-hour must at the optimum be twice that of a labor-hour. To put it another way, a dollar's worth of machine-hours yields the same addition to total product as a dollar's worth of labor-hours.

It is plain that the firm's behavior in making its optimum purchases of variable inputs is exactly symmetrical with the behavior of the consumer. Both the firm and the consumer buy things in such quantities as to equate marginal importance with price. Just as the consumer adjusts a budget so as to equate increments of satisfaction from the last dollar spent on each commodity, so the firm adjusts its expenditures so as to get equal incremental amounts of its product from the last dollar spent on each input.

MANY INPUTS The next step is to generalize the results of the one- and two-variable analyses. To handle three inputs, a three-dimensional diagram would have to be drawn. For four and more inputs, exact analysis requires calculus. But the purchase of many inputs does not cause the behavior of the firm to differ in any important way. The optimum choices of quantities of many inputs can be indicated by extending the two-variable analysis.

Let the firm's inputs be *A*, *B*, . . . , *N*. By extension of previous results, it is true that

$$\frac{MP_A}{P_A} = \frac{MP_B}{P_B} = \cdots = \frac{MP_N}{P_N}.$$

It is also true that

$$\frac{P_A}{MP_A} = \frac{P_B}{MP_B} = \cdots = \frac{P_N}{MP_N} = MC.$$

And since $MC = P_O$, where P_O is the price of the firm's output, it follows that

$$\frac{P_A}{MP_A} = \frac{P_B}{MP_B} = \cdots = \frac{P_N}{MP_N} = P_O.$$

This last set of equations says that the value of the marginal product of *each* input (e.g., $MP_A \times P_O = P_A$) is equal to the price paid for the input. Accordingly, when the firm minimizes costs and maximizes profits, it buys *all* of its inputs in such quantities that the values of their marginal products are equal to their prices.

Changes in Input Prices

Suppose that there is a fall in the price of one of the firm's inputs. Then the firm buys more of this input, equating the value of the lower marginal product of a larger quantity with the lower price. But the effects of a fall in the price of an input go farther than this. They cause a ripple through the equations relating input productivities, prices, and costs. Several adjustments in inputs have to be made because the price of just one of then has changed. Of course, the farmer does not have to go to the nearest research center and ask to have a mathematical economist solve the problem on a computer. The farmer's experience and knowledge are sufficient to indicate what should be done. And if the farmer does keep costs as low as possible, given the farm's output, the farmer does act as if a computer had presented the solution. (As a matter of fact, farmers who are willing to keep the right kind of records and to cooperate with their state universities can get computer assistance in making their decisions.)

Substitution Effect and Output Effect

A change in the price of a consumer good has a substitution and an income effect for the consumer. This was described starting on page 104. Similar effects prevail for the firm. A fall in the price of an input causes more of it to be used, even if the total output of the firm remains constant. This is the substitution effect. But a cheaper input lowers costs, which causes the firm to expand total output, which in turn increases still more the use of the cheaper input. This is the output, or expansion, effect.

TWO OUTPUTS

So far, the firm has been described as having one output, or product. Nearly all firms, however, produce more than one product. Consider now a firm with two products. How does the firm choose the proportions in which to produce its two products?

The formal answer to this question is symmetrical with the statement of the choice of input proportions. As with two inputs, so with two outputs. The firm produces two outputs, or products, in such proportions that the marginal rate of substitution (or transformation) between the products is equal to the ratio of their prices.

Consider a firm that can produce two different products; call them product X and product Y. Suppose that the firm has some given quantity of resources—plant, equipment, and labor. With this quantity of resources the firm can produce X and Y in different proportions, subject always to the condition that if more of X is produced, less of Y can be produced, and vice versa.

Imagine that the monthly production possibilities for the firm are those shown in Table 10–2.

The hypothetical data of Table 10–2 are diagrammed in Figure 10–4. The curve AD is the firm's monthly production possibility curve. Points B and C on the curve correspond with possibilities B and C in the table. If the firm had a larger quantity of resources, the curve would lie farther northeast. Thus for each quantity of resources, the firm has a different production possibility curve.

The curve is concave to the origin, (the absolute value of) its slope being greater at C than at B. This means that as the output of X is increased, the sacrifice of Y output becomes larger and larger. Similarly, increases in the production of Y are accompanied by ever larger sacrifices of X. The firm's resources are not equally adaptable in producing both X and Y, and when they are concentrated mostly on one of the products, as at point C, the resources are less productive. Or to express it another way: The concavity of the curve

TABLE 10–2

PRODUCTION POSSIBILITIES

Possibility	Output of X	Output of Y
A	0 units	150 units
B	125	125
C	225	50
D	250	0

FIGURE 10–4

A PRODUCTION POSSIBILITY CURVE

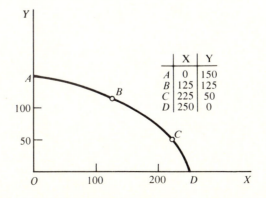

	X	Y
A	0	150
B	125	125
C	225	50
D	250	0

signifies increasing opportunity cost of one output in terms of the other. For each additional unit of Y output sacrificed, the gain in X output becomes smaller and smaller. And of course, vice versa.

Isorevenue Lines

The firm wants to maximize the revenue it gets from selling its two products. Besides its production possibilities, the firm has to take into account the prices it receives for X and for Y. Assume that the demand for both products is perfectly elastic *to the firm* (page 62); then the prices the firm sells at are unaffected by the quantities it sells.

The revenues available to the firm are shown by *isorevenue lines*. They are constructed in the same way as isocost lines. In Figure 10–5, the line FG is an isorevenue line. The quantity OG of product X multiplied by the price of X yields the same ("iso") revenue as OF of Y multiplied by the price of Y. The *slope* of the isorevenue line is $\dfrac{P_X}{P_Y}$, because slope $= \dfrac{FO}{OG} = \dfrac{Y}{X}$, and since $YP_Y = XP_X$, $\dfrac{Y}{X} = \dfrac{P_X}{P_Y}$.

The *position* of an isorevenue line signifies how large is the total revenue. The farther northeast it lies the greater is the total revenue shown by an isorevenue line. Just as there is a family of isocost lines, so too there is a family of isorevenue lines.

The Optimum Combination of Outputs

The optimum for the firm is at point E in Figure 10–5. The firm produces X and Y in the amounts indicated by point E; in so doing, the firm maximizes its total revenue because E is on the highest attainable isorevenue line. If the firm were to produce elsewhere on its curve, at points such as H or K, it would be on a lower isorevenue line, the dashed line in the figure.

At point E the isorevenue line is tangent to the production possibility curve. Therefore, slopes are equal, i.e., the ratio of the prices,

FIGURE 10–5   **OPTIMUM COMBINATION OF OUTPUTS**

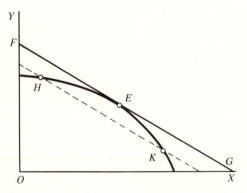

$\dfrac{P_X}{P_Y}$, is equal to the rate of substitution (or transformation) of the two products. Here is another rule of economic efficiency. In another context this rule will be discussed again in Chapter 23.

The ideas discussed in this chapter can be applied to decision making in government. As an example, let us take the area of health research. Suppose that one line of applied medical research aims at preventing coronary disorders and that another has the goal of preventing cancer. The effectiveness—the valuable output—of each of the two research activities can be measured in one dimension, the expected number of lives the results of the research can save.

Suppose that a committee has the power to decide on the allocation of resources between coronary research and cancer research. Each of the two research activities is an input. And each can be combined with the other in various ways. The two inputs are measured in millions of dollars spent on salaries and equipment. Therefore, isoquants for the two research activities can be plotted.

Figure 10–6 displays the isoquants. The figure has four of them—for the expected saving of 10,000, 20,000, 30,000, and 40,000 lives. Each isoquant means that the committee in charge can combine coronary and cancer research in different ways to achieve the same expected result. What should the committee decide? That depends on the budget. The straight line in Figure 10–6 shows the budget that the committee has. With that many million dollars to spend, the committee can choose how much should go to coronary and how much to cancer research. Clearly, the optimum choice is at point E, because that allocation achieves the maximum attainable effectiveness. Any other allocation from the same budget would result in the

FIGURE 10–6   EFFECTIVENESS-COST ANALYSIS

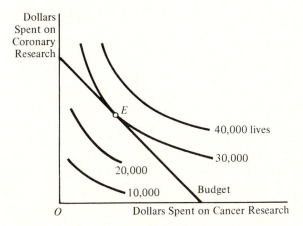

expected saving of fewer lives. Point *E* shows how to get the most from the money available.

Changes and improvements in medical research will alter the shapes and positions of the isoquants. Similarly, a new budget will move the budget line. Hence the optimum point *E* will shift.[1]

This example is simple—only two inputs and only one output. Geometry cannot handle more complicated models; they require advanced mathematical analysis.

SUMMARY

A firm buys inputs in quantities determined by the production function and the prices of the inputs. This chapter deals only with firms having no control over the prices they pay and receive. A firm buys one variable input in such a quantity that *the value of the marginal product of the input is equal to the price of the input.* The price of the input divided by its marginal product is equal to marginal cost which in turn is equal to the price of the output. The total costs of two variable inputs are represented by *isocost lines.* The firm buys two variable inputs in such proportions that the ratio of their marginal products is equal to the ratio of their prices. Minimum costs mean that isoquants are tangent to isocost lines. A firm with many inputs buys them all in quantities whose *VMP*'s equal their prices. A firm with two outputs produces and sells them in such proportions that the ratio of the prices equals the marginal rate of substitution. To maximize revenues, *isorevenue lines* are tangent to *production possibility curves.*

SELECTED REFERENCES

J. R. Hicks, *Value and Capital,* 2d ed. (Oxford, London, 1946), chap. 6; Tibor Scitovsky, *Welfare and Competition,* rev. ed. (Irwin, Homewood, 1971), chap. 8.

Applications: to forest farming—William A. Duerr, *Fundamentals of Forestry Economics* (McGraw-Hill, New York, 1960), chap. 7 (Combining Multiple Labor Inputs) and chap. 12 (Multiple-Product Management); to the national defense—Charles J. Hitch and Roland N. McKean, *The Economics of Defense in the Nuclear Age* (Harvard University Press, Cambridge, 1960), chap. 7; to environmental economics—John H. Makin, "Pollution as a Domestic Distortion in Welfare Theory," *Land Economics,* 47 (May 1971), 185–188.

[1] For an application to decision making in national defense, see Charles J. Hitch and Roland N. McKean, *The Economics of Defense in the Nuclear Age,* Harvard University Press, Cambridge, 1960, pp. 114–118.

1.   Suppose a firm can obtain a valuable input without having to pay for it (e.g., apprentices who receive no pay, or free water or electricity from a municipality eager to encourage new industry). How does the firm decide how much of the free input to take?

2.   For two inputs, draw and explain a diagram showing much more use of one input than of the other. Do this by varying both the isoquants and the prices.

3.   Draw diagrams to prove that a firm would produce one product, not two, if the production possibility curve were convex. Do this for both X and Y.

4.   Suppose the production possibility curve were a straight line with the same slope as the isorevenue line. What then?

5.   Draw diagrams that are variations of Figure 10–1 by assuming: (a) a technological improvement, (b) a rise in the price of the product, and (c) a fall in the price of the input.

6.   Let nuts and chocolate be the inputs of one producer and the outputs of another producer. Construct an isocost curve and an isorevenue curve that show nuts are cheaper. What happens to the curves (or lines) if the price of nuts goes up?

7.   Explain why a point inside a production possibility curve could mean either (a) less than full employment of resources, or (b) fully employed but inefficiently used resources.

8.   With hypothetical data, show how the production possibility curve implies increasing opportunity cost.

9.   Using isoquants and isocost curves, show how an input could be "inferior."

11
Cost
FUNCTIONS

The relations between changes in the costs of a firm and changes in its output will now be examined. The firm's decisions on profit-maximizing outputs depend on the behavior of its costs as well as upon the behavior of its revenue.

COST FUNCTIONS

The general name for the relation between costs and output is *cost function*. The production function of a firm and the prices it pays for its inputs determine the firm's cost function. Since a production function can take different forms, with either one or some or all of the inputs variable, cost functions can take different forms. Price theory gives most of its attention, however, to two cost functions—the short-run cost function and the long-run cost function. On diagrams, these are, of course, the short-run and the long-run cost curves of the firm.

The Short Run and the Long Run

In the short run, some inputs are fixed in amount; a firm can expand or contract its output only by varying the amounts of other inputs. Output can range from zero, if the firm shuts down altogether, to some maximum permitted by the fixed factors. In the long run, all inputs are variable in amount; a firm's output can range from zero to an indefinitely large quantity.

The short run and the long are not definite periods of calendar time. Strictly speaking, they are sets of conditions, not periods of time at all. Still, it is almost impossible to keep the idea of time out of analyses of the short run and the long. Even if it is never mentioned, calendar time lurks in the background, and as an idea might just as well be faced. The fixed factors of the firm in the short run are its plant and equipment and, in some industries, unique kinds of skilled labor. Where plant and equipment are large and complicated, requiring heavy investments and actual construction times of two years or more, the short run can be years in length. But the short run can also be just a few weeks long, if firms can easily procure additional equipment and skilled labor, and if their needs for buildings are modest or minimal. Trucking is probably an example here. Similarly, as a length of time, the long run can vary from a period of two or three decades to just a few weeks. An example of a long run of short calendar duration might be the public relations industry, which needs only ordinary office furnishings and machines as its equipment, and rented space as its plant, and which uses nonspecialized labor, mostly newspapermen. In any large city, this industry should be able to expand and contract with the greatest of speed and ease.

It is not always true that labor is a variable input and equipment a fixed input. In the so-called local service, i.e., regional air carriers, the fleet of aircraft can be expanded much more quickly than the staff of pilots. There is an international competitive market for used aircraft and there exists also an international market where airlines lease aircraft to one another. In contrast, an airline's staff of pilots and copilots can be expanded only slowly. They can be hired fast enough, but before they can fly productively, the new pilots must familiarize themselves with the routes, the particular aircraft, and the procedures of the carrier. This takes much more time than it does to acquire more aircraft. Hence labor can be a fixed factor.

Between the short run and the long run, there can be no sharp or exact distinction. Whether conceived as sets of conditions or as periods of time, the two merge into each other.

SHORT-RUN CURVES

In the short run, the costs of the firm are divided into fixed costs and variable costs. The fixed costs are mainly those of the fixed plant and equipment of the firm. The clearest way to define fixed costs is to say that they are the costs that continue if the firm is *temporarily* shut down, producing nothing at all. Fixed costs include such items as interest on the investment in plant and equipment, most kinds of insurance, property taxes, depreciation and maintenance, etc., and the salaries and wages of those people who would continue to be employed even in a temporary shut-down. The fixed costs of a firm also include, as Chapter 8 explains, the opportunity costs of the owners of the firm, as well as normal profits. The variable costs are those that vary with the volume of output. These costs include wages, payments for raw materials and other goods bought by the firm, payments for fuel, excise taxes (if any), interest on short-term loans, etc.

Many systems of classifying costs have been devised, and in practice it is sometimes not easy to decide whether a particular cost belongs in the group of fixed or variable costs. But economic analysis sets all such difficulties aside, building its explanations on the simple twofold division.

TABLE 11-1

A SIMPLE SHORT-RUN COST SCHEDULE

Output in Physical Units	Total Fixed Cost	Average Variable Cost	Total Variable Cost	Total Cost	Average Cost
0	$1,000	$ 0	$ 0	$1,000	. . . .
1,000	1,000	0.50	500	1,500	$1.50
2,000	1,000	0.50	1,000	2,000	1.00
3,000	1,000	0.50	1,500	2,500	0.83

Constant
Average
Variable Cost

The simplest cost-output relation for the firm in the short run carries the assumption that average variable cost, i.e., variable cost per unit, is constant—that it is the same whatever the volume of output. This means a production function with variable inputs—labor and materials—combined under conditions of constant proportional returns. Suppose that the fixed cost of a firm is $1,000, and that the cost of labor and materials is 50¢ for each unit produced. With this information, a cost schedule can be built, as in Table 11–1.

Because average variable cost in the table is constant, total variable cost increases proportionately with output. The fixed cost is $1,000 at zero output, and remains at this level at any output. The larger the output, the smaller is the fixed cost per unit because it is spread over more units. The last column of Table 11–1 shows the decline in average cost. Average cost means the total cost per unit. Average cost equals average fixed cost plus average variable cost, i.e., $AC = AFC + AVC$.

Notice that with the constant average variable cost, the extra cost of an extra unit, i.e., marginal cost, is the same amount of money. In other words, when it is constant, average variable cost is equal to marginal cost.

The Break-
even Chart

Though simple, Table 11–1 is far from unrealistic. Much business thinking and decision making are based on relations no more complicated. The common device of the *break-even chart* is constructed from the same relations. The only additional piece of information needed for a break-even chart is selling price. Suppose that the same firm can sell its product at $1 a unit and that the firm gets this price no matter how many units it sells (i.e., the demand for the firm's product is perfectly elastic).

Figure 11–1 shows a break-even chart based on the data of Table 11–1 and the $1 selling price. The *TR* line shows the total revenue at any output—$1 multiplied by the number of units of output. The *TFC* line is horizontal at the $1,000 level. The *TC* line shows total costs, fixed plus variable; the line is drawn to start at $1,000, which means that the total variable cost is added to the fixed cost. The

FIGURE 11–1   **A BREAK-EVEN CHART**

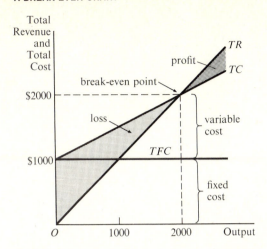

break-even point is the intersection of *TR* and *TC*. With 2,000 units of output, total revenue is $2,000 and total cost is $2,000. A larger output yields a profit, while a smaller one yields a loss.

The break-even chart shown in Figure 11–1 is only one form of this analytical device. It is presumably useful in practice because the chart makes the position of a firm visible with one quick glance. In practice, too, cost figures are often hard to compute, and some doubt and uncertainty may accompany choices about which items to put into the group of fixed costs and which into the variable. Thus, if a firm finds itself operating near the break-even point, the executives might want to see if costs can be reduced, or even if they should be recalculated, or what if anything can be done to increase sales.

Break-even charts are usually drawn with straight lines, though they need not be. The straight lines mean the linear assumption that changes in total costs are proportional to changes in output. For small changes in output above or below the break-even point, the assumption is often correct or so close to the true relation that it can be justified. A firm is not likely to be much interested in cost-output relations for very small or very large outputs when they lie outside the realms of experience and expectation. Why not then draw straight lines over the whole range? For this reason, no importance should be attached to what is obviously an absurdity: The profit area grows and grows without limit as output rises above the break-even level.

Duality of Cost Functions and Production Functions

Cost functions and production functions are the "duals" of each other. That is, one can be converted into the other. Figure 11–2 shows a curve of total variable costs, *TVC*. A look at this curve will show that it is really the *TP* curve on page 158 flipped over, except

FIGURE 11-2   **COST AND PRODUCTION FUNCTIONS**

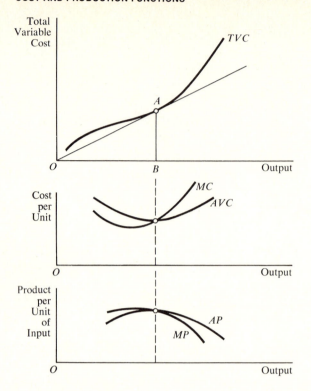

for the declining part of the *TP* curve. The slope of the *TVC* curve is marginal cost, *MC*. In Figure 11-2, slope is indicated at point *A* on the *TVC* curve. At point *A*, the slope of *TVC* is *AB/OB*, which is the marginal cost of *OB* units of output. But *AB/OB* is also the average variable cost of *OB* units—*AB* is the total variable cost of *OB* units, and *AB* divided by *OB* therefore gives the average. Thus *MC* = *AVC* at the output *OB* in Figure 11-2.

When *MC* = *AVC*, *AVC* is at its minimum. That this is true can be seen in the figure. Any other straight line from the origin that intersects *TVC* must be steeper than *OA* and must therefore indicate a higher average variable cost.

Table 11-2 gives a summary statement of the relations between production functions and variable cost functions.

Fixed costs are not included in Figure 11-2. To put them in, all that needs to be done is to displace the *TVC* curve, upward and parallel to itself, by a distance equivalent to the size of the fixed costs.

*The
Conventional
Cost Curves*

The conventional short-run cost curves of a firm are smooth and continuous curves of costs per unit of output. Four curves are to be distinguished. Let *q* be output per day, per week, or some other

TABLE 11–2

THE DUALITY OF PRODUCTION FUNCTIONS AND VARIABLE COST FUNCTIONS

Production Functions	Cost Functions

The counterparts:

TP—total product	TVC—total variable cost
AP—average product	AVC—average variable cost
MP—marginal product	MC—marginal cost

The relations:

1. TP rises first at an increasing, then at a diminishing rate.	1. TVC rises first at a diminishing, then at an increasing rate.
2. AP rises to a maximum, then diminishes.	2. AVC falls to a minimum, then rises.
3. MP rises, then falls, intersects AP at its maximum, and continues to diminish faster than AP.	3. MC falls, then rises, intersects AVC at its minimum, and continues to rise faster than AVC.

appropriate period of time. Let *TVC* be total variable costs, *TFC* be total fixed costs, and *TC* be total costs. Then

$$\text{average variable cost is } AVC = \frac{TVC}{q},$$

$$\text{average fixed cost is } AFC = \frac{TFC}{q},$$

$$\text{marginal cost is } MC = \frac{\Delta TVC}{\Delta q}, \text{ and}$$

$$\text{average cost is } AC = \frac{TC}{q} = \frac{TVC}{q} + \frac{TFC}{q}.$$

The four cost curves are shown in Figure 11–3, which is the standard, or conventional, diagram of the short-run cost curves of the firm. Other cost curves, including simpler ones, will be presented shortly. If there is one set of related curves for the firm, any firm, Figure 11–3 has it, because this diagram contains all that can be put in one set of integrated generalizations. The *AFC* curve is a rectangular hyperbola asymptotic to the axes, i.e., the curve approaches the vertical and the horizontal at each end. For very small outputs, average fixed cost per units is high, and for large outputs it is low. The *AFC* curve is a rectangular hyperbola because average fixed cost multiplied by output is always exactly the same amount.

Table 11–3 throws more light on the meaning of average fixed cost. This table employs the simple numbers contained in Table

FIGURE 11-3   SHORT-RUN COST CURVES

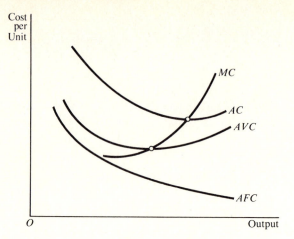

11-1. As output expands, the unchanging total fixed cost is divided by more and more units. Thus *AFC* steadily declines as output expands.

The other curves in Figure 11-3 are *U*-shaped. Notice too that the *MC* curve also intersects the *AC* curve at its minimum point. The explanation is parallel to that for the intersection of *MC* with the minimum point of *AVC*. (See Note 5 in the Appendix to Part 2.)

Marginal cost is independent of the fixed cost. It makes no difference what the fixed cost is, whether it is a thousand dollars or ten million dollars; marginal cost is unaffected. Remember that marginal cost is the *addition* to total cost when another unit of output is produced. One more unit causes nothing to be added to the fixed cost. Marginal cost is associated only with the variable costs.[1]

TABLE 11-3   **AVERAGE FIXED COST**

Output	Total Fixed Cost	Average Fixed Cost
0 units	$1,000	. . . .
1,000	1,000	$1.00 per unit
2,000	1,000	.50
3,000	1,000	.33
4,000	1,000	.25
5,000	1,000	.20

[1] A more formal proof of the independence of marginal cost from fixed cost is this (*q* stands for any volume of output)

$$MC(q) = TC(q) - TC(q - 1)$$
$$= [TVC(q) + TFC] - [TVC(q - 1) + TFC]$$
$$= TVC(q) - TVC(q - 1).$$

190   *The Theory of the Firm*

Just as the area under a marginal utility curve is equal to the total utility of the quantity in question, so too the area under a marginal cost curve is equal to total variable cost. Take any output, q. A line drawn from the MC curve to q is the marginal cost of q. The line can be imagined as a very thin bar. Next to it on the left is another thin bar, the MC of $q - 1$ units. Next to this one is another, the MC of $q - 2$ units. And so on. All the thin bars merge into an area which is the total variable cost of the output q.

The minimum points of the AVC and AC curves have been mentioned more than once. But *all* points on these curves, and therefore also on the MC curve, are minimum points for the outputs they correspond to. Here again we have to go back to the production function, this time to the production function with isoquants, and observe its duality with the cost function. Figure 11-4 shows the duality. The upper part of the figure has three isoquants from the production function for bushels of grain, with pounds of seed and of fertilizer as the variable inputs. The isocost lines are also displayed. The points A, B, and C are the minimum-cost points for each of the

FIGURE 11-4   PRODUCTION FUNCTIONS AND COST FUNCTIONS ONCE MORE

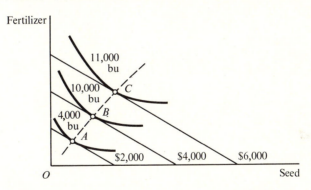

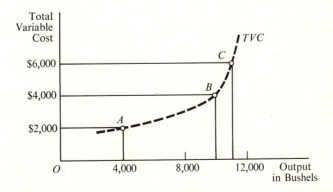

three levels of output.[2] The information about the production function in the upper part of Figure 11–4 is rearranged in the lower part, which exhibits the cost function, i.e., total variable cost. The points *A*, *B*, and *C* now lie on the *TVC* curve. Of course these three points are hardly enough to define the *TVC* curve as it is drawn. But it is easy to visualize the additional isoquants, isocost lines, and the minimum-cost points that could be used to give more points for the *TVC* curve.

OTHER TYPES OF SHORT-RUN CURVES

It was said before that if only one cost curve for the firm in the short run is to be studied, it is the cost curve (i.e., the related group of them) shown in Figure 11–3. The different cost curves of millions of different firms can be thought of as almost endless variants of the one generalization.

The average cost of a firm in the short run always declines to a minimum; then it rises. How much it declines depends on the proportion of fixed to total costs. If the proportion of fixed costs is high, the decline in average cost is rapid. The output whose average cost is the minimum carries the standard definition of the *capacity output*.[3] Capacity here does not mean maximum output but, rather, the designed output. A plant is designed, perhaps by engineers, to produce so many units a week or a month at a minimum cost per unit. In the short run, the plant may be operated below or above the designed output. If a plant is operated at 80 per cent of the designed output, then 80 per cent is its *rate of capacity utilization*. Average cost is higher for outputs below, and higher for outputs above, the designed, or capacity, output. Thus the average cost curve is always *U*-shaped. The two sides of the *U* can be steep, or so nearly flat that the curve looks more like the profile of a shallow saucer. If the capacity output, i.e., the minimum-cost output, happens also to be a physical limit that cannot be exceeded, then the *AVC* and *MC* curves rise vertically at the capacity output.

But the curves of average variable cost and of marginal cost need not have a smooth *U*-shape, as they do in Figure 11–3. In fact, both curves can be horizontal over a wide range of output. When they are, *AVC* and *MC* are equal to each other. That is, if the *AVC* curve

---

[2] Of course the firm has to know *how* to minimize the cost of any level of output. For a debate on whether farmers minimize the costs of fertilizers, see chaps. 15 and 16 in Donald Stevenson Watson, ed., *Price Theory in Action: A Book of Readings,* 3d ed. Houghton Mifflin, Boston, 1973.

[3] Some theorists call it *optimum output*. But to do so can be misleading, because of the implication that the firm always wants to produce this output. The firm wants to produce this output, however, only when it happens to coincide with the profit-maximizing output.

FIGURE 11–5   **DIVISIBLE PLANT**

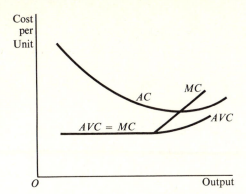

is horizontal, *AVC* is constant; one more unit has the same average variable cost and therefore the same marginal cost.

The firm's plant and equipment and the variable inputs can be combined in varying or in constant proportions. Up to this point, the assumption has been that the proportions are variable, as indeed they often are. But now the constant proportion—e.g., one worker to operate one machine—has to be recognized as a fact of life too and built into the analysis.

Figure 11–5 shows constancy of *AVC* and *MC* over a range of output. Over this range there are constant marginal returns to the variable inputs. Output and total variable cost increase by the same percentage as do the variable inputs. Notice however that *AVC* and *MC* turn up at the right; after some point marginal returns begin to diminish and costs per unit begin to increase.

Several empirical studies of short-run cost functions have found that over the observed range of output marginal cost is indeed constant, or so close to it that marginal cost can be treated as a constant.

Another type of short-run cost curve often appears in the newer literature on public utility economics. At any one time, an electric power plant has a clear-cut capacity it cannot exceed. This fact causes the *AVC*, *MC*, and *AC* curves abruptly to become vertical when output reaches capacity. Figure 11–6 shows this type of short-run cost function. It also displays another characteristic of electric power plants—average variable cost is a small part of total cost per unit. Reflecting the high fixed cost, the *AC* curve lies far above the *AVC* and *MC* curves.

The Learning Curve

The cost curves discussed so far show at each point the minimum cost of the output in question. They do so because of the tangencies

FIGURE 11–6   **SHORT-RUN COST CURVES FOR AN ELECTRIC POWER PLANT**

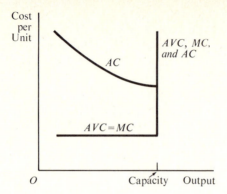

of isocost lines to isoquants. The tangencies signify minimization of costs. Remember too that an isoquant represents the maximum output from the different possible combinations of labor and capital.

But the first batch of a new product produced with a new technology usually has a higher unit cost than later batches. When color TV sets first came out, most people seemed to think that the unit costs of making the sets would fall and thus make it possible for retail prices to be lower. Pocket electronic calculators and digital watches are two more examples. The rapid pace of technology since the end of World War II, together with growing cultivation of analytical techniques, have caused close attention to be given to the costs of new products. The *learning curve* is a generalization about these costs. The expression itself is borrowed from psychology, which has found that any animal, a rat or a human, learns something at some rate by repeated trials.

Also called a *progress function*, a learning curve shows the decline in unit costs as the number of units produced increases. Experience in the aircraft industry has shown that a commonly found learning curve is an "80 per cent curve." Such a curve means that with each doubling of the cumulative number produced, costs fall to (about) 80 per cent of their previous level. In practice, the cost figures employed are usually direct labor only, i.e., just a part of variable costs. To illustrate: Suppose the first 500 units are produced at a payroll cost of $100 each. The cost per unit of 1,000 units falls to $80; and when cumulative production is 2,000 units, the cost per unit is $64 (80 per cent of $80). And so on. Eventually, of course, the unit cost levels out.

The process of learning is one of acquiring greater familiarity with the details of tasks, of modifying tools and procedures, and of improving coordination. The learning curve need not be an 80 per cent curve; apparently its range is between about 75 and about 90 per cent. Analysis of experience is firm enough that the curve can often be used for prediction. Thus if a company gets an order to produce, say, 10,000 units of a totally new piece of equipment, analysts can make a good estimate of the costs of the 10,000th unit, after they know the costs of the 100th one.

So much for the learning curve. All the other cost curves in this book carry the assumption that the learning process, where it might be relevant, has been completed.

LONG-RUN COST CURVES

In the long run, all is variable. The firm's production function has no fixed inputs; the firm has no fixed costs. The firm expands its output by building and operating a wholly new and larger plant. Input-output relations in the production function are those of returns to scale.

Figure 11–7 has three short-run cost curves. The curves for the full average cost of the firm are now labeled *SAC*, i.e., short-run average cost. The curves in Figure 11–7 are for three sizes of plant. Plant *A* is the smallest, with costs SAC_A. Plant *B* is larger and operates at much lower costs, owing to the presence of increasing returns to scale. Curve SAC_B is much lower, except at its extreme left end. Plant *C* is still larger, but the curve SAC_C is higher, because decreasing returns to scale have begun to show themselves.

Clearly, the firm will build and operate plant *A* or a smaller one, if the firm expects to produce a volume of output equal to *OA* or less. If, instead, output is to be in the range of *OB* or *OC*, the firm will decide on plant *B* or plant *C*. Notice that if the firm is to produce an output a little larger than *OA*, it would choose plant *B*, because costs are lower. Take the output *OA'*. This output is the capacity of plant *A* and is the minimum cost from operating plant *A*. Obviously it is better, in producing the amount *OA'*, to run plant *B* at *less* than its capacity. This proposition can be generalized: When there are increasing returns to scale, the minimum cost of any output can be

FIGURE 11–7   **THREE SHORT-RUN COST CURVES**

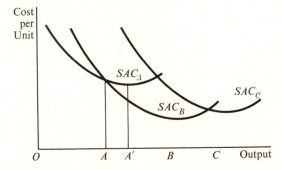

FIGURE 11–8   **DERIVATION OF LONG-RUN COST CURVE**

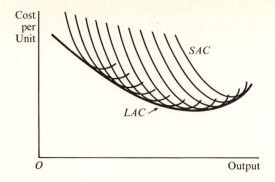

obtained by operating, at less than its capacity, a plant that is larger than the plant whose own minimum cost corresponds to the output in question.

Imagine next that the firm can build many plants, each one just a little larger. The several curves in Figure 11–8 are the *SAC* curves for successively larger plants. The curve *LAC*, long-run average cost, is tangent to the lower portions of the *SAC* curves. Geometrically, the *LAC* curve is the "envelope" of the *SAC* curves.

Economic theorists, like other people, can make mistakes. A famous mistake in the literature of price theory was the one committed by Jacob Viner in his well-known article of 1931 in which he developed the modern theory of the cost curves of a firm. Viner instructed his draftsman, though in vain, to draw the charts for the article so that the *LAC* curve would be tangent to the *SAC* curves at their minimum points. This is possible, however, only if the *LAC* curve is a horizontal line. When the *LAC* curve is declining, it is tangent to the *SAC* curves necessarily to the left of their minimum points. And when the *LAC* curve is rising, it has to touch the *SAC* curves to the right of their minimum points. Viner later acknowledged his mistake with good grace. In reprints of his article, he allowed the error to stand uncorrected so that others can have the pleasure of enjoying a knowledge of geometry superior to his of 1931.

Of course, a firm does not build dozens of plants, just to see what happens to costs. But a firm does have to decide how big its plant should be. In making the decision, the firm surveys the range of minimum costs. The firm knows the range either from experience or from engineering studies. For this reason, the *LAC* curve is often referred to as *the planning curve* of the firm.

It is quite plain that the short-run cost curve of the firm has to be *U*-shaped; the presence of the fixed inputs sees to that. What of the shape of the long-run cost curve? Everyone agrees that the long-run

FIGURE 11-9

CONVENTIONAL COST CURVES

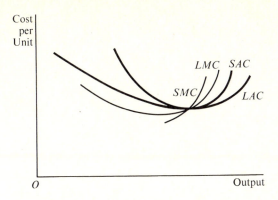

curve first turns down, because of initial economies of scale. But must there be a unique minimum-cost point and an upturn after that?

The conventional shape of the long-run cost curve is shown in Figure 11-9. Here the long-run marginal cost curve is also shown; this curve shows the change in total cost when output is expanded with the construction of successively larger plants. Suppose the firm is producing at the minimum point on *LAC*. Figure 11-9 also displays the short-run average and marginal cost curves for the same output. If it expands output with the same plant, the firm moves along the *SMC* curve. But if it expands output by building a bigger plant, the firm moves along the lower *LMC* curve.

Chapter 14 will show that the logic of profit maximization in the long run and in pure competition requires the *LAC* curve to turn up at the right. The discussion of decreasing returns to scale in Chapter 9 shows that though there is agreement that returns to scale eventually decrease, there is little agreement about just why this must be so. Decreasing returns and a rising *LAC* curve are, of course, the opposite sides of the same coin.

Actually, it is probable that the shape of the curve in Figure 11-10 is typical. Much postwar thinking and empirical research support this version. Observe that over some range of output the curve is perfectly flat. Over this range, all sizes of plants have the same minimum costs. In many industries, in fact, different sizes of plants do coexist and apparently have about the same costs. The length of the initial declining portion of the curve must, however, differ much from one industry to the other.

In brief, the long-run curve is more likely to be *L*-shaped than *U*-shaped.

APPLICATIONS

The chief applications of the cost-output analyses presented in this chapter are as aids to clear thinking. An apparently universal belief

FIGURE 11–10   PROBABLE SHAPE OF MANY LONG-RUN COST CURVES

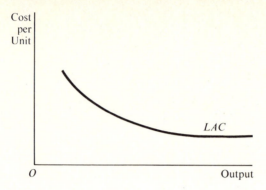

is that larger outputs bring lower costs. This is the everyday doctrine of spreading the overhead over more units so as to cut cost per unit. The doctrine is true—in the short run and over some range of output. But it is not true for outputs beyond the capacity output. Furthermore, how fast unit cost falls with output depends on how large the fixed costs are. If they are a small part of total costs, and if the average variable and marginal costs are constant, then the decline in unit cost with larger quantities of output is not much. At the other extreme, if fixed costs are a large fraction of the total, and if average variable and marginal costs fall over a wide range of output, then unit cost declines rapidly with more output.

Then too, the long-run cost-output relation should never be confused with the short-run relation.

Allocation of Output Between Two Plants

Suppose a firm has two plants. How should the firm allocate output between the two plants so as to minimize cost? The cost to be minimized is the total variable cost. There is no sense in talking about minimizing the fixed cost, in a problem like this, because it is a short-run problem. The fixed cost is fixed and cannot be reduced.

To minimize its variable cost, the firm allocates output between its two plants so that the two marginal costs are equal. This statement is illustrated in Figure 11–11. The figure is so constructed that *OD* is the total output to be allocated. This output is given because this is the amount that consumers take at the price charged by the firm. This output can be produced by *either* one of the firm's two plants—plant *A* or plant *B*. The marginal cost of plant *A* is given by the curve MC_A, which goes from left to right. Plant *B*'s marginal cost curve—MC_B—goes from right to left. The two curves intersect at point *C*. When plant *A* produces the amount *OQ*, and when plant *B* produces the amount *DQ*, total variable cost is minimized. If plant *A*

FIGURE 11-11   **ALLOCATION OF OUTPUT FROM TWO PLANTS**

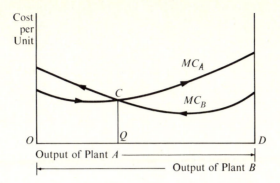

produced more and plant *B* less, cost would be higher, because the *MC_A* curve lies above the *MC_B* curve to the right of point *C*. Similarly, cost would be higher if plant *B* produced more and plant *A* less. Another way of stating that point *C* gives minimum cost is this: Total variable cost is the area under the marginal cost curves. Another look at Figure 11-11 shows that the area for the combined output is least when point *C* defines the allocation of output.

Notice that the curves in Figure 11-11 are drawn so that plant *B* has a lower marginal cost for any given output. Nevertheless, it is rational to have some output from plant *A*. Notice too that both curves are rising at point *C*. This condition is necessary for the solution.

Marginal Cost and Incremental Cost

Marginal cost holds the attention of the rational decision maker. Suppose, however, that the decision maker cannot even in imagination, vary the output by one unit more or less. For many different kinds of practical reasons, outputs are often variable only in batches, or in more or less definite increments of some size. Incremental cost, the cost of an extra batch, is therefore often the closest practical approximation to marginal cost. Rational business decisions, accordingly, can be made on the basis of incremental cost which is compared with incremental revenue, the extra revenue from the same-sized batch of output.

Shape of the Long-Run Cost Curve

It is not much of an exaggeration to say that a good part of the economic foundation of the antitrust laws depends on the shape of the long-run curve of a firm. The antitrust laws attempt to maintain competition. Among other things, competition means the existence of many firms in an industry rather than one or a few. If long-run cost curves would decline and keep on declining indefinitely, then

costs would be at a minimum if only one firm produced each commodity. If this were so, the policy of maintaining competition would
stand condemned on the ground that it would keep costs up; it would
result in economic inefficiency. The shape of the long-run cost
curve, as shown in Figure 11–10, is probably typical of cost curves
in much of American industry.

One of the justifications of the government regulation of the
public utility industries also has to do with the shape of the long-run
cost curve. Some of these industries, e.g., electric power, are
natural monopolies, which can be defined as industries where competition would result in wasteful duplication of facilities. The same
idea can be expressed this way: A natural monopoly enjoys such
great economies of scale that it produces on the declining part of its
long-run cost curve. If two companies were to do business in the
same area, each one would produce less. Each would therefore be
farther up and to the left on its cost curve. The total costs of the two
together would be thus higher than if there were only one firm.

SUMMARY

Price theory devotes its attention to two cost-output relations: the
short run and the long. The simplest short-run relation contains the
assumption that average variable cost is constant. Then marginal
cost and average variable cost are equal. Average fixed cost plus
average variable cost equals average cost. The *break-even chart*
shows the output whose total cost equals its total revenue, as well as
the outputs where profits and losses exist. The family of the conventional *short-run cost curves* consists of the curves for *average fixed
cost, average variable cost, average cost,* and *marginal cost.* The
AVC, AC, and MC curves are U-shaped because of variable proportions in the production function, which has some fixed inputs in the
short run. The MC curve intersects both the AVC and the AC curves
at their minimum points. The MC curve is the key curve because
rational decisions are based on marginal costs. It is possible that
$AVC = MC$ over some range of output. Cost curves for new products typically drop down as the firm gains experience. The *long-run
cost curve* of a firm is derived by drawing a curve tangent to a
succession of SAC curves for ever larger plants. The LAC curve
shows the minimum cost of any output. The LAC curve can be
horizontal over some range of output; it is more likely to be
L-shaped than U-shaped. The theory of the cost-output relations of
the firm has numerous applications, both in business decision making and as a foundation for economic policy in the antitrust and
public utility fields.

SELECTED REFERENCES

On the theory: Jacob Viner, "Cost Curves and Supply Curves," *Zeitschrift für Nationalökonomie,* 1931 [reprinted in *Readings in Price Theory,* ed. George J. Stigler and Kenneth E. Boulding (Irwin, Homewood, 1952)]; George J. Stigler, "Production and Distribution in the Short Run," *Journal of Political Economy,* 1939 [reprinted in American Economic Association, *Readings in the Theory of Income Distribution* (Philadelphia: Blakiston, 1946)]; Edward H. Chamberlin, *The Theory of Monopolistic Competition,* 8th ed. (Harvard University Press, Cambridge, 1962), app. B.

Empirical and statistical investigations of the theory: Joel Dean, *Managerial Economics* (Prentice-Hall, New Jersey, 1951), chap. 5; J. Johnston, *Statistical Cost Analysis* (McGraw-Hill, New York, 1960); George J. Stigler, "The Economies of Scale," *Journal of Law and Economics,* 1 (October 1958), 54–71; A. A. Walters, "Production and Cost Functions: An Econometric Survey," *Econometrica,* 31 (January–April 1963); Donald Stevenson Watson, ed., *Price Theory in Action: A Book of Readings,* 3d ed. (Houghton Mifflin, Boston, 1973), part 3.

Business applications: W. Warren Haynes and William R. Henry, *Managerial Economics: Analysis and Cases,* 3d ed. (Business Publications, Dallas, 1974), chap. 6. Farming applications: Rueben C. Buse and Daniel W. Bromley, *Applied Economics: Resource Allocation in Rural America* (Iowa State University Press, Ames, 1975), chap. 6.

EXERCISES AND PROBLEMS

1. Construct a break-even chart with cost curves like those in Figure 11–2 and with a total revenue curve corresponding to the sloping demand curve of a firm.
2. Show that where *LAC* is rising, the firm is operating at an output in excess of the level where *SAC* is a minimum.
3. Why does *SAC* descend faster than *LAC*?
4. Suppose you publish paperback books which sell at retail for 50¢; of this, you receive 35¢. Suppose that before you can print a single copy of a book, you have to spend $4,500—mainly for typesetting and for the metal plates from which the book is printed. Assume that paper and binding for each copy cost you 20¢. For this one book, what is the fixed cost, the variable cost, the marginal cost? What is the break-even point? Make a cost schedule like that in Table 11–1. Draw a break-even chart for the book.
5. Imagine that the executives of a business firm complain about

the rising costs of labor and materials during the last year. Examination of the firm's cost records reveals, however, that average (business) cost has *not* gone up during the year. How can this be? Draw the diagram. (Hint: The firm's output this year is greater.)

6. When spokesmen for farmers or ranchers complain about a specific price per bushel or per hundredweight, they usually say that the price is below "the" cost of production. Which cost are they talking about—*SMC* or *LMC* or *SAC* or *LAC* or *AVC* or what? And do all the producers have "the" same cost?

7. Explain how cost functions are derived from production functions.

8. Explain the relation between diminishing returns and the following cost-output functions: (a) total cost, (b) total variable cost, (c) marginal cost, (d) average variable cost, and (e) average total cost.

9. Assume that the total fixed costs of a firm amount to $500,000 each calendar quarter and that the output during the period ranges from 1,000 to 100,000 units. Draw a diagram that shows average fixed cost.

10. Economists sometimes assume that the average cost curve is horizontal. Explain what could cause such a cost curve.

11. Explain why average total cost and average variable cost tend to get closer as output increases. Will the curves ever converge?

12
Linear
Programming

From time immemorial, people have made their decisions on how to produce their commodities. Throughout most of history, the decisions were made in the same way year after year in conformity with the patterns dictated by custom and culture. Under the capitalism of the last two centuries, decisions on production began to be increasingly rational, becoming conscious and deliberate choices of the best means to attain clearly defined ends. Price theory is the generalized description of rational decisions in production, as well as in exchange and consumption.

But the theory of the firm, as presented in the last three chapters, shows business people making decisions about one variable at a time or, at the most, about two at a time. Suppose that, as is so often true, a business executive must take dozens or hundreds of variables into account all at once. What then? Economic theory can still give the answer, can still point to the cost-minimizing or profit-maximizing decision. Theory's answers here are not in the simple geometry of the last three chapters; the answers are couched in the language of higher mathematics. Generally speaking, however, the form of the mathematics is such that the answers cannot be put to specific practical use.

Alfred Marshall handled the problem of production decisions with his *principle of substitution*. He saw business people as always studying the production function and input prices. As they change, business people continually substitute one input for another, thus keeping costs as low as possible. Anyone managing a business, said Marshall, "works generally by trained instinct rather than formal calculation."

A method of formal calculation is now available, however. The method can be regarded as an extension and a special case of price theory. At the same time, the method, which is called *linear programming*, can be applied in the solution of a wide range of practical business problems.

LINEAR PROGRAMMING

Linear programming[1] is a technique that uses sophisticated mathematics to solve certain kinds of problems, especially production problems. *Linear* means that the relationships handled are the same as those represented by straight lines. *Programming* simply means systematic planning or decision making. Also called *mathematical programming* and *activity analysis*, the technique was developed in 1947 by the mathematician George B. Dantzig for the purpose of scheduling the complicated procurement activities of the United States Air Force.[2]

Since 1947, linear programming has advanced far both in its theory and in its applications to practical problems in industry. The postwar development of computers has contributed to the growth of linear programming, which in practice usually requires extensive numerical computations. Linear programming has become a set of special cases of the economic theory of the firm. As presented in Chapters 8–11, the conventional theory, as it can now be called, is more general; it covers the short run and the long run, linear and curvilinear relations, and cost-output relations over any range of output.

Because some of its leading ideas are mathematical, a complete description of linear programming cannot be given here. But its economic content can be surveyed along with some of the modifications that it makes in the theory of the firm.

SOME BASIC CONCEPTS OF LINEAR PROGRAMMING

Apart from those that are purely mathematical, the main ideas of linear programming are essentially simple. Both the theory and its applications have concentrated on the short-run decisions about output by firms with given prices for both their inputs and their outputs.

Optimization and Choice

The central feature of linear programming is that it gives actual numerical solutions to problems of making optimum choices when the problems have to be solved within definite bounds or constraints.

Linearity

Linearity is both a simplifying assumption and a useful statement about the input-output relations that often prevail. The linear assumption makes the complicated mathematics of programming simpler than they would otherwise have to be. The economic meanings of linearity are constant returns (marginal products and average products are equal) and, again, the given prices of inputs and outputs (which can be shown on price-quantity diagrams by horizontal

---

[1] A formal definition: Linear programming is the maximization (or minimization) of a linear function of variables subject to a constraint of linear inequalities.

[2] Actually, the Russian mathematician L. V. Kantorovich first formulated linear programming. For this, he was named joint winner of the Nobel Prize in Economic Science in 1975. But Dantzig invented a superior technique of computation.

lines). Though the American economy did not suddenly become linear after 1947, the existence of constant returns over some range of output is common. This of course means that costs per unit are constant over that range and that average variable costs and marginal costs are equal. Linear programming techniques, accordingly, can be applied when cost curves resemble those in Figure 11–5 on page 193. Then too, even if the returns and costs of a firm are not exactly linear, they might be so close to it that the linear assumption is warranted for all practical purposes. Linear assumptions are frequently employed in this book for the sake of simplicity and owing to the influence of linear programming itself.

Not all mathematical programming is linear. Nonlinear, or *curvilinear*, programming techniques set up problems like those in conventional theory, where curves instead of straight lines show the relations. But nonlinear programming raises formidable mathematical difficulties. Still another variant is *integer* programming. Here the problems are set up so that the solutions come out in integers, i.e., whole numbers. No fractions are allowed. The solution to a transportation problem is, say, 8 jet planes, not $7\frac{3}{4}$ or $8\frac{1}{2}$.

Processes

A process is another basic concept in linear programming. A *process*, also called an activity, is a way of doing things. A process is a combination of particular inputs to produce a particular output. A truck driver and a truck are a process—they can carry so many tons so many miles in a week. The *level* of a process means how many trucks with one driver each are used. The linear assumption means that two trucks carry twice as much as one, four trucks twice as much as two, etc.

The notion of a process is essentially technological. A process is a complex, large or small, of workers and equipment. Each process uses factors—labor and capital—in fixed ratios. Thus there is no substitution within a process. In contrast, conventional theory assumes easy substitution among inputs—along a smooth isoquant.

The firm has several processes, each of which can be carried on at several levels to produce the firm's product. One process can be substituted for another. When two or more processes are used together, they do not interfere with one another or enhance one another. This last is another simplifying assumption. A typical linear programming problem is to find the optimum combination of processes, i.e., the combination that minimizes costs when there are constraints. A simple example will be given below.

The Objective Function

Linear programming has fashioned its own language. Simple economic ideas are dressed in new terminology. A good example is *the objective function*.

The objective function, also called the *criterion function*, states the determinants of the quantity to be maximized or to be minimized. Profits, or revenues, are the objective function when they are to be maximized. Costs are the objective function when the problem calls for them to be minimized. Cost minimization is the "dual" of profit maximization, and vice versa. The significance of the dual is that the solution to a firm's problem of minimizing costs can be converted mathematically into the solution for maximizing profits, without having to start the whole analysis from the very beginning. Much deep thought and hard work have to go into just setting up a problem in linear programming.

Constraints

Constraints, also called *restraints*, are limitations. They are things you can't do and things you have to do. The budget of a consumer is a constraint. If a firm is maximizing revenue, then it is limited, or constrained, by the facts that it has, for example, only 10 machines, only so many square feet of floor space, etc. Also, machine *A* has to have 1 operator, machine *B* has to have at least 2, etc. Constraints are also known as *inequalities*. That is to say, 10 or fewer (≤ 10) machines are available and 2 or more (≥ 2) workers are needed to operate machine *B*, and so on.

Feasible Solutions

Feasible solutions can be explored after the constraints are established. Feasible solutions are those that meet, or satisfy, the constraints. Feasible solutions for the consumer are all of the possible combinations of commodities that can be possibly, i.e., feasibly, bought, given the consumer's income and the prices of the commodities. With two commodities, feasible solutions for the consumer are all those combinations of the two goods that are on and to the left of the budget line; for a reminder, see page 65. Similarly, one kind of feasible solution for the firm consists of all the combinations of two inputs that lie on or to the right of an isocost line; see page 176.

Optimum Solutions

The *optimum solution*, of course, is the best of the feasible solutions. Sometimes linear programming results in finding several feasible solutions, all equally good and all better than any others. Then there is no single optimum. Simple examples of this will be given below.

The *simplex method* of solution is not simple but is the name of a commonly used mathematical and computational procedure for finding the optimum solution. In essence, the simplex method, which is a set of successive marginal calculations, consists of successively testing feasible solutions, successively eliminating the poorer ones, until finally the optimum solution emerges.

With geometrical techniques resembling those employed in the preceding chapters, three specimens of linear programming analysis will now follow. One shows how a firm maximizes its profits and two show how a firm minimizes its costs.

The easiest linear programming problem to understand is one of maximizing profits in the production of two products where production is subject to three constraints. This is a *product mix* problem. The two products can be produced in different proportions, or mixes; the problem is to find the profit-maximizing mix.

In the marginal analysis of conventional theory, the firm with two products has a production possibility curve that is smooth and continuous, signifying that the firm can cary the proportions of the two products by infinitesimally small amounts. This is back on page 179. But now we have a firm whose production facilities have fixed physical capacities.

In Figure 12–1, the firm has a plant turning out two products, X and Y. Production is subject to constraints A, B, and C. Monthly output of X is limited by the capacity of machine A; no more than OA of X can be produced. Monthly output of Y is constrained by the capacity of another machine which is B; no more than OB of Y can be produced. The rectangle formed by the axes and by lines AA' and BB' accordingly shows the combined effects of these two constraints. Now comes constraint C, which is, say, the paint shop. Both products have to be painted. The line CC' defines the monthly capacity of the paint shop. The slope of the line indicates that if more units of Y are to be painted, then fewer units of X can be.

The shaded area in Figure 12–1 is thus the zone of feasible production. The three straight lines BE, EF, and FA together form the linear programming version of the production possibility curve. Any combination, or mix, of X and Y on one of the straight lines is feasible; so also is any combination inside the zone. But it is impossible to produce X and Y in a combination shown by a point lying outside the zone.

Now the profits. The two products X and Y sell at certain prices. From their prices subtract for X and Y the unit costs of materials, labor, fuel, power, etc. The differences are the "profits" per unit for X and Y. This definition is really the same as price minus average variable cost. Such a definition of unit profit is customary in this context; no harm is done so long as it is not confused with other definitions. Anyway, let the profit per unit for X be \$10 and the profit per unit for Y be \$40.

Next come isoprofit lines. They are constructed in the same way as isocost lines (page 175) and isorevenue lines (page 180). Three isoprofit lines are shown in Figure 12–1. The line labeled \$40,000 touches the Y-axis at point B. Since Y has a unit profit of \$40, the

FIGURE 12-1

MAXIMIZING PROFITS

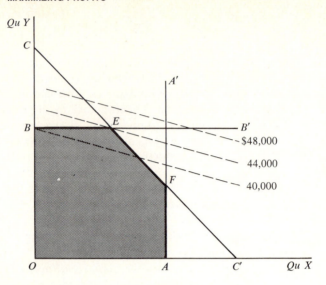

distance *OB* must stand for 1,000 units of *Y*. Where the $40,000 line touches the *X*-axis is not shown, but the point can easily be visualized. It is 4,000 units of *X*, because of *X*'s unit profit of $10. The slope of an isoprofit line is the ratio of the *X* profit to the *Y* profit; here it is 1:4. The farther northeast it is, the greater the volume of profits.

The optimum solution is at point *E* in Figure 12-1. Here profits are a maximum at $44,000 a month. Any other of the feasible combinations of the two products would yield a lower profit. The solution at *E* is a *corner solution*. When there is a unique optimum, linear programming solutions are always at corners. Figure 12-1 has only two corners where both *X* and *Y* can be produced, because there are only three constraints. With more constraints, there are more corners. In the actual uses of linear programming, computers are programmed to find the algebraic equivalent of corners and to search out the optimum corner.

Another look at Figure 12-1 will show that a small change in the slope of the isoprofit line would not alter the optimality of the solution at point *E*. The slope could change because of changes in the prices of *X* and *Y*, in their costs, or both. There would have to be a substantial change in slope to move the solution from corner *E* to corner *F*. In contrast, the firm of the conventional marginal analysis would alter its operations for *any* change in costs or prices, because isocost and isorevenue lines are tangent to smooth curves.

Suppose next that the unit profits from *X* and *Y* would shift in such a way as to give rise to isoprofit lines exactly parallel to line *EF* in Figure 12–1. What then? If this should happen, there is no corner to go to. There are still maximum profits, although they are obtainable from any product mix corresponding to any point between E and F.

Shadow Prices   The linear programming problem just discussed is one of maximizing profits subject to the constraints imposed by the limited capacities of three resources. Such a problem can be reformulated, mathematically, and turned into a problem of minimizing costs. The original or initial problem of maximization is called *the primal* and the associated problem of minimization is known as *the dual*. The calculation of the dual yields *shadow prices* for the limited resources. Another name for shadow prices is *implicit values*.

Shadow prices are the calculated values of increments of the limited resources that are bottlenecks of production.

Another glance at point E in Figure 12–1 will show this: Resource A is not fully utilized. The optimum solution at point E calls for BE units of X, but the capacity of resource A is OA units of X. In contrast, both resources B and C are employed to their full capacities.

Thus resource B and resource C are bottlenecks. If B's capacity could be increased, more of Y could be produced and sold and thus profits could be larger. Although B is a machine, assume that modifications of it can increase its capacity. Now imagine that machine B's capacity can be increased by 1 per cent. The additional profit that would result is called the shadow price of B. Similarly, a 1–per cent expansion of the capacity of resource C, the paint shop, would cause an increase in profit which is the shadow price of C.

What about resource A? This resource has a zero shadow price. The zero shadow price for A does not signify that A is useless or worthless. The zero price means that *more* of A has no value in the circumstances.

If, however, the optimum solution were at the other corner, F, things would be different. Then A and C would be bottlenecks and B would not. B would then be the resource with the zero shadow price. For the solution to be at F, the unit profits obtainable from the sale of products X and Y would have to be quite different from what they are with the solution at E. Thus the shadow prices of the bottleneck resources depend on the profits from the products, as well as on the productive features of the resources.

Shadow prices are not prices actually paid or received. They are the implicit values of increments of bottlenecks. The shadow prices of resources B and C show the values per month (because the example has everything on a monthly basis) of small increments in the resources. Management can compare the shadow prices with estimates of the costs of modifying and expanding the capacities of the two resources. If the cost figures, converted to a monthly basis, are lower than the shadow prices, and if expectations of the future are favorable, it is clear that expansion would be profitable.

The literature on linear programming mentions another way that calculated shadow prices can be used. A large corporation with many divisions each with one or more plants and with decentralized management faces the problem of getting the subunits to pull together in making profits. One manager might increase the profits from a plant at the expense of profits from another plant by, for example, using too much of a scarce resource available to both plants. Such scarce resources could be corporationwide transport and storage facilities, the services of expert engineers, etc. It is not enough to tell each plant manager to maximize profits. There must be a mechanism to ensure that profits from each plant mesh into one grand maximum for the corporation. For the corporation as a whole, a linear programming solution (which would probably be attained only after overcoming the most formidable difficulties) for maximum profits would yield shadow prices for scarce corporationwide facilities. Plant managers would be directed to use these facilities only if they could "pay" for them.

Shadow prices can also be calculated and put to work in decision making in government. Here, shadow prices are the implicit values of unpriced or inadequately priced goods and services produced by governmental units. Imagine a government-owned and operated reservoir whose output is both drinking water and recreation facilities. Suppose that there are constraints on both the production of water and of recreation. Suppose too that production of more water must cause the production of less recreation. Next, assume that the government unit operating the reservoir plans to increase its capacity to produce drinking water. What would be the benefits of carrying out the plan? This is where the shadow prices come in. They should be calculated for both the expansion of water and the contraction of recreation. Then the dollar value of the loss of benefits from less recreation can be subtracted from the dollar value of the benefits from more drinking water. The resulting net benefits can then be compared with estimates of the costs of modifying and expanding the capacity of the reservoir to produce more water. If the government unit does not have a linear programming solution to its problem of shadow prices, it might try to adopt prices, or values, of water and recreation produced elsewhere.

MINIMIZING COSTS

In conventional theory, the firm minimizes the costs of using two inputs by buying them in such proportions that the isoquants are tangent to the iocost lines. The constraints that are central to linear programming techniques have the effect of modifying the shapes of isoquants.

A Simplified Diet Problem

The diet problem was one of the first to be tackled by the linear programming techniques. The problem is to minimize the cost of a diet that has to meet minimum nutritional requirements, which are the constraints. Happily, the diets in question are for animals. Several feedstuffs are purchasable. All have different prices per unit; all possess different amounts per pound of nutrients—vitamins, minerals, proteins, calories, etc. Which combination is cheapest for the purpose?

Consider a highly simplified example. A farmer feeds animals with two varieties of grain. The diet for the animals must give them each day certain minimum amounts of three nutrients. The objective function is the minimization of the cost of the diet. There are two variables, each with a price. There are three constraints. What are feasible solutions? What is the optimum solution?

In Figure 12–2, the horizontal axis shows pounds of grain *A* and the vertical axis measures pounds of grain *B*. The minimum daily requirement per animal of nutrient I is met by *OF* pounds of grain *A*, or by *OE* pounds of grain *B*. Thus the line *EF* shows how to combine grains *A* and *B* to provide nutrient I. The different points on line *EF* represent different combinations of pounds of the two grains; any of the combinations is just as good as any other in meeting the minimum requirements for nutrient I. The steep slope of line *EF* shows that grain *A* is much richer in this nutrient, because in any combination shown by the line, fewer pounds of *A* are needed. Similarly, lines *GH* and *JK* show how the two grains can be combined to provide the minimum daily requirement of nutrients II and III.

FIGURE 12–2   FINDING THE MINIMUM COST OF A DIET

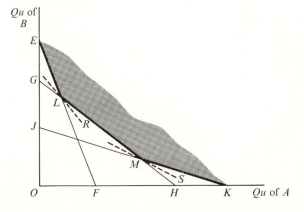

Each point on the heavy line segments *ELMK* is a different pair of quantities of the two grains; each pair meets all three of the nutritional requirements. Any point on the heavy line just meets one of the requirements, but it exceeds the other two. Notice also that the heavy line does look like an isoquant. The line is not, however, a smooth curve; it consists of *linear* segments.

Feasible solutions are points on the heavy line or to the right of it. The stippled area is a zone of feasible solutions. *Any* point in it is feasible, showing that the animals can be fed as they should. But the animals are not pets. Because they are being raised to be sold at a profit, the farmer wants minimum costs.

To solve for the optimum, prices have to be brought in. They come in as isocost lines, whose positions show levels of total costs and whose slopes show the ratios of the prices of grain *A* and grain *B*. In Figure 12–2, the dashed lines *R* and *S* are two possible isocost lines. To minimize costs, the farmer wants to get to the lowest attainable isocost line. Take first the isocost line *R*. In the figure, line *R* occupies its lowest position, touching the point *L*. The point *L* is the optimum when the price ratio is indicated by the line *R*. Here grain *B* has the lower price per pound, the optimum solution being to feed more pounds of *B* than of *A*. Suppose, however, that prices are indicated by the isocost line *S*. Then the optimum would be at *M*, because here *A* is the cheaper grain.

Assume that the price ratio is in fact given by the slope of the line *R*. Then, as was just shown, *L* is the optimum solution. Notice that the solution is not a tangency, but again a *corner*. Figure 12–2 has only two corners because there are only three constraints. With more constraints, there are more corners. If there were several feedstuffs instead of just two grains, geometry fails and higher mathematics takes over.

One more look at Figure 12–2 shows this: The line *R* can pivot a bit while still hitting the corner *L*. That is, the prices can change a little without affecting *L*'s optimality. Suppose, however, that line *R* changes so that its slope is identical with the slope of the line segment *LM*. If this should happen, the one optimum vanishes. Then *either L, M, or any* point between them is optimum.

Linear programming is in fact used by companies that sell feed mixes for livestock and poultry. With many ingredients and many separate nutritional requirements, the problem of finding the actual minimum cost of a feed mix is formidable. It cannot be solved on the back of an envelope. Feed companies employ research organizations, whose inputs of labor and capital—mathematicians and computers—provide linear programming solutions. The prices of some of the ingredients in feed mixes are constantly changing. The feed companies telephone the price changes to the research organizations. In a short time, the feed companies get the instructions they seek—whether and how to alter their feed mixes so as to keep their costs always as low as possible. It is just as if, in Figure 12–2, prices would change from R to S, moving the corner optimum from L to M.

Only one more point needs to be made about feeding the animals. How many pounds of the correctly proportioned feed should they get? No linear programming is required here because that is a straightforward problem in diminishing returns. The more pounds of feed mix per day, the greater the gain in weight (or the more milk or eggs, or whatever it might be). The abundant empirical evidence on this kind of input-output relation always shows diminishing marginal physical product. Clearly the solution depends upon the (minimized) cost of the feed mix, the price of the output, and on how fast the marginal product diminishes. The analysis to be applied here is described on pages 174 and 175.

Note 6 in the Appendix to Part 2 gives a very simple numerical example of the minimization of costs subject to constraints.

Choice of Processes

A firm's labor and equipment are organized in *complexes*, i.e., *processes* or *activities*. One of the firm's problems is how best to combine its processes, how to divide its output among them. A simplified example will now be presented.

First comes the concept of the *process ray*. Figure 12–3 contains three process rays. Consider first the line *OB*, which is a process ray. The horizontal axis measures labor-hours; the vertical axis measures machine-hours. The line *OB* is scaled in units of the firm's output. The marks on the line can be taken to represent, successively, 10, 20, 30, etc. units of output per period, or 100, 200, 300 etc. units. The line *OB* is drawn at an angle of 45°, signifying a

FIGURE 12–3   **THREE PROCESS RAYS**

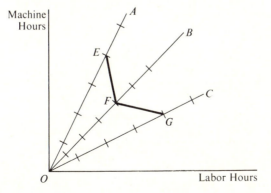

process with equal numbers of labor-hours and machine-hours at any level. The line *OB* therefore stands for a one-worker, one-machine process. In contrast, the line *OA* stands for one worker and two machines; the number of machine-hours is always double the corresponding number of labor-hours on line *OA*. Notice that *OA* is scaled a little differently; process *A* is, say, older and physically less efficient. The line *OC* stands for still a different worker-machine process; here the machine needs two operators.

The kinked line *EFG* in Figure 12-3 is an isoquant or, at least, a portion of one. Any point on the line *EFG* represents a process or a combination of two processes that produces the same quantity of output. An output of 40 (or 400, etc.) units can be produced with process *A* (point *E*), or with a combination of *B* and *C* (points between *F* and *G*), or with process *C*.

In other words: At point *E* in Figure 12-3, the firm is using process *A* exclusively and has an output of 40 units. At point *E*, the firm is on the process ray *A*. If instead the firm is at a point on the line *EF*, the firm is using two processes—both *A* and *B*. Then the firm is part way up the process ray *A* and part way up the process ray *B*. The firm could be halfway up the distance *OF* and halfway up the distance *OE*, or a quarter of one of the distances and three-quarters of the other. The *combined* output from the two processes is also 40 units, i.e., the same as using either process *A* or process *B*. Similarly, if the firm is at a point between *F* and *G*, the firm is part way up both the process rays *B* and *C*. Here too the combined output is 40 units.[3]

Figure 12-4 is constructed similarly. For the time being, let the lines L_M and L_L and the stippled area be ignored. Here are the same three processes and the isoquants *1, 2,* and *3;* other isoquants can be

FIGURE 12-4   CHOOSING THE BEST COMBINATION OF PROCESSES

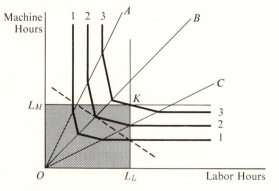

[3] Rigorous proof here is fairly complicated. It is to be found on pp. 805–806 of the Dorfman article cited at the end of this chapter.

visualized. Each one shows processes and combinations of processes that produce the same output. Isoquants farther northeast signify larger amounts of output. The vertical and horizontal portions of the isoquants have no particular meaning; they are shown to display the similarity between these isoquants and those presented in Chapters 9 and 10.

Figure 12–4 also has one isocost line, the dashed line. The isocost line hits isoquant 2 at a corner. If the line is moved parallel to itself, it will always hit an isoquant at the corner on process ray B. Therefore, process B is optimal, being the cheapest one to use when relative input prices are as reflected in the slope of the dashed line. Observe that here too there is no tangency as in conventional theory. Minimum costs are at corners. If the isocost line were nearly flat, it would hit the corner on process C. If it were nearly vertical, the isocost line would hit the corner on process A. In Figure 12–4 also, an isocost line could conceivably have a slope equal to that of one of the line segments. If this were so, there would be no single optimum.

The upshot, so far, is that process B is used if the objective is to produce any chosen level of output at the lowest cost.

Now, let two constraints be brought in.

In Figure 12–4, the lines L_L and L_M express the fact that the firm cannot use more than OL_L of labor-hours or more than OL_M of machine-hours owing, say, to limitations of floor space. These limitations are the constraints. The zone of feasible solutions is the shaded area. If the firm wants to produce as much as possible within its constraints,[4] the highest attainable output is shown by point K, at the northeast corner of the rectangle of feasible solutions. Point K is on isoquant 3 and represents a combination of processes B and C. The input price ratio is the same, but it no longer plays the same role when the objective is to maximize physical output subject to constraints.

With two constraints, two processes are used. Which two depends on what the constraints are. Another look at Figure 12–4 will show that if the labor-hour constraint line were moved to the left far enough, the optimum solution would be a combination of processes A and B.

Step-Shaped Cost Curves

The cost curves of firms in conventional theory are smooth, continuous, and U-shaped. The general shape of these curves is shown in Figure 11–3 on page 190. Even when average variable cost curves

---

[4] The analysis here runs in physical quantities. Physical output is to be maximized subject to constraints. The analysis can be converted to values, by making each point on a process ray correspond to a certain value of output.

FIGURE 12-5   **STEP-SHAPED COST CURVE**

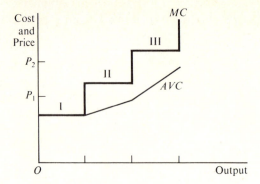

and marginal cost curves are flat over some range, conventional theory requires them to turn upward after some volume of output is reached. See Figure 11–5 on page 193.

When linear programming analysis is converted into the form of conventional theory, the result is a step-shaped marginal cost curve. This follows from the concept of a process. The significance of the step-shaped curve is that the firm makes discontinuous responses to changes in the price of its output.

Figure 12–5 displays one version of a step-shaped cost curve. Here again the firm has three processes, which are now called I, II, and III. For simplicity, each is assumed to be capable of the same maximum output. Cost of output with process I is lower than with II, and lower with II than with III. The step-shaped curve is the firm's marginal cost curve. The horizontal segments reflect the linear assumption and the vertical segments the constraints. The average variable cost curve averages the variable costs when two or more processes are used.

If the price the firm gets for its output is P_1, then it operates process I only. If instead the price is P_2, the firm operates processes I and II. But notice that P_1 or P_2 can move up or down within the range of the vertical segments of the cost curve without any change in the firm's output. The firm is therefore insensitive to certain changes in the price of its output. This statement accords with the finding, earlier in this chapter, that certain changes in input prices do not alter the optimum.

A firm with distinct processes, therefore, responds discontinuously to variations in price.

APPLICATIONS   In its full-blown mathematical form, not in the simplified version presented here, linear programming is applied to a wide range of practical business problems. One class of problems is known as the transportation problem. Here a firm owns several plants from which it ships its product to several destinations. The plants have different capacities, shipping costs per ton vary from one route (from a plant to a destination) to another, and the markets at the destinations have different sizes. With such variables, an exact solution to the minimization of total shipping costs cannot be figured out with everyday methods of calculation. But linear programmers can and do solve such problems. Another class of problems exists in petroleum refining. For example, a type of automotive gasoline must meet definite specifications as to knock rating, etc. The gasoline is produced from several distinct kinds of semirefined oil, called blending stocks. Linear programming shows how to achieve the minimum cost blend for the specified gasoline.

Several of the many applications are discussed in some of the references cited at the end of this chapter.

Frequently, linear programming solutions to practical problems give results that are close to the solutions practical people arrive at by trial and error. Linear programming analyses often come up with plans that will, for example, reduce costs by no more than 3 or 5 per cent. Trained instinct, indeed, usually leads to results as good as those yielded by formal calculation. A trial-and-error solution might be good, but how can anyone be sure it actually is optimum? Here is one of the great achievements of linear programming: Even if it comes forth with the same answer produced by trained instinct, the logic of linear programming can prove that the answer is, in fact, optimum. Business firms, of course, continually face wholly new problems in whose solution the mathematician faces little rivalry from the practical person.

Business executives sometimes decline to act on linear programming solutions. A firm might be told, for example, to eliminate hundreds of items from its line of products if the firm really wants to maximize its profits. The executives of the firm prefer not to do so, for complicated reasons of their own. They might look farther into the future than the analyst and see a long-run advantage in maintaining a full line of products. Another linear programmer might tell a company to cut down on the number of its warehouses to minimize costs. After thanking the programmer, the executives of this company add that they had forgotten to mention that keeping the company's reputation for promptness of deliveries is more important than saving a few thousand dollars on warehousing costs.

Like conventional theory, linear programming can produce clear results only by adherence to the idea of maximizing or minimizing a clearly specified variable. Nor can the solutions be better than the accuracy and completeness of the information fed into the calculations.

SUMMARY

Linear programming is a method of mathematical analysis for the solution of problems of maximization and minimization of variables subject to constraints. Created in the postwar period, linear programming has been applied to a wide range of practical business problems and can be regarded as a special case of the theory of the firm. Input-output, cost-output, and price-output relations are treated as *linear relations*. In producing its outputs, a firm combines *processes*, which are fixed combinations of particular inputs. The minimization of costs or the maximization of profits is the *objective function*, which is subject to *constraints*. Of several *feasible solutions*, one is the *optimum solution*, although sometimes there can be no unique optimum. Simple linear programming analyses can be presented geometrically. Isoquants then become linear-segmented lines instead of smooth curves. Costs are minimized when isocost lines touch *corners*. Profits are maximized when iso-profit lines touch the corners of linear-segmented production possibility curves. Marginal cost curves are linear and can be step-shaped. Linear programming has limitations similar to those of conventional theory.

SELECTED REFERENCES

No mathematics (except for geometry): William Fellner, *Emergence and Content of Modern Economic Analysis* (McGraw-Hill, New York, 1960), pp. 266–274; Robert Dorfman, "Mathematical, or 'Linear,' Programming," *American Economic Review*, 43 (December 1953), part 1, 797–825.

Simple mathematics (elementary algebra): William J. Baumol, "Activity Analysis in One Lesson," *American Economic Review*, 48 (December 1958), 837–_87; Robert W. Metzger, *Elementary Mathematical Programming* (Wiley, New York, 1958).

More advanced: Kenneth E. Boulding and W. Allen Spivey, *Linear Programming and the Theory of the Firm* (Macmillan, New York, 1960).

A classic: T. C. Koopmans, ed., *Activity Analysis of Production and Allocation*, Cowles Commission Monograph No. 13 (Wiley, New York, 1951); Koopmans was joint winner of the Nobel Prize in Economic Science in 1975.

A standard work: Robert Dorfman, Paul A. Samuelson, and Robert M. Solow, *Linear Programming and Economic Analysis* (McGraw-Hill, New York, 1958).

Business applications: W. Warren Haynes and William R. Henry,

Managerial Economics: Analysis and Cases, 3d ed. (Business Publications, Dallas, 1974), chap. 7; Alfred Broaddus, "Linear Programming: A New Approach to Bank Portfolio Management," *Monthly Review, Federal Reserve Bank of Richmond*, 58 (November 1972), 3–11.

A more advanced application to pollution control: Clifford S. Russell and William J. Vaughan, "A Linear Programming Model of Residuals Management for Integrated Iron and Steel Production," *Journal of Environmental Economics and Management*, (May 1974), 17–42.

EXERCISES AND PROBLEMS

1. Construct a diagram like Figure 12–2 on page 211, but with two restraints. Make an assumption about prices, and find a solution. Do the same thing with five restraints.
2. Construct a diagram like Figure 12–3 on page 213, but mark the successive outputs in a different way. Then draw in an isoquant.
3. Construct a diagram like Figure 12–4 on page 214, but modify the constraints so as to show that the optimum is a combination of processes A and B.
4. Suppose the steps in Figure 12–5 on page 216 are made smaller and smaller. What ultimately happens?
5. Draw a step-shaped cost curve to represent this: A firm has a new plant and an old one, which it uses for standby purposes. Both plants can be operated on regular shifts and on overtime.
6. Construct a diagram like Figure 12–1, but with five constraints instead of three. Assume some profits and find the optimum product mix.
7. Describe the symmetry of linear programming and the conventional theory of production. Use both cost-minimizing and profit-maximizing models. Can you see a relation between linear programming and the consumer's choice of the optimum budget?
8. Explain how linear programming can provide estimates of the values of the marginal products of the inputs.
9. Show how linear programming takes opportunity costs into account. Give an example.

Appendix

TO PART 2

MATHEMATICAL NOTES

NOTE 1.

THE MAXIMIZATION

OF PROFITS

The profits of a firm depend on the size of its output. At some volume of output, profits are at a maximum; this book always assumes the existence of a unique maximum.

Let π be profits, q the output of the firm, R the firm's revenue, and C the firm's total costs; π, R, and C are all functions of q.

$$\pi(q) = R(q) - C(q).$$

When profits are a maximum, the first derivative of π with respect to q is equal to zero. Therefore

$$\frac{d\pi(q)}{dq} = \frac{dR(q)}{dq} - \frac{dC(q)}{dq} = 0,$$

or,

$$\frac{dR(q)}{dq} = \frac{dC(q)}{dq}.$$

The first derivative of R with respect to q, $\dfrac{dR(q)}{dq}$, is marginal revenue. Similarly, $\dfrac{dC(q)}{dq}$, is marginal cost. Therefore, profits are maximized at the output whose marginal revenue = marginal cost, i.e., at q_0 where

$$\frac{dR(q_0)}{dq} = \frac{dC(q_0)}{dq}.$$

The second-order conditions require that the second derivative be negative for a maximum. Hence

$$\frac{d^2R(q)}{dq^2} - \frac{d^2C(q)}{dq^2} < 0,$$

or equivalently,

$$\frac{d^2R(q)}{dq^2} < \frac{d^2C(q)}{dq^2}.$$

The above expression requires that the algebraic value of the slope of the marginal cost function be greater than the algebraic value of the slope of the marginal revenue function when profits are at a maximum. Stated another way, with profits at a maximum, marginal costs are increasing more rapidly than marginal revenue.

NOTE 2.

THE PRODUCTION

FUNCTION

The production function is the relation between physical quantities of a firm's inputs and the physical quantity of its output. Let q be output, and a, b, c, etc., be inputs. In general,

$$q = f(a, b, c, \ldots).$$

In econometric studies, the problem is to select the relevant inputs and the mathematical form of the equation. A statistical production function for an auto laundry gave good results with two inputs—the plant and the number of workers. Statistical production functions for Iowa farms required five inputs—land, labor, the improvements on the farms, the farmers' liquid assets, and their cash operating expenses.

For many purposes, no more than two variables are needed to display the properties of production functions. Now let

$$q = f(a, b)$$

and suppose that a is units of labor and b is units of land. If land is held constant and labor is varied in amount, the marginal productivity of labor is given by the partial derivative. Thus,

$$\frac{\partial q}{\partial a} = f_a(a, b).$$

Suppose that the production function is

$$q = 10a - a^2 + ab.$$

Then the marginal productivity of a is

$$\frac{\partial q}{\partial a} = 10 - 2a + b.$$

If $a = 3$ and $b = 6$, the marginal productivity of a is 10. Thus if b is held constant, the limit of the ratio between the increment in output q and the increment in the amount of labor tends to 10 at the indicated level of inputs.

The Cobb-Douglas production function can be applied to a sector of the economy, such as manufacturing, or to the whole economy. This production function is an empirical hypothesis that has given good statistical results.

The function usually takes the form

$$Q = kL^{\alpha}C^{(1-\alpha)}, \qquad k > 0 \quad \text{and} \quad 0 < \alpha < 1,$$

where Q is output, L is the quantity of labor, C is the quantity of capital employed, and k and α $(0 < \alpha < 1)$ are positive constants. The function is linear and homogeneous. Suppose that the quantities of labor and capital are increased in equal proportions. Let L become gL and let C become gC. (If g is 1.10, there is an increase of 10 per cent in each factor of production.) Then

$$k(gL)^{\alpha}(gC)^{1-\alpha} = g^{\alpha}g^{(1-\alpha)}kL^{\alpha}C^{1-\alpha},$$
$$= gkL^{\alpha}C^{1-\alpha} = gQ.$$

Thus output increases in the same proportion. Returns to scale are constant.

Figure 9–3 on page 165 shows the production function as a family of isoquants. So that the language of this note will be consistent with that of Chapter 9, the two inputs are now labor, L, and capital, C. For a given level of output q_o, the isoquant is given by the equation

$$q_o = f(L, C).$$

The slope of the tangent to any point on the isoquant is negative. Minus one times the slope of the isoquant is the marginal rate of technical substitution (*MRTS*)

$$MRTS = -\frac{dC}{dL}.$$

The production function can be described by the whole family of isoquants,

$$q = f(L, C).$$

The total differential of the production function is

$$dq = f_L\, dL + f_C\, dC.$$

Here, f_L and f_C, the partial derivatives of q with respect to L and C, are the marginal productivities of labor and capital, as shown in Note 2 on page 221. But $dq = 0$ for movements along an isoquant. Therefore

$$0 = f_L\, dL + f_C\, dC,$$

and

$$f_L\, dL = -f_C\, dC,$$

and

$$\frac{f_L}{f_C} = -\frac{dC}{dL}.$$

Thus the marginal rate of technical substitution between labor and capital is equal to the ratio of their marginal productivities.

The general form of the short-run cost function of a firm is

$$TC = f(q) + b.$$

That is, total cost TC is some function of output $f(q)$ plus the fixed cost b. This equation and the deductions from it are useful in reinforcing the definitions in Chapter 11 and in explaining the relation between average and marginal cost.

Costs per unit—average cost (AC), average variable cost (AVC), and average fixed cost (AFC)—are defined as follows

$$AC = \frac{f(q) + b}{q} = \frac{TC}{q},$$

$$AVC = \frac{f(q)}{q},$$

$$AFC = \frac{b}{q}.$$

Marginal cost is the derivative of total cost with respect to output

$$MC = \frac{dTC}{dq} = \frac{dVC}{dq} + \frac{dFC}{dq} = \frac{dVC}{dq}.$$

The derivatives of total cost and total variable cost are identical and equal to marginal cost, because b, the fixed-cost term, disappears upon differentiation.

$MC = AC$, when AC is a minimum. For AC to be a minimum, its derivative is set equal to zero

$$AC' = \frac{qTC' - TC}{q^2} = 0,$$

$$= \frac{TC'}{q} - \frac{TC}{q^2} = 0,$$

and

$$TC' = \frac{TC}{q}.$$

Similarly, $MC = AVC$, when AVC is a minimum.

The conventional U-shaped average variable and marginal cost curves of the firm, as shown in Figure 11-3 on page 190, can be represented by making total cost a cubic function of output. For example,

$$TC = aq^3 + bq^2 + cq + d, \quad a, c, d > 0, \quad b < 0, \quad \text{and} \quad b^2 < 3ac.$$

Here $AVC = aq^2 + bq + c$ and $MC = TC' = 3aq^2 + 2bq + c$. Both are U-shaped parabolas. The minimum marginal cost occurs at output level q, where $MC' = 6aq + 2b = 0$. Thus $q = \dfrac{-b}{3a}$. Therefore, minimum MC is $3a\left(\dfrac{-b}{3a}\right)^2 + 2b\left(\dfrac{-b}{3a}\right) + c = 3\dfrac{ac - b^2}{2a}$. Since $a > 0$, to insure that minimum MC is positive, impose the restriction that $b^2 < 3ac$. The fixed cost is d. A change in d would shift the position of the cost curve without changing its shape. Changes in a, b, and c would, however, alter both the shape and the position of the curve.

NOTE 6.
LINEAR
PROGRAMMING

Two examples of linear programming follow. The first shows the solution to a problem of minimizing costs and the second, the solution to a problem of maximizing net revenue.

Minimization of
Cost

Assume that a product is to be produced by mixing two ingredients, A and B, which weigh, respectively, 5 and 10 pounds per unit. The final product must not weigh less than 150 pounds. Costs per unit are $2 for A and $8 for B. This is the problem: What is the mix that will minimize the unit costs of production if at least 5 units of A and 10 units of B must be used to meet production standards?

This information can be written in mathematical language as follows

minimize costs: $C = \$2A + \$8B$, the objective function,
subject to: $\left. \begin{array}{l} 5A + 10B \geq 150 \\ A \geq 5, B \geq 10 \end{array} \right\}$ constraints.

From the equation controlling weight and the minimum input specification, it follows that the feasible input region is the shaded area in Figure A2-1. The feasible region represents the intersection of three constraints. The intersection of the boundary lines is formed by solving $A = 5$ and $5A + 10B = 150$ to get $A = 5$ and $B = 12.5$, and $B = 10$ and $5A + 10B = 150$ to get $A = 10$ and $B = 10$.

The isocost lines are represented by a simple transformation of the objective function

$$B = -\frac{1}{4}A + \frac{C}{8}.$$

MINIMIZING COSTS

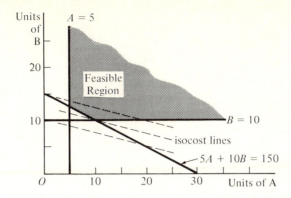

With C as a given cost, B is now a linear function of A, with a slope $-\frac{1}{4}$. Since the slope of the isocost curves $(-\frac{1}{4})$ is less steep than the slope of the line segment between $(5, 12.5)$ and $(10, 10)$, costs are minimized at $(10, 10)$. In other words, because the objective is to minimize costs subject to staying in the feasible input region, the solution is $A = 10$ and $B = 10$. Thus the minimum costs of producing the product and meeting all specifications are $100.

Maximization of Net Revenue   Assume that a drug manufacturer desires to obtain a production schedule to maximize the net revenue from the sale of two drugs (A and B) whose net revenues per unit are 60¢ and 40¢, respectively. Production is limited by the capacity to produce the drugs, the capacity to produce containers, and by the amount of labor available for processing and handling. The limitations, or constraints, on production are these:

1. Capacity to produce drugs is 1,000 units of A and B.
2. Capacity to produce containers is 1,600 units of A, or 800 units of B, or a proportionate linear mix of A and B.
3. Labor is available for 800 units of A, or 1,600 units of B, or a proportionate linear mix of A and B.

By taking into account the fraction of total capacity needed to produce one unit of each drug and container, the following inequalities indicate values for A and B that are permissible.

$$\text{(1)} \quad A + B \leq 1{,}000$$
$$\text{(2)} \quad A + 2B \leq 1{,}600$$
$$\text{(3)} \quad 2A + B \leq 1{,}600$$
$$\text{(4)} \quad A \geq 0$$
$$\text{(5)} \quad B \geq 0$$

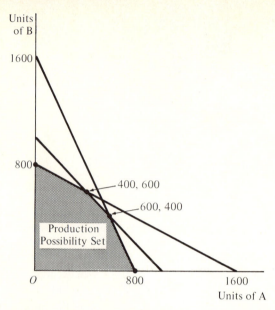

The intersection of the inequalities, along with the nonnegativity restrictions ($A \geq 0$, $B \geq 0$), describes the convex set of all feasible values, i.e., the linear-segmented production possibility set. Then, solving the boundary equations in pairs gives the intersection (or corner) values of A and B. Figure A2-2 shows these values and their locations on the production possibility set.

(1 & 2) $A = 400$, $B = 600$
(1 & 3) $A = 600$, $B = 400$
(2 & 4) $A = \quad 0$, $B = 800$
(3 & 5) $A = 800$, $B = \quad 0$

Notice that the intersection of (2 & 3) falls outside the limitation on drug production, i.e., $\dfrac{1,600}{3} + \dfrac{1,600}{3} > 1,000$, which is impossible.

The net revenue function to be maximized is

$R = \$.60A + \$.40B$.

For (1 & 2) $R = \$.60(400) + \$.40(600) = \$480$
(1 & 3) $R = \$.60(600) + \$.40(400) = \$520$
(2 & 4) $R = \$.60(0) \quad + \$.40(800) = \$320$
(3 & 5) $R = \$.60(800) + \$.40(0) \quad = \$480$.

The maximum net revenue is $520 from sale of 600 units of A and 400 units of B.

Both of these problems could be solved by the graphic method or by the more complicated simplex method.

3
COMPETITIVE
PRICING

13
Short-Run Prices
IN PURE COMPETITION

Demand and supply now come together once more. This chapter, the next two, and Chapter 23 show how demand and supply determine prices and quantities in markets where pure competition prevails. Three simple models of competitive[1] pricing will be constructed. Two will be partial equilibrium models, where one commodity is considered by itself. The third will be a simplified general equilibrium model, which shows the connections among all demands, all supplies, and all prices.

INDUSTRY DEMAND AND FIRM DEMAND

Earlier chapters discussed the subject of demand from the point of view of consumers and their behavior in spending money on commodities. But buyers' expenditures are the same amounts of money as sellers' receipts. A jump to the other side of the market permits a view of demand as seen by the sellers of commodities.

First of all, the demand for the output of an industry must be distinguished from the demand for the output of a single firm in the industry. The distinction is tied to the classification of *market structures*, which will now be given a brief introduction. Later chapters will describe and analyze them more closely.

Market Structures

The standard classification of market structures is simple, being based on just two ideas—the number of firms in an industry and the homogeneity or differentiation of the firms' products.

Pure competition in an industry means many firms producing homogeneous products. How many is "many"? It is any number such that each firm sells so small a part of the total output of the industry that the firm cannot see the effects of its actions on price. Hence the firm ignores these effects. A firm in an industry with pure competition is a price taker, not a price maker. Homogeneity of

---

[1] When used in this book, the word *competitive* always means purely competitive, unless the context clearly indicates otherwise.

product means that each firm's product is, to the buyers, a perfect substitute for the product of any other firm in the industry. Usually this means uniform grades and standards specifying the physical characteristics of a commodity. British economists and some American economists use the expression *perfect competition* instead of pure competition. Nearly always the context is clear enough to prevent possible confusion. But competition can also be pure *and* perfect, and when it is, the word perfect is not a synonym for pure. In *pure and perfect competition*, the number of firms is large, their products are homogeneous; in addition, the firms have perfect (i.e., full) knowledge of the market, and resources are perfectly (i.e., instantaneously and frictionlessly) mobile. Perfection of competition in this sense is not something real, nor has anyone ever pretended that it is. Instead, perfection of competition is a simplifying assumption to use in handling complicated problems.

Pure competition among firms exists in the markets for most farm products and in the markets for some mineral and forest products. Pure competition is not remote. It is, indeed, a fact of everyday experience, for pure competition also prevails among consumers. They too are price takers. They too, as individuals, buy so little of any one commodity that each act of purchase has no appreciable influence on price. The consumer is a price maker only when he or she can bargain effectively and sway a price decision in his or her favor.

Since the word *impure* can possibly suggest irrelevant connotations, competition that is not pure is called *imperfect competition*. It has two forms, monopolistic competition and oligopoly. *Monopolistic competition* in an industry means that there are many firms, each producing and selling differentiated products. The products of the firms are close but not perfect substitutes for one another. The products of different firms within the industry are not identical, as they are in pure competition. *Oligopoly* means a few sellers. Few means a number small enough that each firm knows that its actions visibly affect the whole industry. Rivalry among oligopolistic firms is open and conscious. The products of oligopolistic firms can be physically homogeneous or they can be differentiated. Oligopoly prevails in many American manufacturing industries as well as in many financial and transportation markets.

The literal meaning of *monopoly* is one seller. One definition of monopoly is to identify the firm with the industry. This definition, which is adequate for present purposes, easily applies to industries such as electric power where, in any one market, only one firm is the producer.[2]

---

[2] Chapter 16 goes farther into the problem of defining monopoly.

FIGURE 13-1   INDUSTRY DEMAND AND FIRM DEMAND IN PURE COMPETITION

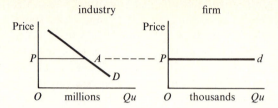

Industry and Firm Demand in Pure Competition

The demand for the output of an industry is the demand for a commodity. Such a demand can be elastic or inelastic. The demand for the product of any one firm in an industry of pure competition is, however, perfectly elastic. Figure 13-1 shows the relations between the two demands. On the left is the industry demand curve whose quantities are marked in millions of, say, bushels. On the right is the demand curve of a firm. Demand is perfectly elastic at price OP. Notice that the quantity axis for the firm is marked in thousands. Though the one curve is horizontal and the other slopes, the two are wholly compatible. The amount PA is some thousands of times greater than the amount Pd. The horizontality of the firm's demand curve means that if it were to sell more, the firm would not have to accept a lower price. The slope of the industry demand curve means that if all firms together would offer substantially more for sale, they would notice an obvious fall in price.

The firm in pure competition can sell any amount, within the range of its own capacity to produce, without perceptibly affecting price. To the firm, the price is given. The firm is a price taker. But the industry's demand is limited, which is only another way of saying that the industry faces a downward sloping demand curve.

MARGINAL REVENUE   The concept of *marginal revenue* will appear frequently in the chapters to come. It can be introduced briefly now. The marginal revenue of a seller is the addition to total revenue when selling one unit more. Or, it is the loss of total revenue when selling one unit less.

For the firm under pure competition, marginal revenue (MR) is identical with price. That is, $MR = P$. If a farmer sells 10,000 bushels at \$2 a bushel, the farmer could also sell 10,001 bushels at the same price. The extra \$2 for the extra bushel is the marginal revenue, and \$2 is also the price.

Industry and Firm Demand in Imperfect Competition

In an imperfectly competitive industry, the demand curves of both the industry and the firm are downward sloping. Of course the firm's demand is smaller than the industry's. Where there are many firms, as in monopolistic competition, one firm's demand is a very small part of the total industry demand. Where oligopoly takes the specific form of *duopoly*—competition between two firms—and where products are homogeneous, then the firm's demand is half that of the industry.

In imperfect competition also, the firm's demand is more elastic than that of the industry. This is true because the products of other firms are close substitutes for the product of any one firm.

Marginal revenue does *not* equal price for firms that are monopolies or are in industries with imperfect competition. All such firms have sloping demand curves, which means that if they sell more than any given amount, they must accept lower prices. If a firm is selling 3 units at $8 each and then sells 4 units at $7, its marginal revenue is $4. That is, total revenue for 4 units is $28, whereas total revenue for 3 units is $24. Observe that the reduction in price from $8 to $7 results in a marginal revenue which is less than price. Except for firms in pure competition, marginal revenue is always less than price.

The full logic of the relations between price, marginal revenue, and elasticity will not be needed until Chapter 16, on monopoly pricing. Further explanation of those relations is therefore postponed. For the chapters immediately to follow, it suffices to know that the expression for the extra revenue from an extra unit of sales is marginal revenue and that marginal revenue equals price for firms in pure competition.

MARKET PRICE

Chapter 2 describes briefly the determination of market price when many buyers and sellers deal in homogeneous products, i.e., when there is pure competition. Only a few additional remarks need to be made at this point.

In the market period (and also in the short run and in the long run), the intersection of the demand curve and the supply curve determines quantity as well as price. Figure 13-2 gives emphasis to this important matter. In this figure, the two supply curves are perfectly inelastic, meaning that the sellers want to sell all they have and will take any price they can get. But the two supply curves stand for different amounts, in, say, two successive weeks. With supply

FIGURE 13-2   **MARKET PRICE: PERFECTLY INELASTIC SUPPLIES**

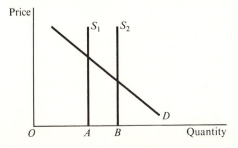

curve S_2, the larger amount OB causes the equilibrium price to be lower.

Figure 13–2 can serve to illustrate something else. Back in 1970, according to *The Wall Street Journal*, hundreds of truckloads of bright red cranberries were dumped into landfill areas in the several states where cranberries grow. Bulldozers pushed piles of earth and mud onto the berries. The cranberry growers had voted for this destruction, or "set-aside," as it is known, and the United States Department of Agriculture had given its approval. Thus, in Figure 13–2, let OB stand for the cranberry crop in 1970. If the growers had sold all of it, they would have received a price determined by the intersection of S_2 with D, or about $7 a 100-pound barrel. But they destroyed AB barrels and received the higher price at the intersection of S_1 with D, or about $11 a barrel. This price, however, was lower than the average in the preceding five years.

The quantity AB in Figure 13–2 happens to exaggerate the destruction of cranberries in 1970. It was "only" about 10 per cent of the crop.

Changes in Demand and Supply

Changes in demand and in supply cause changes in price or in quantity, or both. What happens to price and to quantity depends upon the magnitudes of the changes in demand and supply and upon their elasticities. Figure 13–3 contains two sets of demand and supply curves. They can be paired in four ways, to represent increases or decreases in either demand or supply, or both. Thus, for example, the price is the same when D_1 and S_1 are coupled and when D_2 and S_2 are coupled. But the quantity is larger for the combinations of D_2 and S_2. Notice that each of the figures shows four equilibrium prices and quantities. On the left, where both demand and supply are inelastic, the price differences are greater than the quantity differences. The opposite is true on the right, where both demand and supply are elastic.

Speculation

At any one point of time, the actions of buyers and sellers in organized markets are dominated by expectations of future prices. Since many commodities bought and sold on organized markets are produced seasonally, and since some commodities are consumed

FIGURE 13–3   **CHANGES IN DEMAND AND SUPPLY**

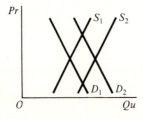

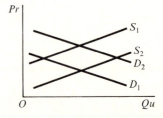

seasonally, fluctuations in market prices would be wide were it not for speculation. A speculator is a trader who buys and sells in the hope of earning a net income from differences in prices. The usual belief is that the activities of speculators, who try to guess what prices will be in the future, cause market prices to be more stable over time than they otherwise would be. Certainly, gross seasonal fluctuations are prevented. Beyond this, however, neither theoretical analysis nor empirical research can establish clearly just what is the price-stabilizing effect of speculation. In the organized markets where homogeneous and storable commodities are traded, there are two sets of prices—spot and futures. Spot, or cash, prices are those paid and received for actual physical quantities of a commodity. Futures prices are prices in contracts for delivery of the commodity at some date in the future. The contracts are paper contracts; with most of them most of the time, physical delivery never takes place, the contracts being bought or sold before their delivery dates. In general, the spread between spot and futures prices of a commodity tends to be close to the costs of storing it. When they make mistakes in judgment, when they are moved by overenthusiasm or by panic, speculators can cause wild fluctuations in prices. Even when they make correct judgments, speculators can cause prices to fluctuate up and down. If, for example, prices fall, speculators who correctly predict further price declines will sell, thus strengthening the downward movement.

Many commodities are traded in geographically separate markets. Price differences between the markets are held exceedingly close to transportation costs by the activities of speculators.

Information

In a competitive market, there can be only one equilibrium price at any one time. This statement, or some version of it, has been repeated by economists for many generations. The validity of the statement, however, depends on an assumption that so far has been implicit, namely, that buyers and sellers have "perfect knowledge." This means only that they know what the price is and what price the same thing is selling for in other markets, if there are any. Complete and accurate information is available in the highly organized markets; computers and other devices provide it. But in many other markets, information is imperfect. It is costly and troublesome to acquire. The many buyers and sellers do not know what all of the offers are. In such markets, there can be several prices at the same time.

EQUILIBRIUM OF THE FIRM IN THE SHORT RUN

The market price of a competitively produced and sold commodity fluctuates. But the fluctuations are not capricious or random. They have a pattern, hardly ever exact and closely predictable, but nonetheless a pattern. The doctrine of short-run equilibrium price is a way of stating the level around which market prices fluctuate in the short run.

The short-run supply of an industry under pure competition is a flow of production from the firms in the industry, producing with their fixed plants and equipment and with their variable inputs. The rate of the flow depends on the price of the commodity and the cost functions of the firms. The *short-run supply schedule*, or curve, shows the volumes of production from the industry at each possible price. The first step in constructing this schedule is to describe the price-output adjustments of a single firm.

How much a competitive firm produces in the short run depends on its marginal cost and the price. Consider Figure 13-4. In this diagram, the price is assumed to be at a level that makes the operation of the firm highly profitable. The price is *OP*. The horizontal line from *P* is the demand curve of the firm. The firm produces the amount *OA*. It does not produce more because additional output has a cost higher than the price. The short-run marginal cost curve—*MC*—shows this; for any output larger than *OA*, *MC* exceeds price. Nor will the firm produce any less than *OA* because if it did, the firm would fail to seize the opportunity to produce and sell units whose marginal cost is less than their price.

The rectangles in Figure 13-4 show the firm's position. *Total revenue* is price times quantity, the rectangle *PA*.[3] *Total cost* is average cost multiplied by quantity, the rectangle *FA*. *Net profit* is the excess of total revenue over total cost. Net profit is the heavily shaded rectangle *PB*. *Total fixed cost* is the difference between total and variable costs; total fixed cost is the lightly shaded rectangle *FC*. *Total variable cost* is the rectangle *OC*. *Net revenue* is the excess of total revenue over total variable cost. Net revenue is the rectangle *PC*, i.e., the two shaded areas together.

FIGURE 13-4   EQUILIBRIUM OF THE FIRM: PRICE ABOVE AVERAGE COST

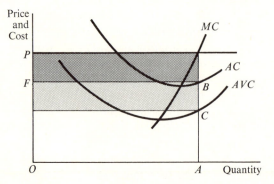

[3] For simplicity, rectangles will be designated by the letters diagonally opposite.

FIGURE 13-5

EQUILIBRIUM OF THE FIRM: PRICE BELOW AVERAGE COST

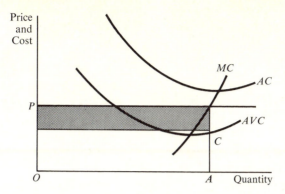

Must the firm earn net profits if it is to produce in the short run? The answer is no. Consider Figure 13–5, which shows an unprofitable price for the firm. The price is below the firm's full average costs. But the firm produces the amount *OA*, whose marginal cost equals the price *OP*. At this price, the firm's net revenue is the shaded rectangle *PC*. Another look at Figure 13–5 shows that net revenue is less than fixed costs, that the firm operates at a loss. But it *minimizes* its loss. If the firm stopped producing and shut down, its loss would be equal to its fixed costs. Producing the output *OA*, the firm's net revenue *PC reduces* the loss that would equal its fixed costs. If, therefore, price is lower than full average cost but higher than average variable cost, output with a marginal cost equal to price gives a net revenue that reduces loss to a minimum.

Here is a simple arithmetic example of the same proposition: Suppose you have a poultry farm and that your fixed costs per week are $100. Your full costs per pound for each fryer you sell are 10¢. Your average variable costs for feed, labor, etc., are 5¢ a pound. Would you temporarily produce at a price of 8¢? Yes, as a rational decision maker you would, because if you were to shut down, your loss would be $100 a week. But if you produce at 8¢, the 3¢ over your average variable costs, multiplied by the number of pounds, recovers for you at least part of your fixed costs. A small loss is preferable to a large one.

The general principle, then, is that the firm in the short run adjusts its output so that net revenue is maximized. If this means a net profit, so much the better for the firm. If maximum net revenue means a loss, then the loss is minimized. Price must exceed average variable cost, and marginal cost must equal price.

If, however, the price is so low that it is below any point on the curve of average variable cost, the firm stops producing. If it did not, the firm would lose, besides the amount equal to fixed costs,

FIGURE 13-6   **SHORT-RUN SUPPLY CURVE OF THE FIRM**

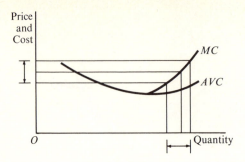

even more—the price would not cover the unit expenses of currently purchased labor and materials.

The supply curve of the firm in the short run, therefore, is that portion of the marginal cost curve that lies above the average variable cost curve. In other words, MC above AVC is the firm's short-run supply curve, because the curve states what quantity the firm will supply at each possible price. Figure 13-6 shows three prices, and the corresponding equilibrium amounts for each price. The arrows indicate the association of amounts with prices.

Rising
Marginal Cost

The short-run equilibrium of the competitive firm, with $MC = P$, occurs in a range of output where the MC curve is rising. If the MC curve were horizontal or falling, it would have to lie below the price line if the firm is to produce at all; but then the firm would find it advantageous to expand indefinitely, and the more it would expand the greater would be the firm's net revenue. For a unique maximum net revenue, therefore, the firm produces with rising marginal cost. That MC must be rising is a so-called stability, or second-order condition ($MC = P$ being a first-order condition).

THE SHORT-RUN
SUPPLY CURVE
OF THE
INDUSTRY

When the marginal cost curves of the firms are combined, the result is the supply curve of the industry. Thus the supply of the industry is based on the costs of the firms. At each possible price, firm A, firm B, firm C, etc., produce amounts corresponding to the equalities of their marginal costs at that price. The total of the amounts is the industry's supply at the same price.

Figure 13-7 shows a short-run supply curve (and a demand curve) for an industry. Suppose the price is OP. Then the output of the entire industry is OQ millions of units. The figure also indicates the adjustments of two of the firms. Firm A has short-run marginal costs of MC_A. Firm B's are MC_B. Observe that firm B has much lower costs for *any* output; for example, output Oa is optimum for firm A, but firm B's marginal cost is about half of A's at the same output. So

FIGURE 13-7

INDUSTRY DEMAND AND SUPPLY, AND FIRM SUPPLY, IN THE SHORT RUN

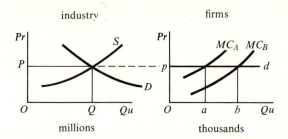

industry   firms

millions   thousands

firm *B* produces much more, namely, *Ob*. But observe that when both firms are in equilibrium, the marginal costs of their equilibrium outputs are equal. The *last* bushel produced on the low-cost farm has the same cost as the *last* bushel produced on the high-cost farm, because both bushels sell at the same price.

EQUILIBRIUM OF THE INDUSTRY IN THE SHORT RUN

An industry is in equilibrium in the short run when the output of the industry holds steady, there being no force acting to expand output or to contract it. A firm is in equilibrium in the short run when it maximizes its net revenue. The firm clearly does not want to change the output that yields its maximum net revenue. If all firms are in equilibrium, then so is the industry.

Demand in the short run is a flow of consumption, the volume of the flow depending on the possible prices. At the equilibrium price for the industry, demand equals supply. The rate of consumption equals the rate of production. In everyday language, consumption and production are in balance.

Changes in Demand

Figure 13–8 shows three short-run equilibrium prices for the industry. If the demand is low—D_1—then the equilibrium price P_1 is low. At this price, many or even most of the firms can be suffering losses. Nonetheless, P_1 is an equilibrium price because demand equals

FIGURE 13-8   **SHORT-RUN EQUILIBRIUM PRICES**

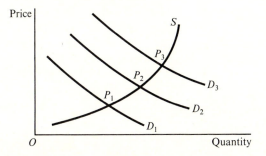

supply. The firms equate their marginal costs with P_1, and total output holds steady despite firms' losses. If demand increases in the short run to D_2, then the new and higher equilibrium price is P_2. At this price, only a few firms, perhaps, are suffering losses. Many might be earning good net profits. And at the high price P_3, perhaps all of the firms are earning net profits.

Short-run equilibrium, therefore, does not denote any one condition of profitability for the industry. Equilibrium is compatible with both widespread losses and widespread net profits. When demand is depressed and when the firms adjust to the lower price caused by the depressed demand, the market price falls to the short-run equilibrium level. An industry with a depressed demand and with many firms suffering losses is often called a "sick industry." In such an industry, much idle capacity exists because the firms losing money operate at less than their capacity outputs. Unemployment of labor can also be at high levels if, in the short run, opportunities to take other jobs are few. Nevertheless, it often happens that a few firms in a sick industry earn good profits. They are the firms with the newest plant and equipment, and the best management. An industry can be sick for many years—the market price continuing to hover about a low equilibrium level. On the other hand, a competitive industry can be in short-run equilibrium with a strong demand, a high equilibrium price, and large net profits for nearly all of the firms. Such a condition is not, however, likely to last for long. As other firms begin to enter the profitable industry, the short run merges into the long.

Changes in Supply

The short-run supply curve can shift, to the right or to the left. Two groups of causes can bring about changes in supply in the short run. One set of causes has to do with the production functions of the firms. In many industries, the physical outputs of firms depend in part upon the weather, upon the amount and the timing of rainfall, upon variations in temperature, upon the frequency and severity of storms, etc. The physical outputs of the agricultural industries also depend on how bad are the effects of insects, pests, and the diseases of plants and animals. Minor improvements in technology can also occur in the short run. Their effects are to reduce the costs of given outputs or to make possible larger outputs with given costs. Another cause of changes in short-run supply is fluctuation in the prices of the variable inputs of the firms. Their marginal cost curves can rise or fall as wage rates, fuel prices, etc., go up or go down.

ADJUSTMENTS OF PRICES AND QUANTITIES IN DISEQUILIBRIUM

So far, the analyses of price formation in pure competition have emphasized the equilibria of prices and quantities. Though one economist has protested that no shadow of approbation should be cast over an equilibrium of price and quantity, his protests have not been heeded. There seems to be something good about it, especially about industry equilibrium under pure competition where equilibrium always goes along with *equality* of quantities demanded and supplied. But must demand and supply and all that they imply always snap into an equilibrium? What is the magic of the intersection of the curves? Is an equilibrium a necessary result? How do price and output get from one position of equilibrium to another?

Prices and outputs in pure competition are, in fact, in constant motion. Changes in tastes and in technology are principal causes. Disequilibrium, rather than equilibrium, is the normal condition of purely competitive markets, certainly over periods of time longer than a few weeks. The pervasiveness of disequilibrium does not, however, make the theory of equilibrium useless. On the contrary, understanding of the movements of disequilibrium must rest on knowledge of the equilibrium conditions. For equilibrium is a shorthand way of referring to the *direction* of the pulling and hauling of the forces working on the prices and outputs of commodities. The forces are not random, or wholly capricious, or arbitrary. They operate within a pattern whose inner tendencies are described by the theory of equilibrium.

In the market period, both demand and supply can shift rapidly. Buyers and sellers can change their opinions about future prices, alter their trading plans, and hence bring new demand and supply schedules into being. In the short run and in the long, demand can often change much more quickly than supply. A new fad or fashion can cause a short-run demand curve to move, within a few days or weeks, to the right and to settle in a new position. Because it is a flow of production, however, short-run supply can usually change only slowly. It takes time to alter physical rates of production, to speed them up, or to cut them back.

Figures 13–9 and 13–10 show the behavior of price in a purely competitive industry when demand changes. Let D_1 and S be the

FIGURE 13–9 **INCREASE IN DEMAND**

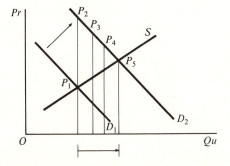

FIGURE 13-10

DECLINE IN DEMAND

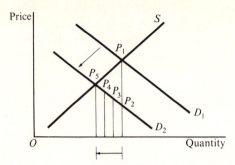

short-run demand and supply curves, and let the industry first be in short-run equilibrium. To begin with, then, price is P_1. Figure 13-9 shows what happens if that demand suddenly shifts to D_2. The price then shoots up to P_2 if the firms cannot suddenly increase their outputs. The price P_2 is highly remunerative because it stands far above the supply curve. The firms expand output as best they can in a scramble to earn still more net revenue. As output grows, the price now falls to P_3, to P_4, and finally to P_5. Then the expansion stops. The industry is once more in short-run equilibrium.

Figure 13-10 shows the effect of a sudden decline in demand. Price drops from P_1 to P_2. The price P_2 is well below the supply curve, causing contraction to take place. As it does, little by little price rises, finally climbing to the new level of equilibrium.

A short-run industry supply curve can shift to the right because of reductions in the costs of the firms or because of a fall in the price of some other commodity that the firms also produce. The supply curve can be imagined as sliding to the right as the firms make their adjustments and coming to rest when the causes of the shift are exhausted. The disequilibrium price slides down the demand curve, also coming to rest in a new short-run equilibrium.

Sometimes, however, supply can change faster than demand. Suppose that the firms, because of a fall in the price of another commodity, increase the short-run supply of the commodity under examination. Imagine that the firms can make their adjustments in production quickly within, say, a few weeks. Imagine also that the demand for a period of a few weeks is less elastic than it is for the short run as a whole. Under these circumstances, price would fall below and then would rise to the new equilibrium level. Figure 13-11 shows this. The original equilibrium of demand, supply, and price is given by the positions of D_1, S_1, and P_1. Supply shifts to S_2, but while it does so, the demand curve for the period is D_2, which is less elastic. Price then falls to P_2. But as the buyers make their

FIGURE 13–11

ADJUSTMENTS TO NEW EQUILIBRIUM

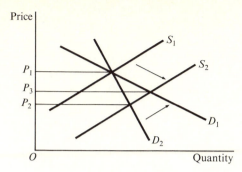

adjustments, demand becomes more elastic. The curve D_2 pivots and swings up, finally assuming the position D_1. In the absence of a fresh disturbance, the equilibrium price becomes P_3.

Changes such as these indicate the many kinds of adjustments constantly taking place in competitive markets.

UNSTABLE EQUILIBRIUM

The equilibrium positions of prices and quantities so far presented are positions of *stable equilibrium*. If something disturbs it, a stable equilibrium is self-adjusting. A billiard ball resting in a bowl on a table occupies a position of stable equilibrium because if somebody gives the ball a little push, it moves back and forth, eventually coming to rest where it was before. If the bowl is turned upside down and the ball is carefully perched on top of the inverted bowl, the ball will stay there. Now, however, it stands in *unstable equilibrium* because if somebody now pushes it, the billiard ball rolls down off the bowl onto the table and drops with a thud to the floor. It does not come back to where it was.

So too, a price-quantity equilibrium can be unstable. When it is, a part of the price mechanism goes awry.

Stability of competitive equilibrium in competitive markets can be taken as the general rule, instability being the exception. Recall the ordinary demand-supply diagram once more. At a price higher than equilibrium, the excess of supply must force price down; at a lower price, the excess of demand must force price up. If demand and supply change (as indeed they do), the result is analytical complication; stability then becomes the stability of moving equilibrium—the tendency of price and quantity to be continually forced to the points of intersection of shifting demand and supply curves.

Whether the equilibrium of price and quantity in a purely competitive market is stable depends upon the slope of the supply curve and on the relation between demand and supply. If the supply curve has a negative slope and if its slope is less than that of the demand curve, equilibrium can be unstable.

The negative slope of a supply curve stands for a particular pattern of sellers' responses to prices. If price falls, they want to sell more, not less. If price rises, they want to sell less, not more. This can happen, for example, to the producers of one crop, who cannot or will not grow any other crop, and whose income, if they operate small family farms, consists almost entirely of wages and contains only a negligibly small element of profit. The lower the price, the lower is their effective wage and the more they have to grow to try to keep their incomes from falling; the higher the price, the less effort they have to put forth. A supply curve can also have a temporarily negative slope for the traders on an organized market in the immediate market period. The sellers possess stocks of the commodity and cash; suppose that their assets comprise only these. Normally, each seller maintains some preferred ratio of his holdings of the commodity and of cash. Suppose next that the sellers in some market at some point of time are caught in such a state of affairs that they desperately need cash. To get it, they have to sell the commodity. The lower the price, the more they have to sell.

Equilibrium is unstable in Figure 13–12. The equilibrium price is *OP*. But if this price should temporarily rise, it will not go back to the equilibrium level but, instead, will keep on rising. It will do this because demand exceeds supply above equilibrium. Similarly, a drop in price sets up a chain reaction of more price declines because supply exceeds demand.

How far can price move away from a level of unstable equilibrium? To this question, no single answer can be given. A diagram like Figure 13–12 leaves the question open. In particular markets, instability is not likely to prevail for long. Stability of equilibrium is restored if the supply curve shifts and becomes steeper than the demand curve. If the supply curve shifts and changes to a positive slope, then of course stability also prevails.[4]

---

[4] The possibility of unstable competitive equilibria has long been the subject of much theoretical speculation and difference of opinion. The treatment here follows the doctrine of Walras and Hicks. But Figure 13–12 can be interpreted as exhibiting a stable equilibrium if Marshall's reasoning is applied—for any quantity that, for example, is less than the equilibrium quantity, the excess of demand price over supply price induces expansion; thus price and quantity adjust *toward* equilibrium. Marshall's context is the long run; that of Walras and Hicks is very short periods of time. Still another theoretical complication is multiple equilibria; if a demand curve and a negatively sloped supply curve are given suitable curvatures, they can be made to intersect more than once.

FIGURE 13-12   **UNSTABLE EQUILIBRIUM**

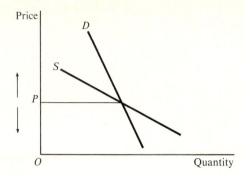

The prices and outputs of many commodities have shown pronounced cyclical movements over long periods of time. Over the years, the prices of these commodities rise and then fall, rise and fall again in a continued wavelike pattern. Production of the same commodities has generally moved up and down in counterwaves. A general explanation for some of the cycles in commodity prices and outputs is furnished by the *cobweb theorem*, as it is called. The *cobweb* name comes from the appearance of the diagrams; see Figures 13-14 and 13-15.

Commodity cycles are, of course, influenced by the forces flowing from the business cycle. Apart from this, commodity cycles have specific causes in the supply responses of producers. Suppose you raise fruit in orchards. The price of the fruit goes up. So you plant more trees. It takes several years for the trees to grow to bearing size. By the time fruit can be plucked from the additional trees, the price is low because you weren't the only one to plant more trees when the price was high.

The cobweb theorem can apply to the prices and outputs of commodities whose production is discontinuous, such as annual crops, or to commodities that take two or more years to produce, such as animals and fruit trees.

The cobweb theorem has still another use because it is the simplest model of the *dynamics* of demand, supply, and price. An often quoted definition of a dynamic theory is that of the Norwegian economist Ragnar Frisch who has said that a dynamic theory connects variables *at different points of time*.

The cobweb model shows demand and supply for a commodity produced and sold under conditions of pure competition. Production takes place in distinct periods of time; for convenience, 1-year periods will be assumed here. The essential feature of the model is that output in year 2 is a response to price in year 1, output in year 3

243   *Short-Run Prices in Pure Competition*

to price in year 2, output in year 4 to price in year 3, etc. Output, then, is lagged 1 year behind price. The supply *curve* stays put in the model; so does the demand curve.

The one-year lag between supply and price is an assumption about the behavior of the producers. Suppose this year's price is high. As the farmers sit near their stoves in the winter making their plans for next year, each one believes that next year's price will be high too, in fact, just as high. Thus each farmer decides to plant, grow, and harvest the size of crop associated with a high price. Each one plans to expand along the marginal cost curve to the point where it meets the *expected* high price. Similarly, a low price this year induces the prediction of the same low price for next year.

The cobweb theorem comes in three standard models. The de luxe, or complicated, models are omitted here. All three standard models have price and output fluctuating around equilibrium. In the first model, price perpetually oscillates from high to low, and output from low to high; equilibrium is never attained. In the second model, price and output flap up and down, but the ups and downs become weaker, then feebler, finally ceasing as equilibrium is reached. In the third model, the movements become wilder and wilder, going always farther away from equilibrium.[5]

Perpetual
Oscillation

Now the first model with its *perpetual oscillation:* In Figure 13–13A, the subscripts for the P's and Q's can be taken to mean successive years. In year 1, OP_1 is the price, let it be supposed. Then in year 2, the quantity OQ_2 is produced. But the demand curve says that OQ_2 can be sold only at the low price of OP_2. The price in year 2 then becomes OP_2. In year 3, the supply curve and the lag assumption

FIGURE 13–13   THE COBWEB THEOREM: PERPETUAL OSCILLATION

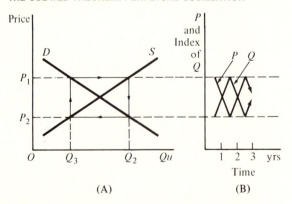

(A)   (B)

[5] Algebraic versions of the models of the cobweb theorem are in Note 2 of the Appendix to Part 3.

say that the quantity produced is OQ_3. But this small quantity sells at price OP_1. Hence in year 3, the price is the same as in year 1. So it continues round and round as the arrows in Figure 13–13A indicate. In this example, the odd-numbered years have high prices and low outputs; the even-numbered years have the opposite.

The immediate cause of the rhythmic alternation between a high and low price is that in the perpetually oscillating model, the slopes of the demand and supply curves are equal. It makes no difference what they are, so long as the slopes are equal. The perpetual oscillation, accordingly, is explained by the constancy of the demand and supply curves and by the identity of the kind of price responses of the buyers and producers.

Figure 13–13B is a schematic times-series diagram. The intervals of time on the diagram are years. The price scale is the same as on Figure 13–13A, but quantity (in bushels or tons, etc.) is expressed by an index, so that price and quantity can be commensurate on the vertical axis.

Damped
Oscillation

The second model has the *damped oscillation*. Let the process start, in Figure 13–14A, with OP_1 in year 1. In year 2, output is OQ_2, which sells at OP_2. In year 3, output drops to OQ_3, which sells at OP_3. And so on. Notice how the prices and outputs come closer and closer to equilibrium. Indeed, they finally reach it, just as a pendulum comes to rest in a vertical position.

In the model with the damping, the slope of the supply curve is greater than that of the demand curve. This means that the producers respond less, relatively speaking, to changes in price than do the consumers. The producers' lesser response causes equilibrium eventually to be reached, provided of course that the demand and supply curves stay put.

Figure 13–14B is also a time-series diagram showing the successive diminution of the fluctuations of price.

FIGURE 13–14   **THE COBWEB THEOREM: DAMPED OSCILLATION**

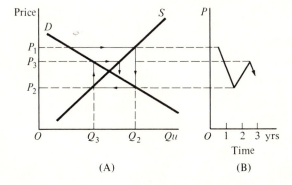

(A)   (B)

FIGURE 13-15   **THE COBWEB THEOREM: EXPLOSIVE OSCILLATION**

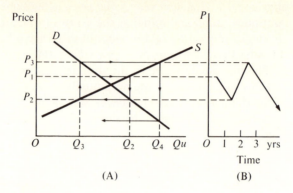

(A)   (B)

Explosive   The third model has the *explosive oscillation*. The cobweb in
Oscillation   Figure 13–15A spins outward, not inward. The fluctuations in Fig-
                   ure 13–15B become ever more violent. Prices and quantities move
                   year by year farther away from equilibrium because the slope of the
                   demand curve is greater than that of the supply curve. The produc-
                   ers' greater responsiveness to price causes the widening oscilla-
                   tions. The buyers always take, at a price, whatever quantity is put
                   on the market. But the producers decide what the quantity is to be.
                        To the mathematical economist, the cobweb theorem models are
                   "beautiful." Their beauty resides in their simplicity and clarity.
                   Though the cobweb theorem does describe something real, the
                   simple models themselves do no more than to execute the logic of
                   their assumptions. When seen in operation for the first time, the
                   explosive model is likely to raise eyebrows, and raise them high.
                   How can such things be? The explosions result from the linearity of
                   demand and supply, from the assumption about slopes, and from the
                   rigidity of the assumption about the lagged-response behavior of the
                   producers. An appropriate modification of linearity can easily muffle
                   or banish the explosions.

Significance   Doctrines of equilibrium probably paint too cheerful a picture of the
                   working of the price system in a private enterprise economy.
                   Equilibrium means that the fundamental forces of wants and of
                   scarcity are precisely balanced by the impersonal mechanism of the
                   market. But with disequilibrium and instability in competitive mar-
                   kets, prices in the private enterprise economy do not unvaryingly do
                   their work with speed and dispatch. Disturbances of equilibrium are
                   not always promptly corrected. Some disturbances, and therefore
                   maladjustments, can persist almost indefinitely.
                        The instability of price and output associated with supply curves
                   whose negative slopes are less than those of the accompanying

demand curves is an instability that can probably be cured. Only brief remarks can be made here. But, in general, the cause behind a supply curve that causes troublesome fluctuations in price is the existence of one-crop cultivation by people accustomed to low incomes. Economic development programs can show such people how to grow other crops and engage in other activities, and can whet their desires for more consumer goods. If the programs are successful, supply curves swing around and take on positive slopes.

Price-output cobwebs can be smashed by more and better information and forecasts if producers act on them. Here too, government and other agencies can, through a variety of means, show producers how to make better estimates of future prices. Informational services have long existed and are steadily improving. Cobweb effects are likely to become much less important.

APPLICATIONS

The prices of most farm products are still determined in free markets that are close to the model of pure competition. For about half of all farm products, price "support" programs of one kind or another have been in operation. The programs differ among themselves and undergo continual modification. But, in general, it can be said that the federal government tries to raise farm prices by manipulating demand and supply.

The Prices of Farm Products

Just *why* the federal government wants to raise some farm prices is a question too complicated to go into here. The price theory covered in this book can, however, throw some light on two of the causes of federal intervention. One cause is the extreme instability of farm prices over time. Most of that instability can be explained by the inelasticity of both the demand and the supply for farm products singly and collectively. Changes in demand and supply, when both are inelastic, cause sharp fluctuations in price.

Another cause of federal intervention to raise farm prices is that adjustments on the supply side are comparatively slow. To say this is really to repeat that over periods of two to five years, supply is highly inelastic. To change from one crop to another, to alter the sizes of herds of animals, to raise fruit trees to maturity—all these similar adjustments do take time. Such slow adjustments are obviously not peculiar to agriculture; they exist in mining and in other branches of the economy where fixed equipment is highly specialized. But, somehow, the difficulties of farmers in adjusting to changing prices command more attention and more sympathy.

Federal efforts to increase farm prices work on both the demand and supply sides. When they are successful, the efforts push demand curves to the right and supply curves to the left. Though in general little can be done to increase the demand for farm products, research is carried on to find new uses and markets for them. Only occasionally does it result in major changes for a particular product; a leading example was the introduction of frozen orange juice concentrate, which came out of federally sponsored research. On the supply side, federal policies tend to work at cross purposes. On the one hand, applied research, education, and related activities have the effect, over longer periods, of increasing supply by improving productivity, that is, by changing farmers' production functions. On the other hand, acreage allotments, marketing quotas, and other techniques of control cause short-period reductions in the supplies of the crops they are applied to. As is well known, however, reductions in acreage hardly ever cause proportionate reductions in output, because farmers take out their poorer acres and fertilize the remaining ones more heavily.

Methods of
Subsidy

In general, the method of subsidy has been to raise prices; with inelastic demands for farm products, farmers' gross incomes are then higher. But this method is open to the objection that resource allocation becomes less efficient. Another method, which used to be called the Brannan plan, is a proposal to let farm prices be wholly free and to pay cash subsidies to farmers when free prices are "too low."

Consider Figure 13–16. Here are demand and supply for one farm commodity in one year. Demand is inelastic; supply is represented as perfectly inelastic to indicate that the farmers throw the whole crop on the market for whatever price it will bring. The equilibrium price is OP_E; let the support price be OP_S. For the support price to prevail, the government has to acquire the amount BA. After buying the amount BA, the government has to keep this quantity off the market by putting it in storage, or by giving it away abroad, or even by destroying it. The cost to the government is BA multiplied by the support price, i.e., the rectangle FA. Production control is a second

FIGURE 13–16   **CONTROL OF FARM PRICES**

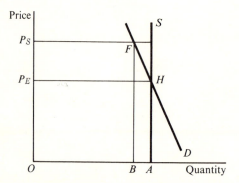

248   *Competitive Pricing*

method of pushing the price up to the support level. If it worked perfectly (which rarely happens), production control would eliminate the quantity BA and would, in effect, establish a new supply curve—the line BF.

Under a policy like the Brannan plan, the price would be the equilibrium price, and the government would make up the difference. Each farmer would get a payment equal to P_SP_E multiplied by the size of his own crop. The total cost to the government of this kind of subsidy would be the rectangle P_SH. The total payments by consumers are less, because they pay the lower equilibrium price and because their demand is inelastic. Under this plan, the cost to the government is higher, because under both methods, the gross income of the farmers is the same—the rectangle P_SA.

The higher cost to the government when the farmer is subsidized directly is not a necessarily strong argument against this method. The total cost to both consumers and taxpayers together is the same either way. But low-income consumers spend larger percentages of their incomes on food than do high-income consumers; low-income consumers pay smaller percentages of their incomes in taxes. It follows that the burden of the price-support program weighs more heavily on those with low incomes than does the burden of the direct-subsidy program.

Effects of a
Tax on Price

The last application here is offered more for its contribution to the understanding of theory than for its usefulness in economic policy.

Suppose that a tax is imposed on the producers of a commodity, the tax being so many cents a unit for each unit they produce. Naturally, the producers wish they could pass the tax on to the consumers. But they could only do so if they could raise their prices. This is impossible in pure competition because individual producers have no control over price at all. The tax, however, is an added cost. It increases the marginal costs of the firms, thus causing them to produce less at any given price. Therefore the industry supply curve shifts upward and to the left. The new equilibrium price is higher than the old. The tax, accordingly, *does* result in a higher price—not because of the producers' wishes, but because of the decrease in supply. The rise in price is not, however, equal to the tax.

Why so? To see this, look at Figure 13–17. The initial equilibrium is with the curves D and S, the price being P_1A and the quantity OA. The tax brings into existence the new supply curve S_t. The vertical distance between the two supply curves is the amount of the tax per unit. The new equilibrium is the price P_2B and the quantity OB. The rise in price is P_2R, whereas the tax per unit is P_2S. The rise in price is less than the tax.[6] Just how much less depends on the elasticities

[6] The same point is proved with simple algebra in Note 1, Appendix to Part 3.

FIGURE 13-17

EFFECT OF A TAX ON EQUILIBRIUM PRICE

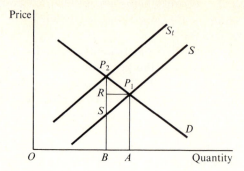

of demand and supply. The more elastic the demand and the less elastic the supply, the smaller is the rise in price as a fraction of the tax. The common sense of it all is this: The more elastic the demand, the less willing are the buyers to pay higher prices for smaller quantities. The more inelastic the supply, the greater is the decline in marginal cost as output is cut back by the tax, which is then added to a lower level of cost.

SUMMARY

The *equilibrium market price* of a commodity bought and sold in a market where pure competition exists is determined by market demand and supply schedules. The equilibrium price equates demand and supply. Equilibrium prices and quantities continually change because demand and supply curves are always in motion. The actions of speculators prevent gross seasonal fluctuations in prices. The flow of production from an industry in the short run is described by the *short-run supply curve of the industry*. This curve is the sum of the short-run supply curves of the firms. Each firm adjusts its output so that marginal cost is equal to price which, in turn, is equal to marginal revenue. The firm produces even if price is less than full cost, provided that price is above average variable cost. The *supply curve of a firm* is the portion of its marginal cost curve that lies above the average variable cost curve. The *short-run equilibrium price* is determined by the equality of industry demand and industry supply. The equilibrium price can be consistent with either widespread losses or profits for the firms in the industry.

Prices and outputs in competitive markets are normally in *disequilibrium*, in motion between equilibrium positions. Short-run demand can shift more quickly than short-run supply. If demand increases, prices rise high, then fall as they approach a new equilibrium. If supply should change faster than demand, prices first fall, then rise to a new equilibrium. Over long periods, price can be below equilibrium if demand grows more slowly than supply. A *stable equilibrium* is one whose deviations are corrected by the accompanying forces. The stability of the equilibrium of a competitive firm requires rising marginal cost. The stability of the equilibrium of a competitive industry requires that demand exceed supply at prices less than equilibrium. Industry equilibrium is unstable if a negatively sloped supply curve is less steep than the demand curve. The *cobweb theorem* describes price and output when supply is lagged one period behind price.

SELECTED REFERENCES

Alfred Marshall, *Principles of Economics,* 8th ed. (Macmillan, London, 1920), book V, chap. 5; Jacob Viner, "Cost Curves and Supply Curves," *Zeitschrift für Nationalökonomie*, 1931 [reprinted in *Readings in Price Theory,* ed. George J. Stigler and Kenneth E. Boulding (Irwin, Homewood, 1952)]; George J. Stigler, *The Theory of Price,* 3d ed. (Macmillan, New York, 1966), chap. 10; Mordecai Ezekiel, "The Cobweb Theorem," *Quarterly Journal of Economics* (February 1938) [reprinted in American Economic Association, *Readings in Business Cycle Theory* (Blakiston, Philadelphia, 1944), chap. 21]; Donald Stevenson Watson, ed., *Price Theory in Action: A Book of Readings,* 3d ed. (Houghton Mifflin, Boston, 1973), chaps. 26–28; Paul A. Samuelson, "Dynamic Process Analysis," in *A Survey of Contemporary Economics,* ed. Howard S. Ellis (Blakiston, Philadelphia, 1948), chap. 10; Reuben C. Buse and Daniel W. Bromley, *Applied Economics: Resource Allocation in Rural America* (Iowa State University Press, Ames, 1975), chap. 9; Marc Nerlove, *Dynamics of Supply* (Johns Hopkins Press, Baltimore, 1958).

EXERCISES AND PROBLEMS

1. Draw diagrams with equilibrium market prices showing various effects of changes in demand and supply.
2. Show that price does not change if demand increases and if supply is perfectly elastic, and that quantity does not change if demand increases and if supply is perfectly inelastic.
3. Suppose both demand and supply were (a) perfectly elastic and (b) perfectly inelastic. What then?
4. Why would a firm in pure competition never want to spend any money on advertising its product?
5. Why does the firm in pure competition operate in the rising portion of its marginal cost curve? Why not the falling portion?

6. Suppose that consumers' tastes change, shifting from commodity A to commodity B. Show how industries A and B are affected, immediately and ultimately.

7. Draw a diagram with a negatively sloped supply curve, but with a stable equilibrium.

8. A firm buys an equilibrium quantity of an input. What makes this equilibrium stable?

9. See if you can draw a single cobweb diagram showing *both* explosive and damped oscillations.

10. See if you can draw a single cobweb diagram with *both* damped and perpetual oscillation.

11. Why are the demand and marginal revenue curves of a competitive firm identical? When are the average and marginal cost curves of a competitive firm identical?

12. What condition prevails when zero output is the optimum output for a competitive firm in the short run?

13. With *total* cost and *total* revenue curves, show (a) the break-even point of a purely competitive firm and (b) the profit-maximizing output of the same firm.

14. With diagrams, show a short-run equilibrium price that is consistent with widespread losses and another equilibrium price that is consistent with large profits for most of the firms in a competitive industry.

15. Explain how a government forecast of a low price for hogs could be acted on by farmers in such a way as to cause higher hog prices. How does your answer modify the assumptions of the cobweb theorem?

14
Long-Run Prices
IN PURE COMPETITION

"In the long run," Lord Keynes once said, "we are all dead." He was talking about money and the price level and about the folly of relying on long-run theoretical propositions in tackling short-run problems.[1] Keynes's remark has been much quoted, with the apparent implication that the long run is far away, a never-never land, a condition of happy adjustment.

MEANING AND RELEVANCE

The implication is not true. The essence of the idea of the long run is the growth of an industry. Industries do grow; new firms enter growing industries, adding their new capital to the expanding stock of the capital of the firms already in the industry. Some industries decline; firms leave them, and the stocks of capital shrink. Nor does the long run have to be a lengthy period of calendar time, though indeed it can be. For industries using readily available, unspecialized, and easily transferable resources, the long run is a comparatively brief length of calendar time.

The long-run equilibrium price of a competitively produced commodity has been a central interest of economic theory for two centuries. In the eighteenth and nineteenth centuries, Adam Smith, David Ricardo, and others sought to explain the "natural values" of commodities, to find the causes of the "natural" level of the price of, say, wheat, when all temporary and ephemeral forces, such as variations in the weather and the effects of wars, are set aside. Karl Marx, the founder of the philosophy of communism, devoted most of the space in *Das Kapital* (1867) to *his* theory of the values of commodities produced in a capitalist ecomony. Smith, Ricardo,

[1] Keynes's next sentence after the one quoted is also worth repeating: "Economists set themselves too easy, too useless a task if in tempestuous seasons they can only tell us that when the storm is long past the ocean is flat again." J. M. Keynes, *A Tract on Monetary Reform*, Macmillan, London, 1923, p. 80.

253

Marx, and others gave explanations of value that looked mainly or primarily to the amounts of labor needed to produce a commodity. When the concept of marginal utility was introduced in the second half of the nineteenth century, it was put to work on the same task; theorists sought to find the ultimate cause of value in consumer demand. Alfred Marshall's contribution to economic theory is often said to consist of having synthesized cost of production and consumer demand as mutual determinants of the value of a commodity.

Price theory used to be called "the theory of value and distribution," i.e., the theory of the exchange rates of commodities and the derived theory of the incomes of owners of productive services. In the past, those parts of price theory having to do with pure competition and the long run had strong philosophical or even ideological associations. Most of the prominent theorists have had strong leanings to conservative positions on issues of economic policy. Since the 1930s, however, price theory has tended to become a box of tools that anyone, conservative or otherwise, can use for varied purposes. Even socialists can draw upon price theory for help in designing a socialist economy.

Because it describes the fullest mutual adjustment of demand and supply, the doctrine of long-run price is still important in modern price theory. The demonstration of the economic advantages of free trade and many of the central propositions of welfare economics are special cases of long-run equilibrium prices in pure competition.

Of current interest are problems like these: At the end of the twentieth century, what will probably be the relative price of beef? Of petroleum products? Of lumber? Answers, in the form of estimates, to such questions are important because they can guide policy decisions in the years to come. Notice the form of such questions. The dollar price of a pound of beef in the year 2000 might reflect more than anything else the change in the general level of prices between now and then. The question asks for the *relative* price of beef—its price relative to the prices of other meats, of dairy products, of cereals. The answers to such questions will also be framed independently of temporary disturbances that might exist in the 1990s, disturbances such as unusual weather or deep depressions. The answers run in terms of the probable growth of demand and the probable changes in the conditions of supply.

EQUILIBRIUM OF THE FIRM

The main task of the analysis is to construct the long-run supply curve of a purely competitive industry. Here too, of course, the behavior of the industry is the collective behavior of the firms. Hence the individual firm must first be put under analysis.

The long-run cost curve of the firm is now brought forward from

FIGURE 14–1   **LONG-RUN EQUILIBRIUM OF THE FIRM**

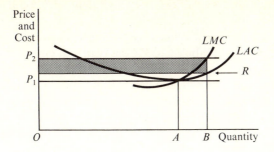

Chapter 11. In Figure 14–1, *LAC* is the long-run average cost curve, with its companion *LMC*, the long-run marginal cost curve. The objective of the firm is to maximize its net profits, the excess of revenue over full cost. The firm does this by adjusting output so that *LMC* = price. Suppose first that the price is OP_2. At this price, the firm adjusts the scale of its plant so as to produce the amount *OB*. Total revenue is the rectangle P_2B. Total cost is the rectangle *OR*. So the net profits are the shaded rectangle P_2R.

Entry and Net Profits

Let it now be assumed that the cost curves of the firms in the industry have the same minimum point. A justification of this assumption will be given shortly. If, then, all the firms in an industry are earning net profits, other firms will be attracted to the industry. In the absence of other events such as a change in demand, the added output from the new firms lowers the price. As the price falls, the net profits of the firms, both the old ones and the newcomers, diminish. When the price equals minimum average cost, net profits are zero. There is then no inducement for new firms to enter. Neither is there any incentive for firms to leave an industry when net profits are zero because all the firms are earning normal profits, which by definition are large enough to keep the firms in the industry. Normal profits, of course, are included in the cost curves.

Just how quickly new firms enter an industry where net profits are to be had is clearly a complex matter. An entrepreneur thinking of going into a new industry needs information on costs, prices, and net profits. The entrepreneur must make an estimate about how long high net profits will continue. He or she must have, or be able to get, the needed know-how and financing. To build a new plant takes time. These and similar analytical complexities are set aside by the assumption that competition is pure *and perfect*. The assumptions of *perfect knowledge* and of decisions under certainty have been implicit all along. To them is now added the assumption of *perfect mobility*, i.e., firms enter and leave an industry quickly and without friction. These perfections greatly simplify the analysis.

Equality of Price and Minimum Average Cost

The entry of new firms lowers the price in Figure 14–1 to OP_1. If the price should go below OP_1, the firm will continue to produce in the short run, provided the price is higher than average variable cost. But in the long run, the firm will not produce at a price below OP_1, because any such price does not cover full cost. The price OP_1 is equal to marginal cost and also to the minimum average cost. And since price is the same as marginal revenue to a firm under pure competition,

$$P = MR = LMC = LAC.$$

One more thing: Observe that, at price OP_1, the firm's demand curve is tangent to the long-run average cost curve at its minimum point.

The importance of the equalities and of the tangency just mentioned will be explained shortly. In the meantime, consider another aspect of the long-run equilibrium of the firm: The firm's marginal cost is rising. Marginal cost *must* rise, for if it did not, there could be no equilibrium, no output with maximum net profits. Imagine that the long-run marginal cost of a firm were either constant or falling, i.e., the *LMC* curve would either be horizontal or declining downward to the right. If there is to be any production at all, the *LMC* curve would have to lie below the price line. So, if *LMC* is either horizontal or falling to the right, the firm would expand indefinitely, without limit. The more it would expand, the larger would be its net profits, which, however, would never reach a maximum. Since all this is absurd, it follows that long-run marginal cost must be rising, in the neighborhood of the equilibrium output.

Observe that this proof of rising marginal cost in the long run holds for firms in purely competitive industries. The doubts expressed in Chapter 9 about the cause of eventually decreasing returns (page 163), and in Chapter 11 about the upturn of marginal and average costs on the right side of the curve (page 197) are settled at least for competitive firms.

Approximate Equality of Full Costs

The next step is to show that the firms in an industry of pure competition can be regarded as having about the same costs. So far their cost curves have been assumed to be similar. The essential feature of the assumption is that each firm has the same minimum cost; even so, the firms can still have different outputs. The assumption is more than a helpful simplification; it rests upon reasoned premises.

Statistical studies of the costs of firms in an industry always show great differences from one firm to another. But such studies of costs are made for a particular point or period of time, and therefore the studies catch the industry in a short-run condition. Besides, the cost figures available for analysis are always in the form of business costs which, as Chapter 8 shows, are always less than full costs. Full costs are relevant in the analysis of the long run. Attention must be focused once more on the difference between them and business costs.

Differences in business costs at any one point of time are due to a multitude of causes, small and large. With opportunity for full adjustment, i.e., in the long run, the small causes disappear or become so negligible that they can be disregarded. But the large cause that remains in the long run is the scarcity of resources. Let the scarce resource be management. In some purely competitive industries, the scarce resource could be a particular type of land or other natural resource. To point to management is to achieve a greater degree of generality, and to say that good management is scarce could hardly evoke disagreement. Scarce here means that in the long run the supply curve of the resource is positively sloped, not horizontal.

Assume first that management is hired by entrepreneurs. Only a few firms in the industry can have the services of the best managers. They bring about low business costs of the firms they work for. But these managers can demand and get salaries equal to the cost savings they cause. If one firm does not pay such a salary, another will. Hence managers' salaries approximately equalize full costs.

Next, assume that the entrepreneurs do their own managing. Part of their implicit costs are the salaries they forego. The entrepreneur-managers look upon their foregone salaries as costs. If they do not earn them, they abandon that particular industry to go into another. Here, too, costs become approximately equal.

EQUILIBRIUM OF THE INDUSTRY

When the firms in a purely competitive industry earn zero net profits, the number of firms is in equilibrium; no firms enter and no firms leave. Each firm is in equilibrium, holding its output steady. Therefore the output of the industry is in equilibrium, there being no force causing the output of the industry either to expand or to contract.[2]

___

[2] The paragraph above conforms to standard modern theory. When the industry is in long-run equilibrium, *each* firm is also in long-run equilibrium. But a moment's reflection will remind anyone that in an industry with a steady rate of output, some firms are expanding their own volumes of production, while others, the ever-present weaker ones, are cutting their outputs back. In a growing industry, some firms grow much faster than others. Every industry has its new firms, its vigorous and progressive firms, and its older and perhaps decaying firms. At stake here is not a contrast

In this equilibrium, all the firms in the industry produce at their minimum average costs. The firms do so more from necessity than from choice. The firms produce their profit-maximizing outputs whose costs are at a minimum.

The next step on the way to the construction of long-run industry supply curves is to take account of external economies and diseconomies.

EXTERNAL ECONOMIES AND DISECONOMIES

External economies and diseconomies are changes in the position of the long-run cost curves of firms when the changes are caused by the growth of the industry. If firms enjoy external economies, their cost curves drop along their entire lengths. Similarly, external diseconomies cause firms' cost curves to be lifted up.

Figure 14–2 has two positions of a long-run average cost curve of a firm, positions *A* and *B*. External economies cause the curve to drop from *A* to *B*, whereas external diseconomies lift the curve up from *B* to *A*. In all likelihood, however, such changes in the position of a firm's cost curve would rarely be so great as they are shown in Figure 14–2.

FIGURE 14–2

EXTERNAL EFFECTS ON A FIRM'S COSTS

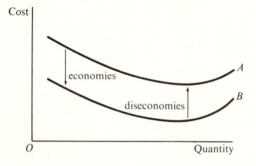

between "theory" and "reality." The issue—whether the full equilibrium of an industry requires the full equilibrium and the equal costs of *all* firms—is an issue between two theories, the modern theory and Alfred Marshall's. To Marshall, long-run equilibrium of the industry meant the equality of long-run demand and supply, nothing more. Some firms could be expanding, others declining, and still others holding their outputs steady. Marshall's famous analogy was the trees of a forest: The forest is growing at some rate, measured in board feet of timber; some trees are being born, some are growing fast, some are growing at the same rate as the forest, some are growing more slowly, and some are dying. A serious shortcoming of Marshall's theory, however, is that he did not demonstrate that for an industry in equilibrium, the outputs of the growing firms are equal to those of the declining firms. It is possible that modern methods of analysis, starting from Marshall's brilliant insights, will much improve the current theory of the connections between the output of an industry and the outputs of the firms in it. See Peter Newman, "The Erosion of Marshall's Theory of Value," *Quarterly Journal of Economics,* 74 (November 1960), 587–600.

The idea of external economies is another of Alfred Marshall's contributions. He drew a contrast with the firm's "internal" economies, which are reflected in the declining, or left, part of the firm's U-shaped long-run cost curve. When they occur, external economies, said Marshall, are the result of the growth of the industry the firm belongs to. As an industry grows, many small changes take place. If auxiliary services such as financing and transportation become cheaper, if materials and semifinished goods bought by the firms become better and cheaper as they are supplied in larger quantities, if the skills of the labor force improve as the result of the spread of training programs paid for perhaps from public funds, if these and similar cost-reducing changes happen, then external economies exist. They do not flow from the introduction of major technological improvements, which also thrust cost curves downward. No, Marshall's external economies arise from the concurrence of many little things, which can include the more efficient application of known technology. The many little things producing external economies as an industry grows can be summed up under two headings: (1) decreases in the prices of some inputs, and (2) increases in the physical productivities of some inputs.

Marshall did not use the expression *external diseconomies* but, instead, wrote about the tendency toward diminishing return. External diseconomies accompanying the expansion of an industry arise from higher input prices or from diminishing physical productivities of the firms' inputs, or from both. Input prices become higher if important inputs to the industry are available to it at rising supply prices. That is, the supply curves of the inputs slope up to the right so that as the industry grows and as its demands for the inputs increase, their prices rise. The industry can get more of such inputs only by bidding them away from other industries. Industries exploiting natural resources—farming, mining, cutting timber, fishing—run into steadily less favorable physical input-output ratios as they expand unless their expansions are accompanied by offsetting technological improvements.

Marshall's concepts are still relevant in the theory of competitive prices in the long run. They will be fitted into the theory shortly. But at this point, a few remarks will be made about the expressions *external economies* and *diseconomies* as they are met in other contexts.

External
Effects in
Modern
Analysis

In the postwar literature on welfare economies and on the development of underdeveloped economies, the expression *external effects* carries a broader meaning. These broader external effects—another name for them is *spillover effects*—will be discussed more fully in

Chapter 15, part of which will touch on the welfare aspects of competitive pricing.

THE LONG-RUN SUPPLY CURVE

The long-run supply curve of an industry in pure competition shows a set of prices and amounts. The prices are equal to the minimum average full costs of the firms. The amounts are the equilibrium outputs of the industry at each price. Long-run supply curves can be horizontal, positively sloped, or negatively sloped. These are the supply curves of *constant-cost, increasing-cost,* and *decreasing-cost industries.*

Constant-Cost Industries

Although no one knows for sure, it is probable that many, if not most, industries are subject to neither external economies nor diseconomies. Or, if both tendencies are present, they counterbalance each other. Such industries have constant cost in the long run. On a diagram, the height of the supply curve is equal to the minimum average long-run costs of the firms. Since the long-run supply curve is horizontal, changes in long-run demand cause no changes in the long-run equilibrium price. When demand increases and when the output of the industry is fully adjusted to the larger demand, the additional output comes from more firms. A doubling of the long-run equilibrium output of a constant-cost industry comes from a doubling of the number of firms in the industry.

To see why this is so, consider Figure 14–3A, which shows a firm, and Figure 14–3B, which shows an industry. Notice that the firm's quantity axis is measured in thousands of units and the industry's in millions of units. To begin, let both the firm and the industry be in equilibrium. The price is OP; the firm (and each of the other firms) produces Oa. The industry produces OB, which is Oa multiplied by the number of firms. The industry demand is D_1, and of course the firm demand is the horizontal line in Figure 14–3A drawn from P. Now let the industry demand increase to D_2. Suppose that

FIGURE 14–3   **CONSTANT-COST INDUSTRY**

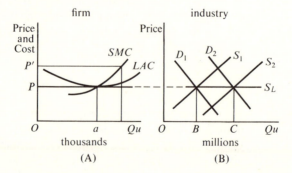

(A)

(B)

the increase in demand is not slow and gradual, but comes fairly quickly. Hence the price rises. All the firms now earn net profits and can earn more by expanding production. To seize the extra net profits, they expand output with their existing plants and do so along their short-run marginal cost curves. Thus if price initially rises to OP'—it could go higher—the firm increases output to beyond Oa. The industry's output expands along the short-run supply curve S_1. The high and profitable price attracts new firms to the industry. The supply curve S_1 shifts to the right. The additions to total output cause the price to fall. As it does, the old firms cut back production along their SMC curves. If demand continues to be D_2, the price finally falls back to OP. When it does, no new firms enter. The short-run supply curve stops shifting and becomes the curve S_2. Each firm, both old and new, again produces the amount Oa. Total industry output is OC, the additional amount BC coming from the new firms. The long-run supply curve of the industry is S_L, drawn through the points of equilibrium of D_1 and S_1, and D_2 and S_2. Should the demand increase again, firms would temporarily expand once more. When the dust would settle on the new long-run equilibrium, it would be found farther to the right on the horizontal line S_L.

Increasing-Cost Industries

In increasing-cost industries, external diseconomies prevail. The expansion of such industries causes the cost curves of the firms to be pushed up. The rise in costs makes the long-run supply curve slope upward to the right.

Figures 14–4A and 14–4B help to tell the story. Initial equilibrium of the firm and the industry is at price OP_1. Each firm produces Oa; all of them together produce the industry output of OB. Then let long-run demand increase from D_1 to D_2. The price goes up; firms expand along their SMC curves; new firms enter; and the short-run industry supply curve shifts to the right. But costs rise. The cost curve LAC_1 is pushed up. In Figure 14–4A, the new and higher cost

FIGURE 14–4   INCREASING-COST INDUSTRY

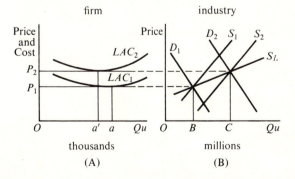

thousands   millions
(A)   (B)

curve is LAC_2. Thus the additional output from the new firm does not eventually cause price to go back down to OP_1, but only down to OP_2, which is the new and higher equilibrium price. The long-run supply curve S_L therefore slopes upward to the right.

In Figure 14–4A, the new and higher cost curve LAC_2 is drawn so that its minimum point corresponds to the output Oa'. This is a smaller equilibrium output. The higher costs force the firms to shrink a little in size. But this result is not necessary. Much depends on what the higher costs are and how the firms can adjust to them.

Decreasing-Cost Industries

Similar reasoning and similarly constructed diagrams can show that external economies cause the cost curves of firms to fall and that therefore the long-run supply curve of the industry slopes downward to the right.

Some economic theorists have objected to the idea that an industry can have a downward sloping supply curve. The objections come in two groups. First, the importance of external economies is belittled; along with this goes the assertion that external diseconomies are always present and always have a heavier weight. An industry can expand only by bidding resources away from other industries; it can bid resources away only by paying higher prices. Secondly, some theorists say that if long-run supply curves slope downward, the stability of the equilibrium can be in doubt. The question of the stability of equilibrium was discussed in Chapter 13.

SUMMARY

The doctrine of *long-run equilibrium price* in pure competition applies to the growth of an industry, to the fullest mutual adjustment of demand and supply. In the long run, the firm adjusts its output and the scale of its plant so as to equate long-run marginal cost with price. If price is such that the firms in an industry earn net profits, new firms enter the industry. All firms have the same costs because payments for scarce resources have the effect of equalizing the long-run average costs of firms. When the industry is in equilibrium, each of the firms is in equilibrium, with $P = MR = LMC = LAC$. Output is at a minimum cost. As an industry grows in response to higher prices caused by increased demand, the firms can be subject to *external economies or diseconomies*, which cause their cost curves to fall or to rise. For a *constant-cost industry*, the long-run supply curve is horizontal at the level of the minimum average costs of the firms. For an *increasing-cost industry*, the long-run supply curve is positively sloped, showing rising minimum average costs of the firms owing to the presence of external diseconomies. A *decreasing-cost industry* has a negatively sloped supply curve owing to external economies.

SELECTED REFERENCES

Alfred Marshall, *Principles of Economics*, 8th ed. (Macmillan, London, 1920), book V; Joan Robinson, *The Economics of Imperfect Competition* (Macmillan, London, 1933), book III.

George J. Stigler, *The Theory of Price*, 3d ed. (Macmillan, New York, 1966), chap. 10.

From George J. Stigler and Kenneth E. Boulding, eds. *Readings in Price Theory* (Irwin, Homewood, 1952): Jacob Viner, "Cost Curves and Supply Curves"; Joan Robinson, "Rising Supply Price."

EXERCISES AND PROBLEMS

1. Draw the diagrams for the firm and the industry for decreasing-cost industries.
2. Does long-run cost *determine* price? Explain.
3. Suppose a competitive industry were given a permanent subsidy in the form of payments for each unit produced by each firm. Draw diagrams to show what would happen to the price.
4. The price of a jacket is always higher than the price of trousers of the same quality. Why?
5. Draw diagrams to show the effects of technological improvements on long-run price.
6. Compare and contrast the relations between prices and costs in the market period, the short run, and the long run.
7. Are long-run opportunity costs likely to be the same as short-run opportunity costs? Explain.
8. Explain why profits are not maximized in the long run when short-run marginal cost is equal to price but is not equal to long-run marginal cost.
9. Describe the relations between input prices, the entry of firms, and increasing or decreasing costs in the long run.
10. Explain why prices are likely to fall in an increasing-cost industry as a result of the exit of firms. What causes the exit of firms?

15
Competitive Equilibrium:
SOME APPLICATIONS

The uses of the theory of the long-run equilibrium of a competitive industry are many. This chapter will cover some of the applications of the theory. The applied theory is generally known as *welfare economics*. The word welfare here does not have its ordinary meaning but, instead, means "efficiency." An efficient economy achieves maximum economic welfare. When this is so, the individuals in the economy enjoy maximum utility from the resources they have.

The examples of welfare economics in this chapter are applied *partial equilibrium* theory, which means that the analysis confines itself to one industry. The demand for the industry's output and the prices of its inputs are assumed to be given. In contrast, more rigorous (and more advanced) welfare economics is applied *general equilibrium* theory, whose attention focuses on the interdependence of all prices, all demands, and all supplies. Chapter 23 presents a nonmathematical version of general equilibrium theory and its associated welfare economics.

Partial equilibrium, or one-industry-at-a-time, theory has the merit of simplicity; the theory extends the ideas covered earlier in this book. The applied welfare economics that deals with real-life problems is always partial equilibrium analysis. It has to be, if real problems are to be tackled at all. But it seems worthwhile just to mention here that some theorists regard partial equilibrium welfare analysis as the "theory of the second best." Although this expression looks as if it conveys faint praise, it does not. Instead, second-best welfare receives only disdain. Although the full reasoning here is too advanced for this book, the story goes something like this: Suppose the widget industry has an optimum output, selling the widgets at a price that just covers full costs. Then the widget industry is efficient and the economic welfare from it is at a maximum. But is it really? Almost certainly not, say the theorists of the second best, because the other industries the widget producers sell to and buy from are probably not efficient. And if they were to become so, the prices the widget industry pays and receives would change, thus throwing the industry out of its efficient position. Therefore, so runs this argument, one industry can be truly efficient only if all other industries are efficient.

Earlier chapters show how consumers and firms individually achieve efficiency. The consumers in equilibrium are maximizing utility. The consumer is in an efficient position, that is, a position that cannot be improved, given, of course, prices and the consumer's income and tastes. When the firm is in equilibrium, it minimizes its costs and maximizes the difference between its costs and its revenue. Thus the firm in equilibrium is also in an efficient position, one it cannot improve.

The efficiencies of the equilibria of the consumer and of the firm, when they are viewed in isolation as units in the economy, hold for whatever are the prices that confront them. These prices can be anything. The prices, however, that make the efficiencies of consumers and firms compatible and that bring their separate efficiencies into one joint efficient position are the prices that prevail in long-run competitive equilibrium.

When both the firms and the industry are in long-run equilibrium, production takes place at minimum cost. The firms earn no net profits; they receive their full costs, nothing more. Output at minimum cost is *optimum*; it stands for "efficiency." Consumers get the commodity at the lowest price compatible with full costs; the total value of the resources devoted to production of the equilibrium amount is at a minimum.

Observe, however, that the firms do not produce the optimum output because it is optimum. The firms are compelled by their price-cost environment to produce that output. In trying to maximize their net profits, the firms find themselves—in equilibrium— earning zero net profits while producing optimum outputs. If they did anything else, they would lose money.

Remember too the limitations surrounding the doctrine that, in the long run, price equals minimum cost. Competition must be pure and also perfect enough that the firms can make their full adjustments. The doctrine assumes away the effects of technological changes. Tastes and technology hold still long enough for the horizontal line of demand to the individual firms to become tangent to the minimum points on the *U*-shaped cost curves.

If the long-run equilibrium price is to be regarded as an unequivocal optimum, two more conditions must hold. Both are discussed more fully a little later on. They can be mentioned briefly here. One of the conditions is that the minimum average cost, which equals the equilibrium price, is a full measure of *all* of the costs of producing the commodity. The other condition is that there be no gross disparity between the average incomes of the producers and the consumers. Some theorists would argue that if the producers are poor and the consumers are rich, or vice versa, the long-run equilibrium is not optimum.

Despite these limitations, the doctrine gives a standard of economic efficiency. As later chapters will show, the standard is used to measure the deviations from economic efficiency that occur in monopoly, monopolistic competition, and the oligopoly.

Efficiency and Equity

The competitive equilibrium is compatible with many different patterns of income distribution. A different constellation of efficient prices and quantities would exist for each distribution of incomes. Imagine an economy where the land, mineral resources, factories, etc., are owned by a small number of families, and where a small minority of persons possess advanced training and education. In this economy the few with the highly productive and therefore valuable resources earn high incomes, the many with the less productive resources earn low incomes. Still, this economy can attain efficiency. In contrast, imagine another economy with widespread ownership of property and with training and education available for all persons. In this second economy efficiency would be accompanied by only moderately unequal incomes.

Can anything be said about which of the two efficient economies is the more desirable? A few economists[1] have conceived of optimum economic welfare as a combination of efficiency and equity. For them equity means a distribution of incomes that approaches as far as it can toward equal incomes without impairing incentives to work. But the orthodox and dominant view of economists is that economic science can say nothing at all about what the distribution of incomes should be, because to do so would require the imposition of a value judgment from outside the domain of economics.

THE SOCIAL RETURN FROM HYBRID CORN

Increases in economic welfare can come from any changes that move industries from inefficient to efficient positions. Gains in welfare can also arise from improvements in technology.

An improvement in technology has the effect of lowering a long-run supply curve. The long-run equilibrium price therefore falls. One of the technological successes of this century was the increase of corn yields from the planting of hybrid corn seed, which was developed from research carried out by the federal and state governments and by private seed companies. The increased yield from hybrid corn has been approximately 15 to 20 per cent.

[1] Two prominent ones are A. C. Pigou, *The Economics of Welfare*, 4th ed., Macmillan, London, 1932; and A. P. Lerner, *The Economics of Control*, Macmillan, New York, 1944.

FIGURE 15–1

SOCIAL RETURN FROM HYBRID CORN

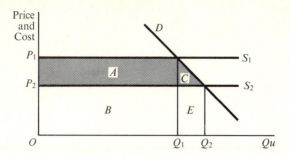

A dollar estimate of the social return from hybrid corn was made by Zvi Griliches, then of the University of Chicago.[2] To keep his estimate low, he took the most conservative figures he could; for example, he used 15 per cent for for the increase in yield. He also assumed that no more than 90 per cent of the corn acres would be planted with hybrid seed. Griliches's estimate was that the annual flow of gross social returns was $341 million for the period following the year 1955. Deducting the projected annual cost of hybrid seed production and research, he obtained $248 million as the annual flow of net social returns. The dollar amount of the research effort leading to hybrid corn had an *annual* rate of return of an astonishing 700 per cent.

The gross social return from hybrid corn can be visualized with the help of Figure 15–1. Griliches assumed that corn is a constant-cost industry. The long-run supply curve is S_2, which is lower than S_1, the supply curve showing costs with nonhybrid seed. The lower equilibrium price is P_2 and the larger production is OQ_2. The total cost of production with hybrid seed is area B plus area E. The total cost with nonhybrid seed is area A plus area B.

The demand for corn is inelastic, the coefficient being about 0.5. It then follows that B plus E is less than A plus B. More corn is produced at a lower total cost. The gain of consumers' surplus is area A plus area C. This is what Griliches called the gross social return. To estimate this in millions of dollars, all Griliches needed were data on prices and quantities, the 15 per cent higher yield figure, the 90 per cent planting figure, and the coefficient of elasticity of demand.

MAINTAINING COMPETITION

One of the firm goals of economic policy in the United States is the maintenance of competition. The instruments of policy are the antitrust laws. For reasons that need not be gone into here, the antitrust

[2] Zvi Griliches, "Research Costs and Social Returns: Hybrid Corn and Related Innovations," *Journal of Political Economy*, 66 (October 1958), 419–431.

laws are not enforced systematically and comprehensively. Nonetheless they have been powerful, one of their strongest effects being their role as a deterrent.

Why maintain competition? Price theory furnishes one of the interlocking elements in the explanation. With the qualifications mentioned already, nothing more need be said at this point except to draw attention once again to the efficiency attained in the equilibria of pure competition.

But many parts of the American economy do not fit the model of pure competition with its homogeneous products, its many consumers and producers, and its absence of price making by anyone. Because of this, some observers have questioned the economic foundation of the antitrust laws. If pure competition outside agriculture is actually rare, if most competition is monopolistic or oligopolistic, why maintain it? Why not seek a wholly fresh approach to the problem of policy for a free and efficient economy?

A good, though not perfect, answer to questions like these is found in the use of the concept of *effective competition*, which has also been called *workable competition*. This concept has come forward in the discussions of antitrust policy since about 1940. The controversies over the fine points and over the emphasis to be given to the elements in the definition will not be gone into here. To put the definition in its barest and simplest form, an industry is effectively competitive if: (1) new firms can freely enter the industry and produce at costs not markedly higher than those of established firms; (2) the firms in the industry are independent and active rivals and do not engage in collusion; and (3) the number of firms is large enough so that none is dominant. When competition is effective, buyers have free choices among alternatives and firms are under constant pressures to keep their costs low.

The concept of effective competition is not so sharp and clear as the concept of pure competition. Also, the emphasis in the concept of effective competition falls on dynamic change rather than on equilibrium. Nonetheless, the concept of effective competition is a bridge between the abstract theory of pure competition and the practical task of maintaining a free and well-functioning economy.

PRICING IN A
SOCIALIST
ECONOMY

In a socialist economy, all material resources, or the greater part of them, are owned by government, which also has unlimited powers of control. Suppose that the sole aim of a socialist government were to operate its economy so as best to satisfy the wants of its people and that the people could freely express their own wants as individuals. What would be the principles of operation of a socialist economy with consumer sovereignty?

With this aim, the socialist government would see to it that the allocation of resources would be as close as possible to the allocation of the competitive model. The people in the socialist society would receive money incomes as workers as well as other money payments corresponding to social insurance benefits. Consumer goods would be sold in shops, the consumers having freedom of choice. The prices of consumer goods, the prices of intermediate goods, the prices of plant, equipment, and labor would all be fixed. They would be fixed to satisfy only one criterion—that demand would equal supply. When demand and supply would change, prices would be changed to preserve equality. The plant managers in the socialist economy would be instructed to adjust production to the prevailing prices. Plant managers would also be instructed to produce amounts whose marginal costs would equal selling prices. In the long run, this rule would assure that productions would take place at minimum average costs. The plant managers would be ordered to keep the costs of any volume of output at a minimum. They would do this by choosing inputs in the same way as a competitive firm in a capitalistic economy.

Much more can be said about the allocation of resources in a socialist economy. The few points just made are enough, however, to show that a consumer-oriented socialist economy would look to the model of pure competition as its ideal. As a group of ideas and of political movements, socialism is well over a century old. But the principles of pricing in a socialist economy were not widely discussed until the 1930s.

The allocation of resources in the United States, and in countries with similar economic and political institutions, is determined not by authority but, instead, by the pattern of prices. Government does directly dispose over more than one-quarter of final output. The composition of the other nearly three-quarters of gross national product results from the market-coordinated decisions of firms and households. The allocation of resources resulting from these decisions is affected in many ways by government price-fixing, taxation, and other kinds of intervention. All these forms of intervention are undertaken separately. They were adopted at different times and as responses to particular pressures and problems. The general economic policy in the United States is still to maintain free institutions and free markets.

DEVIATIONS FROM EFFICIENCY

The efficient economy is the Utopia of the economic theorist. The model of a competitive industry in long-run equilibrium is both static and stationary. It is static because time is absent from the analysis; it is stationary because tastes and technology do not change. Nonetheless, the efficient economy is an ideal that can be approached even if it cannot by fully achieved.

The real world contains many forces causing deviations from efficiency. They can be put into five groups. (1) Consumer tastes and production functions are continually changing. Patterns of resource allocation are always being reshaped by innovations, by economic growth, and by the business cycle. These changes result in constant adjustments toward new positions of moving equilibria. It is easy, however, to exaggerate the role of change. Though of course change does occur, the stability over time of *broad* patterns of resource allocations is remarkably high. (2) Inefficiencies exist because of imperfect knowledge of opportunities and because it often happens that decisions made under uncertainty turn out to be wrong. In monopolistic and oligopolistic industries, competitive pressures are absent or have varying degrees of strength. If these pressures are not strong, firms might not consistently pursue maximum profits and hence minimum costs. Large firms often exhibit "organizational slack" when they are not exposed to strong competitive pressures. In short, then, ignorance, mistakes, and nonmaximizing behavior cause production to be at points away from efficient positions and levels, instead of on them. (3) Inefficiencies are caused by all departures from the norm of the equilibrium of pure competition. Even if they never make mistakes and always maximize their profits, firms producing in other than purely competitive markets do not operate in accord with the rules of economic efficiency. Later chapters deal with monopoly, oligopoly, and monopolistic competition. For present purposes it suffices to say that, when they are in equilibrium, firms in these market structures sell at higher prices and produce smaller quantities than they would if they were subject to the rigors of pure competition. But it does not follow that the antitrust agencies should go out to smash every big firm they can find. The real question is how great are these departures from economic efficiency. No certain answer can be given to this question. When Keynes said ". . . I see no reason to suppose that the existing system seriously misemploys the factors of production which are in use," he expressed a common opinion of economists.[3] Though they have shortcomings, empirical measures of the loss of economic welfare traceable to departures from the norm of competition conclude that this loss is very small. (4) By means of its tariffs and other taxes, through subsidies and a host of other controls, government also contributes to economic inefficiency. At the same time, other actions of government tend to promote efficiency; such actions include the attempt to strengthen competition through the antitrust

[3] J. M. Keynes, *The General Theory of Employment, Interest, and Money,* Harcourt Brace, New York, 1936, p. 379.

laws, the furnishing of vast amounts of information, and the support of research. Most economists would agree that by its high taxes on the rich and through its subsidies to the poor, government brings about a less inequitable distribution of income. (5) Even in competitive equilibrium, efficiency might not be everywhere achieved if *externalities* are present. They will now receive separate attention.

Externalities   *Externalities* are discrepancies between social and private benefits and between social and private costs. *Spillovers* are another often used term for externalities.

Up to now, efficiency has been described as the optimum adjustments of individual consumers and producers, each one maximizing his or her own utility or profits. In other words, each one maximizes private benefits while minimizing private costs. But many activities are interdependent in the sense that consumers and producers can, without intending to, cause other consumers and producers to enjoy additional benefits or to suffer additional costs.

Social benefits are the total benefits from activities of consumption and production. Social benefits can be greater than, equal to, or less than private benefits. Social costs are total costs, to whomever they accrue; they too can be greater than, equal to, or less than private costs.

In this context, economists often speak about costs and benefits to "society." Society seems to be some brooding presence that hovers over us all, bestowing approval and (mostly) disapproval of what goes on in the economy. And it is never quite clear whether society is or is not the same thing as government. The kindest thing to say about society, as an omniscient and benevolent supreme authority, is that the notion is dubious political theory. If, however, the word *society* signifies no more than a group of persons, then the word could mean all of the consumers and producers who are in the economic models of this book. Thus, costs to society are the same thing as social costs, or total costs. And nothing more.

EXTERNALITIES IN CONSUMPTION   There are many relations of interdependence of the utilities enjoyed by consumers. When *A* enjoys the sight of *B*'s well-kept lawn, because it is adjacent to *A*'s, then *A*'s utility level is higher than it otherwise would be. Social benefit exceeds the private, a relation known as an *external economy* in consumption. On the other hand, *C* can be envious of *D*'s higher plane of living. *C*'s level of utility is therefore less, and here is an *external diseconomy* in consumption. Modern urban life seems to abound in external diseconomies. The important diseconomies go beyond such matters as the human propensity to envy others. Noise, pollution, and congestion in housing and on the streets and highways are major causes of external diseconomies in consumption.

EXTERNALITIES IN PRODUCTION   The activities of producers can also be interdependent. Take a firm with an on-the-job training program. The firm plans to raise its employees' efficiencies and thus to improve its production function. The program is undertaken in the expectation that the program will more than pay for its costs, i.e., the program will yield a private benefit to the firm. The training program can normally be expected to have social benefits exceeding the private; the employees will earn higher wages and when they change jobs, their new employers will also receive benefits from the other firm's on-the-job training program. Here, then, is an example of an external economy in production. In contrast to this is pollution as a cause of external diseconomies in production. A firm that pollutes a river or the air thrusts costs onto other firms and persons. If the polluting firm does not compensate others for the damage and losses they suffer, the firm's private costs are lower than the social costs.

The essence of the concept of an externality is interdependence and the absence of compensation. Those receiving benefits in the form of greater utilities or lower costs do not pay for them, and those causing others to have higher costs do not pay anything to offset the higher costs.

Now that externalities have been taken into account, the criterion of efficiency has to be restated. To keep things simple and at the same time to follow common practice, take the criterion, or rule, that marginal cost equals price. That is, in long-run equilibrium, the long-run marginal costs of the firms are equal to the equilibrium price. In the amended version, the rule becomes: For efficient rates of output, marginal *social* cost should equal price. Both the firm operating the training program and the firm causing the pollution have—socially—inefficient sizes of output. From the private MC curve of the firm with the training program should be subtracted the value of benefits going to others. This gives the social MC curve of the firm; since its curve lies lower, the output for social $MC = P$ would be a larger output. The polluting firm, in contrast, produces too much because its MC curve does not include all the social costs. If it had to operate with a social MC curve, which would be higher, the polluting firm would produce less.

The quantitative importance of external economies and diseconomies is hard to gauge. Some economists, who can see them almost everywhere, propose systems of hypothetical taxes and subsidies to firms and industries to bring about closer conformance of prices and marginal social costs. And there are still some people who dislike capitalism on principle. These people can no longer get much of a hearing with talk about the exploitation of the worker or about the injustices of capitalism; but they do echo economists' remarks about external diseconomies.

SOME ECONOMICS OF POLLUTION

Pollution is many things. As a set of problems it is a scientific problem, a political problem, a legal problem, an economic problem, and more. Several intellectual disciplines address themselves to one or more of the problems of pollution. Economics also analyzes the problems and makes recommendations for meeting them. In fact, writers on welfare economics were discussing pollution many decades before it became a matter for widespread concern.

There now follow some examples of theoretical analyses of pollution, examples coming from the field of applied welfare economics.

The Optimum Allowable Amount of Pollution

Pollution is, of course, disagreeable. More than that, pollution imposes many heavy costs on both consumers and producers. The costs of the pollution of air and water run into many billions of dollars a year. Again obviously, pollution can be controlled. But the controls also entail costs; they likewise come to many billions of dollars a year.

How far should the nation go in incurring costs to control pollution? Figure 15–2 gives a way of thinking about the problem. In the figure, the horizontal axis represents the amount of pollution of the air and of water. When read from left to right, the horizontal axis shows the amount of pollution that is permitted. When read the other way, from right to left, the same axis shows the amount of control of pollution. The vertical axis indicates the marginal costs of both the burden of pollution to consumers and producers and of the controls that reduce pollution.

The curve labeled "*MC* of Burden" shows the marginal cost of pollution to everybody. The curve begins at the origin, which means that there is no pollution and therefore none of its costs, because control is at a maximum. Other positions of the curve are possible. For example, the curve could begin slightly to the right of the origin. This would mean that low levels of pollution would have an imperceptible marginal cost. Any movement down the curve, i.e., from right to left, of the marginal cost of the burden of pollution can be viewed as the benefits to consumers and producers from lower levels of pollution.

The curve "*MC* of Control" in Figure 15–2 begins at point *M* and rises to the left. At first the curve goes up gently, suggesting that cleaning up small amounts of pollution can be managed without rapidly rising marginal costs. Beyond some level of pollution

FIGURE 15-2

"OPTIMUM" POLLUTION

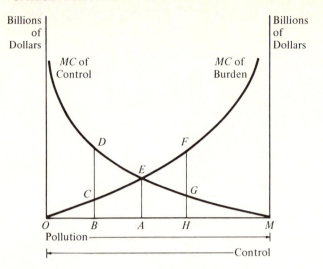

control, however, the marginal cost of control is likely to ascend sharply. The curve's steepness at its left signifies the enormous extra cost of bringing pollution close to zero.

The optimum allowable amount of pollution is at point A. Here, MA of pollution is eliminated and OA of pollution is accepted. At point A, MC of Control = MC of Burden. If more pollution were to be wiped out, say, the amount AB, the marginal cost of doing so would far exceed (by DC billion dollars) the benefit gained. Similarly, if pollution control amounted to only MH, the marginal cost of the pollution is much greater (by FG billion dollars) than the marginal cost of the control.

Remember that the area under a marginal cost curve is total cost. Another way to interpret the optimum allowable amount is this: In Figure 15–2, to reduce pollution as far as point B would cause extra total costs, over and above those needed to achieve the optimum, of $AEDB$ billion dollars. The extra benefits gained would be $AECB$ billion dollars. Thus the costs of the reduction of pollution by AB would exceed the benefits by DCE dollars. Similarly, if pollution were to be cut back only as far as point H, the net loss of benefits, in comparison with the optimum, would be EFG billion dollars.

Polluting Industries and Receiving Industries

Another view of pollution is to look at industries that cause pollution and at industries that receive, i.e., suffer losses from, pollution. Thus there are *polluting industries* and *receiving industries*. In general the polluting industries tend to produce too much because their (equilibrium) prices reflect only their private, i.e., their firms' own, costs. The polluting industries' private costs plus the costs they thrust upon others add up to their social costs. In contrast, the receiving industries produce too little because their (equilibrium) prices reflect the higher costs they must incur because they have to clean up, or purify, or treat some of their damaged or tainted inputs. Some receiving industries are precluded from using some resources that are polluted.

The long-run supply curves of the polluting industries are lower because the curves are formed only by the private costs. Thus the equilibrium prices are lower and the outputs are larger than would be true if the supply curves covered social costs. Therefore, the equilibrium of a polluting industry is not efficient. The consumers of the product of such an industry enjoy a lower price and the larger consumers' surplus that goes with it. The consumers do not pay all of the costs of the product they demand.

Similarly, the long-run supply curves of the receiving industries are higher. True enough, the higher costs are private costs, but part of these are due to the pollution caused by other industries. Thus the equilibrium prices of the receiving industries are higher and their outputs are smaller. The equilibrium of a receiving industry is not efficient either. Consumers pay higher prices because of pollution originating elsewhere.

Pollution therefore causes deviations from efficiency and thus losses of economic welfare.

Strategies for Limiting Pollution

There is more than one way to reduce pollution. Why not simply prohibit it? For some specific kinds of pollution, prohibition is, of course, already in effect. For example, it is unlawful to employ certain chemicals as pesticides or herbicides, to dump untreated sewage into certain bodies of water, etc. As a universal or general remedy, outright prohibition would however have fantastically high costs, almost certainly far in excess of the benefits. The earlier discussion of the optimum allowable amount of pollution explains why this is true.

AN EMISSIONS TAX   One proposal for reducing pollution is for the government to impose an *emissions tax*, or, as it is sometimes called, an *effluent charge*. Figure 15-3 illustrates the effects of an emissions tax. First of all, let the industry be in long-run equilibrium, with price OP_1 and production of OQ_1. The industry's supply curve, reflecting only the private costs, is C_p. Next, suppose that an emissions tax is levied on the industry's output, e.g., a tax of so many dollars a ton. Let this tax be equal to the cost per ton of the pollution caused by the industry. Therefore the new supply curve, C_s, has a twofold meaning—it measures the private costs plus the emissions tax; and it shows the total, or social, costs of the industry.

FIGURE 15-3   **EMISSIONS TAX**

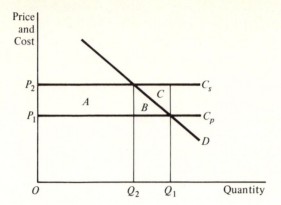

The industry adjusts to the tax and reaches a new equilibrium with the price OP_2 and the quantity OQ_2. The rise in the price is equal to the tax per ton and also to the pollution per ton. Notice that the industry produces less. During the transition from the old to the new equilibrium, some unemployment will have occurred in this industry and the firms will have suffered some losses.

Now look at the effects of this emissions tax. The industry's net profits are unchanged; they were zero in the old and are zero in the new equilibrium. The reduction in output brings less pollution, whose dollar amount is area B plus area C in Figure 15-3. The government collects tax revenue equal to area A. But the consumers do pay a higher price for this product. The burden to the consumers is the loss of consumers' surplus, areas A plus B. If the government uses its revenue, area A, to compensate those who incur losses because of the industry's pollution, that revenue can be called a gain. To sum up, then, the gains are A plus B plus C. The loss is A plus B. Thus the emissions tax brings a net "social" gain equal to area C.

VOLUNTARY AGREEMENTS   There is of course much pollution that government could do something to control but does not, for one reason or another. Economists have speculated about the possibilities of voluntary agreements between polluters and their victims. How much would it cost the victims to pay the polluters to stop it?

Take Figure 15-3 again. The total burden or cost of pollution, with output at OQ_1, is $A + B + C$ dollars. If the industry were to agree to cut output to OQ_2 and to eliminate pollution, the cost of doing so would be A dollars. Therefore, if the victims paid the industry A dollars, the industry would be just as well off as before.

By paying the industry A dollars, the victims save $A + B + C$ dollars of pollution. If the industry insisted on being paid more than A but less than $A + B + C$ dollars, it would be worthwhile for the victims to pay the amount. The point is that, for such clear-cut instances as this one is assumed to be, they would have a net gain if they could come to an agreement with the industry.

If the industry did agree to limit output to OQ_2 and to cut out pollution in return for payments from the previous sufferers, the price would of course have to go up to OP_2, because that is what OQ_2 would sell for. The consumers would be the losers here. Their loss would be the consumers' surplus of $A + B$ dollars. There would, however, still be the smaller amount of C dollars of "social" gain as a partial offset against the consumers' loss.

It is obvious that the kind of voluntary agreement mentioned here could be a reality only if several conditions were met: the victims would have to have an organization representing them all, the industry also would have to be organized, the victims and the industry would have to agree on the facts of pollution and its costs, and so on.

TAXES ON INPUTS   Another way to combat pollution is by taxes on inputs that cause heavy pollution. For example, a tax could be imposed on fuels with high sulphur contents. By changing the relative prices of fuels, the tax would give producers a direct incentive to make substitutions in their inputs, i.e., to use less of the more polluting kinds and more of the less polluting kinds. In principle, too, the revenue from such a tax could be spent as subsidies for the purchase of fuels with low sulphur contents. These subsidies would still further widen the differences between the relative prices of fuels and would strengthen the incentives to use the less polluting forms.

THE USES OF WELFARE ECONOMICS   In the modern economy, the federal, state, and local governments exercise numerous controls over the allocation of resources. This is not the place to review or even to summarize these controls. It suffices to say that the theory of welfare economics does provide a unifying principle for many apparently unrelated kinds of government controls. The principle is to foster external economies and to reduce or eliminate external diseconomies. Public education, basic research, the conservation of soil and other natural resources, urban renewal, zoning laws, workmen's compensation, and many other activities and policies are reducible to the one principle. If they were left solely to private enterprise, education and research would doubtless be produced in small quantities. Yet it would be going too far to hold that, armed with the externalities principle, government can correct the (social) inefficiencies of a faulty private enterprise. Government itself can cause external diseconomies; an example is the damaging sonic boom from government-owned jet planes. And in any event, private enterprise operates within a complex framework of legal institutions. That framework can often be modified to deal with what otherwise would be external diseconomies.

The activities of government itself are increasingly influenced by the theory of welfare economics. In its applications to problems of government, the theory goes under other names—benefit-cost analysis, cost-effectiveness analysis, cost-utility analysis, and planning-programming-budgeting.

SUMMARY

The long-run equilibrium of a competitive industry gives a standard of economic efficiency, with price equal to minimum costs. Economists equate efficiency with economic welfare, viewing equity in the distribution of incomes as a goal whose criteria are noneconomic. Partial equilibrium theory yields models of applied welfare economics. Increases in economic welfare can come from technological improvements, as well as from strengthening competition. Theorists of consumer-oriented socialist economies use the competitive model of a free market economy as their standard. The real world contains many forces causing deviations from efficiency. Even in positions of competitive equilibrium there can be externalities, which are divergences between social and private benefits and social and private costs. Pollution of air and of water can be put to economic analysis, which contributes to clearer thinking on the subject.

SELECTED REFERENCES

On equity and efficiency: Arthur M. Okun, *Equality and Efficiency: The Big Tradeoff* (Brookings Institution, Washington, D.C., 1975).

On welfare economics: Tibor Scitovsky, *Welfare and Competition,* rev. ed. (Irwin, Homewood, 1971).

On private versus social cost: R. H. Coase, "The Problem of Social Cost," *Journal of Law and Economics,* 3 (October 1960), 1–44. On externalities: E. J. Mishan, "The Postwar Literature on Externalities: An Interpretive Essay," *Journal of Economic Literature,* 9 (March 1971), 1–28.

Economic analysis of sexual behavior, marriage, divorce, dying, crime, faculty salaries, etc.: Richard B. McKenzie and Gordon Tullock, *The New World of Economics: Explorations into the Human Experience* (Irwin, Homewood, 1974).

Economics of the environment: Llad Phillips and Harold L. Votey, Jr., ed., *Economic Analysis of Pressing Social Problems*

(Rand McNally, Chicago, 1974); Joe S. Bain, *Environmental Decay: Economic Causes and Remedies* (Little, Brown, Boston, 1973); Joseph J. Seneca and Michael K. Taussig, *Environmental Economics* (Prentice-Hall, Englewood Cliffs, N.J., 1974).

Pricing in a socialist economy is associated with the names of Lange and Lerner: Oskar Lange and Fred M. Taylor, *On the Economic Theory of Socialism* (University of Minnesota Press, Minneapolis, 1938); and Abba P. Lerner, *The Economics of Control* (Macmillan, New York, 1944).

EXERCISES AND PROBLEMS

1.   Speculate about the gross social return from hybrid corn with the assumption that corn production is an increasing-cost industry rather than a constant-cost industry.
2.   Compare the differences between pure competition and effective competition. Can you think of any industries that have all of the characteristics of pure competition? Of effective competition?
3.   Draw diagrams to show the difference between (a) a permanent subsidy per unit of output to help competitive firms clean up pollution, and (b) a permanent tax per unit of output to obtain revenue so that a government body can clean up pollution.
4.   Make a list of the major externalities (economies and diseconomies) associated with the production and consumption of the largest items in your own budget for goods and services.
5.   Speculate on the shapes of the marginal cost curves for the burden of pollution and the cost of pollution control for the following activities: (a) strip mining, (b) oyster and clam harvesting, (c) oil tanker transportation, (d) paper manufacturing, and (e) steel manufacturing. What factors did you include in your estimates of costs and benefits?
6.   Could a zero level of pollution be the optimum level? Or could zero control be the optimum amount of control?
7.   What are the advantages and disadvantages of using the following to control pollution: (a) direct control, (b) voluntary agreements, and (c) taxes?

Appendix

TO PART 3

MATHEMATICAL NOTES

Demand and supply are now brought together in markets where pure competition prevails. What now follows is a partial equilibrium model. It holds for the immediate market, the short run, and the long run. The formal properties of the equilibrium are the same. What differs from one market period to another is the form of the demand and supply functions. Here too, discussion is limited to simple linear functions.

The demand function is now written as $D = A - Bp$, $A > 0$, $B > 0$. The supply function is $S = bp - a$, $a > 0$, $b > 0$. Thus the demand curve is downward sloping and the supply curve is upward sloping. The parameters A, B, a, and b can all represent different values.

In equilibrium, $D = S$. Therefore

$$A - Bp = bp - a$$
$$Bp + bp = A + a$$
$$p = \frac{A + a}{B + b}.$$

Here is a hypothetical numerical example

$$D = 30 - p$$
$$S = 3p - 10$$
$$\therefore p = \frac{30 + 10}{1 + 3} = 10$$
$$D = S = 20.$$

Suppose that demand increases, the demand function changing to $D' = 38 - p$. Then

$$p = \frac{38 + 10}{1 + 3} = 12,$$

and

$$D' = S = 26.$$

Suppose next that a tax is imposed on the producers. Let the supply prices in the supply function be the costs of the producers exclusive of tax, and let the tax be $1\frac{1}{3}$. For example, to produce 10 units, the supply price before the tax is $6\frac{2}{3}$. That is, $S = 3p - 10 = 10$. Therefore $3p = 20$ and $p = 6\frac{2}{3}$. With the tax, price becomes $p + 1\frac{1}{3} = 8$ and therefore $S' = 3(8) - a = 10$, which requires a to be 14 to obtain the supply of 10. Accordingly,

$$D = 30 - p$$
$$S' = 3p - 14$$
$$\therefore p = \frac{30 + 14}{1 + 3} = 11.$$

Observe that the equilibrium price has risen by less than the amount of the tax. The price increase is 1, and the tax is $1\frac{1}{3}$. The result accords with the geometrical demonstration on page 250.

NOTE 2.

THE COBWEB THEOREM

The mathematical model for the cobweb theorem can be expressed as follows

$$D_t = A - Bp_t, \qquad A > 0 \text{ and } B > 0,$$
$$S_t = bp_{t-1} - a, \qquad b > 0 \text{ and } a > 0,$$
$$D_t = S_t.$$

Here the subscript t means a time period, such as a year. Then

$$A - Bp_t = bp_{t-1} - a$$

or

$$p_t = \left(-\frac{b}{B}\right)p_{t-1} + \frac{a + A}{B}$$

$$p_1 = \left(-\frac{b}{B}\right)p_0 + \frac{a + A}{B}$$

$$p_2 = \left(-\frac{b}{B}\right)p_1 + \frac{a + A}{B}$$

$$= \left(-\frac{b}{B}\right)^2 p_0 + \left(-\frac{b}{B}\right)\frac{a + A}{B} + \frac{a + A}{B}.$$

The general solution of this difference equation gives p_t in terms of p_0, the initial price. For any time (t),

$$p_t = \left(-\frac{b}{B}\right)^t p_0 + \frac{a + A}{B + b}\left\{1 - \left(-\frac{b}{B}\right)^t\right\}.$$

Perpetual Oscillation

If $b = B$, $-\frac{b}{B} = -1$ and $p_t = (-1)^t p_0 + \frac{a + A}{B + b}\{1 - (-1)^t\}$.

When t equals zero or any even number, then

$$p_t = p_0 + \frac{a + A}{B + b}\{1 - 1\} = p_0.$$

When t equals an odd number, then

$$p_t = -p_0 + \frac{a + A}{B + b} \{1 + 1\} = 2 \frac{a + A}{B + b} - p_0.$$

Consequently, price alternates between these two price values, and quantities alternate between the two values obtained by substitution of these prices in either the demand or supply functions. This is the model with perpetual oscillation.

Damped Oscillation

If $b < B$, $\frac{b}{B} < 1$ and p_t approaches $\frac{a + A}{B + b}$ as t becomes infinite. This value for price is the same as that for the intersection of the demand and supply functions if the subscripts on price are dropped. Hence, this is the equilibrium price that is approached as t approaches infinity. Once this price is achieved, the variation in price ceases. This is the model with damped oscillation.

Explosive Oscillation

If $b > B$ so that $\frac{b}{B} > 1$, then p_t fails to converge as t increases since $\left(-\frac{b}{B}\right)^t$ becomes infinite as t increases without limit. This is the model with explosive oscillation. Each new value of price and quantity is farther from equilibrium than the preceding one.

4

MONOPOLY

PRICING

16
Monopoly
PRICES

The theory of monopoly price applies to firms having freedom and independence when they decide on their selling prices. Monopolists are price makers, not price takers, as are the firms in purely competitive industries. Monopolists have freedom in price making because they sell to many consumers; they have independence because they need not fear the actions of rivals.

THE DEFINITION OF MONOPOLY

For centuries, people have talked and written about monopoly, usually with condemnation, often with anger. Monopoly has meant many things, each with its own shade of meaning.

In the standard definition, a *monopolist* is the only producer of a product that has no close substitutes. Since the output of an industry consists of products that are either perfect or very close substitutes, the monopolist is therefore the only producer in the industry. Firm and industry are identical. Because, however, the precise definition of monopoly has great practical importance, especially in the enforcement of the antitrust laws, it is well to go farther into the problem of defining monopoly and to look at some other definitions.

Earlier chapters show that a commodity has to be defined for the purpose at hand; several purposes require several definitions. So too with monopoly, and not just on general grounds. The two ideas, in fact, are linked together. A definition of monopoly must specify the commodity that is monopolized.

The literal meaning of a monopolist as a sole seller and the dictionary meaning of exclusive control do not help much. Sole seller of what? Exclusive control of what? When a commodity is distinct in its physical properties and recognized by everybody as distinct, then a firm producing such a commodity can be called a monopoly. Though rough-and-ready, this definition is none the worse for that. To be distinct, the commodity must be a marked gap in a chain of substitutes. Its cross elasticities of demand with other commodities must be low. In his discussion of monopoly, Joel Dean, an authority on managerial economics, calls a monopolized product "a product of lasting distinctiveness." Such a product has no acceptable substitutes; its distinctiveness lasts for many years.

In contrast, Edward H. Chamberlin, whose *Theory of Monopolistic Competition* is an important contribution to price theory, is impressed by the presence of substitutes for *any* commodity and therefore by the *competition* from them. He has advanced the concept of "pure monopoly," which is the control of the supply of *all* commodities and services. But Chamberlin's is too extreme a view to be useful because pure monopoly as he defines it could never exist. Not even the Russian government controls the supply of *all* commodities and services; some of the food sold in Russia is produced by peasants who cultivate little plots of land as independent entrepreneurs.

Still another view is to define a monopolist as any firm with a sloping demand curve. For some purposes, this definition is far too broad because it includes all firms except those under pure competition. Yet the broad definition does have one advantage, namely, that parts of the analysis of monopoly price can be carried over into the theory of pricing in monopolistic competition and in oligopoly.

The essentials of a good definition of monopoly have already been mentioned: There are no close substitutes, and in making decisions on price, the monopolist is independent. The monopolist does not have to allow for the price *policies* of other sellers or take other prices into account because they, as always, help to determine the demand for the product. The position of the monopolist's demand curve is steady, given the buyers' tastes and incomes, and given the prices of the not-so-close substitutes. It is steady because raising or lowering price does not provoke any change in price policy by rivals, a change that would shift the monopolist's demand curve.

One last remark about the definition of monopoly: Many a monopolistic firm sells its product in two or more separate markets. A firm can have a monopolistic position in one market, but not in another. For example, electric power companies are monopolists in selling electric energy for lighting and for certain appliances. The same companies face intense competition as sellers of energy for cooking and heating.

Barriers to entry surround the markets held captive by monopolists. Government sets up many of the barriers by granting patents, imposing tariffs, issuing exclusive franchises, and by furnishing other forms of protection. Some barriers stand because of legal and illegal business arrangements and practices. Still other barriers arise from superior technology and management and the enormous investments that a few industries have to have. Over the years some barriers to entry become higher and stronger while others crumble. The subject of barriers belongs, however, in the domain of antitrust economics and thus merits only this brief mention here.

The demand for the output of a firm under pure competition is always a horizontal line on a price-quantity diagram. The demand for the output of a monopolist always has a negative slope. So do the demands for firms in monopolistic competition and in oligopoly. The purely formal properties of monopoly demand, therefore, hold for monopolistic competition and for oligopoly.

Demand, marginal revenue, and elasticity have all been explained before. What needs to be done now is to probe a little farther into the relations between them. The result will be some useful logical propositions.

The demand curve of a monopolist represents the marketing possibilities. The tastes of the customers and their incomes are built into the demand curve. So are the availabilities and the prices of the substitutes for the product. The monopolist's demand curve is simply the industry demand curve described earlier in this book.

Marginal Revenue of a Monopolist

Marginal revenue is the addition to total revenue by selling one unit more, or the loss of total revenue by selling one unit less. It would of course be unusual, if not strange, to see a firm adjusting its sales one unit at a time, calculating the effect on its total revenue. Firms no doubt make their sales adjustments in batches, in hundreds or thousands of units at a time. But the assumptions of perfect knowledge of the market and of profit maximization require the pinpoint precision of the concept of marginal revenue.

Table 16–1 shows the relation between marginal revenue and price. The first two columns are a monopolist's demand schedule. The third column is total revenue, the numbers being obtained by multiplying those in the first two columns. The fourth column is marginal revenue, the numbers obtained by subtraction. The marginal revenue of 3 units is $6, because these units bring in a total

TABLE 16–1

MARGINAL REVENUE AND PRICE

P	Q	TR	MR
$10	1 unit	$10	$10
9	2	18	8
8	3	24	6
7	4	28	4
6	5	30	2
5	6	30	0
4	7	28	−2

revenue of $24, whereas 2 units bring in $18. Notice that marginal revenue is lower than price and that as price goes down, marginal revenue goes down faster. A monopolist who sells at the same price to all customers, and who lowers the price to sell an extra unit, suffers from that reduced price on every unit—hence the more rapid fall of marginal revenue. In the numbers in Table 16–1, price goes down $1 at a time, whereas marginal revenue goes down $2 at a time. (See Note 1 in the Appendix to Part 4.) The same numbers can be made to say two more things. Observe that when demand is elastic, at prices *above* $5, marginal revenue is positive. When demand has unity elasticity *at* $5, marginal revenue is zero. When demand is inelastic, marginal revenue is negative.

The same relations are shown graphically in Figure 16–1. The demand curve is *D* and the marginal revenue curve is *MR*. The demand curve is linear for the sake of convenience. The *MR* curve always lies to the left of the demand curve whether or not it is linear. This is another way of saying that the marginal revenue of any quantity is less than its price. The *MR* curve is to be read this way: As quantity increases, the height of the *MR* curve above each quantity shows the addition to total revenue from the quantity. In Figure 16–1, the quantity is *OA*, with a price *PA*, and a marginal revenue of *FA*. Total revenue is the rectangle *OBPA*. Total revenue is also the area under the marginal revenue curve, *OCFA*.[1] Because each one describes the same total revenue, the two areas are necessarily equal. Therefore the two triangles—*CBH* and *HPF*—are equal. With a little help from Euclid, it can be seen that *BH* equals *HP*, so that *H* is at the midpoint of the line *BP*. To generalize: *When*

FIGURE 16–1   DEMAND AND MARGINAL REVENUE

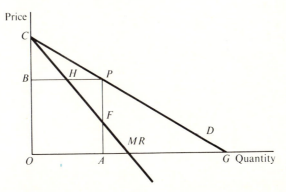

[1] The marginal revenue of *OA* units is the line *FA*. The line that would stand just next to it on the left is the marginal revenue of *OA* − 1 units. And so on. Total revenue is the sum of these lines, that is, the area *OCFA*. Similarly, the total revenue of, e.g., 4 units in Table 16–1 can be found by adding the numbers in the marginal revenue column.

287   *Monopoly Prices*

the demand curve is a straight line, the marginal curve is also straight; it bisects any horizontal line between the demand curve and the price axis.

This property of linear demand is convenient because it makes it easy to draw accurate diagrams and, more important than that, it simplifies the exposition of the economics of monopoly price.

Marginal Revenue, Price, and Elasticity

A convenient formula, that will be used later, is

$$MR = P - \frac{P}{E}.$$

That is, marginal revenue equals price minus price divided by the coefficient of point elasticity of demand at the price in question. Suppose that E is 2, then

$$MR = P - \frac{P}{2} = \frac{1}{2}P.$$

And if elasticity is unity, so that $E = 1$, the formula says that marginal revenue is zero.

The formula can be derived from Figure 16–1. At price PA, elasticity is equal to $\frac{PG}{CP}$. The proof for this is on page 40. Now

$$\frac{PG}{CP} = \frac{BO}{CB}$$

because the two triangles—CGO and CPB—are similar. Therefore,

$$E = \frac{PA}{PF} = \frac{PA}{PA - FA}.$$

But FA is marginal revenue. Hence

$$E = \frac{P}{P - MR}.$$

This can be rearranged as $P = E(P - MR)$, and as

$$MR = P - \frac{P}{E}.$$

(For the calculus, see Note 1 in the Appendix to Part 4.)

Marginal Revenue and Nonlinear Demand

When demand is nonlinear, i.e., when the demand curve really has a curve in it, the marginal revenue line also curves. It too lies between the demand curve and the price axis. For a nonlinear demand, the marginal revenue curve can be found this way: Mark off, say, three prices on the demand curve. At each price draw the tangent to the demand curve. Then for each tangent find the corresponding point

TABLE 16-2

RELATIONS AMONG MR, P, AND E

$$MR = P\left(1 - \frac{1}{E}\right) \qquad P = MR\frac{E}{E - 1} \qquad E = \frac{P}{P - MR}$$

for marginal revenue by following the procedure for straight-line demand curves. The points for the three marginal revenues can then be connected by a curved line that will approximate the curve for marginal revenue. It is well to know that the marginal revenue curve for a nonlinear demand does *not* bisect the distance between the demand curve and the price axis. Bisection holds only for straight lines. The nonlinear marginal revenue curve lies to the left of the line bisecting the distance between the price axis and a convex demand curve. If the demand curve were concave, the marginal revenue curve would lie to the right of the bisecting line.

For the benefit of those readers who do not do algebra quickly in their heads, Table 16–2 sums up the relations among marginal revenue, price, and elasticity.

QUALIFICATIONS

It is customary to conclude a discussion of monopoly pricing with a list of qualifications to the principles set forth. Here, however, the qualifications will come first.

The qualifications amount to saying that monopolists cannot maximize their profits or do not want to do so. They cannot if they are regulated by public agencies unless, as sometimes happens, the regulation is wholly ineffective. Nor can monopolists maximize their profits if they have only the vaguest notions of the demands for their products. This must often be true when the products are new and when consumer tastes for them are still in flux. When they have only a poor knowledge of the demands for their products, business people in positions of monopoly probably sometimes set their prices higher than the level that would bring maximum profits. They are likely to do so because of the common confusion of high prices with high profits, because of the prevailing belief that demand is inelastic, and because to choose a high price may seem the safe thing to do.

Monopolists who deliberately earn less than maximum profits do so because they fear the imposition of public regulation or because they do not want high profits to count against them in a possible antitrust suit. Then, too, they might not wish to encourage potential competition.

Maximizing a Utility Function

Another kind of qualification is to say that a monopolist maximizes a utility function instead of profits alone. The utility functions mentioned briefly in Chapter 8 can be touched upon in this context because a monopolist, who by definition is sheltered from direct competition, can afford to pursue other objectives along with profits. The other objectives can be many things. One way to handle a utility function is to have it contain just two objectives—profits and, say, amenities. These last can take such forms as lavish offices, generous expense accounts, executive aircraft, etc. Such items can add more to total costs than they do to total revenue and thus can reduce profits. But some combination of profits and amenities yields a maximum of utility to the monopolist.

MONOPOLY PRICE IN THE IMMEDIATE MARKET

From now on the assumptions are that the monopolist knows the market and thus the demand for the product, knows costs, and seeks no other goal than to maximize profits.

First of all, consider the monopolist in the immediate market. The monopolist has something to sell, something already produced and ready for sale. Production took place in the past—weeks ago, or months ago. The monopolist does not let the pricing decision be influenced by the costs of production. The pricing decision must be made now. It makes no difference now whether the past costs were high or low. Whether the monopolistic firm sells more or less of what it has for sale, past costs remain unchanged. Therefore, in the immediate market, $MC = 0$.

In the immediate market, the monopolist sells at a price that will yield the maximum *total* revenue. Call this price the monopolist's optimum price. The maximum total revenue attainable at the optimum price might be high or it might be low, when judged by some standard such as the monopolist's earnings in the past. Demand now might be strong or weak, but whatever it is, the monopolist selects the optimum price. Suppose that the demand for the monopolist's product is D, in Figure 16–2. Imagine first that there is an amount OB to sell. This amount is sold at the price it brings, namely, P_2. No more can be sold since there is no more, nor would the monopolist want to sell any less because demand is elastic (as shown by the fact

FIGURE 16–2   MONOPOLY PRICE: IMMEDIATE MARKET

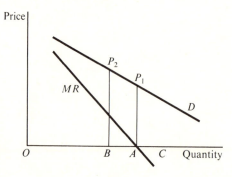

that *MR* is positive at *OB*). Imagine next that the monopolist has on hand an amount equal to *OC*. Not all of it will be sold because the monopolist would have a smaller total revenue than if the amount *OA* were sold. The marginal revenue of any amount larger than *OA* is negative, another way of saying that the total revenue is less. Therefore, with *OA* or more, the monopolist will sell the amount *OA* at the price P_1. The marginal revenue of this amount is zero. And since costs—for decision making—are zero, the condition $MR = MC$ holds.

What does the monopolist do with the unsold amount? If the product is something perishable, like fish or fruit, the monopolist probably destroys the excess amount or lets it rot. If the product is not perishable, the monopolist might hold it hoping that the market will improve in the future. Even a nonperishable product can be destroyed. This in fact has often happened, usually when a monopoly is not a single firm but an organization—a cartel—of firms set up to sell what they all have produced. If the organization is weak and if the firms do not fully trust each other, they might decide on destruction. But notice: When a monopoly has such a quantity that it withholds part of it from a market, perhaps destroying the amount withheld, the demand for the whole quantity is inelastic.

The demand for a product at the monopolist's selling price is always elastic, except that demand can have unit elasticity when the monopolist disregards costs. The profit-maximizing monopolist never sells at a price where demand is inelastic.

When first encountered, these assertions seem to be wrong, somehow. It is well, therefore, to restate and to embellish their proof. Profit maximization means the equality of marginal revenue and marginal cost. Marginal cost can never be negative. It is either zero, as in the immediate market, or positive. Therefore, marginal revenue is zero or positive. Therefore elasticity is unity or greater than unity. Another kind of proof is this: Suppose a monopolist, who has no clear idea of demand, hires consultants to study and measure it. Suppose that they are able to report, with sufficient accuracy, just what the demand is. The monopolist learns that the demand is inelastic at the price being charged. What can be done? The monopolist raises the price, because to do so increases total revenue. Profits become higher owing to the larger total revenue and because total costs are lower, since at the higher price fewer units are sold and produced. So long as demand is inelastic, the monopolist keeps on raising price and increasing profits. This cannot go on forever, because if it did, the monopolist would absorb all the disposable income of the customers. The monopolist's demand must turn elastic at some price. When it does, another price hike will reduce total revenue. When the next price hike would cut revenue more than it would cut costs, the monopolist has attained the profit-maximizing price.

Empirical studies have shown that the demand for local telephone service is highly inelastic and that the demand for long distance service has a coefficient in the neighborhood of $E = 0.5$. Here we have a clear indication that telephone companies do *not* maximize their profits. The companies are of course under regulation that aims at allowing them to earn only "fair" profits.

MONOPOLY PRICE IN THE SHORT AND IN THE LONG RUN

In the short run and in the long, the monopolist is a producer who must balance costs against revenues. In the short run, the monopolist observes the behavior of the marginal cost of more or less output from the plant and other facilities. For the long run, a decision is made on the best size of plant to build. Since the analytical problems of the theory of monopoly pricing are on the demand side, not on the cost side, there is no need to dwell on the differences between pricing in the short run and the long.

Figure 16–3 is the conventional full-dress diagram of monopoly price. The monopolist is in equilibrium when producing the amount OA and selling it at the price PA. Profits are the shaded area, which is total revenue minus total costs. Total revenue is $PA \times OA$ and total costs are $CA \times OA$. Thus the profits are $PC \times OA$. The formula for profits is

$$\text{profits} = (P - AC)Q,$$

where P is price, AC is average cost, and Q is quantity. In Figure 16–3, price is PA, average cost is CA, and the quantity is OA. Marginal revenue equals marginal cost—both long-run marginal cost and short-run marginal cost. In Figure 16–3, the monopolist is fully adjusted. Average cost, CA, is as small as it can be for the output level OA, because the monopolist is on the long-run cost curve LAC.

FIGURE 16–3   **MONOPOLY PRICE: SHORT AND LONG RUN**

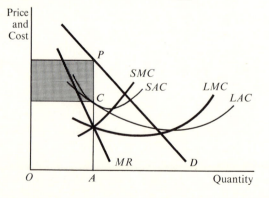

If demand temporarily increases, the monopolist expands production with the existing plant, increasing output to correspond with the intersection of the *MR* and *SMC* curves. If there is a large and permanent increase in the demand for the product, the monopolist will build a larger plant whose size corresponds to the intersection of the *MR* and *LMC* curves.

If, as in Figure 16–3, the demand curve intersects the declining portion of the *LAC* curve, the monopolist is said to have a *natural monopoly*. That is, the cost of the output *OA* is less if a monopolist produces it than if the same market were divided between two or more independent firms; they would have to operate higher up and to the left on their *LAC* curves. Many public utility firms are natural monopolies.

Price and Profit

It must be clear that rational monopolists have no interest in high prices or in high or even maximum profits per unit. They want maximum profits—maximum net revenue in the short run and maximum net profits in the long run. But monopolists, simply because they are monopolists, do not necessarily earn large profits.

The idea of monopoly usually suggests the idea of large and often ill-gotten gains. Here too is an association of ideas, and a common one, that has no foundation of logic. The reason for the association is probably that highly profitable monopolies attract attention; those with slender profits, or with none at all, are simply ignored.

The size of a monopolist's profits depends on the relation between demand and cost. Figure 16–4 shows two possibilities. Let *AC* first stand for a long-run cost curve. If demand is D_1, the monopolist's maximum profit is large. By ordinary business standards, it would indeed be enormous because it would be about a quarter of dollar sales. If demand is D_2, as it could be, the

FIGURE 16–4   MONOPOLY: DEMAND AND COST

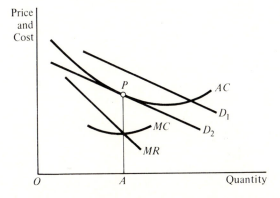

monopolist receives no net profit at all. The curve D_2 is tangent to the average cost curve. There is only one price that can be charged without losing money; this is the price PA, at the point of tangency. The formula for profits can be used again. In Figure 16–4,

$$\text{profits} = (P - AC)Q = 0,$$

because $P = AC$. For any quantity except OA, the formula says that profits would be negative, because AC would be greater than P. Since costs are the full costs that include a normal profit, the monopolist continues to produce the quantity OA. The monopolist is maximizing profits, true enough, but the maximum is zero. Zero profits are bigger than negative profits, i.e., losses. If the monopolist did anything else—raising the price or lowering it—the firm would operate at a loss, because everywhere except at the point of tangency the curve D_2 lies below the curve AC.

For the quantity OA in Figure 16–4, marginal revenue equals marginal cost. They are equal because the price of this quantity equals its average cost. If two average quantities are equal, their marginals are equal. Although the net profits of quantity OA are zero, they are nonetheless the maximum that the firm can attain. And of course, $MR = MC$ when profits are maximum.

If the demand curve would lie below the cost curve, nothing but losses are possible. In the long run, the monopolist would not produce this product. But let the AC curve now be a short-run average cost curve and suppose that demand is temporarily depressed. Provided that price exceeds average variable costs, the monopolist will produce, equating marginal revenue and short-run marginal cost, so as to minimize losses.

Advertising

By advertising, a monopolist tries to make a product more desirable in the minds of actual and potential consumers. If the advertising is successful, it pushes the demand curve to the right and makes the demand less elastic. Advertising causes additional costs that must be weighed against the additional revenue it yields. The subject of advertising is treated at greater length in Chapter 18 on monopolistic competition.

Changes in Demand

When demand increases, the normal effect is a rise in price. This is true under pure competition if supply does not change and with the exceptions of the long-run equilibrium price of a constant-cost or a decreasing-cost industry. If the demand for a monopolist's product increases, will the price be raised? Not necessarily.

With falling marginal cost, a monopolist would lower price when demand increases so long as the new equality of marginal cost and marginal revenue is compatible with a lower price. The rational monopolist is interested, of course, not in the height of the price, but in the size of net revenue or net profits. But even if marginal cost is not falling, the monopolist can gain by lowering the price when demand increases if the new demand is more elastic than the old.

To prove this in the simplest way, let unit cost be constant and let the formula $MR = P - \dfrac{P}{E}$ be put to use. Suppose that the elasticity of the old demand at the old price is 2 and that the elasticity of the new demand at the new price is 3. When these numbers are fed into the formula, the result is that the old marginal revenue is $\frac{1}{2}$ the old price and the new marginal revenue is $\frac{2}{3}$ the new price. The old and the new marginal revenues are equal because both are equal to the same marginal cost. Therefore the new price is lower than the old. With these numbers, the new price is 25 per cent less than the old.[2] Similar results would come from any other pair of elasticity coefficients.

Figure 16–5 shows the lower price that results when a monopolist's demand increases and becomes more elastic. The old demand is D_1 and the new is D_2.

Similarly, if demand declines and if the new demand is less elastic than the old, the monopolist raises prices. Business firms in quasi-monopolistic positions have sometimes raised their prices in periods of slack demand. Public criticism is likely to say, among other things, that such firms do not act even in their own interests. The theory here shows that whatever else might be said about it, a monopolist's action in raising price in the face of a drop in demand is

FIGURE 16–5   MONOPOLY: LOWER PRICE WITH INCREASED DEMAND

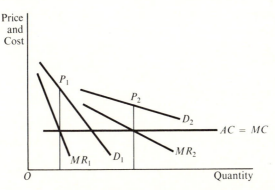

[2] A fuller explanation: Let the subscripts 1 and 2 denote the old and new prices, etc. By assumption, $MC_1 = MC_2$. By the rule of profit maximization, $MR_1 = MC_1$ and $MR_2 = MC_2$. Therefore, $MR_1 = MR_2$. Let $E_1 = 2$, and $E_2 = 3$. Therefore, $MR_1 = \dfrac{P_1}{2}$ and $MR_2 = \dfrac{2P_2}{3}$, and $\dfrac{P_1}{2} = \dfrac{2P_2}{3}$. Hence $\dfrac{P_1}{P_2} = \dfrac{4}{3} = \dfrac{100}{75}$.

indeed rational if the demand becomes less elastic. In a short period of time, that is the very thing that demand is likely to do.

Changes in Cost—the Effects of Taxes

If costs go up, a monopolist can be expected to raise the price. If average full costs rise by 10¢, will the price rise by 10¢? Most people would unhesitatingly say yes to this question and could give plenty of examples to back up their answers. But the rational monopolist raises the price by *less* than 10¢.

The rational monopolist looks only to the equality of marginal cost and revenue. If cost goes up, then there is a new marginal cost curve. Output and price are adjusted so that the higher marginal cost is equal to marginal revenue.

There can be many causes of a rise in costs. For simplicity, assume that the cause is an excise tax of so many cents on each unit sold by the monopolist. Why the monopolist raises the price by an amount *less* than the tax per unit can be seen easily in Figure 16–6. Here, the assumptions of linear demand and constant costs are used again. Before the imposition of the tax, the price is P_1. The tax raises the marginal cost curve to MC_t. The new price is P_2. The difference between P_2 and P_1 is less than the amount of the tax. With the imposition of the tax, MC rises by the amount of the tax. MR must rise by the same amount so that $MR = MC$. But as sales and output are cut back, price rises more slowly than MR—the converse of the faster fall of MR when price is declining. Therefore, price rises by less than the amount of the tax.

Effect of a Tax on Profits

Suppose a tax is levied on the profits of a monopolist. Will the monopolist raise the price and thus pass the tax on to the customers? Confronted with this question for the first time, most people would answer yes. But a rational, profit-maximizing, monopolist would not in fact raise price. The best thing to do is to pay the tax out of maximum profits, rather than out of the smaller profits that would be made if price were to be increased.

FIGURE 16–6   EFFECT OF A TAX ON MONOPOLY PRICE

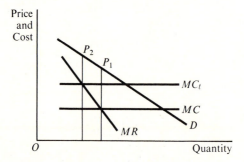

TABLE 16-3

A TAX ON PROFITS

Price	Profits	Profits After 50 Per Cent Tax
3¢	$4,000,000	$2,000,000
2	6,000,000	3,000,000
1	4,000,000	2,000,000

Table 16–3 illustrates this point. Suppose that the monopoly is an unregulated electric power producer and that the tax is 50 per cent of profits. The prices are for a kilowatt hour. It is plain that 2¢ per kwh is the optimum price both before and after the imposition of a tax on profits.

COMPARISON OF MONOPOLY AND COMPETITIVE PRICES

The standard method of comparing prices and outputs under monopoly and under pure competition is to take them both in long-run equilibrium. Imagine that an industry could either be under the control of a monopolist or could consist of many independent firms. Assume that costs are exactly the same whether the industry is monopolized or competitive. It might seem that this assumption is highly debatable, to say the least. Remember, however, that all is adjustable in the long run, that both a monopolist and a group of competitors can have the same production functions (i.e., the same technology), and that both are profit maximizers.

The simplest comparison again uses the linear-demand–constant-cost assumptions. Figure 16–7 compares equilibrium price and output in monopoly and in pure competition. The monopoly price is P_m and the competitive price is P_c. The constant-cost curve stands for the long-run supply curve in pure competition. The competitive price equals the long-run average and marginal costs of the firms.

With the assumptions, the monopoly output OA is exactly one-half the competitive output OB because the marginal revenue curve bisects any horizontal line from the price axis to the demand curve. With other assumptions, i.e., other shapes of the demand and cost curves, the ratio of monopoly to competitive output could be more or less than one-half. Always, however, the monopolist has a higher price and produces less.

The Net Loss of Consumers' Surplus

A firm obviously gains from a monopoly position. The consumers have to pay a price that exceeds cost.[3] In that sense, they suffer a loss. Which is larger—the monopolist's gain or the customers' loss?

[3] In equilibrium, monopoly price exceeds marginal cost by a factor that depends on the elasticity of demand. Since $MR = MC$ in equilibrium, $P = MC \dfrac{E}{E-1}$. (See Table 16–2.) The greater the elasticity, the closer is P to MC, and vice versa.

Some economists hold that this question can be answered with the concept of consumer's surplus. That concept is explained on pages 77 and 78. Figure 5-4 on page 78 can be of some help at this point. In Figure 5-4, the consumer's surplus for an individual consumer is the sum of the three areas A, B, and C, when the price for a particular service or commodity is P_2. When the price rises to P_0, consumer's surplus is the areas A and B. The area C, then, is the difference; it can be called the loss of consumer's surplus from the rise in price.

In Figure 16-7, there are two prices, the competitive price, P_c, and the monopolist's price, P_m. The difference in consumers' surplus is the sum of the two shaded areas; it can also be called the loss of consumers' surplus attributable to the higher monopoly price. (It is assumed here that the consumers' surplus of all of the buyers can be added.) But the monopolist has a net profit, i.e. gain, which is the heavily shaded area. It is clear that the loss of consumers' surplus is greater than the gain to the monopolist. It always is. The excess of the loss to the consumers over the gain to the monopolist is the lightly shaded triangle in Figure 16-7. The excess of the loss is called *the welfare loss* due to monopoly. Economists sometimes call it *the welfare triangle*. The welfare loss can also be expressed this way: Consumers do not buy the amount AB, though they are willing to pay prices higher than the full costs; they lose the consumers' surplus (the triangle) associated with the amount AB and the competitive price P_c.

In Figure 16-7, the area of the welfare triangle is relatively large. So is the area of the monopolist's gain, or profit. The two areas in the figure are intentionally made large, so that they can be clearly distinguished. The figure portrays concepts, not reality. When economists make statistical estimates of the welfare losses from the

FIGURE 16-7   **THE WELFARE LOSS DUE TO MONOPOLY**

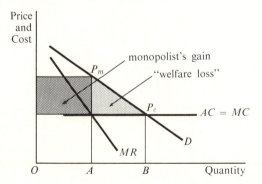

monopolies of the real world, they find that the losses are surprisingly small. The losses are small because the statistical studies show that monopolistic prices, though higher than competitive prices, are in general not much higher.

Equity and the Distribution of Income

Some theorists object to the use of the concept of consumers' surplus in measuring the welfare loss due to monopoly because the concept entails the addition of the utilities lost by the individual consumers. Besides, who is "the" monopolist and who are "the" consumers? The monopolist could be the sales agent for some poor farmers or fishermen, and the consumers could be wealthy people; the product could be something like, say, a rare kind of caviar. Or, to turn things round the other way, the monopolist could be a wealthy and powerful organization and the consumers a group of poor people. Accordingly, if the net loss of consumers' surplus is to have much meaning, it has to be supposed that the producer and the consumers have about the same incomes.

If they do not, then monopoly redistributes income from rich to poor, or from poor to rich. Economists who take the position that a transfer of income from rich to poor accords with the equity standard of economic welfare are then predisposed to soften, perhaps to a whisper, their condemnation of a monopoly that gives this result. Similarly, a monopoly that transfers income from poor to rich receives a charge from both barrels—this monopoly violates both standards, efficiency as well as equity.

The Allocation of Resources

By producing less than a competitive industry, a monopolist causes the allocation of resources to be distorted from the efficiency standard of economic welfare. Remember that when efficiency is at a maximum, price equals minimum average long-run cost and also marginal cost. Thus the last dollar of resources in each industry creates an incremental product value of one dollar. In monopoly, however, marginal cost is less than price; thus the last dollar of resources creates an incremental value product of more than one dollar. If a dollar's worth of resources is transferred from competitive industries to a monopoly, there is a gain. A dollar's worth of competitive output is lost, but more than a dollar's worth of extra monopoly output is achieved. Thus if a monopolist can be compelled to produce more, there is a gain in efficiency up to the point where the monopolist's price equals marginal cost.

An Application: Mergers with Cost Reductions

The concept of the net welfare loss can be used in making judgments of the allocative effects of certain mergers between corporations. Suppose there is a merger of two or more firms whose premerger costs were AC_1 in Figure 16–8, and whose price was P_1. Assume that

FIGURE 16–8

WELFARE EFFECT OF A MERGER

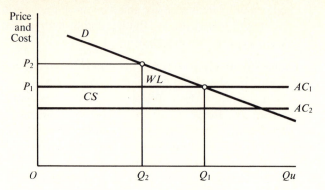

the merger makes it possible to exercise "market power," that is, to raise the price to P_2, which need not, however, be as high as the profit-maximizing monopoly price. Assume further that this merger achieves economies of operation, expressed by the lower post-merger cost curve AC_2. Mergers occasionally do indeed bring about economies.

Remember that many mergers, e.g., of two small firms, are harmless and scarcely noticed. But when two or more large firms enter into a merger, there is often public discussion and sometimes government intervention. In judging a merger, several criteria can be employed, such as possible "substantial" lessening of competition, the possible threat to future competition in the industry, the possible increase of market power, the possible adverse impact on consumers, and possible benefits from new economies of operation.

The last two criteria will be deployed here. In Figure 16–8, the triangle WL is the net welfare loss, which as before is the excess of the loss of consumers' surplus over the gain to the owners of the new firm created by the merger. Thus the net welfare loss results from the higher price P_2. The total reduction in costs is the rectangle CS (cost savings), which is AC_1 minus AC_2 multiplied by OQ_2. The welfare judgment of the merger thus sees both a loss and a gain. The merger yields a net social benefit if the cost savings are greater than the net welfare loss. And, of course, if the opposite were true, there would be a net social loss. As Figure 16–8 happens to be drawn, the cost savings are larger than the net welfare loss. The areas are, in principle, amounts of money in millions of dollars.

A little algebraic manipulation makes it possible to convert the comparison of the dollar amounts of cost savings and of net welfare loss into a comparison of the percentage reduction in costs with the percentage rise in price, taking into account the elasticity of demand. It turns out that the percentage rise in price must be much larger than the percentage reduction in costs if a merger is to cause a net social loss.[4]

A Welfare Function

The ideas that have just been discussed can be summarized by mentioning here a welfare function of the kind that began to appear in the economics journals in the late 1960s and early 1970s. The function is a "partial equilibrium welfare function." The expression *partial equilibrium* signifies that one industry is considered by itself, without regard to its interdependence with other industries. This welfare function is applied in the context of the theory of the regulation of individual public utility industries.

The function can be written this way

$$W = TR + S - TC,$$

where W is welfare, TR is total revenue, S is consumers' surplus, and TC is total costs. The meaning of TC is still the same—these costs include a return on the owners' capital and they include normal profits.

It is clear that welfare is maximized if the competitive solution is imposed on the regulated monopoly. This solution gives $P = MC = AC$, and therefore $TR = TC$. Thus $W = S$, both being at a maximum. Any profits above TC are at the expense of consumers' surplus.

[4] To see the relations between the sizes of the net loss of consumer welfare and of the savings in costs, first set the two magnitudes equal. Then,

$$(1) \quad \Delta(AC)Q_2 = \frac{1}{2}\Delta P \Delta Q.$$

That is, the rectangle CS in Figure 16–8 is set equal to WL, the triangle that is the net welfare loss. Next, divide Equation (1) by Q_2 and on the right side substitute the expression $\frac{E\Delta P}{P}$ for $\frac{\Delta Q}{Q}$ $\left(E = \frac{\Delta Q}{Q}\frac{P}{\Delta P}\right)$. This gives

$$(2) \quad \Delta(AC) = \frac{1}{2}\Delta PE\frac{\Delta P}{P}.$$

Finally, divide Equation (2) by $AC_1 = P_1$. The result is

$$(3) \quad \frac{\Delta(AC)}{AC_1} = \frac{E}{2}\left(\frac{\Delta P}{P}\right)^2.$$

The remarkable thing about Equation (3) is that, to keep the two magnitudes equal, the percentage price increase, $\frac{\Delta P}{P} \times 100$, has to be much larger than the percentage reduction in cost, $\frac{\Delta(AC)}{AC_1} \times 100$. For example, suppose that $E = 2$ and that the price rises by 20 per cent. When these numbers are fed into Equation (3), the cost reduction is just 4 per cent. If the cost reduction were larger than 4 per cent, the merger in this example would be "justified" on welfare grounds. [Source: Oliver E. Williamson, "Economies as an Antitrust Defense: The Welfare Tradeoffs," *American Economic Review*, 58 (March 1968), 21–23.]

The regulating authority might decide, however, to include a "profit constraint," to allow an amount of profits above total costs, so that the company can attract new capital for expansion of its facilities. Such a decision is more likely to be made than not. Accordingly, the welfare function is almost certain to be subject to the constraint of additional profits to provide expansion.

THE DYNAMICS OF MONOPOLY

All that has been said about monopoly so far is static equilibrium theory. Change over time has been ignored. Consumer tastes and technology have been assumed to be known and given.

In a changing and growing economy, the appearance of monopoly undergoes alteration. Consumer tastes shift, technology improves, new products and new industries emerge, some older industries languish and decline. A firm with a monopoly in one period finds itself harried by competitors offering similar products in the next period; monopoly becomes transformed into oligopoly. Even the industries sheltered by public regulation become exposed in time to the inroads on their markets from other products and services. The monopolies of local transportation once enjoyed by interurban electric railways are long since gone. The railroads once had a collective monopoly of intercity transportation.

The "lasting distinctiveness" of a monopolized product seldom endures for long. Most such products go through a cycle. They begin their lives with their distinctiveness, being sold at monopoly prices. Then come the rival products; monopoly shades into monopolistic competition (Chapter 18) or into oligopoly (Chapters 19 and 20). In the end, perhaps, what was once distinctive becomes just another mail order house item.

Short-run monopoly is even an ingredient, though not a necessary one, of effective competition, which is mentioned in Chapter 15. In an industry where several firms are rival producers and sellers of similar products, one firm can make an innovation. Suppose the innovation is an improved product the demand for which quickly increases. The innovating firm can then take advantage of its success, price as a monopolist, and earn monopoly profits—until the other firms imitate the innovation. When they do so, the temporary monopoly of the innovating firm ceases to exist.

MORE APPLICATIONS

The great contribution of the theory of monopoly to applied knowledge is the emphasis that it gives to demand. The analysis presented in this chapter shows that elasticity of demand is the key to the solution of the problem of rational pricing by a monopolist. Cost is important too, of course, but not more so for a monopolistic than for a competitive firm.

When a business firm has a product of lasting distinctiveness, to use Joel Dean's phrase again, and when the firm wants to maximize the profits from this product, then the firm should make the best estimate possible of the demand for its product and price according to the principle of monopoly price. The conscience of the individual firm need not be troubled with qualms about equity and the efficiency of the whole economy.

Pricing is often done by adding percentage margins, or markups, to cost. In many industries, the standard practice, however, is to calculate markups as percentages of price, not of cost. Thus, a markup of 50 per cent is 50 per cent of the price, not 50 per cent added to cost. One of the formulas contained in Table 16–2 can be modified to show how to figure markups that result in profit-maximizing prices. The formula is now

$$P = E(P - MR).$$

Assume that marginal cost is constant, so that marginal cost and average variable cost are equal. For maximum profits, $MR = MC$. Therefore,

$$P = E(P - MC).$$

The difference between price and marginal cost is the markup. Therefore,

$$P = E \times \text{markup}.$$

And

$$\frac{\text{markup}}{P} = \frac{1}{E}.$$

Thus, for example, if E is 2, then the markup is 50 per cent. Suppose the cost is $5.00 a unit. Then the price is $10.00. If instead, E were 3, the markup becomes $33\frac{1}{3}$ per cent, and the price is $7.50. The higher the elasticity, the smaller the percentage markup. This of course is only common sense; the higher the elasticity, the closer is the competition from substitutes and the wiser it is not to be too greedy in pricing.

The only catch here is that the formula requires a precise number for the coefficient of elasticity. In practice, however, good estimates can often be made if enough thought is given to the matter.

Marginal-Cost
Pricing

We turn again to the prices charged by public utility companies. But now the cost assumption is the U-shaped curve, where marginal costs differ from average costs.

The theory of welfare economics explains the conditions for an ideal allocation of resources. Applied welfare economics states rules to improve the actual allocation of resources. One of the rules, though a much controverted one, is marginal-cost pricing. Some economists have proposed that the prices charged by public utilities and by such government enterprises as public power projects be fixed so that these prices are equal to marginal costs.

The prices that the public utility companies are permitted to charge are in general based upon average costs. Profits called a fair return are added to the average business costs of the enterprises. Whether the fair returns and the average business costs are correctly computed in the normal procedure of regulation is a question irrelevant here. The point is that the existing system of regulation concentrates its attention on fair returns, on equity rather than on efficiency. Prices are fixed to bring about an equitable relation between investors and consumers. But the prices also determine volumes of production and consumption. These volumes are probably not "efficient" in the welfare sense.

The marginal-cost pricing proposal would separate the goal of fair returns to investors from the goal of improving the allocation of resources. If all public utility companies and all public enterprises were required to set their prices equal to their marginal costs, then each would be efficient in the long-run adjustment, and all taken together would be efficient. With the $P = MC$ rule, the output of each industry would be optimal and so would their total outputs. One problem, however, would be that some of the enterprises would have falling marginal costs. Therefore, MC would be lower than average cost, and the optimum price would be lower than average cost. Therefore such enterprises would operate at losses. Welfare theorists bravely say that the losses could be made up by subsidies and that the costs of the subsidies would be lower than the gain in welfare. Even so, a proposal to compel some private companies to operate at losses and then to subsidize them with public funds is likely to remain for a long time where it now is—in the ivory tower.

Figure 16-9 shows three possible prices for the output of a public utility enterprise that operates on the declining part of its cost curve. The price P_M is the profit-maximizing price of the output where $LMC = MR$. The lower price P_R, where $D = LAC$, is or could be the price established by the regulating authority. In practice, regulated prices are probably a little higher than P_R. The price equal to marginal cost is P_{MC}, obtained at the intersection of the demand curve with LMC. When the price is equal to marginal cost, as in Figure 16-9, the enterprise operates at a loss. In the diagram the loss is the shaded area—the difference between average and marginal cost per unit at the output OC, multiplied by OC.

Clearly, if the demand curve in Figure 16-9 were to shift to the

FIGURE 16-9

PUBLIC UTILITY PRICING

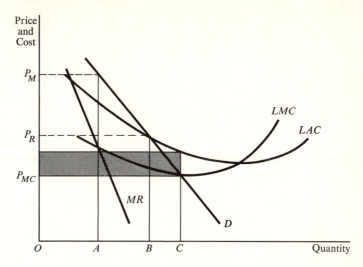

right far enough to cut the *LMC* curve where *LMC* exceeds *LAC*, the price equal to marginal cost would yield profits greater than those yielded by the corresponding price equal to average cost.

The existing system of public utility rate regulation can be defended on the grounds: (1) that some measure of equity is achieved; (2) that the imposition of rates, or prices, that remain constant for months or years at a time gives a strong incentive to the public utility companies to find ways of reducing their costs; and (3) that when prices are fixed at levels corresponding to full costs as defined in this book, they are likely to be well below the monopoly levels. Thus output in fact does come closer to the efficiency ideal. This last point can easily be seen for a public utility with a steeply falling demand curve and gently falling *LAC* and *LMC* curves. If it is set where demand intersects *LAC*, price is far below the height defined by $MR = LMC$.

SUMMARY

A monopolist can set price independently within the limits imposed by the demand for the product. When marginal revenue is positive, demand is elastic; when $MR = 0$, demand has unit elasticity; and when *MR* is negative, demand is inelastic. A useful formula is $MR = P - \dfrac{P}{E}$. In the immediate market a monopolist sets the price to maximize total revenue and to maximize net revenue in the short run and net profits in the long run. The demand at any set price is unit elastic or elastic. Profits depend on the demand-cost relation, not on the mere fact of monopoly. If demand increases, a monopolist lowers price if demand becomes more elastic and if costs are constant. If costs increase, the monopolist raises price by less than the unit rise in cost. With linear demand and constant-cost assumptions, monopoly output in long-run equilibrium is half the competitive. Criticism of monopoly is based on the net loss of consumers' surplus, possibly on grounds of equity, and certainly on grounds of efficiency. When dynamic change is taken into account, monopoly is seen to be temporary. The theory of monopoly pricing is applicable in business and in the evaluation of public utility regulation.

SELECTED REFERENCES

The pure theory: Joan Robinson, *The Economics of Imperfect Competition* (Macmillan, London, 1933), books II and IV.

Theoretical and descriptive: Fritz Machlup, *The Political Economy of Monopoly* (Johns Hopkins Press, Baltimore, 1952); Donald Dewey, *Monopoly in Economics and Law* (Rand McNally, Chicago, 1959); E. A. G. Robinson, *Monopoly* (Nisbet and Cambridge University Press, London, 1941); Donald Stevenson Watson, ed., *Price Theory in Action: A Book of Readings,* 3d ed. (Houghton Mifflin, Boston, 1973), parts 5 and 8.

Business applications: Joel Dean, *Managerial Economics* (Prentice-Hall, New York, 1951), chap. 7; Harold Bierman, Lawrence E. Fouraker, and Robert K. Jaedicke, *Quantitative Analysis for Business Decisions* (Irwin, Homewood, 1961), chap. 18.

Regulation: Richard A. Posner, "The Social Costs of Monopoly and Regulation," *Journal of Political Economy,* 83 (August 1975), 807–827; Richard A. Posner, "Theories of Economic Regulation," *Bell Journal of Economics and Management Science,* 5 (Autumn 1974), 335–358.

EXERCISES AND PROBLEMS

1.   Draw a diagram to show the effect on a monopolist of a subsidy for each unit produced.
2.   What would a monopolist do if a tax were imposed on gross revenue?
3.   Show the relation between elasticity of demand and the excess of monopoly price over competitive price.
4.   Suppose that a monopolist's demand decreases and that E, which had been 1.50, becomes 1.25. Assume constant costs. By what percentage does the monopolist change the price?
5.   Why might a monopolist set a price that is lower than the

profit-maximizing price? Can you draw utility functions that would account for such behavior?

6.   Will a monopolist ever produce if any price that can be set is below average cost? What could cause price to be less than average cost?

7.   Explain how a monopolist, in making the decision on price, could use the concepts of price elasticity, income elasticity, cross elasticity, and elasticity of price expectations.

8.   Draw a diagram that shows the possible prices for the output of a public utility that operates with constant costs over the relevant range. Identify the primary differences between the constant-cost case and the declining-cost case.

9.   Assume that a local government imposes a tax on a monopolist to acquire revenue to clean up pollution. What would be the differences between a tax per unit of output and a lump-sum tax levied without regard to output? If you were the monopolist, which tax would you prefer?

10.   Using *total* revenue and *total* cost curves, show the profit-maximizing output of a monopolist. Do these curves have the same shapes as those of a purely competitive firm? Why or why not?

11.   What determines the size of plant for the monopolist? Is the decision of a monopolist to build a larger plant any different from the same decision of a purely competitive firm?

12.   Explain why the concept of a supply curve is meaningless for monopoly.

17
PRICE
Discrimination

Price discrimination prevails in many of the markets where the sellers are monopolists or oligopolists. In economic literature, *price discrimination* is a neutral term; no odium attaches to it. Neither does the expression *discriminating monopolist* convey any suggestion of approval. In general, price discrimination means that a firm charges two or more prices for the same thing at the same time. It can also mean that the differences in the prices of a firm's products are greater than the differences in their costs of production.

The theory of price discrimination throws almost the whole emphasis on the demand side. Costs, of course, must be aligned with demand, but otherwise costs play the subordinate role. In contrast, business practice usually puts the stress on differences in costs; because it is often hard to estimate, demand tends to be ignored or given scant attention.

Price discrimination is an extention of monopoly pricing, in the broad rather than in the narrow meaning of monopoly. Any seller with a sloping demand curve is a monopolist in the broad and loose sense. A firm that is a price maker can look to the possibilities of price discrimination; this is true of a monopolist who prices independently, or an oligopolist, or a monopolistic competitor.

FORMS OF PRICE DISCRIMINATION Price discrimination comes in so many forms and guises, and even disguises, that only the leading types and examples will be mentioned here. Of these, only the kinds intended to increase sellers' profits will be considered. Hence this discussion excludes predatory price discrimination, i.e., the temporary lowering of prices by a large firm with the intention of bankrupting smaller rivals in a particular location or line of products.

The principal forms of price discrimination, as they exist in the American economy, are listed in Table 17–1.

TABLE 17–1   PRINCIPAL FORMS OF PRICE DISCRIMINATION

Main Classes	Bases of Discrimination	Examples
Personal	Incomes of buyers Earning power of buyers	Surgeons' fees Royalties paid for use of patented machines and processes
Group	Age, sex, military status, etc., of buyers	Children's haircuts, ladies' day at baseball parks, lower admission charges for those in uniform, etc.
	Location of buyers	Zone prices, basing-point prices, lower export prices (dumping), etc.
	Status of buyers	Lower prices to new customers, quantity discounts to big buyers, etc.
	Use of product	Railroad rates, public utility rates, fluid milk and milk for cheese and ice cream, etc.
Product	Quantities of products	Relatively higher prices for deluxe models
	Labels on products	Lower prices of unbranded products
	Sizes of products	Relatively lower prices for larger sizes (the "giant economy" size)
	Peak and off-peak services	Lower prices for off-peak services; excursion rates in transportation, off-season rates at resorts, etc.

Prerequisites   The prerequisites of price discrimination are separate markets and differences of elasticity of demand between the markets. An old example is the monopoly that sells at a high price in the domestic market and at a low price in the foreign market. The two markets are kept separate by a tariff wall; domestic buyers cannot place orders abroad at the lower foreign price and import the commodity. The price is lower in the foreign market because demand is more elastic, owing to the competition from other similar products; such competition is lacking in the domestic market.

A formula from the preceding chapter can show why different elasticities must exist if a monopolist practices price discrimination in two markets. The formula is

$$P = MR\frac{E}{E-1}.$$

Suppose that elasticity of demand in market A is 2 and that in market B it is 1.5. Then,

$$P_A = MR_A\frac{2}{2-1} = 2MR_A \quad \text{and} \quad P_B = MR_B\frac{1.5}{1.5-1} = 3MR_B.$$

Next, suppose that the monopolist's marginal cost is constant, i.e., the MC curve is horizontal. Then if MR and MC are equated, $MR_A = MC = MR_B$, and it follows that

$$P_A = 2MC \text{ and } P_B = 3MC.$$

If marginal cost is, say, $2 per unit, then

$$P_A = \$4 \text{ and } P_B = \$6.$$

Thus the monopolist sets a lower price in the market with the more elastic demand. If the elasticities in the two markets were equal, the two prices would have to be equal, and there would be no price discrimination.

Markets are kept separate in many ways. If a firm cannot keep its markets separate, then all of its buyers will make their purchases in the market with the lowest price, thus frustrating the firm's attempt to increase its profits through price discrimination. The markets for the box seats, the orchestra seats, and the balcony seats in theaters are segregated by tickets and ushers. Because services, as opposed to physical commodities, cannot be resold, their markets can easily be kept apart. Electric power companies use meters and other devices to separate the markets for electrical energy for lighting, cooking, hot water heating, commercial uses, industrial uses, etc. Much price discrimination rests on nothing more than the imperfect knowledge and the sheer ignorance of consumers. Some degree of interdependence often exists, however, between related markets. A resort hotel, for example, might establish lower off-season rates, which might attract some of the regular patrons. This is the problem of leakages between markets, a problem whose complications will not be examined here. The discussion to follow assumes that a firm's markets are watertight compartments.

DEGREES OF DISCRIMINATION

How far can a monopolist go in charging different prices for the same product? What is the limit of the increase in net profit from price discrimination?

First Degree

The limit is defined in the concept of discrimination of the first degree. The expression is employed by A. C. Pigou, the English economist, who created the idea of degrees of discrimination. In discrimination of the first degree, the monopolist knows the maximum amount of money *each* consumer will pay for any quantity. The monopolist then sets prices accordingly and takes from each consumer the entire amount of the consumer's surplus. Joan Robinson calls the same thing *perfect discrimination*, which is perfect, however, only from the point of view of the monopolist.

The simplest kind of discrimination of the first degree is one where, for some reason, consumers buy only one unit each from the monopolist. Knowing exactly how willing they are, the monopolist charges each one a price so high that the consumers almost, but not quite, refuse to pay the prices. If all of the consumers have different tastes, the monopolist has a different price for each one. The lowest price is determined by costs.

When consumers buy more than one unit of the monopolist's product, they are willing to buy more units at lower prices. The monopolist must then adjust the units of sale. Suppose that a consumer who could choose how many units he or she wanted to buy would buy 10 units if the price were $1 each. That is, 10 units have a *marginal* utility of $1, though of course the *total* utility of 10 units is higher. Suppose that the total utility of 10 units to the consumer is $40. The monopolist makes the unit of sale the 10 units; this is an all-or-nothing offer, and the price is $40. Consumer's surplus here is $30, i.e., $40 minus $10.

To put this in another way: Suppose that the monopolist's costs are constant at $1 a unit. A consumer's demand curve is such that he or she is willing to buy 10 units at a price of $1. In the absence of price discrimination, the consumer would pay $10 for 10 units. But the monopolist who practices first-degree discrimination treats the consumer's demand curve as if it were the monopolist's own marginal revenue curve. The monopolist sets $MR = MC$ and charges for the 10 units the entire area under the MR curve, which is also the consumer's demand curve. Therefore the consumer pays the $10 plus his or her consumer's surplus. Why will the consumer pay such a high price? Well, after all, the 10 units are indeed worth that much to the consumer, though just barely.

Discrimination of the first degree is the limiting, or extreme, case. Obviously, it could occur only rarely where a monopolist has only a few buyers and where the monopolist is shrewd enough to see the maximum prices they will pay.

Second Degree   In discrimination of the second degree, the monopolist captures parts of the buyers' consumers' surpluses, but not all of them. The schedules of rates typically charged by public utilities can be regarded as a form of second-degree discrimination.

Figure 17–1 gives a simplified illustration. Let the curve D be the demand of households for electrical energy in a community. The rate schedule, i.e., price list, is such that a high price is charged for the first few kilowatt hours (kwh) consumed per month. At the price P_1 in Figure 17–1, the total consumption is OA kwh. Then the next block of kwh per month is sold at a lower price—the price P_2. At this price, AB kwh are consumed. Similarly at price P_3, BC kwh are consumed. Rate schedules usually have more than three blocks, or

FIGURE 17-1   **SECOND-DEGREE DISCRIMINATION**

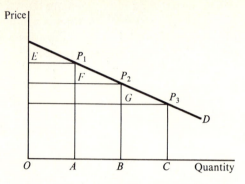

steps, which are usually unequal in size. But the three prices, or rates, in Figure 17–1 are quite adequate for illustrative purposes.[1]

If the monopolist—the hypothetical electric power company here—were allowed to charge only one price and wanted to sell the amount OC, the price would have to be P_3. At the single price, the total revenue would be smaller. It would be the rectangle given by $P_3C \times OC$. But with the three prices, the total revenue is the sum of the three rectangles P_3B, P_2A, and P_1O. The monopolist in this way snatches part of consumers' surplus. The part not obtained is the sum of the three little triangles in Figure 17–1. They are the triangles E, F, and G. Their total is the part of the consumers' surplus that the buyers keep.

Second-degree price discrimination is necessarily practiced in markets where there are many buyers, sometimes hundreds of thousands of them. One rate or price schedule must apply to all buyers. Because tastes and incomes differ, the monopolist can seize only a small part of the consumers' surpluses of those buyers whose desires for the service are stronger, and whose incomes are higher. Second-degree discrimination is furthermore limited to services sold in blocks of small units—cubic feet of gas, kilowatt hours of electricity, minutes of telephoning—that can be easily metered, recorded, and billed.

Third Degree: Allocation of a Given Amount

Third-degree price discrimination means that the monopolist divides customers into two or more classes or groups, charging a different price to each class of customer. Each class is a separate market, e.g., the box seats, the reserved grandstand seats, the unreserved grandstand seats, and the bleachers.

[1] It can be argued that the demand curve in Figure 17–1 should lie a little lower than a conventional demand curve, on which there can be only one price at one time. Because it extracts more money from the consumers, the discrimination has a small adverse effect on their incomes. The discussion above ignores the income effect, because it is almost certain to be negligibly small.

Public utility companies also practice price discrimination of the third degree, by grouping their customers into separate markets such as residential, commercial, and industrial. Each market is further subdivided into submarkets, such as different times of the day and different uses of the service. Prices differ from one submarket to another and, besides, second-degree discrimination is practiced *within* each submarket. The regulatory authorities must approve, of course, the complex patterns of price discrimination chosen by public utility companies. Approval means that the authorities find the patterns to be "reasonable."

The simplest analytical illustration of third-degree price discrimination is that of the monopolist who sells something, already produced, in two separate markets. The problem resembles that of the monopolist selling in the immediate market; because there is some given amount to sell, the monopolist's costs can be ignored. When selling in two markets, the monopolist adjusts the amounts in each so that marginal revenues are equal. Here is another manifestation of the equimarginal principle: The last units sold in each of the two markets make the same addition to total revenue.

Suppose that the monopolist sells 1,200 units in market A and 300 units in market B. In each market marginal revenue is, say, $5. If one unit more was sold in market A and one unit less in market B, total revenue would shrink. The extra unit sold in market A would have a smaller marginal revenue—say, $4. The cutback of one unit in market B would mean the sacrifice of the $5 marginal revenue. There being no sense in gaining less than $5 while losing that amount of revenue, it follows that optimum allocation calls for equality of marginal revenue in each market.

Though the marginal revenues are equal in the two markets, prices are unequal. This time the formula $MR = P - \dfrac{P}{E}$ can be put to work.

Since $MR_A = MR_B$, then

$$P_A - \frac{P_A}{E_A} = P_B - \frac{P_B}{E_B}, \quad \text{or} \quad P_A\left(1 - \frac{1}{E_A}\right) = P_B\left(1 - \frac{1}{E_B}\right).$$

Therefore, the price in market A, i.e., P_A, differs from price in market B when elasticities in the two markets are unequal. If elasticities were equal, prices would be the same; hence there would be no price discrimination.

The simple numbers that appeared a few pages back can throw a little more light on the two prices and the two elasticities. Again let E_A be 2 and E_B be 1.5. Then

$$P_A\left(1 - \frac{1}{2}\right) = P_B\left(1 - \frac{1}{1.5}\right), \text{ or}$$

$$\frac{P_A}{2} = \frac{P_B}{3}, \text{ or } P_A = \frac{2}{3}P_B.$$

With these numbers, therefore, the price in market A is two-thirds the price in market B.

Pricing of Milk The pricing of milk is a good example of price discrimination in practice. In most parts of the United States, milk is sold monopolistically, by producers' associations that act as agents for the dairy farmers in each market area. The federal government lends its benign auspices to this fixing of the prices of milk. Milk is sold in two classes of markets, the markets for "fluid" milk as bought at retail in cities and the markets for "surplus" milk, which is the milk that becomes evaporated milk, butter, powdered milk, cheddar cheese, ice cream, etc. Each of the many producers' associations has a monopoly of the sale (at wholesale) of fluid milk in its own area. But in selling surplus milk, whose markets are much broader, any one producers' association is in competition with others. Therefore, the demand for the surplus milk of any single association is highly elastic. Normally, the price of fluid milk is much higher than the price of surplus milk.

Third Degree: Allocation of Production When looking into the future to plan production and sales, the monopolist must take account of costs as well as revenues. Marginal revenues in each of two markets are equal here too, but they are also equal to the marginal costs of the monopolist's *entire* output. This is easy to see when marginal cost is constant over the relevant range of output; marginal revenues in both markets are equal to marginal cost and therefore to each other. But when marginal cost is a changing function of output, a diagram is needed to show the profit-maximizing division of sales between two markets.

In Figure 17–2, the monopolist has two markets, A and B, with demands D_A and D_B. The demand in market A is smaller and more elastic (in the relevant range) than the demand in market B. The two marginal revenue curves are shown in the figure. The same product is sold in the two markets so that the one marginal cost curve suffices. The analysis holds for both the short run and the long.

The monopolist first determines total output and then allocates sales between the two markets. To decide what total output should be, the monopolist needs to know the combined marginal revenue (*CMR*), which is the addition to total revenue from selling one more unit in *each* of the two markets. Figure 17–2 has the heavy dashed line *CMR*. The line is constructed this way: Take a point on the vertical axis. Then go horizontally to MR_A and MR_B, noting the respective quantities in markets A and B. Add the two quantities

FIGURE 17–2   **THIRD-DEGREE DISCRIMINATION**

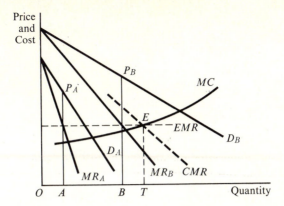

horizontally. This gives a point on *CMR*. Then take another point on the vertical axis, adding the quantities for the two *MR* lines to get the second point on *CMR*.

Total output *OT* is determined by setting *CMR* equal to *MC*; this is at point *E*. From point *E*, draw the horizontal line *EMR*, the line of equal marginal revenue. Then comes the allocation—*OA* is sold in the *A* market at price P_A and *OB* is sold in the *B* market at price P_B. When this is true, $MR_A = MR_B = CMR = MC$. Thus marginal revenues in the two markets are equal to each other, to the combined marginal revenue, and to the marginal cost of the total output.

Since MR_A of output *OA* exceeds the *MC* of *OA*, why not sell more in market *A*? The answer to that, given the sale of *OB* in market *B*, additional sales in market *A* would raise *MC* above *E*. That is, the additional sales would have a higher extra cost than the revenue they would bring. To the right of *E*, *MC* exceeds MR_A, which is what would happen if sales in *A* were greater than *OA*. Similar reasoning holds for sales larger than *OB* in the *B* market.

PEAK-LOAD PRICING   Peak-load pricing is a form of price discrimination where the monopolist charges a higher price for peak use than for nonpeak use. Telephone companies, for example, have long followed the practice of charging more for a three-minute call during the day than they do for the same call during the evening. The demand for telephone service fluctuates predictably during the day, and during the week. So do the demands for many other services, such as those of electric power and gas companies. The demands in the different periods of time have different elasticities. This fact by itself is enough to explain different rates or prices for service during peak and nonpeak periods.

But there is more to peak-load pricing. Public utilities produce nonstorable services; their output is consumed in the very moment it is produced. They have to have the plant capacity to meet the peak demands of their consumers. Typically, the additional cost (long-run marginal cost) of capacity to provide peak service is a large fraction of the total investment of a public utility firm. Higher prices during peak periods, then, have the purpose of thrusting the cost of peak capacity onto the consumers who demand service in peak periods.

Economists have devised elaborate schemes for peak-load pricing. The main purpose of their proposals, and of the methods used by public utility companies, is to save resources. Higher peak prices and lower nonpeak prices reduce the peak quantities demanded and shift some of the demand from peak to nonpeak periods. Therefore, as public utilities expand their plants in a growing economy, peak-load pricing can help them grow at slower rates.

THE PRICING OF MULTIPLE PRODUCTS

The theory of price discrimination just reviewed can be extended to the problem of determining the prices for the multiple products of a firm. The extension of the theory has been carried out in a well-known article by Eli W. Clemens of the University of Maryland.[2] Most firms do in fact produce more than one product. Some produce thousands of products. The multiple products of a firm can be different sizes, models, types, styles, etc., of the same general class of thing. A firm's multiple products can also consist of physically quite dissimilar products. Each single product has a market. In the context of changing markets, changing costs, changing consumer tastes, and changing product designs, alert firms are constantly looking for new markets to invade with existing or with new products. A familiar example is the invasion of each other's markets by drugstores, variety stores, and grocery supermarkets.

What a firm has to sell, it can be argued, is not so much its product or its line of products as its capacity and know-how in production. For this statement to have meaning, certain conditions must hold. One is that the resources of the firm be readily convertible to making a range of products. This means that a good part of the equipment of the firm is general purpose equipment and that management and labor are versatile. Another condition is that the firm normally has some idle equipment or equipment not fully utilized. This amounts to relaxing the assumptions of earlier chapters to the effect that the firm is always locked in a rigid profit-maximizing position.

In his model of the pricing of multiple products, Clemens begins by assuming that a firm has one product and that the firm's plant is being operated at 60 to 70 per cent of capacity. Marginal revenue

[2] See reference to Clemens at the end of this chapter.

and marginal cost for the one product are equal. With its idle capacity of plant, organization, and personnel, the firm can expand production without having to expect much increase in marginal costs. Some of the idle capacity can be used to produce a second product for a second market provided that the demand in the second market is above marginal cost. More of the idle capacity can be put to work on a third product, a fourth, and so on.

Figure 17–3 is simplified and adapted from one of Clemens's diagrams. Here the firm has four products that are sold in four markets. Actually, a firm can have dozens of distinct markets; just think of the firms that put out catalogues. But whatever holds for four markets can also be made to hold for any number. Figure 17–3 lines the four markets up from left to right. The first market has demand D_1, the second has demand D_2, and so on. The quantity sold in the first market is OO_1; in the second market it is O_1O_2, and so on. The firm maximizes its profits when it produces and sells quantities of each product such that their marginal revenues are equal to each other and equal to the marginal cost of total production. The line EMR is the line of equal revenue. In each of the four markets, the marginal revenue curves are the lines lying below the corresponding demand curves. The prices of the four products are shown in the figure. Observe that the fourth product has a price just above marginal cost. The more elastic its demand, the closer would the price of the last, or "marginal," product approach marginal cost. This marginal product is not to be confused with the marginal physical product of an input, which is discussed in Chapter 9. Suppose a company producing rubber footwear finds it worthwhile, though just barely profitable, to put out a line of rubber rafts for swimming pools, etc. Then the rafts are a "marginal" product in the sense used

FIGURE 17–3　　　**PRICING OF MULTIPLE PRODUCTS**

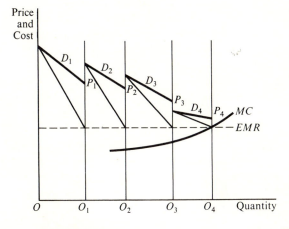

here. For part of its output, therefore, the multiple-product firm operates like the competitive firm, bringing one of its prices close to marginal cost.

Supermarket Prices

We can turn now from the precision of Figures 17–2 and 17–3 to the world of the prices that people pay when they buy in supermarkets. From the complex pattern of these prices, one feature is chosen for mention here. The prices of staples are relatively lower than the prices of nonstaple items. Staples include such products as coffee, soap, cigarettes, sugar, canned soup. Nonstaple items include relatively more expensive specialty foods, imported delicatessen fare, drugs and toiletries. To say that the prices of staples are lower means that the supermarket's markups, or margins, above unit costs are smaller percentages for staples. Why is this so? The basic cause of the difference in markups is the difference in the elasticities of demand for staples and nonstaples. In any one supermarket the demand for staples is more elastic. The causes are the close price competition from rival supermarkets, the advertising that proclaims the prices of staples, and the price consciousness of the thrifty shopper. In contrast, the less elastic demand for the nonstaple items comes from their being occasional or impulse purchases where price does not loom large in the decision. Thus in supermarkets too, lower prices go along with more elastic demands.

OUTPUT UNDER PRICE DISCRIMINATION

If a firm practices price discrimination, is output larger or smaller than if it did not? The answer to this question is important, because of course one of the functions of prices is to determine the quantities of goods and services produced and sold. The answer also has to do with the relation between monopolistic and competitive outputs. But no single generalization about output under price discrimination can be made. The total output of a monopolist with two or more prices can indeed be larger or smaller than total output if the monopolist would sell at one price. Conceivably, too, a monopolist could have an output equal to the output corresponding to conditions of pure competition.

Some commodities and services might not be produced at all if sellers were not able or were not allowed to practice price discrimination. The standard and simple example is the physician in the small community. If he or she charges the same fees to all patients, the physician's income would be too low, let it be supposed, to induce the physician to stay in the community. If, however, the physician charges well-to-do patients more than others, he or she can earn enough to stay in the community. In this example, therefore, the continued availability of medical service in the community is contingent upon price discrimination. So, too, railroad service on a particular route might depend on the ability of the railroad to charge higher rates to some groups of shippers than to others.

If there were ever a monopolist able to practice the perfect discrimination described earlier, that firm would have an output as large as the purely competitive output with the same demand and cost functions. This is because the consumers' demand curve is treated as the monopolist's own marginal revenue curve. The area under the marginal revenue curve of a "non-discriminating" monopolist is total revenue (see page 287). In contrast, the "perfectly discriminating" monopolist takes the area under the demand curve as total revenue; thus the consumer's demand curve plays the role of marginal revenue. This monopolist equates this marginal revenue with marginal cost, thus equating demand with marginal cost, as in the equilibrium of pure competition.

Since discrimination of the second degree is an approach to discrimination of the first degree, it follows that output is larger than if the monopolist had a single price. When a monopolist practices third-degree discrimination, output can be equal to, or less than, or greater than, output at a single price. It depends on the shapes of the demand curves in the monopolist's two or more markets. If the demand curves in the separate markets are linear, then total output is the same as with a single price. With two markets, this means that the reduction in the market with the less elastic demand is equal to the expansion in the market with the more elastic demand. Proof of this is exceedingly complicated and will be omitted here.[3] In her authoritative discussion of price discrimination, the British economist Joan Robinson comes to the conclusion that, in all likelihood, output is larger with price discrimination than without it.[4]

APPLICATIONS

The theory of price discrimination has numerous applications of varied kinds. The contribution of price theory to decisions on price discrimination, whether decisions are for or against discrimination, is to draw attention to differences in elasticities of demand. In contrast, practical decision makers usually concentrate their thoughts on costs—on cost differences, or their absence, as justification, or the lack of justification for price differences.

Business Pricing Decisions

Clemens's model of multiple pricing is a leading example of how a business firm should conceptually tackle the problem of setting prices for its product line. The model, of course, is essentially simple: Profits are the only objective, pricing is independent of

[3] It can be found in Joan Robinson, *Economics of Imperfect Competition*, Macmillan, London, 1933, pp. 190–195.
[4] *Ibid.,* pp. 201, 202.

possible reactions from rival firms, and cost complications are ignored. The lesson taught by the model is the irrationality of the common business practice of setting prices on different products by adding uniform percentages of costs. To do this is convenient. If elasticities differ, as they nearly always seem to do, then the practice of uniform markup pricing results in smaller profits than are attainable. In his *Managerial Economics,* Joel Dean has a long discussion of how the business firm should establish its price "differentials." He rails against uniform markup pricing, urging the business executive to look to the incremental costs of each product, to its actual or probable demand, and to its probable elasticity. In the short run, the firm should select the structure of prices and outputs of its several products that maximizes the excess of total revenue over total variable cost. Lack of data and the uncertainties of the future are barriers to firm estimates of demand. Still, they should not prevent analytical thought.

Economic
Policy

Price discrimination has long been a problem in American economic policy. Elaborate systems of price discrimination prevail in the rate structures of the railroads and of the public utilities. Anything smacking of first-degree, or perfect, discrimination is prohibited in the pricing practices of firms and industries subject to special regulation by the federal and state governments. Such discrimination is personal. In general, classifications of buyers and of markets must meet legal tests of "reasonableness." Price differences must also be "reasonable," which usually means that they must conform to demonstrable differences in costs as measured by accounting standards. Differences in elasticities of demand are hardly ever put on an equal footing with differences in costs. The recognition given to elasticities is oblique or implicit. A regulated company may be allowed to charge a lower rate for some part of its service where it faces obvious competition, and where, accordingly, demand is more elastic. Railroads are often allowed to quote low rates on routes where they face serious competition from other common carriers.

The Robinson-Patman Act of 1936 prohibits, with certain exceptions and qualifications, price discrimination between classes of buyers when the effect of the discrimination is to injure competition. The main purpose of this law is to protect the independent retailer from the competition of the mass distributor (e.g., mail order house) who can often buy from manufacturers at very low prices.

The rates charged by the United States Postal Service are discriminatory. The pattern is based neither upon the costs of the different classes of services nor upon demand, let alone elasticity of demand. Instead, postal rates are set so as to promote the ends of policy as Congress sees them—ends such as mail service for all persons, the dissemination of knowledge (e.g., low rates for books), the subvention of advertising and periodicals, etc. If rates were fixed with the sole purpose of maximizing the net revenue of the Postal Service, their structure would be far different.

During the 1930s, some agricultural economists tried to invent forms of price discrimination that would benefit farmers. If industry has discriminatory prices, they argued, why shouldn't agriculture? If government is going to raise farm prices anyway, why not work in a little discrimination? The notion was that food prices should be made higher to the rich, whose demand is highly inelastic, and be made lower to the poor, whose demand is less inelastic. If the gain to the urban poor and the gain to the farmers would exceed the loss to the rich, discriminatory prices for farm products would be justified. Such was the argument. What came of it were certain programs, some of them still in effect, to make a few farm products available at low prices to selected groups of consumers. Low-priced milk for school children has been one on-again-off-again program. At one time, families on public assistance could buy "surplus" foods at low prices. The food stamp program, however, does indeed reduce the effective prices of food to the millions of low-income people who are entitled to buy the stamps.

Welfare

In the ideal economy of the welfare theorists, there would be no price discrimination. In this economy, the prevailing market structure would be pure competition under which price discrimination is impossible anyway. The natural monopolies in the ideal economy would set their prices equal to their marginal costs. Price differences between products would exactly equal differences in marginal costs, which is another way of expressing the absence of price discrimination. That consumers pay the same prices at the same time for the same products is one of the marginal conditions for maximum economic welfare.

Price discrimination takes on another hue when it is looked at in the context of a partial welfare analysis. *Partial welfare* means the economic welfare flowing from one commodity or industry, considered by itself, and without regard for possible cross effects with other commodities or industries. It was shown earlier that demand-cost relations can be such that without discrimination a particular commodity or service will not be produced at all. Where government controls prices, it may permit or even encourage discrimination if the result is the production of something considered important—rail transportation, for example. Another general reason for government to practice or to encourage price discrimination is to reduce inequalities of personal real incomes. The equity criterion pushes aside the efficiency criterion. Tenants in public housing projects, who must have incomes below specified levels, pay rents that are in general well below full costs. Military personnel and their families can buy groceries and other items in post exchanges at prices generally below those prevailing in ordinary retail establishments. Books in Braille are mailed free to the blind.

SUMMARY

The prerequisites of price discrimination by a monopolist are separate markets and differences of elasticity of demand between the markets. In *first-degree discrimination*, the monopolist captures the entire consumers' surplus of the buyers. In *second-degree discrimination*, the monopolist sets successively lower prices for successively larger quantities, seizing a part of consumers' surplus. In *third-degree discrimination*, the monopolist divides customers into classes or groups. In the immediate market, sales between two markets are allocated so that *marginal revenues are equal*. The difference in price depends on elasticities. In allocating production between two markets, the monopolist equates the two marginal revenues with the marginal cost of the firm's entire output. A firm with many products maximizes profits by selling each product at a price that results in equality of marginal revenue with the marginal cost of total production. Output can be larger with price discrimination than without it. Sometimes output is possible only with price discrimination. The theory of discrimination has wide application in business decisions and in the analysis of economic policy.

SELECTED REFERENCES

A good discussion of the many forms of price discrimination is given by Fritz Machlup, "Characteristics and Types of Price Discrimination," in *Business Concentration and Price Policy,* National Bureau of Economic Research (Princeton University Press, Princeton, 1955), pp. 397–435. Degrees of price discrimination are introduced by A. C. Pigou, *The Economics of Welfare,* 4th ed. (Macmillan, London, 1932), chap. 17. The most rigorous treatment of the pure theory is found in Joan Robinson, *The Economics of Imperfect Competition* (Macmillan, London, 1933), chaps. 15 and 16. A less difficult though thorough discussion is in Joe S. Bain, *Pricing, Distribution, and Employment,* rev. ed. (Holt, New York, 1953), chap. 9. The discussion of multiple-product pricing is based on Eli W. Clemens, "Price Discrimination and the Multiple-Product Firm," *Review of Economic Studies,* vol. 19 (1950–1951), 1–11 [reprinted in American Economic Association, *Readings in Industrial Organization and Public Policy* (Irwin, Homewood, 1958)]. How business firms can benefit from the theory of price discrimination is explained by Joel Dean, *Managerial Economics* (Prentice-Hall, Englewood Cliffs, N.J., 1951), chaps. 8 and 9. How dairy farmers do benefit is shown by Edmond S. Harris, *Classified Pricing of Milk,* Technical Bulletin No. 1184, United States Department of Agriculture (U.S. Government Printing Office, Washington, D.C., 1958).

Also: F. M. Scherer, *Industrial Pricing: Theory and Evidence* (Rand McNally, Chicago, 1970), chap. 6; Reuben A. Kessel, "Price Discrimination in Medicine," *Journal of Law and Economics,* 1 (October 1958), 20–53.

EXERCISES AND PROBLEMS

1.   Suppose a monopolist has two markets, and that the demand schedules in them are as follows:

Market A		Market B	
P	Q	P	Q
$50	400	$60	600
40	600	50	800
30	900	40	1,100
20	1,000	30	1,400

Suppose that the monopolist has 1,400 units to sell. What prices will be set in the two markets? Why?

2.   A business firm charged with price discrimination in violation of the Robinson-Patman Act may offer a cost defense. The accused firm is exonerated if it can prove that cost differences are at least as great as price differences. Under the law, the costs are business costs, measured by cost accounting standards; roughly speaking, they are average costs. Suppose now that the law would allow *marginal* cost calculations as a defense against charges of price discrimination. What do you think the result would be?

3.   Draw a diagram to illustrate third-degree discrimination in the immediate market.

4.   Suppose that $E = 2$ in one market and $E = 1.5$ in another market in which a monopolist can sell the product. What is the percentage ratio of the prices charged?

5.   Why is it easier for a firm to practice second-degree price discrimination than first-degree, or perfect, discrimination?

6.   Compile a list of items that you purchase whose prices are discriminatory. How many of the items carry the lowest price? Does compiling this list make you think of changing your buying habits? Of the items you knowingly pay a higher price for, which can you change, i.e., shift from one group to another?

7. Explain how peak-load pricing could reduce the plant and equipment required by a public utility.

8. Why does a purely competitive firm never engage in price discrimination?

9. Explain why, in the absence of price discrimination, some goods and services would not be produced and would therefore not be available to the consumer.

10. Assume that a monopolist has three separate markets. Explain the following possibilities: (a) the highest price in the smallest market, (b) a lower price in another but larger market, and (c) destruction of some output before selling in the third market.

11. Explain the symmetry between third-degree price discrimination in the immediate market period and the behavior of the consumer in the allocation of time. Why are both examples of the equimarginal principle?

12. Should urban transit companies engage in price discrimination if to do so means avoiding a loss? Speculate on the various prices the transit system could charge. What price structure would avoid hurting low-income users? How might that affect the relation between total revenues and total costs?

Appendix

TO PART 4

MATHEMATICAL NOTES

The monopolist's demand curve is

$$q = f(p).$$

That is, the amount sold depends on the price charged. The total revenue (R) of the monopolist is price multiplied by the quantity of output sold

$$R = pq.$$

Marginal revenue (MR) is the derivative of total revenue with respect to output

$$MR = \frac{dR}{dq} = p + q\frac{dp}{dq} = p\left(1 + \frac{q}{p}\frac{dp}{dq}\right).$$

But $-\frac{q}{p}\frac{dp}{dq} = \frac{1}{E}$, where E is the coefficient of price elasticity of demand. Therefore

$$MR = p\left(1 - \frac{1}{E}\right) = P - \frac{P}{E}.$$

Table 16–1 on page 286 shows that the linear function for the marginal revenue declines twice as fast as price. This can be generalized for linear demands as follows

$$p = a - bq$$
$$R = aq - bq^2$$

$$MR = \frac{dR}{dq} = a - 2bq.$$

The slope of $MR(-2b)$ is twice the slope of demand $(-b)$.

Let the subscripts 1 and 2 denote the revenues and the quantities sold in two markets. The monopolist's profit is the difference between revenues from both markets and total costs

$$\pi = R_1(q_1) + R_2(q_2) - TC(q_1 + q_2).$$

R is revenue, q is quantity sold in a market, and TC is total cost. For maximum profits, the partial derivatives are set equal to zero

$$\frac{\partial \pi}{\partial q_1} = R_1'(q_1) - TC'(q_1 + q_2) = 0.$$

$$\frac{\partial \pi}{\partial q_2} = R_2'(q_2) - TC'(q_1 + q_2) = 0.$$

Therefore, the two marginal revenues are equal to each other and to the marginal cost of the entire output. The same product is sold in both markets, and the one cost function holds. The two partial derivatives, TC' above, are thus identical.

5

PRICING IN
IMPERFECT
COMPETITION

18
Monopolistic Competition

Competition among firms setting their own prices, products that are branded and trademarked, competition with quality and service, competition with advertising—these are the ingredients of the *theory of monopolistic competition*. For some time after it first appeared in 1933, the theory of monopolistic competition seemed to be pushing the theory of pure competition to one side. Enthusiasm for the new theory's realism ran high for a while. But time has shown that the theory of pure competition still has important uses and a wide range of applications. The theory of monopolistic competition is there to provide models of specific forms of competition.

PRODUCT DIFFERENTIATION The theory has the job of explaining price and output in market structures where sellers are many and where each seller has a product differentiated from those of rival firms. Monopolistic competition prevails in retailing, in the service industries, and in some branches of manufacturing. Products are differentiated by brands, trademarks, distinctive designs, packaging, and by a myriad of other devices and artifices. Even if the products sold by several sellers are physically homogeneous—e.g., fuel oil—there can still be differentiation if credit terms, promptness and reliability of delivery, etc., are important to consumers. A known and respected brand confers upon its owner a position of monopoly when it is sold to customers who will buy no other brand. But there are other known and respected brands that furnish the competition for the purchases by consumers who shop around among the several brands of a commodity. *Product differentiation*, which can range from strong to weak, is effective only to the extent that it has an impact on the minds of consumers. The subjective, not the objective, features of product differentiation are what count.

Product differentiation shapes the demand for a firm's product, determining the strength of that demand and its elasticity. Figure

FIGURE 18-1   **PRODUCT DIFFERENTIATION AND ELASTICITY OF DEMAND**

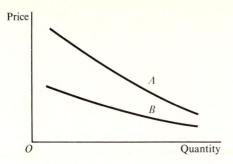

18-1 contains two demand curves, *A* and *B*. Imagine them as the demands for two branded products sold by two different firms. Except at very low prices, both curves are elastic because both products are in close competition with each other and with still other brands. Demand curve *A* is less elastic than curve *B*. Curve *A* also shows a much stronger demand, i.e., at any one price more of brand *A* would be sold. Curve *A* could represent, say, the demand for Old Grandfather bourbon whiskey, a popular and respected brand. In its turn, curve *B* could stand for Old Overshoes, an obscure brand. Product differentiation achieves results like this. Suppose either firm would raise its price. If the firm selling brand *A* did so, it would suffer a much smaller loss of sales, because its demand is less elastic.

Edward H. Chamberlin of Harvard University is the architect and the builder of the theory of monopolistic competition. In a simplified and abbreviated form, his presentation of the theory will be followed here. One of Chamberlin's achievements is to classify all of the adjustments that a firm can make under just three headings. They are *price, product,* and *selling effort.* In seeking to obtain maximum profits, the firm under monopolistic competition can review its price policy, or it can review its policy on the quality of its product, or it can review its policy on advertising or other sales effort. The three kinds of adjustments, or policies, will now be taken up in order.

PRICE ADJUSTMENTS

The firm under monopolistic competition is one of many. No single firm, accordingly, dominates the industry. Each firm produces and sells its product in close competition with other similar firms. The elasticity of demand for the product of each seller is high because the products are close substitutes for one another.

The Firm

Consider first one firm by itself, without regard, for the moment, to the competitive environment of the firm. Assume that the quality of the firm's product is given and that the firm conducts no advertising.

Let the context be the long run. The conclusions applicable to the long run are easily transferable to the short run; all that has to be done is to take account of the shapes of the firm's cost curves. The demand curve of the firm reflects consumers' tastes (for *its* product), their incomes, and the *given* prices of the products of the other firms. Under these conditions, the firm behaves as a monopolist, setting its price accordingly. The equilibrium of the firm, when it is viewed in isolation, is the equilibrium of a monopolist.

The firm, however, is likely to have only a small amount of pricing discretion, because its demand curve is almost horizontal. Monopolistic competition is really closer to pure competition than it is to monopoly. Though the firm in monopolistic competition possesses one of the formal properties of monopoly—the sloping demand curve—it lacks the substance of monopoly.

The Group

Chamberlin calls the several firms whose markets are closely interwoven a *group*. Though a group can be identical with an industry for some purposes, the connotation of the word is that an industry—in the everyday sense of the word—can consist of two or more groups of closely competing firms. Suppose the industry is called "books." One group of firms publishes western, detective, and adventure paperbacks; another group publishes highbrow paperbacks; still other groups produce other kinds of books. Within any one group, close competition exists, though between them competition might not be keen. Another example is gasoline retailing in a large metropolitan area. Gasoline retailing is the industry, but each filling station competes closely with those in its area. The group concept is unavoidably somewhat vague because it is hard to draw sharp lines between groups. The analysis here will proceed on the assumption that a group is definite enough to be discussed.

A supply curve cannot be drawn for a group of firms under monopolistic competition because a supply curve shows the amounts forthcoming at different prices when, as under pure competition, all firms produce the same thing and receive identical prices. But each firm in a group has a different product, and at the same time there are usually several different prices.[1]

Consequently, the behavior of a group must be reflected in the behavior of one firm. The simplest model is one embodying what Chamberlin calls his heroic assumption, namely, that each firm has identical demand and cost curves. If the demand curves are identical, it has to be supposed that the firms have equal shares of the market; if there are 100 firms, each has 1 per cent of total sales.

[1] This is formally correct. Yet if the products of the firms are very similar, as they often are, and if the price differentials are small, something like a group supply curve does make sense. For some purposes, it can be useful.

FIGURE 18-2

DEMAND AND COST

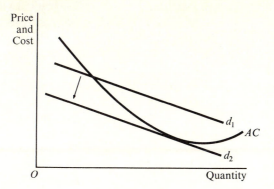

Figure 18-2 can be made to exhibit both individual equilibrium and group equilibrium. Suppose first that each firm has the demand d_1 (the reason for switching the label from D to d will appear shortly). With long-run full costs of AC, each firm can make large net profits. There is no need here to draw in price, marginal cost, marginal revenue, and profits; they can be easily visualized in the imagination. Since all firms are alike, by assumption, net profits for the whole group are high. Since the context is the long run, new firms can enter and put new products on this market. As they do so, the curve d_1 moves down and to the left, because the new products reduce the sales of the existing firms. The firms, old and new, have to lower their prices. All this goes on so long as net profits are to be had. The process comes to an end when the demand curve slides far enough left to become tangent to the cost curve—d_2 is tangent to AC. Another simplifying assumption in this model is that the cost curve AC stays where it is, that the entry of new firms causes no external economies or diseconomies in the group (Chapter 14, pages 258–259).

In Chamberlin's theory of monopolistic competition, the solution to the problem of group equilibrium, when the strongly simplifying assumptions are used, is always a tangency. Tangency simply means that price equals full costs. With tangency, the firm can neither raise nor lower its price without suffering losses. Net profits are maximum at zero.[2] There being no net profits, no outside firm wants to enter the group. Because full costs include normal profits, no firm in the group wants to leave.[3] Hence the group is in equilibrium. Notice that the tangency of the demand curve to the cost

[2] Tangency of the demand curve to the cost curve in pure competition is shown on page 255, and in monopoly on page 293.
[3] This means the further assumption that firms outside the group, that could enter it, are always earning only normal profits.

curve is symmetrical with the tangency of demand to cost in the long run under pure competition. The difference between monopolistic and pure competition is that under monopolistic competition, the demand curve slopes slightly. Because the slope is always negative, price is a little higher and output is a little smaller.

In a rough-and-ready sense and apart from the precision of Chamberlin's analysis, all this means that where entry is free, the long run contains a tendency for prices to be pulled down to full costs. This is true despite the "monopoly" each firm has of its own brand.

Shortsighted Price Cutting

The adjustment to equilibrium just described has taken place through the entry of new firms. The number of firms, however, can be correct, but the price can be higher than the equilibrium level. If so, equilibrium can be established as the result of a price war. Consider Figure 18–3. This figure has two kinds of demand curves. The d curves, for any one firm, are drawn on the assumption that the other firms' prices remain unchanged while the one firm changes its price. In contrast, the D curve shows what happens to the sales of one firm when its rivals do in fact change their prices at the same time and by the same amount. The D curve is much less elastic than the d curve. The D curve is also a miniature of the demand curve for the whole group. Suppose again that there are 100 firms. When the quantities that can be read off the D curve are multiplied by 100, the result is the demand curve for the whole group

Imagine now that one of the firms is at point A in Figure 18–3. Though the firm is enjoying a large net profit, it could earn still more if it could expand its sales along curve d_1. Imagine too that the owners of the firm are shortsighted business executives who believe that if they were to cut price, their competitors would *not* lower their prices. So they cut their price in the expectation of much larger sales

FIGURE 18–3 **SHORTSIGHTED PRICE CUTTING**

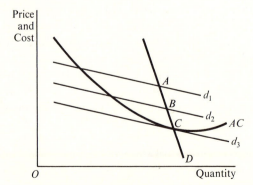

and profits. But the business executives are frustrated because their competitors cut their prices too. The firm moves from A to B, down the D curve. Though sales at B are a little larger, profits are lower. The d curve has slid down from d_1 to d_2. Suppose next that the price cutting firm does not benefit from its experience, and initiates another price cut, which again the other firms promptly imitate. Once more the d curve slides down. When it gets down to the position d_3, it can go no farther, because then more price cuts would bring nothing but losses, even for the shortsighted. This kind of price war, then, establishes the equilibrium of the firm and the group. Price equals full cost, and the curves are tangent.

Diversities of Demands and of Costs

Let the assumption of uniform demands and costs now be dropped. All the firms in the group now have different costs, different demands, and therefore different prices, volumes of output, and profits. Figure 18–4 shows such differences, in hypothetical form, for firms A, B, C, and D. The positions of firms E, F, G, etc., can easily be imagined. Though diversity exists from one firm to another, the group as a whole nearly always shows some definite pattern of profits or losses. Suppose that the group as a whole is profitable, even though a few of the firms are suffering losses. Firms outside decide that the group's markets are worth invading. They do so. As the new firms put their products on the market, the old firms suffer some losses in sales. But not all are affected equally. Perhaps firm A scarcely feels the new competition at all, because its brand is solidly established. Perhaps firms C and D are hit hardest by the invading brands. Eventually the entry of new firms comes to an end and the group's markets offer no more attractions to outsiders. Smaller net profits are now scattered about the group, but their pattern does not offer any incentive to entry.

FIGURE 18–4   DIFFERENCES WITHIN A GROUP OF FIRMS

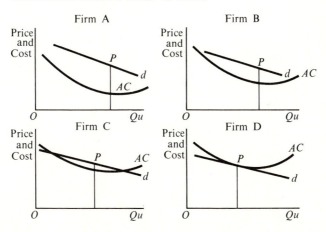

Much of the competition that is monopolistic is nonprice competition, whose two main forms are *product variation* and *advertising*. Product variation is Chamberlin's term for *quality competition*. In nonprice competition, the pushing and jostling among firms takes the forms of manipulating the qualities of their products and their advertising activities. While they do so, their prices remain constant for months or even for a few years at a time. Prices remain constant for many reasons: Some prices stay long at 5¢ or 10¢ or 25¢ simply because these are the denominations of the common coins. Other prices stay at $1, or hover near it, because buyers and sellers are accustomed to this price. Still other steady prices for particular classes of products are the consequence of custom and (sometimes) inexplicable practice.

Here are two examples of prices that remained steady for long periods of time: In 1971 and again in 1974 the Wrigley Company raised the wholesale price of its chewing gum. Before that, the price had been increased in 1960, after having been constant for about four decades. The other example is the Hershey bar. Late in 1969 Hershey abandoned its smallest chocolate bar, which had retailed at five cents for many, many years. Hershey's "product variation" consists of varying the number of ounces in its candy bars.

The Firm

Take a firm selling its product at a price fixed by custom or inertia. Because it is differentiated, the product can be changed this way and that in color, or durability, or workmanship, or design, or in the services that go with it. Assume that consumers will buy larger quantities of a product that is "improved." This last word has to be enclosed in quotation marks to convey the idea that an improvement in a product might or might not be a gain in a measurable, objective sense. An improvement is whatever is intended to make consumers buy more for whatever reason, laudable or otherwise. A lurid picture on a paperback novel is there to increase sales; it probably costs more than a dignified cover. The increased revenue from larger sales must be balanced against increased costs. Hence the firm adjusts its quality so as to maximize profits. Notice the parallel with price adjustments: If it lowers its price, the firm increases its total revenue; but the firm also increases its total costs, because it sells more units.

The optimum adjustment for the firm, when its product is the variable, is indicated in Figure 18–5. The diagram is awkward, because output sold has to be inserted arbitrarily. In the figure, *OP* is the customary price. The horizontal line drawn from *P* is a horizontal line, nothing more. It is not a demand curve. For a product of quality *A*, the curve C_A is the long-run, average-cost curve for variant *A*, or quality *A*, of the firm's product. When the

FIGURE 18–5

PRODUCT VARIATION

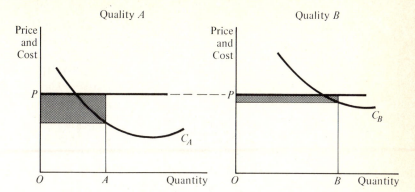

firm chooses quality A, it sells the amount OA. The net profit is the shaded rectangle at the top. On the right, quality B of the firm's product has costs shown by cost curve C_B. More of B is sold, i.e., the amount OB. But it is quite evident that the net profit from B is less than that from A. For other qualities, C, D, E, etc., the firm can calculate costs, sales, and net profits. One of the qualities must be the one that yields maximum net profits, just as when price is the variable, one of the possible prices is the optimum.

Chamberlin's product variation must not be confused with changes in quality induced by technological improvements over time. Almost any durable consumer good is better than it was 10 or 20 years ago. It is likely to be better in its design and in its engineering features. This kind of product improvement comes from changes in tastes and from technical and business innovations. In contrast, Chamberlin's theory deals with the firm's use of existing techniques to modify its product in a context of existing tastes. The analogy is to hold demand and cost curves constant.

The Group

When product is the variable, the solution of the problem of group equilibrium is also tangency, upon the assumption that all firms have the same costs and shares of the market. Suppose that all the firms in a group are alike and that all are making net profits. Then new firms will enter the group, thus causing the sales of old firms to fall off. In efforts to offset their losses of sales, the firms make further improvements in their products. As a result, their cost curves rise and keep on rising until they are tangent to the horizontal line that indicates the price. When sales adjust themselves so that they are equal to the amount corresponding to the tangency position, the firm is in equilibrium. So is the group, because here too tangency means equality of price and full costs, and, therefore, the absence of incentive for firms to enter or to leave the group.

Selling costs are incurred to increase the demand for a product. The term *selling costs* is broader than *advertising* because selling costs include those salesmen, of allowances to retailers for displays, and in fact of any kind of promotional activity. Chamberlin distinguishes selling costs from *production costs*. The costs that must be incurred to make a product, transport it, and have it available to consumers with *given* wants are production costs. The costs of *changing* consumers' wants are selling costs. Though it is useful, the distinction cannot always be sharply made. For example, is attractive packaging a production cost or a selling cost? It probably does not matter that questions of this sort cannot be easily answered. The analysis to follow will assume that Chamberlin's distinction can always be made. Anyway, the difficulty just about vanishes when the expressions *selling costs* and *advertising expenditures* are employed interchangeably; Chamberlin himself does this.

The Curve of Selling Costs

Advertising is a black art. Its mysteries, its great problems, are bypassed here. One of them is how to advertise and, in particular, what media give best results. Instead, let it be assumed that expenditures on advertising do increase the demand for a product, all other things—price, quality, buyers' incomes—being equal. Let the word *increase* also be understood algebraically; that is, the increase in demand could be infinitesimal, perhaps zero, or perhaps even negative if it should happen that the advertising is repellent rather than enticing. The task now is to set up a relation between the advertising expenditures of a firm and the unit sales of its product. The relationship is given in the curve of selling costs, which is another of Chamberlin's contributions to economic theory.

Figure 18–6 contains a curve of selling costs, *ASC*. Though in appearance it is just another *U*-shaped cost curve, the curve of selling costs has its own meaning. The curve shows the *average* cost per unit of selling any given amount of the product. It costs an average of *AA'* cents each to sell *OA'* thousands of units, *BB'* cents

FIGURE 18–6   **CURVE OF SELLING COSTS**

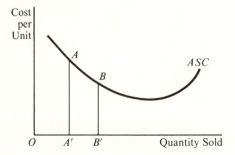

each to sell *OB'* thousands, etc. The curve first declines, because of initial economies of scale in advertising; advertising expenses that are too small are said to be wasteful. Sooner or later, after reaching a minimum somewhere, the curve must rise to indicate the mounting costliness of expanding sales. Here is one cost curve whose eventual rise can never be in doubt.[4] In all likelihood, the curve finally becomes vertical, at which volume of sales there would be the "saturation" so often mentioned in sales discussions. Selling costs can be very high or very low. No generalization is possible. In one year in the 1950s, a major automobile company was said to have spent $700 in advertising *each* car of its luxury make that the company was able to sell.

The shape and position of the curve of selling costs for a firm's product in a given period of time reflect the play of the other variables. They are, of course, the price of the product and of its substitutes, the quality of the product and the qualities of its substitutes, the incomes of the buyers, and their resistance, such as it might be, to having their tastes changed by the advertising. Change one or more of these variables and you change the shape and position of the curve. Raise the price, and up goes the curve, meaning that the costs of selling any quantity of the product are higher. Improve the quality and down goes the curve. If consumer tastes are veering away from the product and other similar products, the curve will curl up sooner and faster.

The Optimum Advertising Expenditure

How much should a firm spend on advertising? The profit-maximizing firm spends an amount such that the combined marginal cost of production and of advertising is equal to the price the firm gets for its product. The last unit sold is just worth the cost of producing and selling it.

Figure 18–7 expresses this idea more fully. Here the firm is considered by itself. The price of the product is *OP*. The horizontal line from *P* can be viewed as if it were a marginal revenue curve because by advertising, the firm can sell more without having to lower its price. Average production costs per unit are shown by the curve *APC*. The curve of average selling costs is superimposed on the curve of average production costs; the curve *APC* + *ASC* is thus total costs. The *MC* curve gives the marginal cost associated with average total cost. The equilibrium, or optimum, level of sales is *OA*, because $MC = P = MR$. With sales at *OA*, the firm's advertising volume is optimum because profits are maximized.

A diagram like Figure 18–7, or an adaptation of it to the short

---

[4] Remember that a little doubt attaches to the eventual rise in the ordinary long-run cost curve of a firm. See pages 196–197.

FIGURE 18-7   OPTIMUM VOLUME OF ADVERTISING

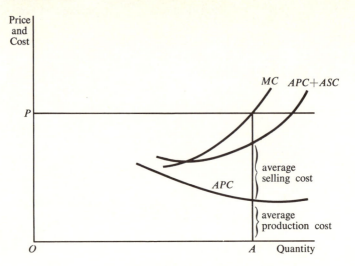

run,[5] has some practical application. Business firms that advertise usually follow rules of thumb, such as operating with fixed advertising budgets, or spending a predetermined per cent of their sales dollars on advertising, or spending as much as their competitors spend, or spending as much as they think they can "afford." Such methods can be safe and certainly they require little thought; thus they do have their virtues, but they are not rational. The marginal approach illustrated in Figure 18-7 is rational; it aims at the profit-maximizing advertising outlay. Only rarely, however, can the relation between advertising expenditures and sales be measured with some degree of confidence. Yet a relation not easily measurable is still relevant. It is better to make the best guess you can of the results of the right course of action than to follow the wrong course just because it poses no problem of measurement.

Advertising and Group Equilibrium

The perpetual controversies over advertising always throw up the question about what part of all advertising satisfies the desire for more information and what part merely diverts sales from one product or product group to another. No attempt will be made here to answer this difficult question or even to suggest the outlines of an answer. Instead, attention here goes to competitive advertising, to advertising as a variable such as price and quality of product.

When it advertises, a firm seeks to increase its own sales. Sometimes the effect is to add to the sales of the firm's competitors, when

[5] Then the production costs are the variable costs.

the advertising increases the desire of consumers not so much for the firm's own product, as for the general class of product.

A simple model of advertising competition, adapted from Chamberlin, is this: Suppose the firms in a group are in equilibrium, none earning any net profits. To begin with, none of them does any advertising. Then imagine that one of them, like the shortsighted price cutter of a few pages ago, thinks that it can earn some profits by advertising, and that it believes it will be the only one to do so.

Figure 18–8 shows what happens. Let the assumption that firms are alike be used again, to keep things simple. Hence the figure stands for any one firm, thus representing all of them. The production cost curve is PC. The price is OP. The initial equilibrium is the output OA. Since price equals average cost of production, there are no net profits. Then one of the firms draws up an advertising plan, shown by the curve SC_1. This curve shows how the firm can increase sales, if it alone advertises. If it is the only one to do so, sales would increase to OB, an optimum output (where marginal cost—not shown—would equal price). But the eager firm is mistaken. It does not achieve the output OB and the net profits that go with it. Its rivals follow the example and also advertise *their* products. The sales of each firm increase only a little just as they do when all firms cut their prices. Now, all of the firms are advertising some amount. Then the eager but shortsighted one tries again. It is more costly now to increase sales with more advertising. Thus the new selling cost curve is SC_2, which does offer the prospect of profits if the eager firm is the only one to expand advertising. Once more, however, frustration ensues. Stable equilibrium comes about only when all firms produce and sell the amount OC and have selling cost curves SC_3. Here too tangency holds. No firm can now hope to earn profits by increased advertising, even if it were the only one to act. Notice that in this mode, advertising does increase sales, from OA to

FIGURE 18–8   ADVERTISING COMPETITION

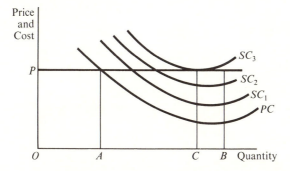

OC. In the end, however, the firms are no better off for having started their advertising war.

Earlier chapters show that the long-run equilibrium of the firm under pure competition is a point of efficiency, that it is one of the conditions of maximum economic welfare. If, then, monopolistic competition causes a deviation from that point, it reduces economic welfare. An aura of suspicion therefore falls on brands, trademarks, advertising, and all of the other means of creating product differentiation. Is the suspicion justified? No one can be sure unless it can be determined *by how much* price and output under monopolistic competition differ. Consider Figure 18–9. Both 18–9A and 18–9B are fully compatible with Chamberlin's reasoning. In both, P_1A is the price and *OA* is the output under monopolistic competition. In pure competition, price and output are P_2B and *OB*; price equals minimum average cost. In Figure 18–9B, the difference is small. Obviously, the shapes of the curves give the two results. The steepness of the cost curve has nothing to do with monopolistic competition, only the steepness of the demand curve, because it indicates the strength of product differentiation. Many economists believe that price and output in most markets with monopolistic competition are closer to the relations shown in Figure 18–9B than to those in 18–9A.

The Wastes of Competition

The theory of monopolistic competition does make an important contribution to the understanding of a facet of a private enterprise economy. That there is some waste in the economy can hardly be denied. The waste takes many forms—too much effort devoted merely to selling things, too many brands, too many retail stores. These excesses are not negligibly small, they are normal and persistent, existing even in equilibrium conditions. They are the wastes of competition, of monopolistic competition to be more precise, of the monopolistic part of monopolistic competition, to be quite precise. Such wastes do not occur under pure competition.

FIGURE 18–9   PRICE AND OUTPUT IN MONOPOLISTIC AND IN PURE COMPETITION

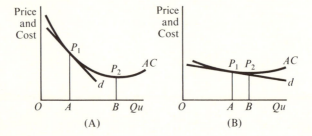

Much controversy and honest doubt surround these issues. Some economists think that the wastes due to monopolistic competition are, in fact, small. Others argue that product differentiation satisfies consumers' desires for variety and breadth of choice. If pure competition prevailed everywhere, homogeneity of products would mean lower costs. Would not life then be drab? If the whole population were put into uniform clothes and made to live in uniform barracks, vast quantities of resources would be released, but what for?

One possible relation between consumers' preferences and economic efficiency is shown in Figure 18–10. Here the demand for the firm's product is D_1. Assume that the consumers have perfect information about the product, i.e., about its quality and about the prices and qualities of all alternative products. The consumers buy the quantity OA at the price P_1. The efficiently produced quantity is OB, whose minimum price is P_2. But the consumers are unwilling to pay price P_2 for the quantity OB; their demand curve plainly says so. They prefer to pay a higher price for a smaller quantity. *If* their demand curve were D_2, which it is not, the consumers would be indifferent between the two choices.

From time to time, observation of events and practices in the Soviet Union can throw new light on features of a private enterprise economy that tend to be taken for granted. In the 1950s, trademarks, brands, and advertising began to appear among the consumer goods sold in Russia. Their purpose and effect seem to be to raise standards of quality. Alternatively, quality in a socialist economy would be maintained by bureaucratic administration. Perhaps the extra costs of product differentiation are less than the cost of enforcing standards of quality. Anyway, it is arguable that American

FIGURE 18–10   **PREFERENCE AND EFFICIENCY**

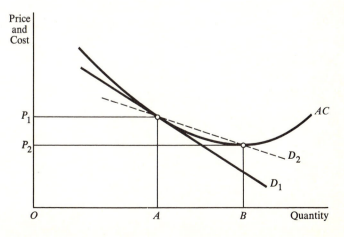

economists have taken quality in private enterprise too much for granted.[6]

SUMMARY

In monopolistic competition, each firm has a *differentiated product* with a highly elastic demand. When it adjusts its price, the firm prices as a monopolist does. In the simple model of the group, where all firms are alike, equilibrium comes about through the entry or exit of firms. Firm and group are in equilibrium when demand curves are tangent to cost curves. When it adjusts the quality of its product, the firm does so to maximize profits. *Product variation* is symmetrical with price adjustment. The *curve of selling costs* relates the expense of advertising per unit with the number of units sold. A firm's *optimum advertising expenditure* is such that the combined marginal cost of production and advertising is equal to price. Group equilibrium with advertising as the competitive variable is also a *tangency solution*. Long-run equilibrium in monopolistic competition is probably close to that attained in pure competition.

SELECTED REFERENCES

The standard work continues to be Edward Hastings Chamberlin, *The Theory of Monopolistic Competition,* 8th ed. (Harvard University Press, Cambridge, 1962). The first edition was in 1933; see especially chap. 5, 6, and 7. A collection of essays by Chamberlin is contained in *Towards a More General Theory of Value* (Oxford University Press, New York, 1957).

A theory of imperfect competition, which also puts the spotlight on the firm rather than on the industry, is found in Joan Robinson, *The Economics of Imperfect Competition* (Macmillan, London, 1933). Robinson offers a box of tools, rather than an integrated theory. Useful analyses of both Chamberlin and Robinson are contained in Robert Triffin, *Monopolistic Competition and General Equilibrium Theory* (Harvard University Press, Cambridge, 1940), especially chap.1.

The view that the theory of pure competition is a more useful model is presented by George J. Stiger, *Five Lectures on Economic Problems* (Macmillan, New York, 1950), lecture 2; Chamberlin's counterargument is in *Towards a More General Theory of Value* (cited above), chap.15.

---

[6] See Marshall I. Goldman, "Product Differentiation and Advertising: Some Lessons from Soviet Experience," *Journal of Political Economy,* 68 (August 1960), 346–357.

EXERCISES AND PROBLEMS

1. Draw sets of diagrams, like those in Figure 18-4, to represent (a) a group of firms whose total pattern of profits and losses is such as to cause exit from the group; and (b) a group of firms with profits and losses such that the group is in equilibrium.

2. Show how a firm might increase its profits by cheapening, instead of improving, its product.

3. Construct an arithmetic table showing, for a firm, different combinations of prices, advertising expenses, and profits.

4. Draw curves of selling costs for different sets of assumed conditions.

5. Should the government establish and enforce grades and standards for ordinary branded products?

6. Draw a diagram that shows an average selling cost curve for a product whose market is saturated.

7. Explain why two kinds of demand curves are important in monopolistic competition.

8. Why do high price elasticities of demand induce firms in monopolistic competition to engage in nonprice competition?

9. Of the many retail establishments you buy from, select five and describe the kinds of competitive behavior they employ.

10. Why do some economists believe that monopolistically competitive industries are "sick industries" and other economists believe that monopolistic competition is wasteful?

19
Oligopoly—
SOME MODELS WITH
PROFIT MAXIMIZATION

Many of the markets in the American economy are oligopolistic. The prices and volumes of production of several important products, such as aluminum, automobiles, heavy electrical equipment, tires, and steel, are determined by the few companies in each of the industries that produce them. Unfortunately, there is no one satisfactory theory of price and output under oligopoly. A satisfactory theory would consist of a few related generalizations commanding substantial agreement and capable of application to policy and welfare problems. Instead of this, there exists a welter of theories about oligopoly. Accordingly, it is well to look first at the difficulties that the subject of oligopoly presents to economic theorists.

PROBLEMS IN THE THEORY OF OLIGOPOLY

To explain the behavior of prices, the behavior of consumers and producers has to be described. This is done by setting up demand curves and cost curves. When they are brought together, equilibrium prices and quantities are determined. In a market with only a few sellers, however, the demand curves of each lose their definiteness. They do not stand still to be analyzed. They flit hither and thither. Suppose that a market has just three sellers, *A*, *B*, *C* and that their products are close substitutes. What is *A*'s demand curve? It can be imagined only by assuming that *B* and *C* charge unchanging prices for their products. If they do, then *A*'s demand curve can be drawn, and as usual, it shows the different quantities *A* can sell at different prices. When *A* alters the price, causing *B* and *C* to change theirs, the result is different. Changes in *B*'s price and in *C*'s price immediately *shift* *A*'s demand curve either to the right or to the left. The same reasoning applies to the demand curves of *B* and *C*. The three demand curves are *interdependent*, so much so, so inextricably, that it makes little sense to try to think of them separately.

The same thing holds if a few firms compete as buyers—when there is *oligopsony*. As an example, take three research firms whose main inputs are the services of particular kinds of engineers and scientists. If one firm raises the salaries it pays to attract better technical talent, the costs of the two other firms are likely to be raised because to keep their staffs, they probably have to raise their salaries too. The cost curves of oligopsonistic firms are therefore interdependent. One of them can be clearly described only on the assumption that the others remain constant.

The theory of pure competition, the theory of monopoly, the theory of monopolistic competition—all come to clear and precise conclusions about equilibrium prices and outputs. Each of the theories is constructed with demand curves, cost curves, and the profit-maximizing assumption. Each of the theories yields equilibria that are said to be determinate, that is, the equilibria are the logical consequences of the assumptions. Some theories of oligopoly, however, yield indeterminate results—they cannot say what price and outputs are. To illustrate this point, the theory of *bilateral monopoly* will now be discussed. As a theoretical problem bilateral monopoly is closely akin to oligopoly.

Bilateral Monopoly

In bilateral monopoly a single seller faces a single buyer. The commodity traded has no close substitute; the seller has no other outlet, the buyer has no other source. The standard theoretical problem here is not that of selling the prize bull or the yacht or the painting, that is, not the problem of exchanging one unit of a commodity. Instead, the problem is that of finding what quantities of a homogeneous commodity will be exchanged, and at what price. The seller is a producing firm. The commodity is its output which it produces, in the usual assumption, at rising average cost. The commodity is an input to the buyer; its value to the buying firm depends upon its (diminishing marginal physical) productivity and upon the demand for the product that the buying firm sells in another market.

Therefore, both seller and buyer view the commodity with their price-quantity schedules. Each wants to maximize money gain from the transaction. Suppose that the seller begins the negotiations by asking a high price. The buyer responds by offering a low price. The higgling proceeds until an agreement is reached. But it is *not* possible to say, with logical analysis based upon the assumptions, just what the agreement is. Price and quantity are indeterminate. Of course, when two firms negotiate a price and when firms and unions negotiate wage rates, they almost always do in fact come to definite agreements. Indeterminacy means that general reasoning, by itself, is unable to say even theoretically what such agreements are.

Theorists have beaten their heads against the problem of bilateral monopoly for decades. Despite their efforts, mostly mathematical, they have not succeeded in finding the principle that determines price in an exchange between two traders, who can be persons, or firms, or a labor union and a business corporation. There is a fair amount of agreement, however, that quantity is determinate in bilateral monopoly, though price is not. To confine the problem, let it now be assumed that seller and buyer can agree on a quantity and that analysis establishes the proposition that the agreed quantity is one compatible with maximum *joint* profits for the two. At this quantity, the lowest price acceptable to the seller throws the whole profit to the buyer; the highest price the buyer is willing to pay gives the whole profit to the seller.

What is the result when they confine their negotiations to price? It is too easy to take refuge in the answer that bargaining strength and skill decide the result. It is even easier to say that the particular facts of each actual transaction determine the result. But these are evasions, digressions from the search for valid generalizations.

The solution to the theoretical problem might come from a theory combined from economics and psychology. Researchers who have done some work along this line have tentatively concluded that the tendency is for buyer and seller to split the joint maximum profit. The tendency becomes stronger when buyer and seller are well informed about each other. Information, then, can be a controlling force. Furthermore, the *levels of aspiration* of seller and buyer also influence the result. Level of aspiration is a concept of psychology; it means the intensity of the desire to maximize. A trader who has been successful and who expects more success possesses a higher level of aspiration than one who has suffered failures.

The Mass, the Individual, and the Group

The theories of pure competition and of monopoly, even the theory of monopolistic competition, pose no difficult problems of appropriate assumptions of human behavior. In pure and monopolistic competition, the behavior of a mass of people is handled with the profit-maximizing assumption. It makes no difference whether this entrepreneur or that one is slow to react to a rise in price, or habitually makes mistakes, or is unusually greedy. The profit-maximizing assumption blankets them all, cancels their individual differences, and gives good results. At the other extreme stands the sole individual, the monopolist. As a pure type, the monopolist too maximizes, always acting so as, in the traditional phrase, to charge what the traffic will bear.

The theory of oligopoly is a theory of group behavior, not of mass or individual behavior. There can be two in the group, or three, or four, or seventeen. Whatever the number, it is few—each one knows that anything he does will have some effect on the group. Unfortunately, there is no generally accepted theory of the behavior of a group. Do the members of a group agree on common goals? If they do, how do individual goals tie in with the common goals? Does the group have a recognized organization, however informal, with recognized rules of conduct? What are the power relations in the group? Is the group dominated by a leader? If it is, how does the leader get the other members to follow? These are just some of the questions that a theory of group behavior would answer.

Market Structures

Oligopolistic markets can have many different structures. The small number of sellers is only one characteristic of an oligopolistic market. Other characteristics are homogeneity or differentiation of the product, the kind of concentration in the industry, and the height of the barriers to entry faced by new firms. *Concentration* refers to the pattern of the relative sizes (measured here by output) of the firms; there can be, for example, two or three or four firms of equal size, or there can be a few large firms with several small competitors. Still another feature of oligopolistic markets is the kinds and amounts of information (about one another) available to the firms. Important also is the pattern of behavior—the goals of the firms and the ways they react to one another.

COURNOT'S MODEL

Augustin Cournot published his theory of the behavior of two competing sellers over a century ago, in 1838. But no one paid any attention to his work until the 1880s nor did his ideas become widely known and discussed until the 1930s. Economists continue to be fascinated by Cournot's model; it is often a point of departure in modern analyses.

Although Cournot's is a model of duopoly, its results can be extended to three, four, etc., sellers. Hence by extension, his model can be transformed into a model of oligopoly.

Here are the assumptions for a simplified version of Cournot's model: The two producers, company *A* and company *B*, produce identical products and do so at identical costs. Their unit costs are constant over any range of output that would come into question. The total demand in the market they share is linear. Both companies know exactly what the total demand is—both can see every point on the demand curve.

Both producers behave in the same way. Both want to maximize the profits attainable, whatever the circumstances happen to be. They do not conspire, they do not agree, even tacitly. Each one sees what the other is doing, assumes the other will continue to do the same thing, and then acts accordingly. Both companies adjust their outputs, not their prices.

It will be recalled that if demand is linear and unit costs are constant, the profit-maximizing monopoly output is exactly half the competitive output (page 298). For present purposes, the competitive output, where of course price equals marginal (and average) cost, can be called the *opportunity output* of a monopolist. The monopolist never wants to produce more than the competitive, or opportunity, output because doing so would cause unit cost to exceed price. Optimum output, of course, is half the opportunity output.

Now let the process of price formation in Cournot's model begin. Company A is the first to take action. It looks over the market, i.e., looks at the demand curve, and produces and sells half the opportunity amount because by doing so, it maximizes its profits. Next company B appears on the scene and sees what company A's output is. Company B simply takes it for granted that company A will continue to produce and sell the same volume of output. The other half of the opportunity therefore belongs to company B. To maximize its profits, it produces and sells an amount equal to half of the half, i.e., a quarter, of the opportunity. Then company A turns and sees that company B is now selling a quarter of the opportunity. Because company B's action has brought down the price, company A has to recalculate its position. It assumes that company B's output will stay at a quarter. Hence company A's chance is the other three-quarters of the opportunity. Half of this is three-eighths. So company A cuts its output back. Then company B expands its. . . . So it goes, and at the end of it all, each one is producing exactly one-third of the opportunity, or competitive output.[1]

Table 19-1 contains an arithmetical illustration of the simplified model of Cournot. For numerical convenience, the competitive, or opportunity, output—where price equals marginal and average cost and where net profits are zero—is set at 6,400 units. Company A begins by selling 3,200 units. Company B follows with 1,600 units. Company A keeps cutting back while company B keeps expanding. When they are selling equal amounts, they stop adjusting their sales. They therefore reach a stable equilibrium and a determinate result.

Cournot's two sellers produce two-thirds of the competitive output. It can be shown that three produce three-quarters and that n would produce $\dfrac{n}{n+1}$ of the competitive output. The greater the number of sellers, the larger does this fraction become. Accordingly, as the number of sellers increases, their combined output and their price come closer and closer to the competitive levels.

If the two sellers in the Cournot model should agree to act

[1] Just why the output of each seller becomes one-third of the competitive output is explained in Note 1 of the Appendix to Part 5. This Note also contains a mathematical version of Cournot's model.

TABLE 19-1

ILLUSTRATION OF COURNOT'S MODEL OF DUOPOLY (assumptions: linear demand and constant costs; competitive output is 6,400 units)

Scene	Output Company A	Output Company B	Explanation
1	3,200 units		$\frac{1}{2}$ of 6,400 units
2		1,600 units	$\frac{1}{2}$ of (6,400—3,200)
3	2,400		$\frac{1}{2}$ of (6,400—1,600)
4		2,000	etc.
5	2,200		
6		2,100	
7	2,150		
8		2,125	
. . .	. . .	. . .	
Last	2,133	2,133	

together and to divide between them the maximum profits attainable, they would decide to sell jointly an amount equal to one-half the competitive output. Each of them would then have an output equal to one-quarter of the competitive output. This contrasts with the one-third that each produces, in equilibrium, when they do not collude but instead adapt to each other. If there were more than two firms making an agreement, they would still divide the one-half of the competitive output among themselves.

Leaders and Followers

In the Cournot model, each seller passively adapts its output to that of the rival. Each follows the other. Suppose, however, that each of the sellers would try to seize all or part of the market. Each would want to dominate, to be the leader. Theoretical work on how sellers react to each other, on what their "reaction functions" are, has led to certain conclusions.

First, if two sellers take their cues from each other, if each thinks the other is going to behave in a definite way, and if, then, each adapts to the other, the result is stable levels of prices and outputs. Of course prices and outputs are not exactly the same as in the simplified Cournot model, but the follower-follower reaction yields generally similar results.

Secondly, if one firm is the leader and the other is a follower, and if each one knows this and acts accordingly, then the results are also stable levels of prices and of outputs. Price leadership is widespread in American industry. More will be said on it in the next chapter.

Thirdly, if both firms try to be the leader, the result is price war or chaos. The lower cost firm would in the end drive the other one out of business.

In the language of part of the literature on oligopoly, the sellers in the older classical models display "zero conjectural variation." This means that each firm assumes that a change in its price or output will *not* induce a change in the prices or outputs of the other rival firms. When, however, each firm assumes that its price or output depends on its rivals' prices and outputs in *some* way, then the conjectural variation is nonzero.

Guessing about the actions of rivals leads to planning courses of action, i.e., *strategies*. The idea of strategies, in turn, brings up the theory of games. When *The Theory of Games and Economic Behavior* was first published by John von Neumann and Oskar Morgenstern in 1944, it was widely thought that their new theory would greatly advance thinking on oligopoly. A *game* is an activity with definite rules whose outcome is controlled jointly by players with incompatible objectives. Games in this sense include the matching of coins, checkers, poker, etc., as well as military combat and the actions of oligopolistic business firms. Although game theory has developed far since 1944, its contribution to the theory of oligopoly has been disappointing.[2]

Product
Differentiation

In the Cournot model, the two firms have homogeneous products. When both are selling, they necessarily have the same prices, and they always divide the market exactly between them. This assumption—pure oligopoly is its usual name—does put a strain on the imagination because it requires the buyers to be wholly indifferent about the sellers, as if they had no personalities at all. Products can be physically homogeneous, but sellers, when few, never are.[3] When product differentiation is introduced into oligopoly, when therefore the products become close but not perfect substitutes, much is changed. A price cut by one seller does not deprive the other of all of his sales, only of part of them.

With product differentiation, the two prices do not have to be equal. They only have to be in line. Only by coincidence would Fords and Chevrolets carry exactly the same sticker prices, but their prices are never far apart. Similarly, the price differential between the gasolines sold by the outlets of major oil companies and by independent distributors is normally stable. The oligopolistic interdependence of sellers sees to that.

Product differentiation also means competitive activities directed

[2] Note 2 in the Appendix to Part 5 describes a simple model of duopoly as constructed in game theory.
[3] Do not wheat farmers have personalities, too? Yes they do, but purely competitive markets are so organized that in each transaction, buyers and sellers are, in Chamberlin's phrase, "paired off at random." And in competitive markets *all* sellers are "followers."

to the qualities of products and to sales promotion. Just as in the theory of monopolistic competition, oligopolistic firms can have three variables to manipulate—price, product, and advertising.

Uncertainty   The discussion of bilateral monopoly earlier in this chapter shows the importance of information, i.e., the absence of uncertainty. Information also plays a part in monopoly and in pure competition. To maximize, monopolists have to know at least the relevant part of their demand curves; consumers and pure competitors have to know prices. The fluctuations described by the cobweb theorem (pages 243 to 246) are the result of producers' reliance on stale information. In oligopoly, information is even more important because it must include knowledge of rivals and of their courses of action. In Cournot's model, the sellers act with certainty because they have or think they have complete information on demand and on how their rivals behave. When these assumptions are relaxed, uncertainty prevails. A seller thinking of changing the price is uncertain of the consequences. The seller cannot be sure what the market is even if rivals do nothing. Nor can the seller be sure whether in fact they will do nothing.

All this frays the nerves of entrepreneurs and leads to the possibility of collusion in oligopoly. Collusion here means cooperation, or common patterns of action, rather than outright agreements on prices and outputs.

CHAMBERLIN'S MODEL   Chamberlin's model of oligopoly gives a result quite different from those of Cournot's model. This holds even though Chamberlin assumes the same market structure—homogeneous products, firms of equal size and with identical costs, no entry by new firms, and full knowledge of demand. Chamberlin's model, to which he gives the name "mutual dependence recognized," differs because the firms are assumed to have full and farsighted recognition of their interdependence and its consequences. Furthermore, each firm knows that the others have the same costs and that all firms in the industry are profit maximizers.

Chapter 18 contains a model of shortsighted price cutting by firms in monopolistic competition. In the model, a firm faces two demand curves. The first one (*d*) assumes no changes in the rivals' prices; the second demand curve (*D*) assumes that all firms move their prices up or down together. In oligopoly, however, shortsighted price cutting can hardly occur—each of the firms knows the other will meet a price cut. Therefore the only relevant demand curve is the second one. Because the products are homogeneous, the firms must charge the same price. With identical demand curves, i.e., shares of the market, and with identical costs, the common price preferred by one firm is also preferred by every other firm. Without even tacit agreement, then, the firms set identical prices, at the monopoly level, that maximize their individual profits. Thus they also maximize their joint profits. The profits, of course, need not be large because demand-cost relations might not permit large profits. Whether they are large or small, however, individual and joint profits are at a maximum.

The equilibrium in Chamberlin's model is stable, stable as granite, because each firm, in looking to its ultimate interest, never gives a moment's thought to any other possible course of action. In this model, there is no collusion in any meaningful sense. Each firm acts independently, while it recognizes the mutual dependence of all of the firms in the group.

Oligopoly is a form of competition. The significance of Chamberlin's model is that it shows the possibility that this form of competition can yield the same results as monopoly. As a representation of reality, this model is certainly not an impossibility. Noncollusive behavior of this kind, based on good if not perfect information, must sometimes occur. But there is no way of knowing empirically how important it is.

The *perfect cartel* model, which will be examined next, also contains the price and output of monopoly. The perfect cartel is usually looked upon as a merely temporary form of oligopoly.

CARTELS

A *cartel* is an explicit agreement, usually formal, among independent firms on prices, output, and often on other matters such as division of sales territories. In general, cartels are unlawful in the United States. The exceptions are, however, not unimportant because, for example, the price of milk in many communities is fixed by associations—cartels—of producers who make their price decisions under the benevolent auspices of the federal government. The United States participates in the International Air Transport Association; this cartel tries to keep international air fares high.

Why discuss cartels under the heading of oligopoly? Oligopoly is a form of competition. The firms in an industry either compete or they do not. If they do not, if they act in concert, should they not be analyzed as a monopoly? But the convention of treating cartels under the heading of oligopoly is firmly established. Cartels are often short-lived. Firms do have the desire for large joint profits; this desire gives the impulse to form cartels. Firms are likely, however, to quarrel over the division of joint profits; this propensity is the leading cause of the breakup of cartel arrangements. Some industries in the United States have a history of alternate periods of illegal price fixing and of intense competition among the firms.

Perfect Cartels   A perfect cartel is an agreement among the firms in an industry that results in the maximization of the joint profits of the member firms. The board of control, established by the cartel, has full knowledge, let it be assumed, of the demand for the output of the industry at each possible price. Therefore the board of control can calculate marginal revenue for the industry. The board also knows the marginal costs of all of the firms and can calculate the marginal cost of each volume of output for the industry. (The industry's *MC* curve is found by adding, horizontally, the *MC* curves of the firms, just as the short-run supply curve of a competitive industry is derived; see page 236.)

The board of control of the perfect cartel then sets industry marginal revenue equal to industry marginal cost. This gives the price and output for the industry. Then the board allocates to each firm that output at which the firm's marginal cost equals the level of industry marginal cost selected to maximize the joint profits of the industry.

Cartels are often children of depressions. The impulse to joint action is stronger when demand is depressed than when it is expanding. If a cartel is established when the demand for the industry's output has fallen and when the firms have much excess capacity, the board of control might decide to tell the high-cost firms to shut down altogether, though these firms would still receive an agreed-upon share of the joint profits. The board would then allocate the industry's output so as to minimize costs. Each producing firm would then have the same marginal cost. (This point is explained in Chapter 11, pages 198, 199 for a firm allocating output between two plants.) The minimization of industry costs insures the maximization of joint profits.

Imperfect   In a collection of theoretical models of cartels, the perfect cartel
Cartels   stands as a polar extreme. It does indeed maximize joint profits. But it means the abject surrender of decision making by the firms. A cartel is always defined as an agreement among firms that retain their identities and independence. Mutual distrust among firms and their unwillingness to give up all of their sovereignty make it most unlikely that perfect cartels could long endure.

It can be taken then that cartels are always imperfect, which here means only that though they raise prices and profits, they do not reach the levels of monopoly. Though there are many models of imperfect cartels, they will not be reviewed here. Instead, a few general remarks about them will now be made.

After fixing a price, a cartel usually has to set sales or output quotas. This does not have to be done if industry demand is growing as fast or faster than the expansion of industry output. But, ordinarily, output quotas have to be set to maintain the cartel price. Methods of setting the quotas and of dividing the joint profits are sources of friction. If the cartel agreement is illegal besides, good ways of enforcing compliance are hard to find.

A member of a cartel can find advantage in making secret price concessions. Even if the industry demand is inelastic, the demand to any one firm at prices lower than the cartel price is highly elastic. Additional sales at covertly negotiated lower prices can therefore be profitable enough to offer strong temptation to a firm.

THE KINKED DEMAND CURVE

Perhaps the most popular of the models of oligopoly is the model with the kinked demand curve, because it offers an explanation of price rigidity under oligopoly.

Once established, oligopolistic prices often remain constant for months at a time, occasionally even for a few years. A familiar example is the durable consumer good whose quoted wholesale price remains unchanged for an entire model year. Quoted prices, however, are not always the actual prices paid and received; in periods of slack demand, open or hidden concessions from quoted prices are often made.

Oligopolistic prices that long remain unchanged are said to be *rigid*, in contrast to the *flexibility* of market prices in industries behaving like the model of pure competition. Rigid prices are changed infrequently and usually by small amounts. An implication of the concept of rigidity is that rigid prices are resistant to changes in demand and in costs. There can be no strong reason, from the points of view either of the profit-seeking firm or of the theory of welfare economics, that prices should move up or down with every little quiver in demand and every little flutter in costs. For a large firm, a change in prices can be expensive; new catalogues and lists have to be issued, dealers must be notified, and so on. Constancy of prices must, accordingly, be distinguished from rigidity—the lack of movement when changes occur in demand or in costs, or in both.

The kinked demand curve and the argument that goes with it describe a pattern of business behavior such that the firm has no incentive to raise its price or to lower it. The firm's attitude rests on an estimate of what its rivals will and what they will not do. The firm believes that though its rivals will not imitate an increase in price, they will indeed follow a price reduction. Acting on this belief, then, the firm adheres to its price, seeing no reason to change until some upheaval occurs such as a major movement in demand or in costs.

Figure 19–1 shows a firm's demand curve with a kink in it. The kink is at *P*, the price at which the firm is producing and selling the amount *OQ*. Above the price *P*, the demand curve as seen by the

FIGURE 19–1   THE KINKED DEMAND CURVE

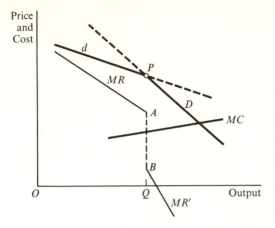

firm is *dP*. This portion of the curve is highly elastic; notice that the corresponding part of the marginal revenue curve *MR* is positive. The *dP* portion of the curve is elastic because the firm believes that its rivals will *not* follow suit if the firm raises its price. Thus the firm thinks its losses in sales from a price increase would be heavy, that its total revenue and its profits would fall off. The *dP* curve and its dashed extension can be recognized as Chamberlin's *d* demand curve (page 332). The other part of the kinked demand curve is *PD*; this curve and its dashed extension are Chamberlin's *D* curve. The *PD* curve is much less elastic; at lower prices the *PD* curve is inelastic, as shown by the fact that its marginal revenue curve, *MR'*, is negative after a point. The firm thinks that a reduction in price below *P* will cause the rival firms to reduce *their* prices. Though the firm would enjoy some increase in sales, its profits would be smaller.

The peculiarity of the diagram of the kinked demand curve is the gap in marginal revenue, which comes from the abrupt change from the more elastic to the less elastic parts of the demand curve. The gap is shown by the dashed line *AB* in Figure 19–1. The marginal cost curve intersects the gap, which can be regarded as if it were a vertical section of the marginal revenue curve.

With its assumptions about the firm's vision of the demand for its product and of the reactions it expects from its competitors, the kinked demand curve therefore explains price rigidity. The kinked demand curve is often called *subjective*—it exists in the decision maker's mind. The actual demand curve, the *objective* one, might be different. But the rigidity imposed by subjective demand is reinforced by cost. Look again at Figure 19–1. If the marginal cost curve rises, but not above point *A*, and if it falls, output and price do not change. This is because *MC* still crosses the vertical part of the *MR* curve.

The kinked demand curve model of oligopolistic behavior gives an appearance of rationality to the maintenance of rigid prices by firms. The model has a serious flaw. There is nothing in the model to show how the rigid price is established. Nor does the model explain how a new kink forms around a new price.

SUMMARY

The interdependence of the demand curves of the firms in oligopoly poses serious difficulties in establishing a theory of the determination of prices and outputs. The theoretical problem is closely akin to that of *bilateral monopoly* to which there is no agreed-upon determinate solution. The behavior of a few competing firms is also group behavior, which can assume many patterns. In *Cournot's model*, each firm adjusts its output in the belief that the other's will remain constant. With linear assumptions, their combined equilibrium output is two-thirds of the competitive. Thus if firms adjust to each other, prices and outputs can be stable. But if each firm tries to dominate, the result can be price war or chaos. Efforts to create a satisfactory theory of business strategy have not succeeded. In *Chamberlin's model* of oligopoly, the prices and outputs of the firms are identical at the monopoly level, though there is no agreement among the firms. A *perfect cartel* also achieves the maximum joint profits. *Imperfect cartels* can increase the profits of their members by fixing prices and production quotas; cartel agreements are likely to be temporary. The prices set by oligopolistic firms tend to be rigid. An explanation of price rigidity is offered by the hypothesis of the *kinked demand curve*. The firm facing such a curve has no incentive either to raise or to lower its price because of its estimate of its rivals' actions.

SELECTED REFERENCES

On bilateral monopoly: Sidney Siegel and Lawrence E. Fouraker, *Bargaining and Group Decision Making* (McGraw-Hill, New York, 1960).

On the older classical models: Edward H. Chamberlin, *The Theory of Monopolistic Competition*, 8th ed. (Harvard University Press, Cambridge, 1962), chap. 3. An excellent and thorough presentation is in Fritz Machlup, *The Economics of Sellers' Competition* (Johns Hopkins Press, Baltimore, 1952), chap. 12.

On the general theoretical problems raised by oligopoly: Machlup (cited above), chap. 11; William Fellner, *Competition Among the Few* (Knopf, New York, 1949), chap. 1.

George J. Stigler, "The Kinky Oligopoly Demand Curve and Rigid Prices," *Journal of Political Economy*, 55 (1947) [reprinted in *Readings in Price Theory*, ed. George J. Stigler and Kenneth E. Boulding (Irwin, Homewood, 1952)].

EXERCISES AND PROBLEMS

1. Construct your own model of oligopoly: Suppose that three car washes are opened up at the same time in the same large suburb. Assume that the owners do *not* get together to agree on the prices they will charge. Set up reaction functions, i.e., patterns of competitive response, for the three owners, and then show what happens as they compete for customers.
2. Work out a Cournot model with the price, not the output, as the variable.
3. Suppose that the three firms in an industry form a perfect cartel. The firms produce the same product at different costs. Draw a diagram to show how the cartel determines price and allocates output among the firms.
4. Draw a kinked demand curve. Then draw a decrease in demand and prove that a price reduction will not occur.
5. Draw an increase in demand for a demand curve with a kink. Show that a price rise can happen.
6. Using the model of the kinked demand curve, compare the effects of a tax on profits with those of an excise tax per unit of output.

20
Oligopoly—
SOME MODELS WITHOUT
PROFIT MAXIMIZATION

One of the obstacles to the building of better models of oligopoly is strict adherence to the assumption of profit maximization. Economic theorists have been giving increasing attention to multiple goals of business firms. Chapters 8 and 16 mention *utility functions*, in which some amount of profit is sacrificed in pursuing one or more other objectives. In large business firms controlled by management rather than by their owners, the managers can be said to maximize their *managerial utility functions*. Not enough however is known about such functions to permit useful generalizations in a broad discussion of oligopoly. And to say that business people maximize utility functions is a statement that usually carries little more meaning than the implication that they do not have the sole objective of maximizing profits.

RESTRAINTS ON PROFIT MAXIMIZATION

In Chapter 19, the models of oligopoly have the profit-maximizing assumption built into them. This assumption must be relaxed and modified so that more can usefully be said about oligopoly.

Three distinct kinds of forces may prevent any firm from attaining maximum profits. Remember that maximum has no meaning apart from the relation between demand and cost; the attainable maximum can be zero profits or minimum losses. One force blocking a firm's attainment of the maximum is lack of information about prices and the market; sometimes, firms do not even have clear information about their costs. A second force, already mentioned, can be the presence of other objectives. A monopolist who has a secure position might prefer the quiet life to the continuous effort of adjusting price to the profit-maximizing level. A monopolist who is insecure may keep profits lower than they could be for fear of government regulation or of potential competition. The third force is the restraint that oligopoly itself can put on the maximization of profits by firms.

The restraints that oligopoly places on the behavior of firms in

FIGURE 20–1

PRICES AND PROFITS

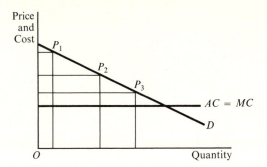

seeking profits are: (1) considerations of safety, (2) desires for stable profits, and (3) tendencies toward conservative policies in large corporations where ownership and management are separated. These restraints can be stated only in a general form because specific patterns of group behavior can vary much from industry to industry and from time to time. Oligopolistic interdependence creates the urge to play it safe, the willingness to accept "reasonable" profits, and the atmosphere conducive to common courses of action.

An assumption in the discussion to follow is that less than maximum profits are associated with prices lower than monopoly prices. Figure 20–1 shows demand and cost for an industry. The optimum monopoly price is P_2. The rectangle of profits drawn from P_2 is the largest inside the triangle bounded by demand and cost. The rectangles of profits drawn from the higher price P_1 and the lower price P_3 are much smaller. The assumption, accordingly, is that smaller profits go along with prices lower than P_2 in Figure 20–1. One justification for the assumption is the common practice of calculating prices on a cost-plus basis. Cost-plus pricing will be discussed a little later.

SALES MAXIMIZATION

A model of oligopoly in which the firm makes a compromise between dollar volume of sales and profits has been constructed by William J. Baumol of Princeton University. This model gives still another way of modifying and relaxing the assumption of profit maximization.

Although Baumol does not refer to a utility function, the decision. maker in Baumol's model can be said to maximize utility when the firm produces and sells the output yielding the maximum revenue that is consistent with the earning of a minimum profit. The model has been criticized on the ground that Baumol does not allow for the interdependence of the prices of oligopolistic firms. To those economists who see interdependence as the key to all pricing in oligopoly, the criticism is serious because it points to a major flaw in the model. Baumol relies on his experience as a business consultant to claim an inside view of decision making in large corporations. He argues that oligopolistic interdependence actually plays a small part in the month-by-month decisions of large firms. Anticipated reactions from competitors influence the strategy of a firm, he thinks, only when a major change is imminent, such as the marketing of a wholly new line of products or the launching of a new kind of advertising campaign. Baumol supports his contentions by pointing to the clumsy slowness of decision making in large firms, to their reliance on the same rules of thumb, and to the prevalence of the live-and-let-live attitude.

Baumol's argument is that an oligopolistic firm looks upon its dollar sales, i.e., total revenue, as an end in itself. The executives of a large firm want dollar sales to grow. Declining sales are dreaded because of the fear that there will be trouble in arranging bank financing, that consumers will shy away from products that are losing their popularity, that the firm will lose distributors and big dealers, and that other disadvantages will ensue. Large sales mean large size, which in turn, so runs a common belief, means large profits. But after some point—where marginal revenue equals marginal cost—increases in sales can be had only at the sacrifice of profits. Though it wants sales to be large, the firm also seeks a minimum level of—business—profit. Minimum profits must vary in relative and absolute size from one firm to another, from one industry to another, and from depression to prosperity. Baumol offers no one clear definition of the minimum acceptable profit. But he and other economists who have discussed the same thing point to the elements that make up an acceptable minimum. They are the funds to pay some satisfactory rate of dividends, the funds to be reinvested for growth, and the funds to ensure financial safety and to retain the confidence of lenders in the capital markets. It suffices for the working of Baumol's model if minimum profits are defined as any amount less than maximum profits.

Figure 20–2 presents Baumol's model; the figure is adapted from one of Baumol's diagrams. The vertical axis shows total revenues and total costs in millions of dollars. The horizontal axis shows output. Total revenue is *TR*, which the firm adjusts by changing its price. Total cost is *TC*. (Since *TC* starts from the origin, the diagram presumably shows the long run. But the diagram can easily be converted to the short run by dropping the horizontal axis by an amount equal to fixed costs.) Total profit is the curve *TP*, which states the difference between *TR* and *TC*. The horizontal line is the acceptable minimum profit. If the firm had no objective but to maximize its profits, output would be *OA*, because *OA* corresponds

FIGURE 20-2

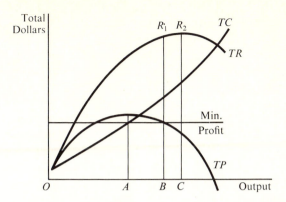

to the top of the *TP* curve. If the firm did nothing but maximize its total revenue, output would be *OC*, which corresponds to R_2, the top of the *TR* curve. Baumol's firm produces and sells *OB*, thus earning the minimum profit and setting revenue at the highest level—R_1—that is, consistent with the minimum profit.

Thus the firm in Baumol's model of oligopoly produces and sells more than profit maximization dictates. Just how much more depends on the shape and positions of the curves.

Baumol's model seems to have a resemblance to cost-plus pricing, in which the firm adds a minimum profit figure to business costs to arrive at selling price. But as he shows, the resemblance is superficial because the firm in his model makes marginal calculations. The firm adjusts its output for maximum revenue subject to the profit constraint and, in doing so, prices some of its products to earn more and others to earn less than the minimum profit. In contrast, most cost-plus pricing methods are rules of thumb which cannot predetermine volumes of output.

As earlier chapters show, the profit-maximizing firm ignores its fixed costs in coming to pricing decisions. Changes in fixed costs do not affect marginal costs, which together with marginal revenue determine output and therefore price. But Baumol's firm does indeed react to a change in fixed costs, just as business people generally seem to do. If fixed costs rise, the result is, all other things being equal, to reduce total profit. The *TP* curve in Figure 20-2 falls, and thus the minimum profit line cuts it at a point indicating a smaller optimum output. This, in turn, means a rise in price.

PRICE LEADERSHIP

Price leadership means of course that the firms in an industry follow the lead of one firm. If the products of the firms are physically homogeneous, prices are usually uniform. If the products are differentiated, prices can be uniform or can conform to a definite pattern of differentials. From time to time, the leader announces a price change, e.g., a rise of 10 per cent. The next day, or the next week, the other firms raise their prices by 10 per cent.

It is now customary to distinguish *barometric* price leadership from *dominant* price leadership where one firm actually dominates the industry. In barometric price leadership, one firm is simply the first to announce a price change. This firm does not dominate the others. Suppose that the industry's inventories have been piling up while consumption of the industry's product remains sluggish. A price reduction is then in order; all firms come to understand that it is due. The barometric firm is the first to announce the change. This firm does little more than to establish the prices that would, in time, be set by the forces of competition.

The bases of dominant price leadership can be the lower costs of the leader, or its larger size, or its aggressive behavior, or some combination of these. If one of, say, three firms with physically homogeneous products has the lowest costs, this firm can act as if it were a monopolist. This firm can set its price so as to maximize its profits. The other two firms must set their prices at the same level and, therefore, accept less than maximum profits. This means that they produce more than they otherwise would and that, therefore, the output of the whole industry is larger than under monopoly.

One form of price leadership, based on lower costs, is shown in Figure 20–3. Here are two firms, A and B, with different costs and with homogeneous products; the firms must therefore sell at the same price. Assume also that they are fully aware of their inter-dependence. In Figure 20–3, the total demand in the market is D_T. Since they share the market, each firm has the demand D, which is half (horizontally) of D_T. Each firm, then, has the same marginal revenue. Firm A has the lower costs, MC_A. Firm A sets the price P_A, which maximizes A's profits. Firm B, however, does *not* maximize its profits, because firm B must also sell at price P_A, instead of at price P_B. The output of the two firms together is twice OA, instead of OB plus OA. In Figure 20–3, the firms have full knowledge of demand. When, as is nearly always true, firms do not know their demands exactly, they must guess.

Price leadership by the largest firm in an industry is common. The other firms follow the lead with motives ranging from fear to con-venience to laziness. Here, too, the leader can act as if it were a monopoly. It can maximize its profits. To choose the price that maximizes for it, the firm must be certain that the other firms will set the same price or, if products are differentiated, that their prices will be in line with its prices. If there are several small firms in the industry, they can look upon the leader's price as given to them. If products are physically homogeneous and if the market is well

FIGURE 20-3

ONE FORM OF PRICE LEADERSHIP

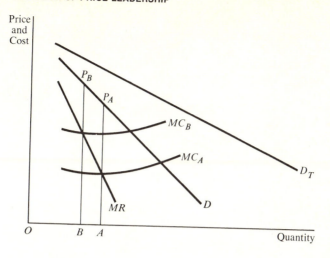

organized, the small firms can treat the leader's price as if it were their marginal revenue. Then they adjust their outputs so that their marginal costs equal the leader's price and, therefore, maximize their profits.

Unless the firms in the industry have uniform costs and market shares, price leadership does not give results identical with those of Chamberlin's model. Though prices can be close to the monopoly level, the output of the industry is bound to be a little larger.

Dominant price leadership is sometimes called *partial monopoly*, especially when the dominant firm is large and the other firms are small. The partial monopolist is more than just a price leader. Because such a firm wields monopoly power, it becomes a problem—a difficult one—in the enforcement of the antitrust laws.

QUASI AGREEMENTS

When they knowingly behave in the same way, oligopolistic firms can be said to have entered into *quasi agreements*. Other terms to express the same idea are *conscious parallelism of action, imperfect coordination, collusion,* and the like. Quasi agreements can take many forms. A few of them are: mutual adherence to the belief that price cutting is unethical, respect for one another's market shares and sales territories, the use of the same methods of calculating prices, and reliance on the continuity of patterns of prices and of competitive behavior that have gone on for some time. As a method of quasi agreement, *cost-plus pricing* will now be singled out for attention. It can be called quasi agreement if all the firms in an industry set their prices on a cost-plus basis, and if each firm believes that the others will continue to do so.

Cost-Plus
Pricing

Cost-plus pricing is a common method of determining the selling prices of products. A firm computes the selling price of its product by adding, say, 30 per cent to the average total cost of the product. Cost here is business cost, not the full cost as defined in this book. Alternatively, the firm can add, say, 60 per cent to the average variable cost of the product; the higher percentage here is to take care of overhead, as well as to earn a business profit. The percentages added to cost are called *margins* or *markups*. Thus, cost-plus pricing is also known as *margin pricing* and *markup pricing*.

The business world employs many systems of cost-plus pricing. They range from simple rules of thumb to sophisticated formulas. The simple rule of adding a customary markup seems to be common. With a sophisticated formula, a company estimates future sales, future costs, and arrives at a markup that will achieve, so it is hoped, a *target return* on the company's investment.

Economists generally regard cost-plus pricing as a practice that might or might not result in the maximization of profits. Only by accident could maximum profits come from the simple rule-of-thumb method, which takes demand for granted and makes no allowance at all for elasticity of demand. Even the pricing methods that aim for a target return on the investment are a kind of satisficing rather than maximizing behavior. Cost-plus pricing need not, however, be inconsistent with maximum profits. If average variable costs are constant over the relevant range, cost plus some amount could indeed give a price identical with that determined by rational behavior (see pages 303, 317). And if shifts in demand are accompanied by no changes in elasticity, cost plus would continue to give profit-maximizing results.

As a form of oligopolistic behavior, cost-plus pricing by all firms in an industry results in stable patterns of prices. In some industries, the firms use uniform systems of cost accounting. If their input prices and production functions are identical and if they add the same percentage markups, the firms can have identical prices for their products. Whether or not the firms have identical prices, their practice of cost-plus pricing also causes them to make uniform changes in prices. If excise taxes are imposed, or increased, or abolished, the firms change their prices by the corresponding percentages. They act similarly if wage rates rise throughout the industry and if materials prices go up.

**ENTRY AND
LIMIT PRICING**

It has been implicit all along that the number of firms in an oligopolistic industry is fixed, or given. This is so in the short run. But what of the long run? It is probably well to modify the definition of the long run for the purposes of the theory of oligopoly. Generally, the long run is long enough for a firm to expand its whole plant and equipment. Now let the long run also be a period long enough for a firm to introduce a new product. Thousands of American firms are large enough and diversified enough that they can invade new fields with new products in periods of time much shorter than those needed to increase their total capacities by significant amounts.

The model of multiple-product pricing described in Chapter 17 can be made to show one kind of entry. Portraying a common and readily observable business practice, the model shows the invasion of markets by firms with new products they can produce with their existing facilities and organization. Suppose that several firms produce and sell components for stereo equipment for consumers. Suppose that their prices are established through a process of quasi agreement. Then imagine that a large manufacturer of diversified electrical equipment designs a line of stereo components and sells them at comparatively moderate prices. Such an invasion of the market for stereo components can be as fully effective as if two or three new firms were to come into existence. If the manufacturer succeeds in gaining a noticeable share of the market, the existing firms might be compelled to lower the prices, or improve their products, or both.

Where oligopolistic markets can be invaded by the new products of firms with diversified facilities and by new firms, the result is similar to the groping toward group equilibrium in monopolistic competition. Profits are reduced. Prices may also fall. To the extent that they do, output becomes larger. With a stable total demand for the products of the firms, an oligopolistic industry can reach a low-profit or a no-profit equilibrium. Prices and outputs are by no means the same as under pure competition. But they are likely to be much closer to the competitive than to the monopolistic levels.

Entry to oligopolistic industries is often, however, not effective. The barriers to entry can be legal. Some public utility industries are oligopolies; the public regulating bodies usually bar outside firms by denying them the requisite franchises or licenses. Another legal barrier can be thrown up by the operation of the patent law; the firms in an industry sometimes have patent arrangements among themselves and do not admit outsiders to them. Barriers can be illegal, too. The wide variety of means, in violation of the antitrust laws, that have been used to restrict entry is beyond the scope of discussion here. Entry to industries in which individual firms require large amounts of capital is restricted by the difficulties of raising the capital and of assembling the organization and the specialized talents essential for success. When, therefore, entry is either blocked or where the obstacles are not easily surmounted, the firms in an oligopolistic industry can have prices well above the competitive level.

Limit Pricing

The fear of potential entry often appears as a reason given for quasi agreements that result in lower-than-maximum profits. In general, such profits accompany lower prices and larger outputs. Hence fear of entry can drive prices and outputs down from monopoly toward competitive levels. If joint profits are held down by quasi agreements, it is still possible, by stretching a point, to say that they are "maximized" over a longer period of time. Suppose that expected joint profits in an industry are at a maximum at $50 million in year 1, and that beginning in year 4, the entry of new firms reduces joint profits to $10 million a year. With these assumptions, joint profits over a 10-year period are $220 million (3 × $50 million plus 7 × $10 million). But suppose that quasi agreement holds joint profits in year 1 and in succeeding years to $30 million a year, and that this level attracts no new firms. Then the total profits over a 10-year period would be $300 million, a larger amount.

A *limit price* is one that limits the entry of new firms; here, to limit means to prevent. At a limit price the firm expects to sacrifice short-run profits but to earn larger profits over longer periods of time. Theory cannot say precisely what the level of a limit price is, except that it must lie between what would be the competitive equilibrium price and the profit-maximizing price before the entry of new firms. Much depends on how easy or how hard it is to enter the industry. The firms already in the industry must be able to cooperate in setting limit prices and must therefore have similar views on the potentialities of entry and on streams of future profits.

NONPRICE COMPETITION

Nonprice competition in oligopolistic industries has certain similarities to the nonprice competition in industries characterized by monopolistic competition. Conventionally, nonprice competition is divided into two forms, product variation and sales promotion. The difference between the theory of oligopoly and the theory of monopolistic competition is the stress that has to be laid on interdependence in oligopoly.

Price can be the competitive variable in oligopoly. So can quality of product. And so can be the amount and kind of sales promotion activities. Most of the models of oligopoly already described could be easily reformulated by substituting "quality of product" or "volume of advertising" for "price." The reformulation would not give results different in any essential respect. The knowledgeable and steady-nerved firms in Chamberlin's "mutual dependence recognized" model would unerringly select the qualities of products and the volumes of advertising that would maximize individual and therefore joint profits.

This point is more important than it might seem at first. A common opinion is that, though they lack price competition, the oligopolistic industries make up for the lack by vigorous rivalry in product and advertising policies. But the parallelism of price, product, and advertising competition means that any one of these variables can be manipulated to shackle the strength of competition. Chamberlin's model was just mentioned again; in the model, individual and joint profits are maximized, as in monopoly. Product or advertising can also be the key variable in a leadership model. One firm sets a standard for product design and quality, and the other firms in the industry follow. Similarly, there can be collusion, quasi agreements, and cartels on product quality and sales promotion, as well as on price. Similarly, a firm maximizing its sales, subject to the restraint of a minimum profit, can do so by adjusting its advertising outlays. Such a firm sells more and advertises more than if it tried to do nothing but maximize its profits. All this means that deeper exploration of nonprice competition would only follow paths of analysis parallel to those investigated in the last two chapters.

Nonprice competition, however, does raise difficult problems of welfare economics.

On the other hand, quality competition in some industries is much more intense than price or advertising competition. Successful quality innovations such as a new automobile can be imitated much less quickly than changes in prices and in outlays for advertising.

OLIGOPOLY AND ECONOMIC WELFARE

Since the equilibrium of pure competition provides the standard of efficiency in the allocation of resources, it follows easily that oligopoly is inconsistent with maximum economic welfare. Price seems to be higher and output seems to be lower under oligopoly, given of course the same demand and cost functions. Hence oligopoly causes a loss of economic welfare, just as monopoly does. How great is the loss? How strong is the accompanying implication that, somehow, something ought to be done about oligopoly?

Here again are questions with no certain answers. The welfare loss due to monopoly can be stated precisely, with the assumption of profit maximizing behavior by the monopolist. Since oligopoly can have so many shapes, no single precise statement can be made. Some help, however, can be obtained from the array of models of oligopoly presented here. These models range from those with prices and outputs identical to monopoly to those with prices and outputs approaching the levels of pure competition. The loss of welfare from oligopoly must accordingly vary from one model to another. If prices and outputs would lie between those of monopoly and of pure competition, it would follow that the welfare loss from oligopoly is less than that from monopoly.

The welfare aspects of nonprice competition in oligopolistic industries present difficult analytical problems. Suppose that the firms in an industry incur larger costs to produce a product of higher quality, and that the demand for the higher quality product is larger. Suppose also that though the price is unchanged, the result is larger profits for the firms. Hence the firms gain. The consumers gain also; otherwise they would not buy more. Is the gain to them as great as the additional costs incurred by the firms? Perhaps it is, but it need not be. Still another welfare problem of product competition is the variety of products of the same type. Consumers generally seem to prefer variety—of models, designs, sizes, etc.—to standardization. Is the gain from variety greater than or less than its costs? Are the degrees of variety optimum? That is, does the proliferation of product types make consumer choices wider or does it confuse consumers and make choices more difficult? Most people have strong opinions on these and related matters. So far, however, economic theory has little to contribute.

THE DYNAMICS OF OLIGOPOLY

Just as monopoly changes its appearance when viewed in motion over time, so does oligopoly. With the exception of the long-run entry model, the theories of oligopoly reviewed here are all of the short-run variety. The long run is long enough for an industry to grow or to decline. The long run is also long enough for resources to move from one industry to another, for investors and for persons entering the labor force to choose among industries. In the long run also, and above all, in many of the big oligopolistic industries in the American economy, technological change occurs and consumer demands shift. New products for consumers come on the market; new machines, new processes, new materials appear in the production functions of firms. In the long run, demands are more elastic.

It follows that over longer periods of time, there is a tendency toward a uniformity of levels of business profits among industries. This of course is by no means the same thing as the universal condition of zero *net* profits in the static general equilibrium model. Still, the tendency toward uniform levels of business profits in the oligopolistic (and other) industries must prevail, given the mobility of resources over time. The tendency is rough, because some barriers to entry persist, because investors make mistakes, and because rates of growth among industries are unequal. In brief, then, the monopolistic elements in oligopoly become less important in the long run. Interindustry competition for markets and for resources in the long run shapes the short-run contexts that oligopolistic decisions are made in.

Though the complexities of dynamic change preclude rigorous proof, it can be concluded, as a matter of judgment, that the allocation of resources under oligopoly is, by and large, tolerably close to efficiency—pressures to reduce costs are strong and production is responsive to consumer demand. Islands of exception probably exist even over longer periods; deviations from the ideal of efficiency can occur in the short run. Yet the forces of the long run keep pushing price and output toward efficiency.[1]

SUMMARY

The models reviewed in this and the preceding chapter show prices and outputs ranging between the monopoly and the purely competitive levels. For oligopoly to have the same price and output as monopoly, the necessary assumptions are uniformity of costs and products, perfect knowledge, no objective other than profit maximization, and either the mutual recognition of uniformity and interdependence or the actions of the perfect cartel. The significance of Chamberlin's model and of the perfect cartel model seems to be only that it is conceivable, that it is not logically impossible, for the equilibrium of oligopoly to be identical with either that of monopoly or of pure competition.

Table 20–1 displays the leading models reviewed in this chapter, together with Cournot's. The important models are those showing prices and outputs intermediate between the poles of monopoly and pure competition. The price leadership, the imperfect cartel, and the quasi agreement models *can* give results close to monopoly, or to pure competition. They can give prices and outputs between the extremes. General analysis cannot be more precise. This is unfortunate because it means that theory cannot say much that helps in assessing the performance of oligopolistic industries.

Nonprice competition in oligopoly functions in about the same way as price competition; quality of product or volume of advertising can also be the competitive variables. How nonprice competition affects economic welfare is a difficult analytical problem. Over

---

[1] Empirical measures of the welfare loss due to monopoly and oligopoly have found it to be very small. See Harvey Leibenstein, "Allocative Efficiency vs. 'X-Efficiency,'" *American Economic Review*, 56 (June 1966), 392–415. Extracts from the empirical studies of Harberger and Schwartzman are contained in Donald Stevenson Watson, ed., *Price Theory in Action: A Book of Readings*, 3d ed., Houghton Mifflin, Boston, 1973.

TABLE 20-1

**SOME LEADING MODELS OF OLIGOPOLY CLASSIFIED BY RELATION
OF PRICE TO THE LEVELS OF MONOPOLY OR PURE COMPETITION**

Equilibrium Prices	Name of Model	Remarks
Monopoly prices	Chamberlin	Products and costs must be uniform.
	Perfect cartels	
Close to monopoly price	Price leadership Imperfect cartels Quasi agreements	If firms seek maximum profits, prices are close to the monopoly level. But if they seek smaller profits, prices are closer to the competitive level.
Close to purely competitive price	Cournot	Price approaches the competitive level as the number of sellers increases.
	Long-run free-entry model Baumol	Deviation from competitive price depends on elasticity of demand.

Notes: Models with indeterminate or fluctuating prices are excluded. The monopoly price maximizes individual firm and joint profits when demand and cost functions are known. The competitive price is the equilibrium price consistent with zero net profits.

longer periods of time, oligopoly takes on a different hue, just as monopoly does; the long-run allocation of resources probably does not deviate far from standards of efficiency.

SELECTED REFERENCES

Fritz Machlup, "Theories of the Firm: Marginalist, Behavioral, Managerial," *American Economic Review*, 57 (March 1967), 1–33; William Fellner, *Competition Among the Few* (Knopf, New York, 1949), chap. 7; Joe S. Bain, *Industrial Organization* (Wiley, New York, 1959); Fritz Machlup, *The Economics of Sellers' Competition* (Johns Hopkins Press, Baltimore, 1952), chaps. 13, 14, 15; William J. Baumol, *Business Behavior, Value and Growth* (Macmillan, New York, 1959), chaps 4–8; Donald Stevenson Watson, ed., *Price Theory in Action: A Book of Readings,* 3d ed. (Houghton Mifflin, Boston, 1973), parts 5, 6, and 7; F. M. Scherer, *Industrial Pricing: Theory and Evidence* (Rand McNally, Chicago, 1970).

On the dynamics of oligopoly: Joseph A. Schumpeter, *Capitalism, Socialism, and Democracy,* 3d ed. (Harper, New York, 1950), chaps. 7 and 8.

1. Draw a diagram to show how entry to an oligopolistic industry can cause prices to be forced down to the levels of average costs.
2. In Baumol's model, a rise in fixed costs causes the firm to reduce output. Draw a diagram. Why would a profit-maximizing firm *not* reduce its output?
3. Suppose the firms in an industry follow different methods of cost-plus pricing. Is there still a quasi agreement that results in stability?
4. Would the standardization of the essential features of differentiated products improve economic welfare? Standardization ought to reduce costs and, eventually, prices. Consumers would gain from lower prices and would lose by having less variety of choice. Which would be the greater, the gain or the loss?
5. Annual model changes are often criticized. Would consumers benefit if annual model changes were eliminated?
6. Price theory judges oligopoly by the criteria of levels of prices and output. Should other standards be brought in too? What are they?

Appendix

TO PART 5

MATHEMATICAL NOTES

In Chapter 19, Cournot's two producers are in equilibrium when each produces exactly one-third of the opportunity, or competitive, output.

Company A begins with $\frac{1}{2}$, then cuts back to $\frac{3}{8}$, then to $\frac{11}{32}$, etc. This can be written as

$$1 - \tfrac{1}{2} - \tfrac{1}{8} - \tfrac{1}{32} \ldots,$$

which is the same as

$$1 - (\tfrac{1}{2} + \tfrac{1}{8} + \tfrac{1}{32} + \ldots) = 1 - [\tfrac{1}{2}(1 + \tfrac{1}{4} + \tfrac{1}{16} + \tfrac{1}{64} + \ldots)].$$

The numbers in brackets are in an infinite series, whose sum to the limit is of the form $a(1 + r + r^2 + r^3 + \ldots)$, which sums to $a/1 - r$, if $0 < r < 1$. In the brackets above, $a = \frac{1}{2}$ and $r = \frac{1}{4}$. Since $\frac{1}{4}$ lies between zero and unity,

$$\frac{a}{1 - r} = \frac{\frac{1}{2}}{1 - \frac{1}{4}} = \frac{2}{3}.$$

Therefore, Company A's equilibrium output is $1 - \frac{2}{3} = \frac{1}{3}$.

Company B starts with $\frac{1}{4}$, then expands to $\frac{5}{16}$, then to $\frac{21}{64}$, etc. Its infinite series is $\frac{1}{4} + \frac{1}{16} + \frac{1}{64} + \ldots$, whose sum to the limit is

$$\frac{a}{1 - r} = \frac{\frac{1}{4}}{1 - \frac{1}{4}} = \frac{1}{3}.$$

There are many modern versions of Cournot's model. The simple one now to follow is adapted from William Fellner.[1]

First, let the demand function be linear and let costs be zero. Let the market demand function be $p = a - bQ$, where p is price, Q is the total output of two duopolists, and a and b are positive constants. The outputs of the two duopolists are q_1 and q_2. Therefore,

[1] William Fellner, *Competition Among the Few*, Knopf, New York, 1949, pp. 60n.-62n.

$p = a - b(q_1 + q_2)$. Dupolist 1 treats q_2 as a constant, and vice versa.

The total revenue of duopolist 1 is $pq_1 = aq_1 - bq_1^2 - bq_1q_2$, who equates MR and MC so as to maximize profits. Because $MC_1 = 0$

$$MR_1 = \frac{dpq_1}{dq_1} = a - 2bq_1 - bq_2 = 0.$$

Similarly, the profit-maximizing output of duopolist 2 is given by the equation

$$a - 2bq_2 - bq_1 = 0.$$

The solution of these two simultaneous output equations yields $q_1 = q_2 = \frac{a}{3b}$. Then total output is $q_1 + q_2 = \frac{2a}{3b}$. If there were n producers instead of two,

$$Q = \frac{na}{(n + 1)b}.$$

The monopoly output is found by setting $q_2 = 0$ in the equation $a - 2bq_1 - bq_2 = 0$. Thus the monopoly output is

$$q = \frac{a}{2b}.$$

The competitive output is found by setting price = costs. Since costs are zero, $p = 0$. Therefore $a - bQ = 0$. The competitive output is then

$$Q = \frac{a}{b}.$$

Thus with the linear functions, the monopoly output is half the competitive, as is also shown on page 298.

If constant costs C are introduced, then the foregoing has to be modified by writing $a - C$ instead of a.

With nonlinear demand functions, the results are about the same. The duopoly output is less than the competitive, but greater than the monopoly output. The larger the number of producers, the larger the output of oligopoly.

NOTE 2.

GAME THEORY

The theory of games has contributed little to the advancement of knowledge about oligopolistic behavior. The theory does offer some simple models, one of which will be described here.[2]

---

[2] This note is based on the discussion in Robert Dorfman, Paul A. Samuelson, and Robert M. Solow, *Linear Programming and Economic Analysis,* McGraw-Hill, New York, 1958, chap. 15; and in William J. Baumol, *Economic Theory and Operations Analysis,* 3d ed., Prentice-Hall, Englewood Cliffs, N.J., 1972, chap. 23.

A PAYOFF MATRIX

Strategy of Firm A	Strategy of Firm B				
	1	**2**	**3**	**. . .**	**n**
1	a_{11}	a_{12}	a_{13}	. . .	a_{1n}
2	a_{21}	a_{22}	a_{23}	. . .	a_{2n}
3	a_{31}	a_{32}	a_{33}	. . .	a_{3n}
.	. . .	. . .	. . .	. . .	. . .
.					
.					
m	a_{m1}	a_{m2}	a_{m3}	. . .	a_{mn}

The subject of game theory is rational behavior in situations of conflict—parlor games, military combat, and the struggles of firms for profits. Games have definite rules, known to and adhered to by the participants. A standard problem of game theory is the *two-person, constant-sum* game. For the economic application, this means a pair of duopolists who compete for some *given* total profit. What one of them gains the other loses.

Each of the two firms has its *strategies*, which are all of the courses of action, the moves and countermoves, that one firm can take in the light of what the other firm does. The strategies of the two firms are aligned in a table called a *payoff matrix*.

Table A5–1 is the general form of a payoff matrix. Firm *A* has *m* strategies, listed vertically in columns. Firm *B* has *n* strategies, listed in rows. The entries in the body of the table are the profits of firm *A*. Thus, if firm *A* selects its strategy 3, and if firm *B* selects its strategy 2, the table says that firm *A*'s profits will be a_{32}.

The payoff matrix is set up from the point of view of firm *A*. The profits of firm *B* are some constant minus firm *A*'s profits in the table. Firm *A* would like the maximum number in the table. Firm *B* would like the minimum number in the table because that would mean the maximum profits for firm *B*.

Table A5–2 gives hypothetical data for a payoff matrix in duopoly. The strategies of the firms are their choices of how many units of their products to sell. In the table, each firm can have 3 strategies—to sell 100, or 200, or 300 units of its products. The dollar figures are the profits of firm *A* for each combination of strategies.

What will the two competing firms do? They will each offer 100 units for sale. Such happens to be the solution of this duopoly problem. Here is a "strictly determined" game.

Why do both firms choose the strategy of selling 100 units? The profits of firm *A* are \$4,000. Firm *B* also sells 100 units and thus prevents firm *A* from getting any more than \$4,000. With firm *B*

TABLE A5–2   **PAYOFF MATRIX FOR TWO RIVAL FIRMS**

Strategy of Firm A	Strategy of Firm B			Row Minimum
	100 units	200 units	300 units	
100 units	$4,000	$5,000	$4,500	$4,000 ("maximin")
200 units	3,000	3,500	3,800	3,000
300 units	2,000	2,500	2,800	2,000
Column Maximum	4,000 ("minimax")	5,000	4,500	

selling 100 units firm *A* has no incentive to sell 200 units or more, because to do so would lower profits.

Formally, this game is strictly determined because the *maximin* is equal to the *minimax*. (They are also called *maxmin* and *minmax*.) The maximin is the greatest row minimum, and the minimax is the smallest column maximum.

Firm *A* follows a maximin strategy. That is, it seeks the maximum of the minimum payoffs. Firm *B* follows a minimax strategy of holding its rival to the minimum of the maximum payoffs.

The strategies are conservative. They mean that each firm assumes the worst and acts accordingly. The solution, where the maximin equals the minimax, is an equilibrium solution. Both firms are motivated to adopt and to hold to the mutually compatible strategies.

But the maximin does not have to be equal to the minimax. Nor do firms necessarily employ such cautious strategies. Nor is it usually true that two firms fight over a pot of profits of a fixed size. In more complicated games, where the number of players, or firms, is greater than two, and where the prizes, or profits, do not add to a constant sum, the conclusions reached by game theory are much less definite.

6

PRICES OF
FACTORS

21
Prices
of Factors
OF PRODUCTION

In modern economic theory, the *factors of production* are labor and capital. The factors of production are also known as *productive services* or *resources*. In much economic literature they are also called *inputs*. In this book, however, the word *input* means all of the things bought by the firm—fuel, raw materials, etc., as well as labor and capital.

FACTORS OF PRODUCTION

Early in the nineteenth century, economists distinguished three factors of production, namely, land, labor, and capital. The owners of the factors of production were landowners, wage earners, and capitalists whose incomes were rent, wages, and profits. Thus the theory of factor pricing was the theory of the determination of three kinds, or three functional forms, of income. In nineteenth-century England, the landowners, the capitalists, and the wage earners were more than economic groups. They were also distinct sociological and political classes—upper, middle, and lower. Late in the nineteenth century, economists added a fourth factor of production. This was enterprise; profits then became the incomes of entrepreneurs, and interest became the income of the owners of capital.

Whether there are two, or three, or four factors of production does not matter very much. Classification is a matter of convenience and relevance. The British class system with its three kinds of incomes was never relevant in America. Conflict and discussion in this country have centered on the division of total income between labor income and property income, on the supposed tension between "human rights" and "property rights," as if the owners of property were not human beings, too. Another important reason for holding to two factors in price theory is that macroeconomic theory operates with two factors. In its special and narrow sense as a component of gross national product, the national income is the sum of factor incomes—of (1) the compensation of employees, and (2) the incomes of proprietors of farms and unincorporated businesses, together with the incomes of the owners of rental properties, of fixed-income securities, and of the stocks of corporations. The incomes of millions of Americans, who are both workers and owners, are combinations of labor incomes and property incomes.

As every student of economics knows, the gross national product consists of the values of final or finished goods and services only. To avoid double counting, the values of intermediate products are excluded. After the exclusion of depreciation and of indirect business taxes, the value of national product thus reduces to the value of the services of the factors of production. Similarly, "value added" by a firm or an industry is its dollar sales minus its purchases of intermediate products from other firms or industries. Value added is thus the value of the services of the workers and of the owners in the firm or industry.

The structure of the theory of factor pricing will now be briefly sketched. The structure has four main parts. (1) As Chapter 10 shows, each firm uses inputs and factors in such amounts that the money values of their marginal productivities are equal to their unit costs to the firm. (2) Each firm has a demand curve for factors of production, the curve sloping downward because of diminishing marginal productivity. When the demands of the firms are added, the result is the demand functions for factors in each market and in the economy as a whole. (3) The supplies of factors, at various prices, are determined by decisions about quantities of the factors offered by their owners. Factor prices are determined by demand and supply. (4) The theory of product prices (Chapters 13-20) and the theory of factor prices are parts of one whole. The costs of firms depend on factor prices as well as on technology. The demands of consumers depend on their tastes and on their incomes, which they receive from the sale of their factors, i.e., their productive services. Consumer demands, in turn, along with technology, determine the marginal productivities of factors. Accordingly, the combined theory of product and factor prices shows how, within the limits imposed by technology and the tastes of consumers, the factors of production are directed into their many uses by their prices.

A consumer's demand for a commodity rests on the utility of the commodity. In contrast, a firm's demand for a factor depends on the factor's productivity or, more specifically, on the factor's value productivity.

The theory of factor pricing is generally known as the *marginal productivity theory* of distribution. This name is not fully descriptive because the idea of marginal productivity comes in only on the demand side. And in every pricing process, supply is just as important as demand.

The first step is to define the demand for factors of production. This will now be done in two stages, first in pure competition and second in monopoly and imperfect competition. Although all factors of production are put in two classes, labor and capital, there are many kinds of each. In the discussion to follow, the word *factor* is to be understood as meaning one of several kinds of labor or of capital.

THE DEMAND
FOR FACTORS IN
PURE
COMPETITION

Some of the ideas developed in Chapter 10 can now be brought forward and adapted for present purposes. The emphasis in Chapter 10 is on the quantities of inputs and factors that the firm buys. The emphasis here goes to the demand curves for factors.

Demand of the Firm

Let A, B, etc., stand for factors. Let MP_A, MP_B, etc., stand for the marginal productivities of factor A, factor B, etc. The prices of A, B, etc., are P_A, P_B, etc. Marginal cost is MC, and P_0 is the price received by the firm for its output. On pages 177 and 178 it is shown that

$$\frac{P_A}{MP_A} = \frac{P_B}{MP_B} = \cdots = MC = P_0.$$

This equation, or statement, says in effect that the firm minimizes costs and maximizes profits when it adjusts quantities of each factor so that the value of its marginal product (VMP) equals the price paid for it. That is, $\frac{P_A}{MP_A} = P_0$, and therefore $P_A = MP_A \times P_0 = VMP_A$.

In the short run, the competitive firm might be in a position where only one factor is variable in amount; this could be, for example, unskilled labor. When this is so, the firm's demand curve for the one variable factor is identical with the curve of the value of the marginal product (VMP).

The marginal product of a variable factor (or input) diminishes as more units of the factor are employed. The *value* of MP also diminishes, because MP is multiplied by a constant, the price of output. In pure competition, nothing that the firm does can alter the price of a unit of its output. The hypothetical numbers in Table 21–1 give an illustration of diminishing VMP; the table is a modification of Table 10–1 on page 175.

The fourth column in Table 21–1 gives the schedule of the value of the marginal product. That schedule is the firm's demand schedule for the factor. In the table there is only one price for the factor; at this price the firm of course employs 20 units of the factor. But it is easy to see that, at other factor prices such as $37.50 and

TABLE 21-1

A FIRM'S DEMAND SCHEDULE FOR ONE VARIABLE FACTOR

Units of Factor	Marginal Product	Price of Unit of Output	Value of Marginal Product	Price of Unit of Factor
19	5 tons	$7.50	$37.50	$30.00
20	4	7.50	30.00	30.00
21	3	7.50	22.50	30.00

FIGURE 21-1

FIRM'S DEMAND FOR ONE VARIABLE FACTOR

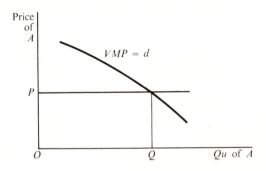

$22.50, the firm would employ, i.e., demand, fewer or more units of the factor.

When only one factor is variable in amount, then, the firm's demand for the factor is the value of the marginal product of the factor. The firm's demand curve is the factor's *VMP* curve.

In Figure 21-1, price is on the vertical axis, and quantity of factor *A* is on the horizontal axis. The curve *VMP* is the demand curve of the firm for *A*. The firm buys (or hires) the amount *OQ* of the factor when the price is *OP*. The amount *OQ* is the amount for which $OP = VMP$ (i.e., $MP_A \times P_0$). At a lower price, the firm would use a larger amount of *A*. At a higher price, less would be used.

The demand curve can shift to the right or left, and if it does, the firm will use more or less of the variable factor. The curve will shift to the right if either or both of two things happens. One is a rise in the price of output, i.e., a rise in the *V* of *VMP*. The other is an improvement in methods of production that increases productivity.

Two Adjustments

To complete the theory of a firm's demand for a factor, two adjustments must be made. The first adjustment is called here the *multifactor adjustment*. It allows for changes in the quantities of other factors when one factor varies in quantity. In other words, the multifactor adjustment drops the assumption that only one factor is

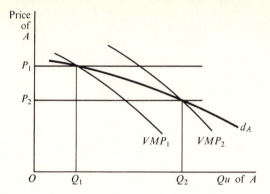

variable. The second adjustment is called the *industry adjustment*. It allows for changes in the industry that affect the firms.

THE MULTIFACTOR ADJUSTMENT   The task now is to derive the demand for A, when both A and other factors B, C, D, etc., are variable. If the price of A falls, more of it is used. The other factors complementary to A will also be used in larger quantities, with the result of increasing A's MP. The substitutes for A will be used in smaller quantities; this too has the effect of increasing the MP of A. Suppose, for example, that an earth-moving firm finds that it can lease large power shovels at a lower rate. So it plans to employ more of them. If the firm also hires more operators (the complements) and uses fewer small power shovels (the substitutes), it will get more work (a higher MP) out of the larger power shovels than if the firm simply leased more with no change in the work force and line of equipment.

In Figure 21-2, let the price of A at first be P_1. The firm is in equilibrium, using the quantity OQ_1. Then the price of A falls to P_2. The changes in the quantities of the other factors shift the VMP curve to the right. It becomes VMP_2 instead of VMP_1. The firm then equates P_2 and VMP_2, to arrive at the amount OQ_2 of factor A. The curve d_A, joining the points defined by P_1Q_1 and P_2Q_2, therefore describes the demand for one factor when the quantities of others are also variable.

The curves VMP_1 and VMP_2 are unadjusted. The curve d_A contains the multifactor adjustment.

THE INDUSTRY ADJUSTMENT   The demand curve of an industry for a factor of production is the sum of the demand curves of the firms in the industry. If the price of a factor falls, the firms use more. Other things being equal, their outputs expand as

FIGURE 21-3   FIRM'S DEMAND FOR ONE FACTOR: INDUSTRY ADJUSTMENT

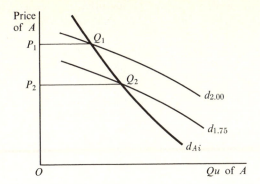

their costs fall. The supply curve of the industry shifts down and to the right, with the result that the equilibrium price of the product decreases. Hence, *VMP* has to be revised downward. Suppose, for example, the price of fertilizer falls. The farmers use more, produce more, and so receive a lower price for their grain. The fertilizer still has the same marginal *physical* product in bushels per season, but because a bushel now sells for less, the *value* of the *MP* is less.

In Figure 21-3, the demand curves $d_{2.00}$ and $d_{1.75}$ are constructed in the same way as the demand curve d_A in Figure 21-2. The 2.00 and the 1.75 are product prices in dollars per bushel (or other physical unit). The firm's demand for a factor is less when the price of the product is lower, because *MP* is multiplied by a smaller number. The curve d_{Ai} contains the industry adjustment and is drawn to show the firm's demand when changes in the price of the product are allowed for. The demand of all the firms of the industry is the sum total of the d_{Ai} curves of each of the firms.

The adjustments described with the help of Figures 21-2 and 21-3 are probably often small. The important thing to keep in mind is the *VMP* curve (in Figure 21-1) as the competitive firm's demand for a factor.

THE DEMAND FOR FACTORS IN MONOPOLY AND IMPERFECT COMPETITION

Firms producing and selling in monopoly and in imperfect competition generally have some control over their selling prices. Sometimes they have some control over the prices they pay. The unregulated profit-maximizing monopolist calmly chooses the optimum price. Many regulated monopolists must, however, sell at given prices, fixed by public authorities. Oligopolists also commonly sell at rigid prices. The firms in many industries characterized by monopolistic competition likewise sell at prices dictated by custom. Certainly in the short run, therefore, many firms *not* in pure competition can share a feature of competitive firms, namely, given product prices. To avoid more complication, this matter will henceforth be overlooked. It will be assumed that firms vary their selling prices, that they know their demands, and that they maximize their profits.

Variable Prices for Products and Factors
To sell more of its product, a monopoly firm as well as one in imperfect competition has to accept lower prices. Instead of a given price, the firm faces a schedule of prices. Thus the demand curve for the firm's product comes into the calculations, and so does its marginal revenue. Accordingly, when the firm produces more by adding more units of a variable factor, the additional (i.e., marginal physical) product must be multiplied by the additional revenue it brings. *Marginal revenue product* is the name for marginal product multiplied by its marginal revenue.

The calculation of marginal revenue product is illustrated in Table 21-2. To obtain marginal revenue product, multiply marginal product by the corresponding marginal revenue. Or, what amounts to the same thing, the marginal revenue product of, say, the eleventh worker is found by calculating (by subtraction) the addition to total revenue that is caused.

Since marginal revenue equals price to the firm under pure competition, it follows that marginal revenue product (MRP) equals the value of the marginal product (VMP). That is, $MRP = VMP$, where $MR = P$. But for firms whose product demand curves are sloping, MRP is always *less* than VMP, because marginal revenue is always less than price.

The price paid for a factor or an input can also vary with the level of activity of the firm. Suppose a small firm in a small town has 10 employees at work on the same task and that each has a daily wage of $30. Suppose that if the firm hires another worker to do the same kind of work, circumstances are such that the firm has to pay all 11 workers $32 a day. Ten workers at $30 equals $300, and 11 workers at $32 equals $352. The extra wage cost of 11 workers is $52. The extra cost of 1 more unit of a factor is called *marginal factor cost*. In this example, marginal factor cost rises if the firm buys more units of

TABLE 21-2   MARGINAL REVENUE PRODUCT

Units of Factor	Total Product	Marginal Product	Selling Price	Total Revenue	Marginal Revenue	Marginal Revenue Product
10	15	5	$100	$1,500	—	—
11	19	4	99	1,880[a]	$95	$380
12	22	3	98	2,156	92	276

[a] This number has been rounded off.

TABLE 21-3

MARGINAL FACTOR COST

Number of Workers	Wage per Worker	Total Daily Wages	Marginal Factor Cost
10	$30	$300	—
11	32	352	$52
12	34	408	56
13	36	468	60

the factor, and rises faster than average factor cost—$52 versus $32. On the other hand, marginal factor cost can fall. Suppose the firm can rent trucks, which are driven by its own employees, and that the rental per truck is lower the larger the number of trucks. If 1 truck is $20 a day and 2 are $18 each, then the marginal factor cost for 2 trucks is $16 ($36 minus $20). When marginal factor cost declines, it goes down faster than average factor cost.

A schedule of rising marginal factor cost is illustrated in Table 21-3. The daily wage per worker in the second column is *average factor cost*. The first two columns together are the supply schedule of labor to the firm. The relation between average and marginal factor çost is parallel to that between price and marginal revenue (see Table 16-1 on page 286).

If the price paid for units of a factor is the same regardless of the amount bought by a firm, then average factor cost and marginal factor cost are identical. Figure 21-4 shows average and marginal curves for two factors as one firm would see them. The average factor cost curves are really supply curves to the firm. In Figure 21-4A, factor *A* is available to the firm at a constant supply price *OP*. In Figure 21-4B, factor *B* is available at rising supply prices, shown by the curve *AFC*.

A firm facing rising supply prices for a factor (or any input) is often called a *monopsonist*. The literal meaning of this word is of course *sole buyer*; so to label such a firm carries no more meaning

FIGURE 21-4   **AVERAGE AND MARGINAL FACTOR COST**

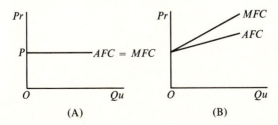

(A)   (B)

than to say that any firm with a downward sloping demand curve is a monopolist.

Demand of the Firm

If the firm has just one variable factor, its demand curve is the curve of marginal revenue product for that factor. If two or more factors are simultaneously variable, the firm's demand curve for a single factor is constructed in the same way as that of the competitive firm. Thus in Figure 21-2, on page 382, *MRP* curves can be substituted for *VMP* curves.

Assume first that average and marginal factor costs are constant to the firm. When it is in equilibrium, the firm with a sloping demand curve pays each of its factors less than the values of their marginal products. Suppose that the firm in Table 21-2 has 11 employees. The eleventh worker adds 4 units of the firm's product per week. The selling price of the product is $99 and marginal revenue is $95. Then, $MP = 4$, and $VMP = \$99 \times 4 = \$396$. But $MRP = \$380 =$ weekly wage cost. In other words, the eleventh employee is paid $380 a week during which he or she helps produce something the firm sells for $396.

Earlier chapters show that a firm with a sloping demand curve produces less and sells its product at a higher price than a competitive firm. The comparison, of course, is made under the assumptions that both types of firms have the same cost curves and that both are in full (i.e., long-run) equilibrium. The comparison is now drawn for the employment of factors. The firm with the sloping product-demand curve produces less and employs smaller quantities of factors because $MRP < VMP$. In contrast, $VMP = MRP$ for the competitive firm.

Assume next that average factor costs are rising to a firm with a sloping demand curve. When this is so, the firm pays the factors less than their marginal revenue products. This is shown in Figure 21-5. Here the demand d is either the *MRP* schedule directly or is derived from it by the adjustment previously described. The *AFC* curve is

FIGURE 21-5   EMPLOYMENT OF A FACTOR BY A MONOPSONISTIC FIRM

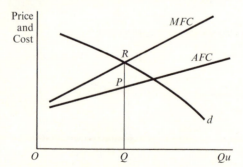

the supply curve to the firm of a factor; the curve AFC exhibits the actual prices the firm has to pay for different quantities. The firm employs OQ units of the factor, paying the price PQ. The marginal revenue product of OQ units is RQ. The firm does not employ more than OQ units because if it did, the extra units have an extra cost higher than their revenue productivity. Beyond OQ, as can be seen in Figure 21-5, $MFC > MRP$.

The gaps between VMP and MRP and between MRP and AFC have consequences for the allocation of factors, or resources. *Monopolistic* firms do not employ resources in quantities as large as do competitive firms, all other things being equal. *Monopsonistic* firms put an additional brake on their uses of resources. Thus the price system fails, on the factor side, to allocate resources in accordance with the conditions of efficiency. Here, of course, is the other side of the coin of monopoly as a cause of loss of economic welfare.

Table 21-4 summarizes the discussion so far.

TABLE 21-4   **THE DEMAND FOR FACTORS OF PRODUCTION**

Firm or Industry	Factor	Demand	Supply of Factor	Equilibrium
Firm in pure competition	one variable factor	demand curve = VMP	AFC = MFC	VMP = AFC = MFC
	several variable factors	demand for one factor equals its VMP adjusted for effects of changes in quantities of other factors	AFC = MFC	adjusted VMP = AFC = MFC
Industry in pure competition		industry demand is sum of firm's demands further adjusted for changes in product price caused by variations in employment of factors		
Firm with sloping demand curve for its product	one variable factor	demand curve = MRP curve	AFC = MFC MFC > AFC	MRP = AFC = MFC MRP = MFC
	several variable factors	demand curve for one factor equals its MRP curve adjusted for effects of changes in quantities of other factors	AFC = MFC MFC > AFC	adjusted MRP = AFC = MFC adjusted MRP = MFC

In modern analysis, the theory of capital and interest belongs in both microeconomics and macroeconomics. Since the publication of Keynes's *General Theory* in 1936, economists have devoted much more effort to the macroeconomic aspects of capital and interest. They have done so because of the importance of business investment for the stability of the whole economy and of the rate of interest as an instrument of stabilization policy. Discussion of capital and interest here will be kept brief and confined to a partial equilibrium analysis. Because capital is a factor and interest a cost to the firm and the industry, the basic theory has already been covered. It remains only to point to the special features of capital.

*Discounting
Future Yields*
The special feature of capital goods is that their yields are available over a period of time. The services of buildings and of machinery extend over many years, depending on how durable they are and on how quickly technological change makes them obsolescent. In deciding on the purchases of a capital good, the firm looks to the stream of outputs that will be produced in the future with the aid of the capital good. The stream of outputs will be sold in year 1, year 2, year 3, etc.; thus the firm visualizes a stream of gross dollar yields in successive years in the future. From the stream of future gross yields, certain costs are deducted to arrive at the net yields. Interest and depreciation are not included in these costs; interest appears elsewhere in the calculations, in which depreciation is ignored so as to avoid double counting. Suppose the capital good is a motel. The owners can expect some average rate of occupancy, some average price per room, and some expenses of operation. Uncertainty about the future, of course, beclouds any estimates made in the present. But the complications, theoretical and practical, of uncertainty will be bypassed here.

The future net yields must be *discounted* to the present. A dollar that will not be received for 5 years is not as good as a dollar that will be received in 1 year. The present value of the future net yields is calculated at the going or market rate of interest by a standard formula.[1] For example, the present value of $10,000 a year for 10 years discounted at 9 per cent is $64,176.58. The market rate of interest enters the calculations because if the firm borrows the

---

[1] If y_1 is the net yield in year 1, y_2 in year 2, etc., and if r is the rate of interest expressed as a decimal, then the discounted present value PV of the stream is

$$PV = \frac{y_1}{(1 + r)} + \frac{y_2}{(1 + r)^2} + \frac{y_3}{(+ r)^3} + \cdots \frac{y_t}{(1 + r)^t}.$$

Year t is the last year of the planning period, e.g., the tenth year or the twentieth. Given y_1, y_2, etc., as well as r and t, PV can be found from prepared tables.

money to buy the capital good, future net receipts must exceed or at least equal interest payments. If the firm buys the capital good with its own funds, it sacrifices the interest income it could earn with these funds.

The next step is to compare the present value of the expected net yields from a capital good with the cost, or the supply price, of the capital good. If the cost is less than present value, it pays the firm to acquire the capital good. If cost and present value are equal, it just barely pays.

Observe the three elements in the firm's decision on adding another capital good—its cost, the expected yield, and the rate of interest. The first and third elements are given to the firm. That is, capital goods and funds are in perfectly elastic supply. This statement might not hold for very large firms, which sometimes face rising costs of borrowed funds and perhaps rising costs of capital goods.

THE SUPPLY OF FACTORS

The supply functions of factors *to the firm* have already been discussed. In general, factors are available in perfectly elastic supply to individual firms, competitive and noncompetitive alike. Rising or falling supply curves to firms are the exception, though they are by no means rare.

The supply of labor is discussed in the next chapter, whose subject is the theory of wages. Much of the material on the supply of capital and on the rate of interest now belongs to the domain of macroeconomics. All that can be said about the supply of factors, when their natures are not made specific, comes under the heading of *elasticity of supply*.

To the industry and to the economy, elasticity of factor supply takes on an aspect different from elasticity to the firm. Imagine a large area devoted to varied farming activities. Suppose that much of the land is leased on annual terms and that there is a market for the leases. Acres of land could, therefore, be in perfectly elastic supply to any one farmer; by paying the going rate, the farmer can lease as many additional acres as wanted. But for an industry, i.e., all the farmers who grow the same crop, supply is less than perfectly elastic. If the price of their crop rises, and if the farmers all bid for more land, its lease value will rise because the land is transferred from other crops. Suppose next an increase in the demand for *all* of the farm products produced in the area. Because the total amount of farm land is fixed once and for all, its supply is perfectly inelastic.

The same factor, then, can have supply curves ranging from the horizontal to the vertical, depending on which demand curve is coupled with supply—the demand of the firm, of an industry, of a

FIGURE 21-6

SUPPLY OF FACTORS

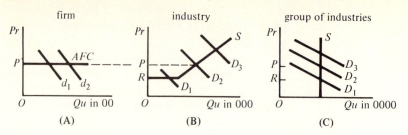

group of industries. Figure 21-6A displays an increase in the demand of one firm, the increase coming, for example, from an improvement in technology. Because the factor is in perfectly elastic supply to the firm, the price of course does not rise. Notice that the quantity axis in Figure 21-6A is scaled in hundreds. The same axis is scaled in thousands in Figure 21-6B, which shows supply to the industry and demand from the industry. The price OP to the firm is the industry equilibrium price, given by the intersection of the supply curve and demand curve D_2.

The supply curve in Figure 21-6B is perfectly elastic, however, for a small range of quantities at price OR. This means that if the industry is small with, e.g., demand D_1, the industry can get more of the factor without paying more per unit. The meaning of the price OR is that other industries use the same factor. Figure 21-6C, with quantities in the tens of thousands, shows group demand D_1 and supply resulting in the equilibrium price OR.

If industry demand increases, as in Figure 21-6B, the price of the factor rises, as more of the factor is employed by the industry. The horizontal AFC curves of the firms rise in step with the industry price. But when group demand increases, as in Figure 21-6C, price goes up and quantity remains constant.

In general, the supply price of a factor to an industry is equal to or above the price the owners of the factor could obtain in an alternative employment. In Figure 21-6B, this other price is OR. This other price can also be called the opportunity cost, or the transfer earnings, of the factor.

Rents

The foregoing example is that of a factor whose total amount is fixed and cannot be increased. Its total supply (S in Figure 21-6C) is perfectly inelastic. Land, of course, is the leading example of such a factor. When demand increases, the long-run equilibrium price paid for the services of land rises without limit, with nothing to check the rise.

In contrast, the long-run supplies of particular kinds of capital goods—to firms, to industries, to groups of industries—are elastic at prices equal to the full cost of producing the capital goods. This proposition is subject to one major qualification: Capital goods produced in monopolistic or oligopolistic industries can have long-run prices above full costs. There is, however, no limitation on supply; whether larger quantities of capital goods are sold at higher or lower prices depends on the shapes of demand functions and cost functions in industries producing the capital goods.

The incomes of owners of factors in less than perfectly elastic supply are called *rents*. In this sense, the word *rent* is not confined to land, nor does it have anything to do with leasing things or hiring them. The factor owner can receive rent from land, or from capital under certain conditions, or from labor under certain conditions.

The essence of the idea of rent is that it cannot be competed away. This is clear for land. When demand for the services of land grows, rents rise. Nothing on the supply side makes them fall, even in the long run. In contrast, more capital goods can always be built in the long run. An increase in demand for office space, for example, leads in the long run to the erection of more office buildings. When, however, the demand for particular capital goods *in the short run* increases, the incomes of the owners of existing capital goods rise. Nothing on the supply side makes these incomes fall because, by definition of the short run, the short-run supply of capital goods is perfectly inelastic or nearly so. Because their short-run behavior resembles the behavior of the rent of land in the long run, the incomes of the owners of capital in the short run are called rents, or *quasi rents*.

The net revenues of firms in the short run are mentioned often in earlier chapters, especially in Chapter 13. These net revenues are quasi rents, but they are not so referred to earlier in this book; there is no need to do so, and it has to be admitted that the term rent can easily cause confusion. Anyway, given a firm's plant and equipment, i.e., its capital goods, the size of its net revenue, or quasi rent, depends on current demand. If demand is high, quasi rent is high, and can be far, far above the earnings that had been expected when the plant and equipment were built. Quasi rent can also be low if demand shrinks much. Quasi rent, in short, is at the mercy of short-run demand, just as the income from land in the long run depends on long-run demand.

Rents and Profits

What is the difference between rents and profits? It is this: Rents cannot be competed away, whereas profits can. Rents are present in the long-run equilibrium of pure competition; (net) profits are not. Recall the long-run equilibrium of the competitive firm and the industry (Chapter 14). The firms earn zero net profits. The adjustments of the firms and the entry and exit of firms to the industry

FIGURE 21-7

SUPPLY AND RENT

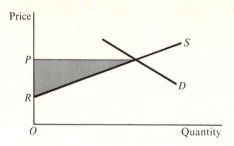

cause net profits to be zero. But the firms all have similar cost curves (page 257). They are similar because costs are approximately equalized by the firms' payments—rents—for the services of scarce managers.

In Figure 21-7 the *S* curve is the long-run supply curve for managers in a particular industry. The demand for managers depends on their productivity. In the long run, given adequate information and mobility, the managers all receive the same salary, which is *OP*. The supply curve says that all but one of them would be willing to work for less than *OP*, if the demand were a little less. No one, however, would work for less than *OR*. The shaded area in Figure 21-7 is the total rent element in the incomes of the managers. Rent is the excess of the incomes they receive over the minimum incomes they would accept if they had to, the minimum incomes being determined by what they can earn elsewhere. If the supply curve were flat, the shaded area would disappear. There is no rent when supply is perfectly elastic.

Net profits, the excess of total revenue over full costs, are the result of disequilibrium and monopoly. When they are negative, i.e., when there are losses, net profits are also the result of disequilibrium. Monopoly here means monopoly in the broad and loose sense—the sloping demand curve. As Chapter 16 demonstrates, monopoly can, but it does not have to, result in profits. When monopoly is temporary, and is brought into existence by a firm's innovation that is later imitated by other firms, then net profits, which are also temporary, arise from innovation. The existence of uncertainty has been assumed away in this book because of the formidable theoretical complexities that uncertainty causes. Some theorists link profits with the entrepreneurial function of bearing uncertainty.

THE ALLOCATION OF FACTORS

Their demands, supplies, and prices mutually determine the allocation of factors among all their possible employments. Suppose that a change in consumers' tastes causes the demand for a consumer good to increase. Whether or not its price rises, which depends on the kind of competition in the industry, more of the consumer good is produced, the demand for factors increasing. Some of the factors are of unspecialized types, employed in many industries. Except perhaps in the short run, such factors are available in perfectly elastic supply to the expanding industry. Their prices do not go up, but the increase in demand allocates more of them to the industry. Other factors are scarce, their supply curves rising, even in the long run. The larger demands for the scarce factors cause their prices to rise, to the expanding industry, as well as to other industries. These higher prices lead to substitutions among factors, causing still more changes in factor demands, supplies, and prices. So it goes—just one shift in consumer demand results in a ripple of changes in the allocation of factors.

AN APPLICATION

The theory of factor pricing surveyed in this chapter has the traditional name of the *marginal productivity theory of distribution.* The theory has been embroiled in much controversy, mainly over the social ethics of the pattern of incomes in a private enterprise economy. Most of the controversy has had to do with wages. Further consideration of the marginal productivity theory of distribution is therefore postponed to the next chapter.

Capital Budgeting

One of the important decisions that periodically confront the executives of a business enterprise is how to allocate their investment funds among the many projects that are always proposed. Which projects for expansion are needed most?

The idea of the need for capital expansion is, however, just as useless as the idea of a consumer's need for a commodity. *Need* conveys nothing about intensity. But the concept of demand does do so, both for the consumer and the firm. The concept of the firm's demand for capital can be applied as a useful device in capital budgeting.

Consider Table 21-5, which ranks the proposed investments of a hypothetical firm at some point of time when decisions have to be made on investments in new capital. The several proposals up for examination and decision are arrayed by estimated yield and size. A few have high yields, whereas many offer low yields. The planning period is, say, 2 years. Suppose next that the firm has, from internal sources on which it alone relies, funds for capital expenditure amounting to $4 million. A glance at Table 21-5 shows that only proposals promising 15 per cent or more should be acted on. The cutoff rate of return is 15 per cent.

(Why does the firm not rush out to sell its bonds at, say, 8 per cent, and expand its new investments to $6.5 million? Here again are

TABLE 21-5   A FIRM'S DEMAND SCHEDULE FOR CAPITAL

Estimated Yield (per cent)	Proposed Investments	Cumulated Demand
	(thousands of dollars)	
Over 50	$ 200	$ 200
35–50	800	1,000
25–35	1,200	2,200
15–25	1,800	4,000
10–15	2,500	6,500
5–10	5,000	11,500
Less than 5	7,000	18,500

the difficult problems raised by the profit-maximizing assumption and by the uncertainties surrounding the estimates of future yields. Then too, borrowing alters a firm's financial structure, making for still more complications.)

Suppose that a wholly new investment proposal comes up in the deliberations of the firm. If its estimated yield is below the cutoff rate, the new proposal can be summarily rejected. If, however, the new investment has a yield higher than the cutoff, it can displace other investments that had been decided on.

SUMMARY

The prices of the factors of production are connected with the prices of consumer goods through the actions of firms and households. The demand curve of a competitive firm for one variable factor is the curve of the value of the marginal product of the factor. The firm's demand for one factor, when several are variable, is found by adjusting *VMP* to allow for changes in the employment of other factors. Still another adjustment has to be made to allow for variations in the price of the product as the industry expands or contracts. The demand of firms with sloping demand curves is based on *marginal revenue product*. Factors can be available to firms at rising or falling supply prices. Then the rational firm looks to *marginal factor cost*, equating it with marginal revenue product. A firm's demand for capital is based on the present value of expected net yields. A factor can have supply curves ranging from the horizontal to the vertical, depending on time and on whether demand is from a firm or an industry or a group of industries. *Rent* is the name for the income to the owners of a factor in less than perfectly elastic supply. The net revenues of firms in the short run are *quasi rents* because the supply of capital is inelastic in the short run. Rents cannot be competed away, whereas net profits can.

SELECTED REFERENCES

General: American Economic Association, *Readings in the Theory of Income Distribution* (Blakiston, Philadelphia, 1946).

Edward H. Chamberlin, *The Theory of Monopolistic Competition*, 8th ed. (Harvard University Press, Cambridge, 1962), chap. 8; Joan Robinson, *The Economics of Imperfect Competition* (Macmillan, London, 1933), book VII.

William J. Baumol, *Economic Theory and Operations Analysis*, 3d ed. (Prentice-Hall, Englewood Cliffs, 1972), chap 17; George J. Stigler, *The Theory of Price*, 3rd ed. (Macmillan, New York, 1966), chap. 14–17; Donald Stevenson Watson, ed., *Price Theory in Action: A Book of Readings*, 3d ed. (Houghton Mifflin, Boston, 1973), part 9.

Orris C. Herfindahl and Allen V. Kneese, *Economic Theory of Natural Resources* (Merrill, Columbus, 1974), chaps. 3 and 5.

EXERCISES AND PROBLEMS

1. Upon what does the elasticity of demand for a factor depend?
2. Describe the effect on the prices and on the allocation of factors of a decline in the demand for a consumer good.
3. Describe the effect of a technological improvement on a firm's demand for capital.
4. Make up a set of numbers to show the relation between quantities of a factor and of a firm's product. Calculate the marginal product. Make up a demand schedule for the firm's product. Calculate marginal revenue product. Assume a price for the factor and find the amount the firm employs. Show why the firm would not use more, or use less.
5. Explain how the following influence the value of the marginal product of an input: (a) a change in the price of the product sold, (b) a change in the quantity of substitute inputs, (c) a change in the quantity of complementary inputs, and (d) a change in the quality of the input itself.
6. Explain why it is possible for competition to eliminate profits but not rents in the long run. Are normal profits eliminated in the long run?
7. Speculate on the sizes of the economic rents received by: (a) students working in the college library, (b) neurologists practicing in

New York City, (c) trash collectors in San Francisco, and (d) farm-hands in Iowa.

8. Expenditures for education are viewed by economists as investments in human capital. What should you take into account if you would measure the present value of the expenditures on your own education?

9. Why do monopolistic and monopsonistic firms tend to hire fewer resources than competitive firms?

10. How can opportunity cost be used in estimating the present value of an investment?

22
Wages

The title of one of the popular essays of a French economist of the last century, Frédéric Bastiat, was "Things Seen and Things Not Seen." That price theory looks more to things not seen than to things seen must now be fully evident. In particular, the theory of wages describes many things not seen.

The theory of wages deals with the slowly changing underlying forces, with the background. In the foreground stand the day-to-day practical problems that must be dealt with by employers, personnel administrators, workers, and union officials. The theory of wages describes the forces causing different levels of wages. Practical men and women take the levels for granted while they wrestle with problems such as systems of wage payments—time wages, piece wages, incentive wages, overtime wages, bonuses, length-of-service increases, etc. Other problems include wage inequities within plants and between plants operated by the same company. Wage disputes often turn on fringe benefits, which must be considered as additions to wages, and which include vacations with pay, paid sick leave, paid travel time, clothing allowances, pensions, health and other insurance, as well as recreational facilities.

Thus *wages* can mean many different things in different contexts. The word *wages* will be used here in the comprehensive sense of labor cost to the employer, per unit of time or per unit of output. This usage therefore means that the current values of fringe benefits and of similar costs to the employer are included. The word wages here is also assigned its customary meaning in economics as the one expression for payments for personal services, embracing alike the salaries and bonuses (etc.) of the corporation executive, the fees of the surgeon, the income of the entertainer, the pay of the soldier, and the earnings of the unskilled manual worker.

As a branch of the theory of prices, wage theory has the purpose of explaining persistent differences in wages as well as the role of wages in allocating human services among occupations, industries, and areas. Wage theory is also a part of macroeconomics, where one of its main tasks is to explain the relations between the aggregate level of wages and total employment. Partial equilibrium analysis ignores the role of wages as income, because even if the employees of a firm or an industry are consumers of the product, their contribution to demand is negligibly small.

The marginal productivity theory of wages applies to a firm and to an industry. And when all labor and all capital are regarded as if they were homogeneous, the theory applies to the whole economy, giving an explanation of the share of wages in the national income.

THE SHARE OF WAGES IN THE NATIONAL INCOME Statistical estimates of national income in the United States go back many decades. A remarkable fact is the fairly stable ratio of wages to the total of national income. In most years, wages have been about 75 per cent of the national income of the private domestic economy. How can this relative stability be explained?

A favorite hypothesis is based on the marginal productivity theory with the accompanying assumption that the production function for the whole economy is linear homogeneous; that is, returns to scale are constant. If the quantities of labor and capital each increase by 10 per cent, output and income increase by 10 per cent. Labor and capital are combined in such a way that their contributions to income (i.e., their marginal products and their quantities) have a constant ratio of about 3 to 1, i.e., 75 to 25. Because the ratio of the prices paid to factors is equal to the ratio of their marginal products, it follows that the incomes of labor and capital are in the same constant ratio. (See Note 1 in the Appendix to Part 6.)

This hypothesis, based on the Cobb-Douglas production function (page 155), does have some empirical foundation. If the hypothesis is valid, notice that the influence of unions on the ratio of aggregate wages to other incomes reduces to zero, that the presence of monopoly and imperfect competition does not affect the result, and that changes in technology must improve the efficiency of labor and capital about equally.

The Adding-Up Controversy and Euler's Theorem Quarrels between labor and capital still go on, but among theorists the great controversies over the meaning of the division of income between labor and capital have long since subsided. One of the controversies over the marginal productivity theory of distribution, when it first became widely discussed about three generations ago, was whether capital received a share of total income greater than that corresponding to the value of its marginal product. Suppose that each of the two factors is paid an amount equal to the value of its marginal product. Does the sum total of labor's income and of capital's income then equal total income—which is the same as total product? Or is there something left over after both factors are paid the values of their marginal products, some income that falls into the hands of exploiting capitalists?

A proposition known as *Euler's theorem*, after Leonhard Euler (1707–1783) the Swiss mathematician, states that

$$\text{Total product} = L \times MP_L + C \times MP_C.$$

That is, total product (of a firm, an industry, or the entire economy) equals the quantity of labor, L, multiplied by the marginal product of labor, MP_L, plus the quantity of capital, C, multiplied by its marginal product. In this equation, the price of the product is omitted. To do so is customary because the price just multiplies all the terms in the equation by the same number.

Euler's theorem is valid in the equilibrium of pure competition, and when the production function is linear homogeneous, when returns to scale are constant. The proof of Euler's theorem is a simple matter of the differential calculus. The significance of the theorem is that no one is exploited—in competitive equilibrium with constant returns. The controversies over the theorem mostly centered about the legitimacy of the constant-returns assumption. If firms have constant returns to scale, a competitive equilibrium is impossible (Chapter 14, page 256). The rejoinder here is that in long-run competitive equilibrium, price equals minimum average cost, the firms's cost curve *at that point* being horizontal. The momentary constancy of unit cost corresponds to a momentary constancy of returns to scale at the point of equilibrium. Thus, at the exact point of equilibrium, it can be argued that constant returns exist.

Marginal Productivity and Social Ethics

In the past, the marginal productivity theory of distribution was both defended and attacked owing to its implications for social ethics. Because it says that a person's income is equal to (the marginal productivity[1] of) what that person produces, the theory was defended by some as exhibiting the justice of the working of free markets. Workers and owners deserve what they get; markets mete it out to them. This accords with the ethics of private property—that anyone is justly entitled to the fruits of her or his labor. Early in the twentieth century, some economists pushed the doctrine of marginal productivity too far, however, making it into almost a natural law.

Opponents of the doctrine protested that it is cruel and harsh, because it puts a stamp of approval on low wages, and because the

---

[1] This terminology is customary in this context. Strictly, it should be marginal revenue productivity, which when $MR = P$, includes the value of the marginal product.

doctrine is incompatible with distributive justice—the principle that people have a just claim to income according to their needs. It is true indeed that many persons—the aged, the blind, the disabled, for example—have low or zero productivities. It is also true that in industries and areas where the supply of labor is large relative to the demand for it, the marginal product of labor can be low and result in wages far beneath standards of needs.

In the present age, however, the problem of low incomes is met by government programs that include social insurance, public assistance, and other social service activities. The principle of distributive justice is in actual operation, although economists would agree that the operation has many a shortcoming. Most incomes are determined in markets where marginal productivity governs the demand for labor and other productive services. The social justice inherent in market-determined incomes continues as the widely accepted criterion. Thus both principles reign in the present age, each in its place. Violent and divisive controversy has subsided. The marginal productivity theory of wages has become a neutral instrument of analysis.

THE SUPPLY OF LABOR

Supply curves for labor can have almost any shape. The shapes depend on whether the context is the short run or the long and on whether the labor is that of one person, or of a group, or of all employed persons.

The theory of the supply of labor of one person rests upon the analysis of households as sellers of service to business firms. The analysis uses indifference curves. They are similar to the indifference curves in Chapter 6, where consumers, or households, are buyers of commodities.

The Supply of Services from Households

Consider the attitude of a household toward its income. In general, the more income the better. In general also, more income is to be had, in given circumstances, only by more work—only by the household's selling more services during a period of time. More work means the sacrifice of some leisure, which is also desirable. The gain in utility from more income has to be balanced against the loss of utility from less leisure.

Let it now be assumed that the members of a household can freely vary the size of their joint income by varying the number of hours per week that they work. It might be objected that this assumption is not realistic, because millions of people are employed at fixed working hours over which they have not the slightest control. Still, many such people can choose whether or not to work overtime, can take leave without pay, can play games with their allowances for sick leave, and can in fact make other adjustments.

Besides, many people have two jobs. And since the economic unit here is the household, rather than one person (although some households consist of one person), it must be clear that a household of two or more persons does have some flexibility in deciding how many hours to work in a week. Shall both husband and wife work? Part time or full time? Shall one take on a second job in the evenings or on weekends? A few second thoughts, therefore, show the possibility of flexible choice of income even where most of the income of a household comes from salaried employment at fixed hours. Then, too, millions of other people in the American economy can and do make their own choices about how many hours a week to work. These others are farmers, business proprietors, independent professional people, and others who are self-employed.

Indifference Curves for Income and Leisure

The next step is to construct indifference curves to show income and leisure as substitutes. A week has 168 hours. Suppose that 12 hours a day are used for sleeping, eating, dressing, traveling to and from work, etc., so that the maximum amount of "leisure"—time not spent in working—is 84 hours a week. Figure 22-1 exhibits 3 indifference curves from a whole map of them. The vertical axis is money income in dollars per week. The horizontal axis, when read from left to right, shows hours of leisure per week. When read from right to left, the horizontal axis shows hours of work per week. Take indifference curve *1*. It shows combinations of income and leisure that are equally desirable. Point *A* indicates one such combination, and point *B* another. To go from *A* to *B*, the individual sacrifices income but gains enough leisure to compensate, so that the person is indifferent between these 2 combinations and between any others on the same curve. But always, other things being equal, more income is preferable to less. Accordingly, any combination on indifference curve *2* is preferable to any on curve *1*. And curve *3* is, of course, still higher and still more desirable than curve *1*.

FIGURE 22-1   **INDIFFERENCE CURVES FOR INCOME AND LEISURE**

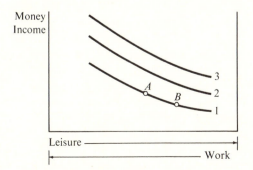

401   *Wages*

FIGURE 22–2

INCOME AND WORK

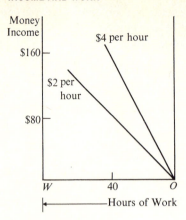

What about the shape of this kind of indifference curve? Observe that those in Figure 22-1 descend fast at first (i.e., on the left), and then flatten out a bit. This means that the utility of an hour of leisure is high when the hours are few, and that when the hours of leisure are many, not much income is sacrificed to get more hours of leisure. The indifference curves would be perfectly flat for someone who wanted no leisure at all. They would be very steep for someone who wanted to loaf as much as possible. Accordingly, variations in the shapes of the indifference curves can be made to describe many patterns of attitudes toward income and leisure.

Differing hourly payments—fees, wage rates, etc.—can be represented in the diagram through the slopes of straight lines, as shown in Figure 22-2. In this figure, OW represents 84 hours. The line marked $2 shows the weekly income attainable by working various numbers of hours at $2 an hour. The line marked $4 shows that twice as much income can be earned with any given number of hours of work. Thus the slopes of these lines reflect the hourly rates of pay.

The Optimum Choice

Now to solve for the optimum. The rational person, who surveys all possibilities and who coldly calculates what is best, wants to be on the highest reachable indifference curve. In Figure 22–3, the line LA represents one hourly wage rate. If this rate prevails, the highest indifference curve is curve *1*, which is tangent to the straight line at point A. Then the person works LM hours a week; by choosing to work any other number of hours, the person would be on a lower indifference curve. Higher wage rates are shown by the slopes of the lines LB and LC. The points B and C are also points of tangency. The line ABC joins points of tangency. Its meaning is that as the wage rate rises, the individual first works more hours and then works fewer. The line ABC need not have the shape exhibited in

FIGURE 22-3   **OPTIMUM COMBINATIONS OF INCOME AND WORK**

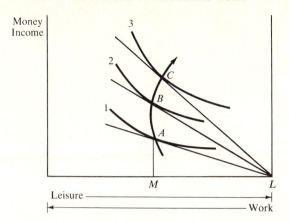

Figure 22-3. The shape can be almost anything, because the shape depends on where the indifference curves touch the straight lines; this in turn depends on the shapes of the indifference curves.

The Back-
ward-Sloping
Supply Curve

The information conveyed by an indifference diagram such as Figure 22-3, can be rearranged and presented in an ordinary price-quantity diagram. This is done in Figure 22-4. Here the curve *CBA* is a supply curve, one that shows the relation between wage rates (price) and the number of hours (quantity) worked at each.[2] A curve like the one in Figure 22-4 is called *backward-sloping*, even though only part of it—the part *BC*—slopes backward, i.e., up and to the left.

The backward-sloping supply curve in Figure 22-4 is derived

FIGURE 22-4   **SUPPLY CURVE OF LABOR FOR A PERSON**

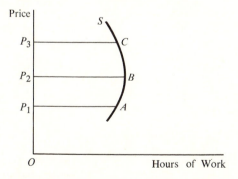

[2] The curve *ABC* in Figure 22-3 and the curve *CBA* in Figure 22-4 face in opposite directions, like two boomerangs with their middles toward each other. The reason for this is that Figure 22-3 measures work from right to left, whereas Figure 22-4 measures work from left to right.

from Figure 22–3, and therefore is the supply curve for an individual. But the same curve can also be made to stand for a group of persons in a labor market, when the supply curves of different persons are added. All that needs to be done is to restate the numbers implied by the horizontal axis.

A curious thing about the backward-sloping supply curve is that it has sometimes been looked upon as an insult to the people whose behavior it describes. People in developing or "precapitalist" economies sometimes are accustomed to a definite plane of living and want no more money than is needed to acquire their customary goods and services. When, therefore, such people begin to work in newly established commercial ("capitalistic") enterprises, they typically work only long enough to earn the money that is enough for them. Then they quit. Accordingly, to get more work out of people who behave this way, their wages must be lowered. But when such people begin to learn about new goods and services and abandon their old customs, they come to take on the "capitalistic" virtues—acquisitiveness, rationality, and insatiability of wants. Then their supply curves take on positive slopes.

As the foregoing indifference curve analysis shows, however, the backward-sloping supply curve can apply to highly sophisticated as well as to simple people. It is only a question of the shapes of indifference curves, i.e., of the importance attached to income and leisure. Backward-sloping supply curves for labor are probably fairly common. When incomes are low, supply curves are positively sloped. But when incomes rise above some level, leisure begins to compete strongly with income; then supply curves alter their slopes to become backward-sloping. The steady drop in length of the average workweek in the last several decades is one indication.[3]

[3] The income and the substitution effects apply also to the income-leisure choice. In Figure 22–3, take the two rate-of-pay lines, LA and LC. The change from LA to LC is an increase in the rate of pay. The total effect of the increase is the movement from point A to point C. The substitution effect can be found in this way: Draw a straight line parallel to line LC and make it tangent to indifference curve 1. The new line signifies an imaginary income tax that keeps the person on the original level of utility. On the right the new line will cut the vertical axis below point L; the (negative) distance between the intersection of the vertical (income) axis and point L is the size of the imaginary tax on weekly income. Because it is steeper than line LA, the new line must be tangent to indifference curve 1 at a point to the left of point A. The difference in hours between point A and the point of tangency is the substitution effect. Here it is always positive, i.e., a higher rate of pay (compensated by an imaginary tax that keeps the person on the original indifference curve) always causes the choice of more hours of work. But the income effect can work both ways—to increase hours or, in swamping the substitution effect, to decrease the number of hours. The income effect in the income-leisure choice is much more important than in the purchase of goods and services, because most people have only one or two kinds of services they can sell to others.

Do income taxes cause people to work less? No plain answer can be given to this complex and much debated question because the answer depends mainly on the shape of the supply curves for labor. If they all have positive slopes, then the income tax does indeed reduce the number of hours of labor people want to work because the tax lowers the price (i.e., income) received. On the other hand, if all supply curves have negative slopes, the effect is the opposite: The income tax causes people to offer *more* labor, not less. But in the present state of knowledge, no one knows how many million persons have the one kind of supply curve and how many million the other. Nor does anyone know how many million persons have curves that first slope up to the right and then slope backward; the effects of the income tax depend on where these persons are on these curves. Then, too, attitudes toward leisure and income change over time, just as do the tastes for consumer goods. The effects of income taxes are therefore further complicated by changes and shifts in the supply curves for labor.

The Aggregate Supply of Labor

The aggregate supply of labor is often identified with the labor force, which is officially defined as the total, in any one week, of all persons, 16 years of age and older, who are self-employed, or employed by others, or are unemployed, or are in the armed forces. Of this total, many millions are independent owners and entrepreneurs. What is the probable shape of the short-run supply curve for the labor force? The supply curve can be visualized as a relation between average real wage and the number of hours of work offered in a year. To express the quantity in hours is to make allowance for part-time and seasonal employment, as well as for those persons who hold more than one job. Economists who have speculated about the short-run supply curve for the labor force have generally concluded that this curve has a negative slope. Figure 22–5 exhibits a supply curve for the labor force in the short run. At an average real

FIGURE 22–5   **SHORT-RUN SUPPLY CURVE FOR LABOR FORCE**

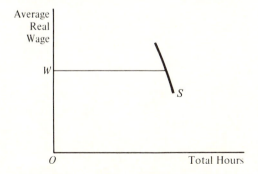

wage above OW, the number of hours offered is smaller than at OW, signifying such responses as earlier retirement, shorter workweeks, longer vacations, longer periods of schooling, etc. The growth of the labor force can be represented by the rightward shift of the supply curve in Figure 22–5.

WAGES IN DIFFERENT OCCUPATIONS

One of the traditional jobs of the theory of wages is to explain persistent differences among the wages paid to different groups. Analysis here can begin with the exercise of just a little imagination, so as to see what conditions would have to hold if all wages were to be exactly equal.

If all wages were to be exactly equal, then: (1) all occupations, industries, and employers would have to be equally attractive; (2) perfect mobility of labor would have to prevail, with no costs of mobility; (3) labor would have to be homogeneous; and (4) pure competition would have to exist everywhere. Each firm in each industry would face the same horizontal supply curve. Differences in demand would not have any effect at all on the level of wages. Demand would, however, determine the numbers of persons employed in each occupation; demand would perform the allocating function.

These conditions will now be examined. By the attractiveness of an occupation is meant its nonmonetary advantages, with advantages having an algebraic meaning, i.e., the net of the occupation's positive and negative attractions. To cut through a maze of sociological considerations, let it be said simply that people have different tastes for occupations, just as they do for consumer goods and services. The supply prices in the more attractive occupations are lower. But the supply prices in all occupations are rising, at least after some point. This means, of course, that to attract more people to any one occupation, the wage rate has to be higher. With rising supply prices, it follows that differences in demand do indeed help to cause differences in wage rates. These differences are usually called *equalizing differences* because such wage differences equalize the attractiveness of all occupations—the money advantage (or disadvantage) offsets the nonmonetary disadvantage (or advantage).

Consider next the mobility of labor. *Mobility* means transfer from one occupation, industry, etc., to another. Although it attracts attention, geographical mobility is only one form, and not everybody has to move when wages change. To act as an equalizer, mobility need only bring about adjustments at the margin. Less than perfect mobility is more pronounced in the short run than in the long. But even in the long run, less than perfect mobility is another cause of differences in wages, a cause operating on the supply side. In the nineteenth century, the English economist J.E. Cairnes (1823–1875) advanced the concept of *noncompeting groups* as part of the explanation of observable differences in wages that continue generation after generation. According to this idea, the whole labor force can be divided into groups such as professional and executive employees, clerical workers, skilled manual workers, unskilled manual workers, etc. Just how such groups should be defined and how they should be classified are complicated matters. Happily, there is no need to go into them here. The point is that mobility is high *within* each group, but low *between* them. Still on the assumption that labor is homogeneous, *intragroup* mobility tends to uniformity of wages within groups, modified only by differences in the attractiveness of occupations. *Intergroup* immobility results in differences of wages between groups.

In a society composed of socioeconomic classes with rigid barriers between them, intergroup wage differences would be permanent and perhaps large. In the United States, the barriers between groups are not rigid, and there is much socioeconomic mobility. Nonetheless, this mobility is so far short of perfect mobility that the thesis of noncompeting groups can still be held to apply. Even though they have been steadily diminishing, unequal educational opportunities continue to be a principal cause of self-perpetuating noncompeting groups.

Next, let the assumption of homogeneity be dropped. Each worker is a unique human being. In any group of workers, there are nearly always differences in efficiency among them. (The *productivity* of a worker is the capability of the person to work in a complex of machinery and equipment. In contrast, *efficiency* is the individual's personal skill, diligence, speed, reliability, etc.) But if this idea is emphasized enough, the labor of every individual worker would have to be regarded as a separate factor of production. If the workers in a group are not of equal efficiency, then the marginal product of labor cannot be defined at all. Because marginal product is the loss of output by removing one worker, the loss would depend on which one is removed. To take account of the uniqueness of each worker means, therefore, that few generalizations are possible. Instead, the way to proceed is to divide large groups into smaller groups and to assume that the persons within the small groups have equal efficiencies as workers. This means more supply curves coupled with more demand curves and therefore still more differences in wages.

Dropping the assumption of pure competition means, among other things, dropping the companion assumption of freedom of entry to occupations. Within any one noncompeting group, freedom of entry to some occupations is barred or limited by, for example, the policies of some labor unions, the licensing requirements of governments, the prejudices of some employers. These and similar barriers alter the shapes of supply curves, making them less elastic; by so doing, the barriers tend to raise wages in some occupations.

Because Chapter 21 surveys the theory of the firm's employment of factors, all that needs to be done here is to draw attention to certain special features of the firm's employment of labor. For all firms under pure competition and for many firms under imperfect competition, wage rates are given and thus beyond the control of the firm. The wage rates are determined by industry demand curves and industry supply curves. To the firm, the various types of labor are available in perfectly elastic supply at the going rates of wages. Imperfections of labor markets can make it possible or necessary, however, for a firm to pay a little less or a little more than prevailing rates of wages.

*Some Features
of the Firm's
Demand for
Labor*

Although the shorthand version of the theory of wages holds that a wage rate depends on the marginal revenue product of labor, it is possible for the line of causation sometimes to run the other way. Marginal revenue product can, under unusual circumstances, depend on the level of wages. Consider Figure 22-6. Suppose initially that the demand for labor is D_1 and that the wage rate is W_1. Then imagine that something happens to cause the wage rate to rise to W_2. The higher wage rate can *cause* the demand curve to shift to D_2. If it does, there need be no decline in employment but, instead, as in Figure 22-6, some gain in employment. Several different combinations of circumstances could produce such a result. Just to indicate: In the short run, the higher wage could result in an improvement in the morale of the workers and, thus, in their productivity. In the long run, a rise in wages from a low level could mean, among other things, better health and physical vigor and, hence, greater productivity.

This feedback effect, from wages to productivity, must be distinguished from the "gospel of high wages," as it was often called in

FIGURE 22-6   **HIGHER WAGE CAN INCREASE DEMAND FOR LABOR**

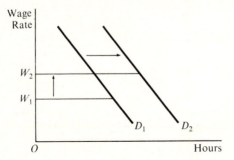

the 1920s. A single employer who pays more than the rates of wages prevailing in a labor market can be more selective in hiring and can choose the more efficient of the workers attracted by the higher wage. Employers also differ in their efficiencies. The more efficient of them can get higher marginal products from workers of superior efficiency. Employers of lesser abilities cannot pay higher wages to superior workers.

The demand for labor by business firms is a derived demand, derived from the consumers' demand for the firms' products. This proposition deserves repetition lest its significance go unnoticed. Differences in product markets can cause substantial differences in wages. At least they can in the short run. In the same city at the same time, the hourly wage rates established in negotiations with the same union for the same kind of labor can differ widely. The hourly wage for a truck driver in one industry can be twice as high as the hourly wage for a truck driver in another industry. Some industries are expanding while others are standing still or contracting. Product demand-cost relations differ at any one time from one industry to another. Differences in wage rates for the same kind of labor in the same market area tend to persist. They are not so much the result of market imperfections as they are of continuing differences in product markets.

One of the points of criticism of the marginal productivity theory of wages has been that employers do not, so it has been argued, adjust the numbers of their employees when wages rise or fall. When such criticism is based on actual observation, the facts that are seen might not be the kind relevant for testing the generalizations of theory. The employers in question are perhaps not ardent profit seekers; they do not have all the information they need for rational decisions. In short, a business firm at any one point of time is by no means necessarily in a position of profit-maximizing equilibrium.

If a business firm fails to adjust employment in face of a rise in wages, its behavior need not, however, be inconsistent with the theory—certainly not in the short run. It is enough to recall the proposition that demand in the short run is always less elastic. A firm's demand for labor in the short run can easily be perfectly inelastic, or nearly so. The short-run demands for the products of firms in imperfect competition are less elastic and can be inelastic. For an oligopolistic firm with a kinked demand curve, the relevant portion of the marginal revenue curve is vertical (page 355). The possibility of substituting capital for labor in the short run is likely to be small and is often zero; office equipment, however, is an example where short-run substitution is relatively easy. If, then, a firm's short-run demand for labor is highly inelastic, a change in wages causes little change in employment.

The Supply of Labor to a Firm	The supply curve of labor to a large firm is usually drawn as a curve rising to the right. A rising curve states that to get more workers, the firm must pay higher wages or that the number of workers potentially available to a firm is an increasing function of wages. It can be argued, however, that a rising curve exists only when the level of unemployment in the market area is exceptionally low. Often, the level of unemployment is such that a firm can expand its work force, without changing its wage rate, simply by hiring more of the people who daily apply for jobs. Over some range, then, the firm's supply curve may well be horizontal rather than rising in the short run.
COLLECTIVE BARGAINING	Collective bargaining between a union and an employer is the leading form of negotiation between one seller and one buyer. The theory of bilateral monopoly is accordingly the theory relevant to collective bargaining. Chapter 19 shows that, despite the intellect lavished on it, the theory of bilateral monopoly does not give a determinate solution. General reasoning based on the profit-maximizing assumption cannot say exactly what price and output will be in transactions between one buyer and one seller. At best, theory can point to a range of outcomes, a range within which bargaining decides the actual outcome.

So, too, with collective bargaining. In practice, of course, the thousands of collective bargaining agreements encompass thousands of details, ranging from seniority rules to grievance procedures to conditions of work, as well as to details of wage scales. Relevant to price theory is the collective bargaining over the general or average level of union wages in a firm or industry. If the demand for a firm's product increases and if, as a result, the curve of marginal revenue product of the firm's labor shifts to the right, the union may then demand an across-the-board wage increase. Given the new demand, what will be the rise, if any, in wages that will be negotiated in collective bargaining? This kind of question cannot be given an exact theoretical answer, even if, let it be noted, all the pertinent information is assumed to be known.

Just as economists have constructed many models of oligopoly, so also have they designed many of collective bargaining. Here, too, no single model or any set of models commands agreement. The problem peculiar to models of collective bargaining is how to set up the hypothesis for the goal of the union. Are unions economic, or political, or politicoeconomic organizations? Do they try to maximize some quantity? Of the many possible hypotheses, three can be mentioned here because they have forms that make it possible to analyze them with the usual methods of price theory. (1) It can be assumed that the union acts in the same way as a business monopoly, that the union is a sales agent for the services of its members. If this were so, the union would try to set an optimum wage which would maximize the income of its members. Because the short-run demand for labor is generally inelastic, it seems likely that the union would strive for a high wage to increase the total income of the members of the union. But if demand is elastic, as it can be—when payroll is a large part of total costs, when capital can be easily substituted, and when product demand is elastic—the rational union has a modest desire for a higher wage level. (2) Another possible kind of behavior is that the union tries to maximize the number of its members. It can be supposed that at each wage rate the union can negotiate, there are so many persons who will belong to and owe allegiance to the union. The higher the wage, the larger the number; thus a special kind of supply curve (a *membership function*) can be imagined. Upon the assumption that the union knows the demand curve for the services of its members, the wage sought is at the intersection of the demand curve and the supply curve as just defined. (3) Still another way of defining the behavior of a union is to imagine it as seeking an optimum combination of wages and employment. Different combinations of wages and employment can be represented through families of indifference curves. To develop this analysis would be to go too far afield here, but some of the results of the analysis can be presented. The analysis can give an exact theoretic basis to the common view about a union's reaction to a change in the demand for an employer's product. If this demand increases and if, therefore, the demand curve for labor shifts to the right, the union will seek a wage increase. The union *could* seek the gains of more employment for its members, but it *prefers* to get a wage increase, accompanied by perhaps only a small amount of additional employment. On the other hand, the union's reaction to a decline in demand is to resist a reduction in wages even if wage cuts would mean laying off fewer workers.

For employers also, systems of indifference curves, or preference functions, can be constructed, showing profit levels related to wages and output. When the indifference curves of a union and of an employer are brought together, a range of bargaining can be defined. But only a range. Theoretical reasoning cannot specify a determinate wage. In some of the models, however, the range within which bargaining takes place is narrow; this result confirms the general opinion about the complementary interests of unions and employers.

MINIMUM WAGES

Does the imposition of a minimum wage rate cause unemployment among the workers for whose benefit the minimum is established? No single valid answer can be given to this question. Much controversy has centered over the applicability of theoretical models to this problem. Economists who have argued that minimum wages do in fact cause unemployment have sometimes drawn conclusions too hastily from the theoretical models. Not that the models are wrong. They might be irrelevant to some problems. In any event, many qualifications must be introduced when models are applied.

Take the simplest case, the imposition of a minimum wage on a competitive industry. If all the firms are in equilibrium, each one equates *VMP* with the wage of the type of labor in question. A higher wage means rising up and to the left on the *VMP* curve; at the new equilibrium, less of the labor is hired. Therefore, some unemployment ensues; its amount depends on how high the wage is raised, the slope of the *VMP* curves, and on the number of workers and firms. Even in this simple case, qualifications have to be brought in. At the time when a minimum wage is introduced, the competitive industry might be expanding in response to a higher price caused by growing demand. If so, the *VMP* curves are shifting to the right. In the same period of time, many of the firms might be improving their methods of production, and this too would shift the *VMP* curves. It is quite possible, therefore, for the imposition of a minimum wage to be accompanied by more, not less, employment. The minimum wage does, however, have the effect of putting a brake on the expansion of employment.

It was shown earlier in this chapter that the short-run demand of firms for labor can be highly inelastic. This, too, means that the short-run effects of a minimum wage are likely to be slight. In the long run in a dynamic economy, innovations shift the demand curves for labor. Still another effect of a minimum wage deserves brief mention. Chapter 21 explains the derivation of a firm's demand curve for a factor of production when more than one factor is variable. Suppose a firm employs two kinds of labor, skilled and unskilled, that the two are substitutable, and that the minimum wage affects only the unskilled workers. If, in consequence, fewer of them are employed, the productivity of the skilled workers increases, i.e., their *VMP* (or *MRP*) curves shift to the right. Hence, more skilled workers are employed. The substitution of more efficient for less efficient workers is, in fact, an often observed effect of minimum wages.

SUMMARY

The *marginal productivity theory of wages* offers an explanation of the relatively constant share of wages in the national income, when it is assumed that the production function for the whole economy has constant returns to scale. With the same assumption, it can be shown with the aid of *Euler's theorem* that the sum of the marginal

products of labor and capital is equal to total product in the equilibrium of pure competition. The marginal productivity theory can be
aligned with the social ethics of private property; the theory conflicts, however, with the principle of distributive justice. Supply
curves for the labor of a person can be derived from indifference
curves for income and leisure. The supply curve for the whole labor
force probably has a negative slope. Persistent differences in wages
are due to the unequal atttractiveness of occupations, to the imperfect mobility of labor, to the nonhomogeneity of labor, and to
imperfect competition. The demand for labor by business firms is
derived from the demands for the firms' products. The short-run
demand for labor is likely to be highly inelastic. Theory cannot state
the wage rate that is the outcome of collective bargaining. Though
they can cause some unemployment, minimum wages do not always
yield this result.

SELECTED REFERENCES

On the share of wages in the national income: Allan M. Cartter,
Theory of Wages and Employment (Irwin, Homewood, 1959),
chap. 11.

On the levels of wages: J. R. Hicks, *The Theory of Wages*, 2d ed.
(Macmillan, London, 1963), part I; John T. Dunlop, ed. *The Theory
of Wage Determination* (Macmillan, London, 1957), parts I and IV;
K.W. Rothschild, *The Theory of Wages* (Macmillan, New York,
1954), parts 1 and 2.

On wages and the firm: Allan M. Cartter, cited above, chaps. 4
and 5.

On the theory of collective bargaining: Allan M. Cartter, cited
above, chaps. 7, 8, and 9; John T. Dunlop, ed., cited above, parts
III and V.

On how schooling affects earnings: Paul Taubman, *Higher Education and Earnings: College as an Investment and a Screening
Device* (McGraw-Hill, New York, 1974).

On the supply of labor and related topics: Glen C. Cain and
Harold W. Watts, eds., *Income Maintenance and Labor Supply*
(Markham Press, Chicago, 1973).

EXERCISES AND PROBLEMS

1. Draw diagrams to show how a union can raise the wage level in
an industry by influencing the supply of labor.
2. Show how a union can increase wages by influencing the demand for labor—by encouraging employers to increase the degree of

mechanization (for example, the bituminous coal industry in the postwar period).

3. Why are men often paid more than women for doing the same kind of work?

4. Why are wages low in some of the most disagreeable of occupations?

5. Suppose that a high (e.g., $3.00 an hour) minimum wage were imposed on *all* employers. Trace the short-run and long-run effects on (a) employment, (b) capital-labor ratios, and (c) the composition of output of consumer goods and services.

6. Why do economists think of leisure as a good? How does the substitution effect influence the amount of leisure of a person?

7. Explain the possibility that during one's working life there might first be an income effect, then a substitution effect, and then again an income effect.

8. Speculate on the success and then the effects on wages and employment of unions representing: (a) highly skilled technicians, (b) elementary school teachers, (c) state government employees, and (d) semiskilled laborers.

9. Why are most athletes and rock stars paid more than university professors?

10. Can a change in technology, making capital more efficient or cheaper, affect the marginal product of labor?

11. The professions of law and medicine are generally held in high esteem by the American public. How do you explain income differentials within each profession and between the two professions? What role does mobility play? And what of the roles of the American Bar Association and of the American Medical Association?

12. Can you explain why laws requiring equal pay for men and women doing the same work can enhance the wage received by a few women, but at the same time can result in unemployment for many other women?

13. Are there any similarities between a supply curve for labor and a supply curve for a commodity? Between a demand curve for labor and a demand curve for a consumer good?

14. See if you can explain the following relationships: (a) increases in fuel prices and changes in farm wages, (b) government price support programs and changes in farm wages, and (c) faculty salaries and grade inflation.

15. Explain why some economists urge that minimum wage legislation not be applied to the teenage labor market.

Appendix

TO PART 6

MATHEMATICAL NOTE

Note 3 in the Appendix to Part 2 gives the Cobb-Douglas production function as follows

$$Q = kL^\alpha C^{(1-\alpha)}, \ 0 < \alpha < 1 \text{ and } k > 0,$$

where Q is aggregate output, k is a factor of proportionality (a constant), L is the quantity of labor, and C is the quantity of capital. The text on page 398 states that the ratio of the incomes of labor and capital is constant. It is shown below that this constant is $\alpha/(1 - \alpha)$. Recall that the ratio of the prices of labor and of capital is equal to the ratio of their marginal products.

In the Cobb-Douglas production function, the marginal product of labor is given by

$$\frac{\partial Q}{\partial L} = \alpha k L^{\alpha-1} C^{1-\alpha} = \alpha \frac{Q}{L}.$$

Similarly, the marginal product of capital is

$$\frac{\partial Q}{\partial C} = (1 - \alpha)kL^\alpha C^{-\alpha} = (1 - \alpha)\frac{Q}{C}.$$

Let the price of labor be P_L and the price of capital be P_C. Then

$$\frac{\dfrac{\partial Q}{\partial L}}{\dfrac{\partial Q}{\partial C}} = \frac{P_L}{P_C} = \frac{\alpha \dfrac{Q}{L}}{(1 - \alpha)\dfrac{Q}{C}} = \frac{C\alpha}{L(1 - \alpha)}.$$

The income earned by labor is $P_L L$, i.e., the price of labor multiplied by the number (L) employed. Similarly, the income of capital is $P_C C$. Therefore,

$$\frac{P_L L}{P_C C} = \frac{\alpha}{1 - \alpha}, \text{ a constant.}$$

Thus labor receives α of total output Q, and capital receives $(1 - \alpha) Q$.

7
ECONOMIC
EFFICIENCY

23

GENERAL EQUILIBRIUM AND ECONOMIC WELFARE

APPENDIX TO PART 7 MATHEMATICAL NOTE

23

GENERAL

Equilibrium

AND ECONOMIC

Welfare

So far, prices have been studied one at a time, each in isolation. The price of any one commodity is of course influenced by the prices of other commodities. Other prices have been let into analysis only to help fix the shapes and positions of demand and supply curves. Once being admitted, other prices have been held constant by assumption and could then be ignored. Besides, attention has been paid only to the prices of commodities closely related to the commodity under analysis. Such is the method of partial equilibrium theory, the method long followed by American and British theorists. Partial equilibrium theory is simple; it also has the great advantage of giving results applicable to a great range of uses. Partial equilibrium theory is applied in industry studies, in analyses of foreign trade and the taxation of individual commodities, and in investigations of price-support programs for farm products.

But prices are in fact interdependent. The demands, supplies, and prices of commodities are interconnected—through the substitutions that households make in their budgets and in their sales of productive services; prices are connected also through the substitutions that firms make in their purchases of inputs and in their sales of outputs. When turning attention to the behavior of the entire system of prices, the theorist uses the method of general equilibrium theory. Although this method is nearly a century old, it was cultivated for many decades solely by a small number of theorists on the continent of Europe. Only since just before World War II have American and British economists become interested in general equilibrium theory.

THE THEORY OF GENERAL EQUILIBRIUM

The French economist Léon Walras (1834–1910) was the first to design a model of the general equilibrium of a purely competitive economy. Others have constructed refinements of Walras's model,

418

but no radical modifications have been made. Walras's general equilibrium model is simple, that is to say, the economic ideas that are its building blocks are simple; modern versions of them have been presented earlier in this book. But the building blocks are put together mathematically. To a mathematician, Walras's mathematics are not complex. But full and easy understanding of the mathematics of the general equilibrium of prices is denied to many students of economics. It is indeed quite possible to simplify the mathematics too; see Note 1 in the Appendix to Part 7. The references at the end of this chapter show where other simple versions can be found. The description of Walras's model now to follow is literary—a word used with scorn by the Italian economist Vilfredo Pareto (1848-1923), who also contributed to the mathematics of general equilibrium theory. The mathematics gives a vision of the interdependence of prices that is clear, precise in detail, complete, and self-checking in its logical consistency. Though the view opened by a literary exposition is a little cloudy, it is better than none at all.

Walras's model has households and firms in a self-contained economy. Pure competition prevails in all markets whose prices connect the actions of all households and firms. The firms sell commodities to the households which, in turn, sell resources, or factors of production (i.e., labor, the services of land and of equipment), to the firms. There is no unemployment of labor or of other resources.

Households

The tastes of the households, or consumers, are assumed to be constant. Stability of tastes means that the indifference maps of the consumers are stable. Each household buys quantities of each commodity in accordance with tastes, income, the price of the commodity, and the prices of *all* other commodities. This last point is the special emphasis of general equilibrium theory. In buying any one commodity, a household assesses *all* commodity prices. A change in any one of them affects the entire budget, causing the household to reappraise and to rearrange it. For example, a rise in the price of shoes causes a change in a household's demand for butter. This is clear enough because the household buys both shoes and butter. But the higher price of shoes is traceable to changes in the prices of other commodities, those the household does not buy. In this sense, then, a household's demand for any one commodity depends on the prices of all commodities. Of course, many of the repercussions from the other prices are exceedingly small.

The households in Walras's model spend their entire incomes on consumption. Their incomes are derived from the sale of their resources, which also have prices. Thus each household's budget is also determined by the prices of resources. Any one household sells one or two resources, perhaps several of them. A change in the price of one resource causes a change in the price of another, because households can make substitutions in their capacities as sellers, just as they can in their capacities as buyers. Thus the prices of resources are connected in a network.

The demands of households for commodities depend, accordingly, on two networks of prices. One is the network of the prices of commodities; the other is the network of the prices of resources. The two price networks are connected through the actions of the households.

The market, or total, demand for each commodity is the sum of the demands of the households. The market demands, of course, also depend on the same two networks of prices.

Firms

The commodities produced by the firms sell at prices equal to full costs of production, because pure competition exists everywhere and because the context is the full adjustment of the long run. Unit costs are constant in the simple Walrasian model. Thus average costs and marginal costs are equal and constant. Because this also means constant returns to scale, the price of each commodity is the sum of its cost components. They are the amounts of each resource needed to make a unit of the commodity multiplied by the prices of the resources. Thus if a suit of clothes requires 10 minutes of one kind of labor at $3 an hour, 15 minutes of another kind at $4 an hour, etc., the price of a suit of clothes is equal to 50¢ plus $1, plus etc. In this example, the 10 minutes of one kind of labor and the 15 minutes of another kind are called *coefficients of production*. In the simple model, they are assumed to be fixed.

As suppliers, the firms govern their actions by the prices in the network of commodity prices. As buyers of resources, the firms govern their actions by the prices in the network of resource prices, which along with the coefficients of production determine the costs of the firms. The two networks are therefore also connected by the actions of the firms.

Equalities of Demands and Supplies

There being no unemployment in the model, the demand for each *resource* must equal its supply. The demand comes from the firms, supply from the households. The network of resource prices is a set of prices making each demand equal to each supply, and making all of them compatible with one another. Each resource market is in equilibrium; all together are in a general equilibrium.

The demand for each *commodity* equals its supply. The demand comes from the households, supply from the firms. The network of commodity prices establishes an equilibrium in each market and the compatibilities of the equilibria in all commodity markets.

Because the two networks of prices are doubly interconnected, the equilibria in the resource markets and in the commodity markets are joined in one grand general equilibrium.

In the general equilibrium of all prices, demands equal supplies, and all households and firms are in equilibrium. For each household, the ratio of the prices of any two commodities equals their marginal rates of substitution (Chapter 6). For each household, the marginal rate of substitution between income and leisure is equal to the price ratio between income and work (Chapter 22). For each firm, the marginal cost of each commodity equals its price (Chapters 10 and 14). For each firm, costs are at a minimum (Chapters 10 and 14).

The essence of general equilibrium is that the tastes of the households and the technologies available to the firms mutually determine the quantities of the commodities produced.

How do all the equalities of demands and supplies come about? Walras himself described the reaching of general equilibrium as a process of *groping*. Imagine that the price of commodity *A* is out of equilibrium, that the price is below the equilibrium level in the market for *A*. Then the excess of demand at that price forces the price of *A* up. But—and here is the emphasis of general equilibrium theory—the rise in the price of *A* causes an expansion of the demands for *B*, for *C*, etc. Besides, the rise in the price of *A* causes a decline in the supplies of a whole group of other commodities. Therefore, other prices change too, and these changes reflect back on the demand for *A* and the supply of *A*. During the process of groping, the price of *A* may fall for a while. But in the end, it dances its way up to its own equilibrium, one that is consistent with those in all other markets. The simplifying assumptions in the model, and above all, Walras's mathematics, ensure this result. True enough, many of the changes in other demands, supplies, and prices that are caused by a change in the price of *A* are exceedingly small. They are so small that for some purposes they can be ignored, just as partial equilibrium theory ignores them. The comprehensive mathematical equations do not, however, ignore small changes; they embrace the small and the large, tracing and relating all effects to the end.

Limitations of the Model

Any model has its limitations. The simplified Walrasian model described here has several, even as a model of an economy with pure competition in all markets. The model is static—it operates with the assumptions of fixed tastes and coefficients of production, and allows for no processes of change over time. The households and the firms in the model are busy enough, but they everlastingly consume and produce exactly the same things, in exactly the same way, and in exactly the same proportions. There are no leads and lags in the relations between production and consumption, between demand, supply, and price. Everything happens instantaneously, as in electric circuits. But the efforts of theorists to construct good models of dynamic systems of relative prices have not yet been successful. Hicks and others have gone a little beyond Walras because they have investigated the *stability* conditions of the general equilibrium of prices.[1] They have developed the theory of what happens when changes occur in interlinked demands, supplies, and prices.

The simple model has other but less serious limitations. The assumption of fixed production coefficients can be removed, and, in much more intricate models, replaced with an assumption of variable coefficients. More complicated models can also be constructed to contain increasing and decreasing returns to scale, money and securities, and even certain forms of imperfect competition.

Uses of General Equilibrium Theory

Despite their limitations, despite their air of unreality, models— even the simplest—of the general equilibrium of prices have important uses.

Such models advance the understanding of a private enterprise economy. Most of the praise and the blame strewn on private enterprise consists of repetition of phrases so worn as to retain little meaning. Those who praise private enterprise point to its efficiency, to the tendency for costs of production to be low, to the responsiveness of production to the wants of consumers. Those who have found serious fault with private enterprise include socialists and communists; they have long argued that private enterprise means production for profit, not for use, and that a private enterprise economy is a chaotic and unplanned system.

The simple general equilibrium model is a model of a private enterprise system at rest, all of the consumers and producers having made their best adjustments. The model shows indeed that production is both efficient and responsive, and that the satisfaction of consumers' wants is maximized. In the domain of the discussion of economic and social philosophies and systems, the general equilibrium model is the strongest of the serious arguments for private enterprise and against collectivism. But remember, maximum satisfaction means no more than the maximum attainable under the circumstances, whatever they might be. The economy might be poor, with meager resources, a primitive technology, and an ill-trained labor force. But with free markets and the eager pursuit of self-interest, the poor economy would still approach the maximum satisfaction of its consumers that is consistent with its limited resources.

Some admirers of private enterprise might not like the fate of

[1] The stability of competitive partial equilibria is discussed in Chapter 13.

business people in the model. The entrepreneurs in Walras's model are drones. They control no prices; they exert no power over other persons; they fulfill no social responsibilities. In their efforts to maximize profits, they are able to earn no more than the normal profits included in their full costs. They are compelled by the system of prices to be efficient, to produce at the lowest attainable costs. In fact, if their singular function is to be innovators and risk takers, entrepreneurs do not exist at all in Walras's model. Neither do labor leaders.

General equilibrium theory has furnished the conceptual foundation for *input-output analysis* which was created by Wassily Leontief of Harvard University. Input-output analysis is the statistical measurement of the inputs and the outputs of all industries taken together in an interdependent system of commodity flows. Input-output has been developed far, lending itself well to planning for mobilization and to planning for the economic development of countries and regions.

ECONOMIC WELFARE

In modern economic literature the expression *economic welfare* usually refers to a combination of two criteria. They are efficiency and equity; terminology here, however, is not hard and fast, because economic welfare often signifies efficiency alone. When efficiency is optimum, as in the general equilibrium of competitive prices, no resources are wasted or put to less than their best possible uses; there cannot be more production of one good without less production of another; and one household cannot consume more unless another consumes less. In this context, equity means the distribution of personal income. And what is an optimum or ideal distribution of income? Most economists take the position that this question cannot be answered with economic analysis, and that all judgments about equity are necessarily ethical and political value judgments. Nonetheless, there is a way to bring equity into economic analysis; this way will be demonstrated shortly.

A TWO-SECTOR MODEL

To probe more deeply into economic efficiency and economic welfare, a model of a *two-sector economy* will now be presented.[2] Though this economy has only two dimensions, instead of thousands, its logic is both exact and general.

The two-sector model of economic welfare has two persons, two commodities, and two inputs, or factors of production, in a simple, self-contained economy. The problems to be solved in the model include the requirements for *efficiency in exchange*, for *efficiency in*

---

[2] The discussion to follow, as well as some of the terminology, is adapted from the first part of the well-known article by Francis M. Bator, "The Simple Analytics of Welfare Maximization," *American Economic Review*, 47 (March 1957), 22–59.

production, and for joint *efficiency in both exchange and production*. To be solved also is the problem of the quantities of the two goods that provide for the maximum of economic welfare that combines efficiency and equity.

The two persons in the model are *A* and *B*. The two commodities are food and clothing; let it be assumed that units of food and clothing are both meaningful and homogeneous. The inputs are labor and machines, the total amount of each being a fixed quantity. The labor is furnished by *A* and *B*. The units of labor, in hours, are also assumed to be homogeneous. So are all machine-hours. *A* owns some of the machines, *B* the rest of them.

The analysis to follow draws upon the indifference curves of Chapter 6, the isoquants of Chapters 9 and 10, and the production possibility curve of Chapter 10. Few new concepts need to be developed here. But there will be one new and important graphic device. This is the *Edgeworth box diagram*, named after its inventor, the Oxford economist F. Y. Edgeworth (1845–1926).

*Efficiency
in Exchange*

The first problem is to define *efficiency in exchange*, that is, the optimum distributions (notice the plural) of two commodities between two persons. Assume that the two persons engage in barter transactions in the absence of money and prices. The problem is old and important. Is trade or exchange always mutually advantageous?

Figure 23-1 is the first Edgeworth box diagram. At the southwest corner is *A*'s origin. Units of food for *A* are on the horizontal axis, and are measured from left to right. Units of clothing for *A* are on the vertical axis, and are measured from bottom to top. The preferences of *A* for food and clothing are shown by the convex indifference

FIGURE 23-1   **EXCHANGE CONTRACT CURVE**

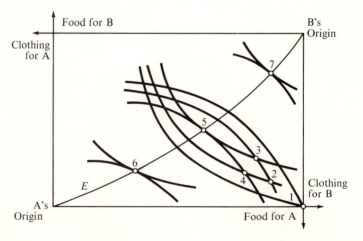

curves, five of them being shown in the diagram. Any move northeast puts *A* on a higher level of utility.

For *B*, everything is turned around 180 degrees. *B*'s origin is at the northeast corner. Increasing quantities of food are measured from right to left, and increasing quantities of clothing are measured from top to bottom. Notice the arrowheads in the diagram. The indifference curves for *B* are convex to *B*'s origin; thus they appear as concave to *A*'s origin. Any move southwest puts *B* on a higher level of utility.

The dimensions, i.e., the height and the width, of the Edgeworth box in Figure 23-1 are certain arbitrary quantities of food and clothing. Assume, to begin with, that *A* has as many units of food as the width of the box and that *B* as many units of clothing as the height of the box. Any point in the box represents the result of an exchange of food and clothing between *A* and *B*. The midpoint of the box would signify equal amounts of food and clothing for each of the two persons.

Both *A* and *B*, then, begin at point *1* in Figure 23-1. Point *1* is on one of *A*'s indifference curves and also on one of *B*'s. The two persons can exchange units of food and clothing, with the aim of making themselves better off, i.e., of getting onto higher indifference curves.

What agreement will they come to, what will be the outcome of their bargaining? In general, it is not possible to say, because, for one thing, much depends on the bargaining skills that the two persons possess. Even so, however, several statements can be made about the properties of the agreements that *A* and *B* could come to.

Imagine that *A* and *B* make offers and counteroffers before they come to a final agreement. Suppose that one of them makes an offer that is equivalent to point *2* in the figure. This would mean that *A* would give up some food and would acquire some clothing and *B* of course would get some food by giving up some clothing. Both *A* and *B* would be better off at point *2* than at point *1*, because each one of them is on a higher indifference curve. Each would gain from this exchange, each would have more utility.

Consider next an offer that would put *A* and *B* at point *5*. Because point *5* lies on indifference curves for both *A* and *B* that are higher still, point *5* means still more utility for both than point *2*. Exchange, or trading, can therefore be mutually advantageous.

Exchange also, however, can take place in such a way that only one of the parties benefits. Suppose that after *A* makes an offer that leads from point *1* to point *2*, *B* counters with an offer that would put them at point *4*. Here, *B* is on a higher indifference curve than at point *2*. But *A* is not. In fact, *A* is on the same indifference curve at both points *4* and *2*. But we can say that point *4* is an improvement over point *2*—*B* is better off and *A* is no worse off. Similarly, point *3* is an improvement over point *2*—*A* is better off, *B* is no worse off.

By the same reasoning, point *5* is an improvement over points *3* and *4*. Notice that at point *5*, one of *A*'s indifference curves is tangent to one of *B*'s. Point *5* is on the curve *E*, which connects all of the points of tangency of all of *A*'s and *B*'s indifference curves. The curve *E* is called *the contract curve,* or better still, *the exchange contract curve*. The slope of an indifference curve is the marginal rate of substitution (*MRS*), or trade-off rate, between the two commodities. The slopes of *A*'s and *B*'s curves are equal at their points of tangency. The exchange contract curve therefore is a locus of equal *MRS*. And since the contract curve is not a straight line, the *MRS* vary all the way along it.

The special meaning of the contract curve is that, if the parties reach a point on it, they can no longer make offers of other trades that would either benefit both or would benefit one and not hurt the other. To repeat, the movement from *1* to *2* benefits both *A* and *B*; so does the movement from *2* to *5*; and so of course do many other possible movements. And then there is the other kind of movement, such as from *4* to *5*, that puts one person on a higher indifference curve and continues the other person on the same curve. But once they arrive on the contract curve, improvement can no longer take place. Any moment *off* the contract curve would be worse for one or both. Any movement *along* the contract curve would benefit one and be worse for the other.

Any movement along the contract curve is a gain of utility to one person and a loss to the other. Any movement northeast is a gain for *A* and a loss for *B*. But since the subjective utilities of *A* and *B* cannot be compared, there is no means of measuring the sizes of the gains and losses.

Another way to think of the exchange contract curve is to imagine a third person who has the power to decide how much of the available stock of food and clothing should be distributed between *A* and *B*. The third person would pick a point on the curve; any point on the curve is efficient, or "Pareto-optimal." The meaning of efficiency, of Pareto-optimality, is that one person cannot be made better off without making another person worse off. The third person really has to make two decisions. One is to find all of the efficient distributions and the other is to select from among the plenitude of efficient distributions the one that person—the third person—regards as the most equitable.

Here, then, are the two essentials of economic welfare, efficiency and equity, that can be seen on the exchange contract curve.

Any point inside the box diagram is a combination of units of food

FIGURE 23-2

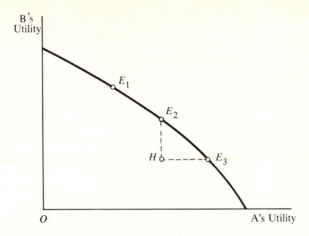

and clothing. The space inside the box can therefore be called *commodity space*. Points on the exchange contract curve show more or less utility for *A* or *B*. Let us now move from commodity space to *utility space*. This movement is made from Figure 23-1 to Figure 23-2.

In Figure 23-2, the horizontal axis is *A*'s utility, and the vertical axis is *B*'s. The curve in the figure is a *utility frontier*; it corresponds in utility space to the contract curve in commodity space. A move over to the right along the contract curve means more utility for *A* and less for *B*. So then, isolate this idea, forget about the food and clothing for the time being, and concentrate on the utilities of *A* and *B*. Such is the meaning of the utility frontier in Figure 23-2.

It has already been said that the utilities of *A* and *B* are not commensurable. The axes represent rankings of utilities rather than quantities. The points E_1, E_2, and E_3 correspond to points 6, 5, and 7 in Figure 23-1. Point *H* in Figure 23-2 is inside the utility frontier. A movement from *H* to E_2 is similar to the movement from point 3 to point 5 in Figure 23-1. *B* gains in utility and *A* does not lose. Thus all points on the utility frontier are efficient.

Efficiency in Production

The rule for *efficiency in production* is symmetrical with that for efficiency in consumption. If production is to be efficient, producers who use the same two inputs must have equal marginal rates of technical substitution (*MRTS*) between the inputs.

Figure 23-3 illustrates efficiency in production. The figure is another Edgeworth box diagram, but this one has two producers and their isoquant curves. The two producers employ two homogeneous inputs, which are labor measured in labor-hours per week and capital measured in machine-hours per week. Labor is on the horizontal

FIGURE 23-3   **PRODUCTION CONTRACT CURVE**

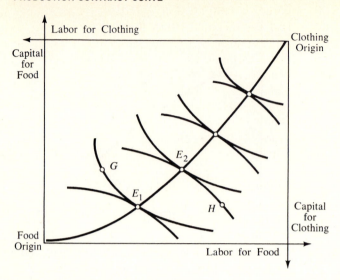

axis and capital is on the vertical axis. Thus any point in this diagram is a point in *input space*. The two dimensions of the box signify that there are fixed quantities of labor and capital available to the two producers.

One of them produces food and the other produces clothing. For both food and clothing, there are given technologies, whose properties are shown by production isoquants. The food producer has the isoquants convex to the origin at the southwest corner. The clothing producer's isoquants are convex to the origin at the northeast corner. Only four isoquants for each producer are shown, but they will suffice.

The labor and the capital can be employed to produce both food and clothing. Imagine that quantities of labor and of capital can be easily and quickly shifted from food production to clothing production and vice versa. Imagine too that the labor and the capital are not equally suited to the making of both food and clothing. Suppose that labor is more important in producing food than in making clothing; then if food production is expanded, relatively more labor, in proportion to capital, has to be employed.

The problem is to allocate labor and capital to food and clothing. In the two-sector model the task is to see just what is the pattern of efficient allocations. More generally, the process of allocation can be imagined in different ways. A firm producing both food and clothing would want to make efficient allocations of labor and capital. In a competitive market system, the prices of food and clothing, and of labor and capital, would determine one efficient allocation.

Consider point G. This point is down toward the southwest corner, signifying that the food producer is using much less labor and capital than the clothing producer. In other words, point G represents some definite allocation of labor and capital in the production of food and clothing. This allocation is inefficient, because a change from G to E_1 would keep food production at the same level and would increase clothing production. The shift from point G to point E_1 means that less capital and more labor are used in food production, and that more capital and less labor are employed in the production of clothing. It can be seen, too, that H is another inefficient point; a reallocation from H to E_2 would maintain clothing production at a constant level, and would increase food production.

Points E_1 and all other points on the *production contract curve* are efficient points. Any movement, i.e., reallocation *along* the curve signifies more food and less clothing or the opposite. Any movement *toward* the curve signifies more food or more clothing or more of both. The production contract curve passes through points such as E_1 and E_2. At these points, the isoquants of the two producers are tangent. This being so, the marginal rates of technical substitution are equal and therefore the ratios of the marginal products of labor and capital are equal. (This relation was explained earlier on pages 166 and 167.)

Efficient allocation of inputs, then, requires that a point on the production contract curve be attained. Just where cannot be determined until more information is brought into the analysis. In a competitive economy, the equilibrium prices for labor and capital determine the optimum point on the production contract curve. The ratio of these prices gives the slope of an isocost line, which must be tangent to each of a pair of isoquants that are tangent to each other.

The next step is to transfer the information given by the production contract curve to a *production possibility curve*. From point E_1 to E_2 in Figure 23-3, food output increases and clothing output declines. Any other points on the curve show other quantities of food and clothing that can be produced efficiently. Figure 23-4 has a production possibility curve, or *frontier*. The change from Figure 23-3 to Figure 23-4 is from *input space* to *commodity space*. The axes of Figure 23-4 are food and clothing.

The production possibility frontier displays the maximum quantities—from efficient combinations of output—that can be produced with the resources available. All points on the curve are efficient. Points inside the frontier represent possible combinations of food and clothing; but inside points are inefficient, because production of one good can be increased without sacrifice of the other. This is illustrated in Figure 23-4 by the movement from G to E_1 and from H to E_2. Points outside the frontier are unattainable.

FIGURE 23-4

PRODUCTION POSSIBILITY FRONTIER

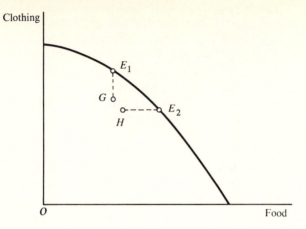

The slope of the production possibility curve is negative, which means more food, less clothing, and vice versa. The slope of the curve at any point is the trade-off between food and clothing, or the *rate of product transformation* (*RPT*). The curve is concave to the origin, which means that if food output is increased by constant increments, the sacrifices of clothing output become larger and larger. The increasing sacrifice, or trade-off, of clothing for food means increasing marginal costs. Another unit of food can be had only at an increasing cost of units of clothing given up.

Each of the efficiently produced combinations of units of food and clothing can be divided between *A* and *B* in many ways. Efficient distribution of the two commodities between them means that they must be on their exchange contract curve.

The Grand Utility Frontier

The utility frontier in Figure 23–2 corresponds with the exchange contract curve of Figure 23–1, which was for some arbitrary quantities of food and clothing. But now we have the production possibility frontier. *Each point* on it is an efficient combination of food and clothing. For *each efficient combination* a box diagram could be drawn; *each box* has its contract curve; and to *each contract curve* there corresponds a utility frontier. Imagine now many curves showing utility frontiers. They will be pretty much alike, though not identical. The next step is to construct a *grand utility frontier*. This curve in utility space traces the farthest (farthest east and north) points on the many utility frontier curves. The curve of the grand utility frontier is an envelope of the other curves, just as the long-run cost curve of the firm is an envelope of many short-run cost curves.

The curve in Figure 23–5 is smooth and continuous. Such a curve is often drawn with waves in it. Hardly anything in fact can be said about its shape because the only assertion the curve can contain is

FIGURE 23-5

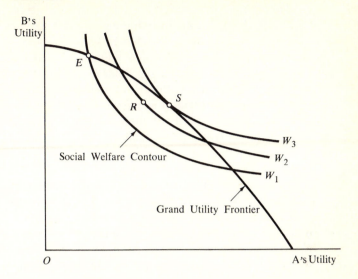

that, if you take utility away from either *A* or *B* and give it to the other, one gains and the other loses. And remember, the utilities of *A* and *B* (U_A and U_B) are not comparable.

The grand utility curve is related to the production possibility frontier and the exchange contract curve in this way: The grand utility curve shows the utilities associated with every conceivable combination of efficiencies in *both* production and exchange. Each point on the curve states the maximum of U_A for any given level of U_B and vice versa.

The Social Welfare Function

Where is the optimum? The grand utility curve has an infinite number of points, all of them efficient in both production and in commodity distribution. The way to find the one optimum point is to bring in, from outside the domain of pure economics, a *social welfare function*, which can be written

$$W = W(U_A, U_B).$$

That is to say, social welfare is a function of the levels of utility of *A* and *B*, or more generally, of all persons in a society. The social welfare function can be thought of as a set of agreed-upon ethical value judgments, or as a vision of national well-being, or even as the aims of a dictator, or as the result of firm tradition in social policy. If Robinson Crusoe makes decisions for himself and imposes decisions on his man Friday, he is employing a social welfare function for his society of two persons.

Figure 23–5 has three curves, W_1, W_2 and W_3, from the family of curves that can represent the social welfare function. The curves have the same properties as the indifference curves of consumers. The solution at point S has the name *constrained bliss*, the constraints being the given technology and the fixed quantities of inputs. The solution combines judgments on equity (as between A and B) and the efficiency criterion. To illustrate: Take a point R between E and S on welfare curve W_2. Point R is below the utility curve, and is therefore inefficient. But in contrast to the efficient point E, point R has a higher content of social welfare, because it lies on a higher W curve. In plain words, though point E is efficient, whoever or whatever promulgates the social welfare function decides that other efficient points, and even some inefficient ones, are better.

Consider next the properties of the solution at the point of constrained bliss. The solution settles the question of the deservingness of A and B. More for one and less for the other would result in lower social welfare. Anyway, the bliss point corresponds to a point on the production possibility curve. This point establishes the quantities of food and clothing. The slope of the curve at this point is the rate of product transformation (RPT), the trade-off between the outputs. This rate must equal the marginal rates of substitution (MRS) for both A and B. Why? Suppose the rates differ, that RPT is two to one, and that MRS is one to one. Then you could reduce food output by one unit and get two units of clothing. Leaving A alone, you could take one unit of food from B and replace it with a unit of clothing. But then you have a unit of clothing left over. This you could give to either A or B, increasing utility. Therefore inequality between RPT and MRS means inefficiency.

With, then, $RPT = MRS$, there is some particular MRS corresponding to the grand solution. Therefore there is some one optimum point on the exchange contract curve. This point decides the distribution of food and clothing between A and B.

Similarly, the optimum point on the production possibility curve corresponds to a point on the production contract curve, a point determining the quantities of labor and capital used in producing food and clothing.

So far, eight quantities of the constrained bliss solution have been determined. They are food and clothing for A and for B, and labor and capital in food and clothing. Four more variables can be determined. They are P_F and P_C, the prices of food and clothing, and w and r, the wage of labor and the rental value of machinery.

The first eight variables can be determined graphically, i.e., from the slopes of points on the contract curves, which are the solution ratios for MRS and $MRTS$. The last four variables are found algebraically.[3]

[3] Cf. C. E. Ferguson, *Microeconomic Theory*, Irwin, Homewood, 1966, pp. 389–390.

$$(23\text{-}1) \quad MRS = \frac{P_F}{P_C}, \text{ or } P_F = P_C(MRS), \text{ and}$$

$$(23\text{-}2) \quad MRTS = \frac{w}{r}, \text{ or } w = r(MRTS).$$

Chapter 10 also shows that the competitive equilibrium price of an input equals the value of its marginal product. Let MP_{KF} be the symbol for the marginal product of capital in producing food, with other symbols accordingly. Then $P_F MP_{KF}$ is the value of the marginal product of capital in producing food. Thus

$$(23\text{-}3) \quad r = P_F(MP_{KF}) = P_C(MP_{KC}), \text{ and}$$
$$(23\text{-}4) \quad w = P_F(MP_{LF}) = P_c(MP_{LC}).$$

The next step is to take Equation (23-3) and to substitute in it the value of P_F from Equation (23-1). This gives

$$(23\text{-}5) \quad r = P_C(MRS)(MP_{KF}).$$

Then if Equation (23-2) is substituted in Equation (23-5) the result is

$$(23\text{-}6) \quad w = P_C(MRS)(MP_{KF})(MRTS).$$

The values of the three expressions in parentheses in Equation (23-6) come from the geometry of the constrained bliss solution. To get values for P_F, P_C, r, and w only one more thing needs to be done and that is to select one of the commodities as the unit of account, or standard of value. Walras's expression is still used—the *numéraire*. Let this be food. Then the price of food can be set equal to unity. $P_F = 1$. Then the numerical values of P_C, r, and w can be found by solving the equations.

In the two-person, two-good, two-input model it is not really necessary to solve for the two prices and for the wage and rental rates. The ratios furnish all of the information needed for the solution. But the prices and the ratios contain the essentials of a general equilibrium. Except for the fixed (by assumption) quantities of labor and capital, all of the variables are sensitive to changes in one another; they are interdependent. Suppose there is a change in the technology of food production. This alters the food isoquants, bringing about new points of tangency with the clothing isoquants. A new production contract curve yields a new production possibility frontier, which in turn yields a new grand utility frontier. The constrained bliss solution is therefore different. So are the quantities, the ratios, and the prices.

Suppose there were no social welfare function. What then? Then the market solution with the four prices would be the solution, which would be at some point on the grand utility frontier. The critical values would be w and r. Imagine that the productivity of a machine-hour is much higher than that of a labor-hour and that A owns many more machines than B. Then r would be much higher than w and A would have a higher income than B. The point of the social welfare function is that "society" would put a tax on A and with the proceeds give a subsidy to B. The result would be a different pattern of prices and quantities and a solution at a different point on the grand utility frontier.

**EFFICIENCY IN
THE GENERAL
EQUILIBRIUM OF
COMPETITIVE
PRICES**

The rules, or necessary conditions for economic efficiency are quite general, being applicable in any kind of economy—Robinson Crusoe's, socialist, or capitalist, or any other type. The rules are thus independent of particular economic institutions and ways of organizing economic activity. Linear programming versions of the rules, together with the capabilities of modern computers, open the possibility of actually using the rules to improve efficiency in the conduct of the affairs of government and, in socialist countries, to conduct various types of economic planning. The computers would have to be programmed with whatever data would be available, they would have to handle thousands of equations, and they would have to print out millions of numbers; but in principle it can be done, so some economists believe.

The prices and patterns of resource allocation in a competitive capitalist economy behave as if they had been generated by a properly programmed computer, as if some brain were seeing to it that the rules of efficiency are being followed. But of course no one brain directs a competitive economy. That economy is directed by the free choices of millions of persons who seek to maximize utilities and profits. The theory of general equilibrium describes the competitive economy. In stable equilibrium this economy is efficient throughout, the configuration of inputs and outputs is everywhere efficient.

For these statements there are important qualifications. Chapter 15 covers them.

*The Marginal
Conditions*

The rules, or conditions, of economic efficiency can be recapitulated in this way:

Rule 1: The marginal rate of substitution between any two commodities is the same for any two consumers. The *MRS* is equal to the ratio of the prices of the two commodities. With prices identical to consumers, they have no incentives to engage in trade among themselves.

Rule 2: The (marginal) rate of product transformation between any two commodities is the same for any two producers who produce both. The *RPT* is equal to the ratio of the prices of the two commodities. Here also any two producers receive the same prices in competitive equilibrium.

Rule 3: For any two commodities, the *MRS* of the consumers are equal to the *RPT* of the producers. This follows from Rules 1 and 2 and from the identities of prices to consumers and producers.

Rule 4: The marginal rate of technical substitution between any two inputs is the same for any two producers who use both inputs. Again, identities of prices and thus equalities of price ratios insure this result.

Rule 5: The marginal product of an input in the production of a commodity is the same for any two producers. This really follows from Rule 4, because *MRTS* equals the ratio of the marginal products, which in turn equals the ratio of the prices. When firms must pay the same wage rate, each firm producing a given commodity will employ labor up to the point where marginal products (and values of marginal products) are equal. In another guise, Rule 5 can take this form: The marginal costs of any two producers for any commodity are equal because they are equal to the same price.

In an extended analysis, more rules for efficiency could be added to the foregoing list. But they can all be summed up in one fundamental theorem, which is: "Every competitive equilibrium is a Pareto-optimum; and every Pareto-optimum is a competitive equilibrium."[4] A Pareto-optimum, it will be remembered, is another expression for an efficient point or solution.

SUMMARY

In the general equilibrium model, the demands of households for commodities depend on the prices of all commodities and of all resources. The supplies of commodities from firms depend on commodity prices, the coefficients of production, and the prices of resources. The demand for each commodity equals its supply, all demands and supplies being compatible because of their interconnections through the networks of prices. Economic welfare combines the criteria of efficiency and equity. In a two-sector model, efficient distributions of two goods between two persons are defined by the *exchange contract curve*. Efficient allocations of two inputs in the production of two goods are defined by the *production contract curve*. All points on the *production possibility frontier* are efficient. The *grand utility frontier* defines the maxima of the utilities that can be divided between two persons, when both distribution and production are efficient. The *social welfare function* permits the solution for a maximum of economic welfare, the solution combining both efficiency and equity. The *general equilibrium model* gives standards of economic efficiency.

[4] Robert Dorfman, Paul A. Samuelson, and Robert M. Solow, *Linear Programming and Economic Analysis*, McGraw-Hill, New York, 1958, pp. 409–410.

SELECTED REFERENCES

Even those with little mathematics can benefit from Léon Walras, *Elements of Pure Economics*, translated by William Jaffe and published for the American Economic Association and the Royal Economic Society (Irwin, Homewood, 1954). A modern version of static general equilibrium theory is contained in J. R. Hicks, *Value and Capital*, 2d ed. (Oxford, London, 1946), chap. 8. An extensive treatment of the economics and mathematics of general equilibrium is to be found in Robert Dorfman, Paul A. Samuelson, and Robert M. Solow, *Linear Programming and Economic Analysis* (McGraw-Hill, New York, 1958), chap. 13.

Several writers have expounded general equilibrium theory with mathematics simple enough for anyone who remembers a little algebra. Among these are: Gustav Cassel, *The Theory of Social Economy*, trans. Joseph McCabe (Harcourt Brace, New York, 1924), chap. 4; John F. Due and Robert W. Clower, *Intermediate Economic Analysis*, 5th ed. (Irwin, Homewood, 1966), chap. 18.

On welfare economics: Howard R. Bowen, *Toward Social Economy* (Rinehart, New York, 1948); Tibor Scitovsky, *Welfare and Competition*, rev. ed. (Irwin, Homewood, 1971).

More advanced: A. C. Pigou, *The Economics of Welfare*, 4th ed. (Macmillan, London, 1932); J. E. Meade, *Trade and Welfare* (Oxford University Press, London, 1955); Hla Myint, *Theories of Welfare Economics* (Harvard University Press, Cambridge, 1948); William J. Baumol, *Welfare Economics and the Theory of the State*, 3d ed. (Harvard University Press, Cambridge, 1972); E. J. Mishan, "A Survey of Welfare Economics, 1939–59," in *Surveys of Economic Theory*, American Economic Association and Royal Economic Society (St. Martin's Press, New York, 1966), vol. I.

Applications of welfare economics to government programs: John V. Krutilla and Otto Eckstein, *Multiple Purpose River Development* (Johns Hopkins Press, Baltimore, 1958); Jack Hirshleifer, James C. DeHaven, and Jerome W. Milliman, *Water Supply, Economics, Technology, and Policy* (University of Chicago Press, Chicago, 1960); Charles J. Hitch and Roland N. McKean, *The Economics of Defense in the Nuclear Age* (Harvard University Press, Cambridge, 1960).

On private versus social cost: R. H. Coase, "The Problem of Social Cost," *Journal of Law and Economics,* 3 (October 1960), 1–44.

Several of the selections in Donald Stevenson Watson, ed., *Price Theory in Action: A Book of Readings*, 3d ed. (Houghton Mifflin, Boston, 1973) deal with topics in welfare economics. They are chap. 26, parts 5, 8, and 10.

1. Take the general equilibrium model as the starting point. Then trace the effects of: (a) one consumer's action in modifying purchases because of changes in personal taste; (b) one person's action in deciding not to work any more and to live with relatives; and (c) one technological improvement.

2. Suppose you have a free hand in setting postal rates and that you want to have the Postal Service operated in accordance with the criteria of economic efficiency. What would you do?

3. Name all of the second-order conditions for the two-sector model of economic welfare.

4. In the general equilibrium model, prices act to allocate resources. Explain how an allocation of goods determined by a rationing system with coupons would affect exchange and production. Would it ever be possible to have a Pareto-optimum with ration coupons allocating resources?

Appendix
TO PART 7
MATHEMATICAL NOTE

The model of general equilibrium to be described now is one of the simplest versions. It is usually called the Walras-Cassel model.[1] To conform a little more closely to the conventions associated with general equilibrium theory, several of the symbols in what follows differ from those used elsewhere in this book.

The economy described by the model has $1, 2, \ldots, n$ commodities and $1, 2, \ldots, m$ resources, or productive services. The quantities of the commodities are $x_1, x_2, \ldots, x_n$. The quantities of the resources are $r_1, r_2, \ldots, r_m$.

The prices of the commodities are $p_1, p_2, \ldots, p_n$. The prices of the productive services are $v_1, v_2, \ldots, v_m$.

In this economy, the commodities are produced directly with the productive services. Intermediate goods do not appear, just as they do not in the national income and product accounts. In these accounts, the final products in the gross national product are produced with the two groups of productive services, labor and capital. To produce a unit of the jth commodity, the physical quantity a_i of the ith resource is needed. A loaf of bread needs so many minutes of the labor time of a baker. Thus, a_{ij} is called a production coefficient, or an input coefficient. In the model, all the production coefficients are fixed. There are mn of them.

All prices are measured in terms of the price of one commodity. Let $p_1 = 1$. Thus prices are the ratios at which commodities 2, 3, $\ldots, n$ exchange for commodity 1, which Walras called the *numéraire*. The economy is really a kind of barter economy, with the *numéraire* serving as a unit of reckoning.

[1] After Walras and Gustav Cassel, the Swedish economist whose translated version was for many years the only one available in English. Treatment of the Walras-Cassel model here is adapted from Robert Dorfman, Paul A. Samuelson, and Robert M. Solow, *Linear Programming and Economic Analysis*, McGraw-Hill, New York, 1958, pp. 351-355.

The Demand Equations

The model has two sets of demand equations. One is that of the households for commodities. The other is that of the firms for resources.

The market demand equations for each commodity are the totals of the demands of each household for each commodity. Each household's demand for a commodity is a function of its utility, its price, the prices of *all* other commodities, and the household's income, which in turn depends on the amounts of productive services it sells and their prices.

The market demand equations are

(A7-1)
$$x_1 = f_1(p_1, p_2, \ldots, p_n; v_1, v_2, \ldots, v_m)$$
$$x_2 = f_2(p_1, p_2, \ldots, p_n; v_1, v_2, \ldots, v_m)$$
$$\cdot \quad \cdot \quad \cdot$$
$$x_n = f_n(p_1, p_2, \ldots, p_n; v_1, v_2, \ldots, v_m).$$

Notice that the resource prices appear in these equations. The resource prices allow for changes in demand when there are shifts in the incomes of the households.

Because the production coefficients are fixed, the demand of firms for units of resources is the sum of the quantities required for each commodity. The firms producing commodity 1, whose quantity is x_1, demand a_{11} units of resource 1, a_{12} units of resource 2, etc. The demand for resource 1 is the sum of the amounts of it used in all commodities, or $a_{11}x_1$ plus $a_{12}x_2$, etc. Then let the total supply of each resource be put equal to its demand because the model has no unemployment. The equations are

(A7-2)
$$a_{11}x_1 + a_{12}x_2 + \cdots + a_{1n}x_n = r_1$$
$$a_{21}x_1 + a_{22}x_2 + \cdots + a_{2n}x_n = r_2$$
$$\cdot \quad \cdot \quad \cdot$$
$$a_{m1}x_1 + a_{m2}x_2 + \cdots + a_{mn}x_n = r_m.$$

The Supply Equations

All markets are purely and perfectly competitive in the model, which also has the adjustments of the long run. Therefore, the price of each commodity equals its cost per unit. Cost per unit is the sum of the payments for the quantities of the productive resources used per unit of a commodity. Production of a unit of commodity 1 requires a_{11} units of resource 1 at price v_1; a_{21} units of resource 2 at price v_2; etc. The equations are

(A7-3)
$$a_{11}v_1 + a_{21}v_2 + \cdots + a_{m1}v_m = p_1$$
$$a_{12}v_1 + a_{22}v_2 + \cdots + a_{m2}v_m = p_2$$
$$\cdot \quad \cdot \quad \cdot$$
$$a_{1n}v_1 + a_{2n}v_2 + \cdots + a_{mn}v_m = p_n.$$

The last step is to tie the supply of resources to the prices. The supply of any one resource depends on its price, the prices of the other resources, and the prices of the commodities. The supply of hours of bakers' services depends on the wage rate, on wage rates in other occupations, and on the prices of bread, cake, cookies, etc. The final set of equations is

$$r_1 = g_1(p_1, p_2, \ldots, p_n; v_1, v_2, \ldots, v_m)$$

(A7-4)
$$r_2 = g_2(p_1, p_2, \ldots, p_n; v_1, v_2, \ldots, v_m)$$

$$\cdot \quad \cdot \quad \cdot$$

$$r_m = g_m(p_1, p_2, \ldots, p_n; v_1, v_2, \ldots, v_m).$$

There are $2n + 2m$ equations for the $2n + 2m$ unknowns x, r, p, and v. But Equations (A7-1) and (A7-4) really contain only $m + n - 1$ independent equations. By setting $p_1 = 1$, however, the number of unknowns is also reduced by 1. Thus a necessary condition for the system of equations to be determinate is satisfied.

INDEX

BCDEFGHIJ–M–7987